THE DOMAIN OF BEING

Ontology

THE DOMAIN OF BEING

OF BEING

ONTOLOGY

CELESTINE N. BITTLE, O.M.Cap.

THE BRUCE PUBLISHING COMPANY
NEW YORK   MILWAUKEE   CHICAGO

Imprimi potest: THEODOSIUS FOLEY, O.M.CAP., Provincial
Nihil obstat: THOS. A. HEIDENREICH, O.M.CAP., Censor Deputatus
Nihil obstat: H. B. RIES, Censor librorum
Imprimatur: ✠ SAMUEL A. STRITCH, Archiepiscopus Milwaukiensis
September, 28, 1938

AUTHOR'S PREFACE

THIS IS a book of acquaintance. As a rule, college students and general readers have had little or no acquaintance with ontology, or general metaphysics, as a science in its own right. Many ideas of an ontological or metaphysical character are, of course, encountered in their daily reading in books, magazine articles, scientific treatises, and professional discussions of all kinds. While the general meaning of such ideas is clear enough, their signification and implication, as an integral part in the structure of philosophic thought, is unknown or hardly felt. They become understood and appreciated in their full value only when studied in the context of the philosophic science of ontology or metaphysics as a whole. Hence the need of correlating these scattered ideas into a basic science, such as ontology, and of fitting them into the fundamental framework of a philosophic system of thought.

It is hoped that this book may be helpful to the student and general reader in accomplishing this purpose. It is primarily a student's book, written from the standpoint of the student's mentality and educational development. While a general education, as a preparatory stage of mental culture, is presupposed, no special previous acquaintance with the subject matter of ontology is expected or demanded.

In accordance with this purpose, the scope of the book is frankly positive and constructive. It attempts to build up an understanding of the matter of ontology in a logical manner, using simple language, illustrating the subjects with copious examples, and extracting the contents of each chapter into compact summaries. Some of the more abstruse problems of ontology, such as the problem of essence and existence, have been omitted; it was felt that the average student would derive little benefit from a lengthy discussion of problems which have

v

taxed the ingenuity and acumen of the most profound intellects. Such problems may be attacked after the student has become acquainted with the ideas and subjects which form the foundation of the science of metaphysics. After all, the student cannot be expected to be a professional philosopher; it should be sufficient if he acquires a thorough grounding in fundamentals, so that he can deepen his knowledge through subsequent reading and study.

It might seem at times that the author is belaboring the obvious. However, one must bear in mind that the average student will not be clear in his ideas and principles until they are reduced to the simplest and most basic terms of evidence. Experience in the classroom proves this beyond dispute. The author, therefore, having the mental needs of the student always in view, has not hesitated to use this method whenever considered advisable. For the same reason, recapitulations of treated material are inserted at various points throughout the book. The subject matter is complex and difficult at times, and the mind of the student may become confused through the multiplicity of details; a certain amount of periodic recapitulation should help the student to obtain a proper orientation as he proceeds on his way. The method and language of presentation is, generally speaking, comparatively non-technical; to have the student grasp the meaning of technical terms and ideas, one must speak the language of the student. While the sharpness and nicety of philosophical terminology will suffer somewhat for the time being, in the end the student will have acquired a technical vocabulary which should be fairly accurate and complete.

That the author's policy and method of presentation is essentially sound, is evidenced by the fact that his logic, *The Science of Correct Thinking,* and his epistemology, *Reality and the Mind,* have been adopted by a large number of colleges and universities as texts. It is hoped that this book will meet with similar favor and will render similar service.

THE AUTHOR

CONTENTS

PART I

BEING AND ITS PRIMARY DETERMINATIONS

CHAPTER

PART III

THE SUPREME CATEGORIES

PART I

BEING AND ITS PRIMARY DETERMINATIONS

CHAPTER I

SCIENCE, METAPHYSICS, ONTOLOGY

MAN'S MIND is never permanently satisfied with a commonplace, obvious, and superficial knowledge of nature. It forever seeks to penetrate the veil of phenomena and to grasp the reality of things. This is due partly to man's insatiable craving for knowledge and partly to his desire to control the forces of nature. No doubt, the practical advantages resulting from such control furnish in most instances the original spur for knowledge; subsequently, however, knowledge for its own sake, for the mental satisfaction it affords, becomes a dominant factor in man's incessant search for the realities which make the wheels of the world go round. And with increased knowledge in widely separated fields comes the need to unify and systematize the scattered truths. Thus is science born.

SCIENCE

Science is not interested in isolated, individual facts and things, except in so far as they represent the traits of a class and of a law. A kettle of boiling water, a flash of lightning, a horseshoe magnet, a ray of sunshine, a sheaf of wheat, a mongrel dog, an Australian bushman — these things mean little to the scientist when taken as individual facts. However, the laws of thermo-dynamics, of electricity, of magnetism, of light, of plant, animal, and human life, manifested by these things, are of great importance. If the scientist can discover the *causes* of such phenomena and the *laws* according to which they operate, he has acquired a knowledge which is the scientific explanation of the working forces of nature.

Each science has its own selected field of research. The material object may be the same for several sciences, but the formal object is different for each. By the *material* object of a science we understand the general object with which it occupies itself in its investigation; and by the *formal* object we understand that special phase or aspect of the general object which forms the subject matter peculiar to this science and which distinguishes it from all other sciences. The bodies existing in the world are the material object of the natural sciences; for instance, of astronomy, geology, physics, chemistry, biology, medicine, mathematics, etc. Each of these sciences, however, views and investigates bodies from its own peculiar standpoint. A particular class of bodies may be the material object of a number of special sciences. Organisms, or living bodies, are the material object of biology, botany, zoology, and anthropology; but while biology treats of life in general, botany treats of plants, zoology of animals, and anthropology of man.

While various sciences are engaged with the same bodies in general, it will be observed that each one examines them from a different standpoint. The fact, however, that their material object is more or less common to them all, shows that no special science is completely isolated from the others. When compared to each other, certain features of reality will be found in them all. For example, all presuppose the existence of bodies, of quantity, quality, relation, cause and effect, relative permanence amid constant change, extension, mass, energy, and the like. Now, just as the single sciences are the result of the unifying and systematizing tendency of man's mind in particular fields of investigation, so the presence of such *common elements in all the sciences* entitles the mind to attempt a further unification and systematization of the various sciences in their more universal aspects, in order to harmonize their differences in a higher unity and synthesis of knowledge. And that, precisely, is the knowledge of *philosophy*.

The sciences seek the knowledge of things in their 'proximate' causes. *Philosophy*, on the other hand, is the science of things in their *ultimate causes, reasons,* and *principles,* acquired by the aid of human reason alone. It endeavors to obtain a more definite, extensive, scientific knowledge of those realities which are the *foundation* of the special sciences and which they accept as granted without previous investigation or proof. That leads us to metaphysics.

METAPHYSICS

The term 'metaphysics' had a peculiar origin. It was coined by *Andronicus of Rhodes* (about 70 B.C.); but the meaning now universally associated with it hardly entered his mind. What he called μετὰ τὰ φυσικά meant only 'that which follows after physics,' in as much as he, when he edited Aristotle's works, placed this particular department of philosophy *after* the parts which followed Aristotle's discourse on physical nature. The term thus had only a systematic value. *Aristotle* (384–322 B.C.) himself called this part of his philosophy 'the theological science,' because it led up to a consideration of God and His attributes; and he also styled it 'the first philosophy,' since it treated of first or fundamental causes which, in his opinion, furnished us with knowledge of prime importance. Due to the curious coincidence that this 'first philosophy' of Aristotle treated of realities which were *beyond* the physical properties of things, being in this sense μετὰ τὰ φυσικά (after or beyond physics), 'metaphysics' came in the course of time to mean that department of philosophy which deals with those features of things that are hyperphysical, suprasensible, immaterial.

In a general way we may define *metaphysics* as the *science of the ultimate principles and properties of real beings*.

Instead of investigating a particular *kind* of being, as the other sciences do, metaphysics inquires into *being as such*, whether material or immaterial, actual or possible, real or mental, and seeks to discover its most general principles and properties. It leaves out of consideration all attributes which are characteristics of physical bodies in so far as they are physical, for instance, light, heat, electricity, color, and sound, and focuses its attention on the most general features of their reality.

The outline just given indicates the scope of metaphysics. It includes the world, the soul, God, being in general. There is a further distinction between *General Metaphysics* and *Special Metaphysics*. Cosmology treats of the material world at large; psychology, of the soul; theodicy, of God: these are the three departments of Special Metaphysics. Ontology treats of being in general; it is the department of General Metaphysics.

ONTOLOGY

Ontology (Gr., ὄν, being, and λόγος, treatise, discourse) is the *science of being in its most general aspects*. It is called a *science,* because it contains a definite body of proved truths, arranged in systematic order. It is the 'science of *being.*' 'Being' is here taken as the opposite of 'nothing,' and it means anything that really is or can be. The idea of 'being' will be analyzed in its various meanings and connections in the following chapters. In the special sciences 'being' in some form or other is also the material object with which they occupy themselves; but they always treat of some particular kind of being, e.g., physics, of the material qualities and forces of objects, chemistry, of the constitutive elements of bodies, biology, of vital functions, and so on. Ontology does not treat of any kind of being in particular; in as much, however, as it treats of 'being,' it agrees with them in its *material* object.

Ontology is the 'science of being *in its most general aspects.*' Here we have the *formal* object of ontology. Being, as actually found in nature, must, of course, be either material or immaterial. Ontology, however, does not consider 'being' from either standpoint; it views it in those most general conditions and aspects which are common to both and are, therefore, attributes or determinations of 'being in general': these are the proper subject matter for ontology as a special philosophic science.

Consider, for example, ideas like 'relation,' 'cause,' 'quality,' 'essence,' 'existence,' 'change,' 'substance,' 'accident,' 'one,' 'whole,' and others. They have so broad a meaning and so wide an application, that they will be found in every sort of being, whether material or immaterial. They transcend the merely physical properties of things, like heat, color, and three-dimensional extension, so that they must be considered as metaphysical and ontological attributes of 'being in general.' And that places them among the proper subject matter of ontology. This being the case, it must be evident that ontology is not a mere summation of the findings of the physical sciences, but is a science in its own right, with a formal object peculiar to itself, irrespective of whether it comes to the final conclusion that the above-mentioned ideas have a valid signification or not. At any rate, the philosopher has the right and the duty to examine the validity of such ideas.

IMPORTANCE OF METAPHYSICS AND ONTOLOGY

A goodly amount of abuse and contempt has been heaped upon metaphysics and ontology by some classes of scientists and philosophers. For them the empirical sciences alone have value as knowledge. They point with justifiable pride to the marvelous results obtained by the exact methods of experimentation as used in science and the vast broadening of human knowledge achieved thereby. In consequence of this, they consider any other knowledge as superfluous, if not impossible of attainment; the knowledge of physical causes and laws alone is truly certain and valid.[1]

This attitude, however, is based on a misconception. There should be no hostility of scientists against metaphysics, because metaphysics is the very basis of true science. Without ontology the fundamental ideas of science cannot be resolved into their ultimate elements, nor can their validity be established. Do not the ideas of 'cause,' 'effect,' 'quality,' 'truth,' 'relation,' and similar ones previously noted, lie at the very

---

[1] As an example of this attitude, see *Modern Science,* by Hugh S. R. Elliot (Longmans, Green, 1912).

root of all scientific knowledge? Science simply *presupposes* the validity of these ideas; consequently, to rob them of their objective value is to rob science of the ground upon which it stands. And to accept these ideas without examination and proof, means to leave the *ultimate* foundation of all knowledge open to question and doubt. Man's mind can never be satisfied with this. If this ultimate foundation is insecure, everything based on it is insecure. It is the purpose of metaphysics and ontology to *prove* this foundation valid. Thereby ontology proves the *rationality of science* in general. Instead of being hostile, then, scientists should welcome such an investigation.

As a matter of fact, scientists themselves cannot avoid metaphysical problems, nor do they actually leave them aside in their scientific discussions. Soon or later they must reach a stage in their researches where metaphysical questions are asked. The deeper they delve into the mysteries of nature the more frequently they come face to face with metaphysical problems which demand a definite solution. The scientist cannot go very far without asking himself: What is quality? quantity? causality? change? energy? What is the ultimate constitution of bodies? of protons? of electrons? of matter? What is the essential difference between truth and error, substance and accident, power and act? These are metaphysical questions, and scientists do actually discuss them. But they usually lack the philosophic knowledge offered them by a thorough understanding of ontology, and as a result they often exhibit an ignorance of fundamental ideas and principles which is harmful to the best interests of science itself. Their very attitude shows that ontology is a science of prime importance for every department of human knowledge.

METHOD AND DIVISION OF ONTOLOGY

If the charge were true that the method employed in metaphysical inquiries is totally divorced from experience and observation, then indeed there were just cause for complaint.

The inductive method of the natural sciences has proved its value beyond the possibility of doubt. The progress made by these special sciences in advancing and broadening man's knowledge of the world gives ample testimony of its worth. A vast body of valuable truths has been discovered and systematized in the course of the last century or two, which must form the essential material for the philosopher in conducting his own researches into those wider problems cast up by metaphysics. He must accept the demonstrated findings of these physical sciences and from them draw the conclusions implied therein concerning the ultimate realities which lie behind the phenomena and laws of nature. To ignore them would indeed be fatal to the very purpose of philosophy.

The metaphysician, therefore, accepts the *facts* proposed by science, if they are unquestionably proved; he also uses the *inductive method* as his implement of investigation. Having traversed the field of these special sciences, using the scientists themselves as his guide, he then attempts to explore the unknown regions of reality which extend beyond the frontiers of the experimental sciences and effect a still greater unification of knowledge by means of a fuller grasp of those general concepts and principles which knit all things together. Having established these general concepts and principles inductively, the metaphysician then deduces other concepts, principles, and truths which flow from the former as necessary conclusions. Thus, truth and knowledge are increased through the *deductive method*. Metaphysics, therefore, uses both induction and deduction as its method. This is done especially in ontology, the science of being in its most general aspects. Thereby a great service will also be rendered to the experimental sciences in return, because ontology will show the essential truth and validity of the fundamental ideas upon which the sciences are based and without which they seek in vain for a final verification of their conclusions. Ontology and science must assist, not oppose, each other. Their interests are mutually related and dependent.

The position of ontology in the scheme of human knowledge having thus been stated and clarified, we must now divide the subject matter in such a manner as to insure the best arrangement of the problems involved. This will be done by going from the more simple to the more complex, from the more known to the more obscure. Correspondingly, ontology is divided into three major parts: (1) *Being* and its *primary determinations;* (2) the *transcendental attributes* of being; (3) the *supreme categories* of being. The subject is avowedly difficult, but its understanding is well worth the mental effort expended.

SUMMARY OF CHAPTER I

Man's mind seeks to discover the reality manifested by the phenomena of nature.

1. *Science* is the knowledge of things in their causes. The empirical sciences look for the proximate causes, while *philosophy* is the science of the ultimate causes, reasons, and principles of things, acquired by the aid of human reason alone. All sciences contain common elements and are, therefore, interrelated.

2. *Metaphysics* is the science of the ultimate principles and properties of real beings. *General Metaphysics,* or ontology, treats of 'being in general.' *Special Metaphysics* consists of three departments: cosmology treats of the material world; psychology, of the soul; theodicy, of God.

3. *Ontology* is the *science of being in its most general aspects.* It investigates realities like 'being,' 'cause,' 'effect,' 'relation,' 'quality,' 'essence,' 'existence,' 'change,' 'substance,' 'accident,' etc.

4. The *importance* of metaphysics and ontology can be seen from the fact that the realities just mentioned are fundamental to all the natural sciences. Ontology proves their validity and thereby furnishes the ultimate verification of the sciences.

5. The *method* employed in ontology is the method of in-

duction and deduction. The *division* of ontology is as follows: Being and its primary determinations; the transcendental attributes of being; the supreme categories of being.

READINGS

Coffey, P., *Ontology*, General Introduction; Rickaby, John, *General Metaphysics*, Bk. I, Ch. I; Baschab, Chas. R., *A Manual of Neo-Scholastic Philosophy*, Ch. XXI; Urráburu, John Jos., *Ontologia*, Introd.; Mercier, D. Card., *A Manual of Modern Scholastic Philosophy*, Vol. I, pp. 407–413; McCormick, John F., *Scholastic Metaphysics*, Ch. I; Aristotle, *Metaphysics*, I, iv.

CHAPTER II

THE CONCEPT OF BEING

THE FIRST thing necessary in any science is to have a clear understanding of the subject under discussion. In ontology it is 'being.' The form 'being' is the participle of the verb 'to be,' and the verb 'to be' means 'to exist,' 'to have existence.' But while the participial form of 'being' means 'having existence,' the term 'being' is usually taken as a noun, and in this substantive form it is equivalent to 'that which exists,' 'that which has existence.' This nominal definition is taken from the etymology of the term and is sufficient as a preliminary designation. There is, however, much more to the meaning of 'being' than this meager content, and it will be our first task to develop the concept of 'being' in its various phases. We have a *direct* and a *reflex* concept of 'being,' and both demand our attention.

THE DIRECT CONCEPT OF BEING

We derive the concept of 'being' from the things around us: they all are 'beings.' A tree is a being; and so is a house, a bird, a dog, a cloud, a lake, a star, a book. All objects, persons, places, facts, qualities, actions, events, are beings or things. Whatever is present in the universe or outside of it in some way or other is a being. Each one is a particular *kind* of being, distinguished from every other by its own degrees of being. But they all have this one feature *in common* that they *exist,* and that is why we can apply to them the same word — 'being.' The mind thus ignores all that in which things differ among themselves and centers its attention on that in which they agree, namely, the common element of 'existence.' 'Being' includes even more than the actually existing things: it embraces also all those things which do not at present actually exist, but which *can exist,* which have 'possible existence.' Thus we would say that the generation of men to be born a hundred years hence are possible 'beings.'

The term 'being,' then, includes anything that has a *positive reference to existence,* whether this existence be actual or merely possible. The common element in actual and possible beings is their *capacity for existence.* Hence, 'being' in general means something capable of existing, *existible;* something capable of being actualized, *actualizable;* something capable of being realized, *realizable.*

Anything that can be positively thought of partakes of this character of 'existibility' — the actual and the possible, the real and the ideal, the necessary and the contingent, the material and the immaterial, the physical and the mental, the finite and the infinite. All fall under the comprehension of 'being'; not in so far as they differ, but in so far as they agree in the one feature of something that is 'existible.' This meaning of 'being' in the sense of 'existible' is the meaning with which ontology occupies itself. 'Being,' then, in this widest, most indeterminate sense, is the special subject matter of ontology.

How does the mind arrive at such an indeterminate concept like 'being'? By *abstraction* or *precision.* Both mean the same thing, namely, the concentration of the mind's attention upon some particular phase of a thing, thereby ignoring and mentally excluding other phases or characteristics actually combined with it. A practical example will illustrate this mental process.

Take 'man.' There are many individual men, and no two are perfectly alike in every respect. Some are children, others adults; some are white, others are brown or black or yellow or copper-colored; some are male, others female; some are healthy, others diseased; some are stout, others slender; some are tall, others short; some are vivacious, others phlegmatic; and so forth. Notwithstanding these many individuating differences, all agree in this that they possess a human 'nature' —

they are 'men'; and a man is a 'rational animal.' Now, the mind can ignore all these *individuating notes* or characteristics and concentrate its attention on that portion of man's being which he has in *common* with every other human being and which constitutes his *essence* as a 'man.' The essence of a thing is its 'whatness' — that which makes it to be 'what' it is and without which it would cease to be 'what' it is; everything else could be changed or missing, and the thing would still remain a member of that particular class of beings. Thus, the essence of man consists in this that he is a 'rational animal.' As long, and only as long, as he is a 'rational animal' is he truly a 'man.' Size, age, sex, color, weight, shape, health, temperament, and similar individualizing traits, may remain, change, or disappear, but that will not affect his essential nature as a 'rational animal.'

Precision, or *abstraction,* therefore, is a process in which the mind fixes its attention upon one or other characteristic of a thing or upon an item common to many things, excluding others which are joined to it in the real order.

Precision may be either subjective (formal) or objective (material), and the difference depends upon the difference in the relation of the abstracted ideas to each other. It will be a *subjective precision,* when the ideas drawn out by the abstractive process are only *subjectively different,* i.e., when these ideas are such that they include each other implicitly, though they do not expressly mention each other. And it will be an *objective precision,* when the ideas drawn out by the abstractive process are *objectively different,* i.e., when these ideas have a different comprehension or thought-content, so that the one does not necessarily include the other. An example will make this clearer.

Man's essence, as we have seen, consists in this that he is a 'rational animal.' This involves a number of constituent elements. Man in his essence is 'rational.' As an 'animal' he is also 'sentient' and 'living.' He is also a 'body' and a 'substance' and a 'being.' We have thus resolved the essence of man into a 'rational, sentient, living, corporeal, substantial being.' Do these ideas mutually include each other, so that they are only subjectively different (subjective precision); or can we define the one without necessarily including the other, so that they are objectively different (objective precision)? Let us see.

The idea 'sentient' means something that is capable of sense-perception; and that does not involve the idea 'rational,' because the brutes (e.g., dogs, lions, eagles, etc.) are sentient, but they are not in any sense 'rational' like man. The idea 'living' means an organism capable of immanent action (vital function); and that does not involve the idea 'sentient,' because plants are living, but they have no sense-perception. The idea 'body' means something that consists of extended matter; and that does not involve the idea 'living,' because inanimate things (metals, etc.) are corporeal, but they are not living. The idea 'substance' means something that exists in itself; and that does not involve the idea 'body,' because God is a substance, but He is not corporeal. These ideas, therefore, do not include each other, even though in man they are found together. They are objectively different, and the abstractive process, whereby they are abstracted from man's essence, is an *objective precision*.

But when we compare these ideas with the idea of 'being,' we perceive an entirely different relation. They all contain within themselves *implicitly* the idea of 'being,' because they evidently are 'beings'; and 'being' *implicitly* contains every one of these ideas, because 'being' involves every sort of reality. The only difference between 'being' and these other ideas is that they do *not expressly mention* each other, although they are and must be implicitly included in each other. The ideas 'rational,' 'sentient,' 'living,' 'corporeal,' and 'substance,' are objectively different among themselves and have a thought-content which is not mutually inclusive; but the idea 'being' includes them all and is included in them all, so that they are only *subjectively* different from 'being' and 'being' from them.

No matter with what other idea we compare the idea of

'being' (except with 'nothing'), they are mutually inclusive: everything is a 'being' and 'being' is everything. Consequently, we arrive at the idea of 'being' by means of a *subjective, or formal, precision.*

THE REFLEX CONCEPT OF BEING

So far we have considered 'being' simply in its direct and immediate meaning, and we have examined the mode of abstraction by means of which we acquire its idea. We must now consider 'being' *reflexly,* i.e., as applied to the various kinds of things, and examine its *relation* to them. This will reveal a number of interesting facts.

The idea of 'being' is *first in the logical order.* By this is meant that it is the first and most fundamental in the order of ideas. Every idea contains the idea of 'being' in some form. An idea must have a content, must be the idea of *something;* and 'something' is always a 'being.' All knowledge is of things. The content of an idea will thus always represent a modification or a certain kind of 'being.' Hence, it is the most basic idea, the one into which all other ideas are ultimately resolved, the one without which nothing can ever be known.

The idea of 'being' is *first in the chronological order.* This statement cannot, of course, be demonstrated in any strict fashion. No one can prove its truth from personal experience, because no one will be able to recall the first idea that he had in time. Nor can it be proved through observation of other minds. Obviously, children would be the only ones who could tell us, and they are incapable of telling us when they obtain their first idea and what its content is. The above statement is made in consequence of a general fact universally observed, namely, that man always passes in his knowledge from the more confused and indeterminate ideas to those more clear and more detailed. Since, however, the most confused and indeterminate idea is that of 'being' or 'thing,' and since this idea is involved in every concept, it is natural to suppose that the child's process of knowledge will have started with the simplest notion of 'thing' ('being') and gone from there to the more detailed modes and kinds of 'being.'

The idea of 'being' is the *narrowest in comprehension* and the *widest in extension*. By the comprehension of an idea we understand the sum total of all the attributes or thought-elements which constitute the idea; it is expressed in the definition of the content of the idea. By the extention of an idea we understand the sum total of all the individuals and groups to which an idea can be applied.[1] The comprehension of 'being' is the simplest of all, since it contains but a *single* element, namely, that which is 'existible,' that which is not 'nothing.' Its extension is the widest of all ideas, because it can be applied to absolutely *everything* that exists or can exist — finite and infinite, God and creature, material and immaterial, substance and accident.

Since the idea of 'being' is composed of but a single element, the 'existible,' it is the *most empty* of all ideas. It ignores every kind and special modification of entity in its comprehension and expresses solely the one element common to all things, namely, their capacity for existence. But while 'being' is the most empty of all ideas, the most indeterminate of all concepts, it has a *positive content of reality*. Hence, it cannot be identified with 'nothing,' as it is done by *Georg Hegel* (1770–1831), the German idealist philosopher. He does this because of the indeterminateness of the idea of 'being.' But indeterminateness does not deprive 'being' of all positive content. If it did, and if 'being' were equivalent to 'nothing,' then there would be no difference between 'being' and 'non-being,' between 'thing' and 'no-thing.' That would be a patent contradiction in terms, a logical and ontological monstrosity. After all, 'being' must always be 'being' and not its opposite. An examination of 'nothing' will show this more plainly.

---

[1] See *The Science of Correct Thinking* (Bruce Publishing Co., 1935), p. 28, where the author gives a more detailed description of these terms.

BEING AND NOTHING

'*Nothing*' is the *absence of being*. It presupposes the knowledge of 'being' to begin with. It is only by having a previous concept of 'being' and then denying its presence that we acquire the idea of 'nothing.' We can even distinguish between different *kinds* of 'nothing,' depending on the different kinds of 'being' which are considered to be absent. Thus, we speak of absolute and relative 'nothing.'

An *absolute nothing* is the *total* absence of being in every conceivable form. It is, obviously, only a mental abstraction. Being actually exists and has always existed, at least so far as God is concerned. There could never have been a time when there was an absolute nothing; because in that case no being could ever have come into existence.

A *relative nothing* is the absence of a definite *kind* of being. This relative nothing will again be either negative or privative. A *negative nothing* is the *mere absence* of some kind of being in a thing: the absence of wings or fins or claws or hoofs in a man; the absence of life or sight or hearing or speech in a stone; the absence of locomotion or feeling or memory in a plant. A *privative nothing* is the absence of some kind of being in a thing that is *fit* to have it and normally *ought* to have it. Cases in point are: the absence of wings in a sparrow, of fins in a perch, of hoofs in a horse; the absence of life in a dog, of hearing in a squirrel, of speech in man; the absence of locomotion in a giraffe, of memory in a lion. In these instances the absence of the perfection mentioned is a real *privation,* since these beings lack something that they ought to have according to their normal constitution.

From the above it is evident that Hegel's contention, that 'indeterminate being' is identical with 'absolute nothing,' is erroneous. If the two ideas were identical in content, then whatever is excluded from the idea of 'absolute nothing' would also be excluded from the idea of 'indeterminate being.' But this is not so. *All* being, of whatever type and kind, is excluded from 'absolute nothing'; but only a definite or *determinate kind* of being is excluded from the idea of 'indeterminate being.' The two ideas are thus seen to be objectively and essentially different. Certainly, both 'absolute nothing' and 'indeterminate being' exclude every determinate kind of being; but 'absolute nothing' is absolutely devoid of *all content* in its idea, while 'indeterminate being' still retains the *positive content* of 'being in general.' The mere fact that both agree in one point does not make them identical and equivalent; just as little as the fact that the ideas of 'plant' and 'animal' exclude the idea of 'rationality' will make the plant and the animal to be the same reality and identical thing. 'Indeterminate being' is still always 'being,' while 'absolute nothing' is never 'being' under any and all conditions.

DEFINITION OF BEING

'Being' admits of *no strict philosophic definition.* Such a definition would demand a proximate genus and a specific difference. The proximate 'genus' includes within its comprehension all the essential elements of the genera above it and therefore includes all the beings that are cognate or similar in nature to the thing which is to be defined. The 'specific difference,' on the other hand, brings in the distinctive element which separates this thing from all others of a similar nature, by showing in what manner it is different from all others with which it might be erroneously identified.

Take as example 'man.' Man is defined as a 'rational animal'; 'animal' is his proximate genus, 'rational' is his specific difference. The proximate genus 'animal' includes within its comprehension all the essential elements of the genera above it, because an 'animal' is a 'sentient, living, corporeal substance'; and this shows all the beings which are in some way similar to man — brutes, plants, inanimate bodies, substances. The specific difference 'rational' is the one distinctive essential element which distinguishes 'man' from every other 'animal'; it thereby makes him a species of his own and separates him from every other 'animal' and also from every other genus or species, including plants and inanimate bodies.[2]

It will be noted that the generic idea must always be *wider in extension* than the idea to be defined; and the idea expressed by the specific difference must always be something not already contained in, but *extraneous* to, the generic idea. A definition, therefore, if it is to be a real and strict one, must be made up of two objectively different ideas — one wider and one narrower than the thing to be defined, so that the combination of both gives the exact designation of the thing. This, however, can never be the case in a definition of 'being.' 'Being' is the supreme idea, the widest and simplest and most indeterminate which the mind possesses; *there can be no wider idea than 'being.'* Consequently, the mind can find no idea which could, in any strict sense of the term, serve as a true genus for 'being.' The most we can attempt, then, is a *descriptive definition,* and even that will not elucidate the idea, since none of the ideas which could be employed will be clearer and simpler than 'being' itself. As was pointed out above, 'being' is the first idea in the logical order, and no other idea is intelligible without a previous understanding of the idea of 'being.'

Viewed positively, 'being' can be described as that *which exists or can exist,* the 'existible'; viewed negatively, it is *whatever is not nothing.* That is the best we can do in describing it.

SUMMARY OF CHAPTER II

The term 'being' is derived from the verb 'to be' and means something that has, or can have, existence.

1. *The Direct Concept of Being.* We form the general idea of 'being' by contemplating the things around us; they are things, 'beings.' All things have a common element — actual or possible existence; they are *existible.*

The mind arrives at the indeterminate idea of 'being' by

---

[2] See *The Science of Correct Thinking,* p. 74; also pp. 56–58.

means of a subjective (formal), not an objective (material), *abstraction* or *precision*.

2. *Reflex Concept of Being.* The idea of 'being' is the first in the logical and chronological order. It is the narrowest in comprehension and the widest in extension; it is the most empty of all ideas. But the idea of 'being' always has a positive content of reality and as such is not identical with 'nothing.'

3. *Being and Nothing.* 'Nothing' is the absence of being. *Absolute* nothing is the total absence of being, while *relative* nothing is the absence of a definite kind of being. A relative nothing is *negative,* when it is the mere absence of some kind of being in a thing; and it is *privative,* when it is the absence of some kind of being in a thing that is fit for it and ought to have it. 'Absolute nothing' is the absence of all being, while 'indeterminate being' is merely the absence of a determinate kind of being.

4. *Definition of Being.* A strict philosophic definition is impossible, because there is no idea wider than 'being' that could serve as its genus; a descriptive definition is the best than can be given, and even this will not elucidate the idea of 'being,' because no idea is more intelligible than this. Viewed positively, 'being' is that *which exists or can exist;* viewed negatively, it is *whatever is not nothing.*

READINGS

Coffey, P., Ch. I; Rickaby, J., Bk. I, Ch. II; Hugon, Ed., *Metaphysica, Ontologia,* Tr. I, Qu. I, art. 1; Urráburu, J. J., Disp. I, cp. I; Phillips, R. P., *Modern Thomistic Philosophy,* Vol. II, Part II, Ch. I; Aristotle, *Metaph.,* IV.

Chapter III

KINDS OF BEING

THE IDEA of 'being' is the simplest, widest, and most indeterminate of all ideas. 'Being' is anything and everything that does or can exist; whatever is not nothing is a 'being.' Such is our concept of it in its most general form. Naturally, 'being' itself can never exist in such indeterminateness; it appears always as some determinate *kind* of being, as something which possesses definite *degrees* of reality, as individual things or *entities*. Every single thing in nature is a 'being,' and we could make a classification of 'being' according to the ordinary types of things which are found in the universe. Such a classification, however, belongs more properly to the special sciences. Ontology considers only those kinds of 'being' which run across the lines of all the sciences, as characteristic of 'being in general.' A classification from this standpoint is the division into *real* being, *ideal* being, and *logical* being.

REAL BEING

A *real being* is anything that has, or can have, *existence independent of man's actual knowing.* By this is meant that it must be able to exist even when not thought of by man. That nothing can exist without the knowledge of God, is true; but it must be existible without dependence on man's knowledge-act. There are a number of subdivisions of real being which are important in this connection, and their general concept will be given.

Actual and Possible Being. The 'actual' being is one that *really exists* at the present moment. We all are aware of ourselves as existing realities, we are conscious of our existence;

we are, therefore, actual beings. The same is true of every article in my room; of the house I live in; of the trees, garden, hills, sky, clouds, sun, etc., which exist in the universe at large, even if we do not know that they exist. They may be visible or invisible, physical or psychical, corporeal or spiritual: so long as they have existence here and now, they are actual.

The 'possible' (potential) being is one that does not actually exist, but is *capable of existence*. Such a being is not present in any way in the existing order of things; but it is such that it is not intrinsically impossible and can receive existence, provided there is a cause that can give it existence. For instance, in the spring, when the seed is placed into the soil, the future crop is not actually present; but it is a possible or potential reality, in as much as the seed has the inherent power (Lat., *potentia,* power) to bring it forth so that it can exist (Lat., *pot-ens, potis esse,* to be able to exist).

Substantial and Accidental Being. A 'substance' is a being that *exists in itself* and does not need another to exist in as in a subject of inherence. Such are the ordinary objects we observe in the physical world — a table, a box, a book; metals and non-metals; plants, animals, men; the rivers and lakes, the hills and plains, the sun and the moon and the stars. These things exist in themselves and have a being of their own.

An 'accident' is a being that cannot exist in itself, but *needs another to exist in* as in a subject of inherence. Such beings are too weak in entity to exist without a subject; they require a substance to support them in their being and existence. Accidents are modifications of substances. Such are color, quantity, quality, action, motion, etc. Motion, for instance, never exists for itself and in itself; it is always a body that moves from place to place. Action cannot exist except in a body that acts. Color is always found in a body that is colored.

Necessary and Contingent Being. A being is said to be 'necessary,' when its *non-existence is impossible.* It may be either absolutely or conditionally necessary.

A being is 'absolutely' necessary, when its non-existence is impossible under any and all conditions. In such a being existence is a constituent of its very essence. Such a being simply *must exist*. An absolutely necessary being can never have been produced, because production implies that there was a moment when it did not exist and then received existence through this production; an absolutely necessary being, however, can never have been non-existent even for a moment. Consequently, such a being cannot be a produced being, but owes its existence to its own infinitely perfect essence (*ens a se*). God is conceived as such a being; His existence is identical with His essence, and as such His essence can never be without actual existence.

A being is 'conditionally' or 'hypothetically' necessary, when its non-existence is impossible under a certain given condition. Thus, no man's existence is necessary; however, given his existence, he must exist as a 'rational' being, because 'rationality' is one of the elements which constitute his existing essence. Again, a plant need not exist; but if it exists, it must have 'life.' So, too, a stone need not fall; but if it falls, it must of necessity have a certain amount of speed in its motion.

A 'contingent' being is one whose *non-existence is possible*. Actual existence, therefore, is not an essential element of its nature. It would involve no contradiction to conceive of such a being as non-existent. Essentially, such a being is indifferent to existence or non-existence. If it actually exists, it could not have received its existence in virtue of its own essence, but must have received it from some other being which produced it. This is obvious. Since its existence is not due to itself, it must be due to another being; this means that it is produced by this other. If it were not produced by another, it would owe its existence to its own essence, and then it would not be contingent but necessary.

Finite and Infinite Being. These are terms which are frequently used, and their exact meaning should be well understood.

A 'finite' being is one whose reality is *limited in perfection*. All things composing this physical world are finite. Not one has being, power, or existence which can truly be conceived as not limited in some manner. They are limited in size, in energy, in time, in space, in quality, in action, in endurance. As long as there is the slightest limitation of any kind in a being, it cannot strictly be accounted as anything but finite.

An 'infinite' being (Lat., *finis,* limit; *infinitum,* without limit, limitless) is one which has *no limit in its entity or perfection*. Our idea of the 'infinite' is negative in form, since it denies a limit; but it is positive in content, because it asserts the supreme fullness of entity and perfection. A being may be actually or potentially infinite.

A. being is 'actually' infinite, when it has *reality without limit*. If this being is unlimited in one definite *kind* of reality only, while limited in other ways, it is said to be 'relatively' infinite. In mathematics, for instance, we speak of an infinite line; we mean thereby that it is limitless in length, but a line is limited in width and depth to such an extent that it is conceived as being without these two dimensions. But if a being were without any limit in the positive fullness of *all perfection,* including every kind and degree without measure, it would be 'absolutely' infinite. A being of this nature must possess the perfections of all other beings and essences within itself, but stripped of their imperfections and limitations; and since a spiritual substance is more perfect than a corporeal substance, the absolutely infinite being must be a spirit whose essence is purest actuality without any admixture of potentiality. It is thus that we conceive God to be.

Something is 'potentially' infinite, when it is always actually finite in the amount of its reality, but is *limitless in its potentiality for receiving more reality*. Its possibility of receiving more reality will never reach an ultimate limit, for the reason that the store of possible reality which it did not yet receive is inexhaustible. A potentially infinite being, therefore, is always actually finite in perfection, and it can never become actually infinite in perfection.

Absolute and Relative Being. That is 'absolute' which can be thought of or can exist *without reference to another.* It is self-sufficient, independent; it does not need another. If it can 'exist' without reference to another, it is *ontologically* absolute. Only the necessary being, God, is absolute in this sense. If it can be 'thought of' without reference to another, it is *logically absolute.* Ordinary objects are logically absolute, because we can form an idea of them without reference to another object; such are the idea of 'dog,' 'clock,' 'star,' 'gold,' 'eagle,' 'man,' etc. Their meaning is clear, and they can be defined by themselves.

That is 'relative' which can exist or be thought of only in *reference to another.* If the existence is relative, the thing is said to be *ontologically* relative. The existence of all creatures is of this kind, because they owe it to God. If the very concept of a thing, as expressed in its definition, involves reference to another, it is *logically* relative. We see this logical relation in ideas like 'father,' 'child,' 'brother,' 'king,' 'president,' 'front,' 'rear,' 'north,' 'east.'

Some of these divisions are the subject of considerable controversy, like 'substance' and 'infinite' and 'absolute.' It is not our purpose here to pass judgment on the validity of such concepts. They, and the problems connected with them, will be treated at greater length in different departments of philosophy. For the moment we are concerned merely with stating these classifications and nominal definitions, because they are commonly used, and their signification should be clearly understood, so as to avoid confusion of thought.

IDEAL BEING

By *ideal being* we understand any object in so far *as it is known.* It is also called *intentional* being. The mind of man in the act of knowledge is not like a mirror in which the known object is simply reflected, or like a photographic plate upon which the object makes an impression, so that the mind is purely passive in the process. The mind itself is actively engaged in this process and contributes its share to the production of the cognitional image of the object. No object leaves its position in external space and passes with its bodily presence into the sense in sense-perception and into the intellect in thought. Nor does the mind pass out of the human person and envelop the physical object. Nevertheless, there must be a union between mind and object in some fashion in the act of knowledge, otherwise the mind could not be aware of its presence and existence. In the act of knowledge, then, there must be a *substitute presence* or image of the object *in the mind.* This *presence to awareness,* this sense-presence or thought-presence, is what we mean by 'ideal being.' An object as 'known,' therefore, obtains a mental or ideal existence whereby it manifests its presence to the perceiving mind; and this 'ideal existence' is entirely different from its real or physical existence which it has as an object in its own right, within the realm of the physical universe.

That the mind is not purely passive in the process of knowledge, can be seen in the fact that the mind can err in its knowledge. If the object were the only active agent in this process, it would always reveal itself as it is, and the mind could never obtain an erroneous impression of it, and thus a false judgment about it would be utterly impossible and unintelligible. The only reason why we can make a mistake about an object is, that the mind itself actively produces an intentional or ideal image of the object, and this image may not always correspond perfectly with the object in its physical being. In epistemology it was shown[1] that sense-knowledge of things is largely a matter of *interpretation* and *subjective construction,* based upon impressions received from the physical objects. Both object and mind contribute their share to the production of the image, and the result is something different

---

[1] See the author's *Reality and the Mind* (Bruce, 1936), Chapters X–XII.

from the physical object itself. In the act of knowledge, then, the object receives a special form of being or existence, characteristic of knowledge itself, which is styled its 'ideal' or 'cognitional' or 'intentional' being.

This ideal being of a thing appears in two forms, *sensible* and *intellectual,* depending on the type of faculty which represents the object. Brutes and men have sense-perception of things, and these known things thus obtain a 'sensible intentional (ideal) being' in this form of knowledge. But men also have an intellect and form intellectual ideas, strictly so called, of these things; the cognitional existence thus obtained by the known things is an 'intellectual intentional (ideal) being.' Many philosophers of a sensist and phenomenalist frame of thought deny the difference between sense and intellect and assert that there is nothing but sense-knowledge in man. It is the duty of the psychologist to investigate this claim. The terms 'sense' and 'intellect,' however, are so current and so generally recognized as essentially different that the ontologist is entitled to accept the distinction, at least in a general way, and give a nominal definition of both. Whether these terms possess ultimate validity, will be a matter for discussion in psychology. So much is certain: man and brute are different in some way, and the difference manifests itself in man's power to think, an activity which is not definitely observed in the brutes. That alone is a sufficient reason for the classification of 'ideal being' into 'sensible' and 'intellectual.'

There is another point to bear in mind in this connection: sense-images are always concrete, individual, vague, and indistinct with complexity and minuteness of detail, while idea-images are abstract, universal, sharp, and distinct notwithstanding complexity and minuteness of detail.[2] This is a further reason to divide 'ideal being' into 'sensible' and 'intellectual,' even though there would be no essential difference between sense and intellect.

---

[2] See the author's *The Science of Correct Thinking,* pp. 24–28, 44–63. Also his *Reality and the Mind,* Chapter XIII, XIV.

LOGICAL BEING

We speak of *logical being* in opposition to real being and ideal being. Our knowledge is naturally of things that are found in external nature, of extra-mental realities. Trees, buildings, birds, animals, earth, stars, are realities independent of our mind and its operations; the mere fact of their being known or unknown does not make them less real. They have their own being, 'real' being. An 'ideal' being, it is true, is dependent on the mind for its existence as known; but the ideal being of a thing always presupposes its real being, and hence is not purely mental.

There are, however, a variety of beings which have no existence and being whatever except as *products of thought,* creations of the mind; they have no objective existence in the world outside. The mind, in acquiring its knowledge of a thing (real being), makes concepts of them (ideal being), and this knowledge represents the thing as it exists in nature. But the mind goes a step further and analyzes these concepts, compares them, relates them, and thus arrives at new concepts which have value only *in the order of thought.*

Such are the concepts of *genus, species,* and others of a similar character. 'Animal,' we say, is the 'genus' of man, and 'rational animal' is his 'species.' There is no such *thing* in nature, as a mind-independent entity, which could be called a 'genus' or a 'species'; the only beings that exist in nature are individuals. But the mind by its abstractive power conceives them as a unit and expresses them in one concept which it then applies to all the individuals as a class. As a 'genus' or a 'species' they have no existence except in the mind, in the logical order of thought. They are *logical beings, thought-beings.*

So, too, the mind in its thinking makes sentences with *subjects* and *predicates, nouns* and *adjectives, prepositions* and *adverbs;* and so on, with the other mental beings we call 'particles of speech.' We do not find such things existing in the world, as we see trees, buildings, hills, lakes, dogs, horses; they are not physical entities, but exist only in the mind.

We are now in a position to define *logical being;* it is *anything that has objective being only in the mind.* Whatever is conceived by the mind as a being, although it has not, and cannot have, any objective existence in nature precisely as thus conceived, is a thought-being, a logical being.

There are two main *classes* of logical being: one without a foundation in reality, and the other with a foundation in reality.

A logical being may be *without a foundation in reality,* and then it is a pure fabrication of the mind. Such would be 'a square circle,' 'a stick with only one end,' 'a corporeal spirit,' and similar contradictory concepts. Each element in such a dual concept actually denies and removes the reality given by the other, and so nothing is left that would represent a positive reality. Yet they are treated by the mind *as if* they represented some positive content and had real being. Obviously, such concepts or thought-beings can exist nowhere except in the mind.

A logical being *with a foundation in reality* is one which cannot exist in nature in the *precise manner in which it is conceived,* but there is a reason in the things of nature why the mind conceives it thus. Such a logical being will be either negative, or privative, or relative.

A *negative* logical being is a concept representing a mere absence of being; for instance, a 'vacuum,' 'sightlessness,' 'lifelessness.' Ideas of this sort have a content which is negative and *as such* is not a reality which can exist for itself outside the mind. Yet there is a foundation in reality for these concepts, because they are negations of some reality.

A *privative* logical being is a concept representing a lack of being. Examples would be 'death,' 'blindness,' 'paralysis,' 'neuralgia,' and similar concepts. If we compare such logical beings with negative logical beings, we will immediately see the difference. 'Sightlessness' signifies the mere absence of sight, while 'blindness' is the privation of sight in one who ought to have it. 'Lifelessness' is the absence of life in a being which is not supposed to possess it, for instance in a stone; but 'death' is the privation of life in a being which formerly was living.

A *relative* logical being is a concept representing some relation between thoughts, sentences, inferences, and any part of them, considered as a being. The relations existing between subjects and predicates, between the premises and conclusion in an argumentation, between parts of speech, between genera and species, etc., are logical entities. So, too, are the mental laws which govern them, for instance, the laws of the syllogism, of induction, of eduction, of predication.

Such things have a foundation in reality. The negative and privative logical beings have their foundation in the physical world, in as much as the objects found therein are limited and imperfect and are affected by negations and privations in some part of their being.

These, then, are the different kinds of being: real, ideal, and logical. They all belong to the extension of 'being in general' and give us a better understanding of what 'being' really is: it includes everything mental and extra-mental, everything in the order of existing or existible things. Our next task will be to investigate how 'being' is found in these different kinds of being. And this brings us to the contraction of being in general to its inferiors.

SUMMARY OF CHAPTER III

There are three main kinds of being: real, ideal, and logical.

1. *Real* being is anything that has, or can have, *existence independent of man's actual knowing*. It includes: actual and possible being; substance and accident; necessary and contingent being; finite and infinite being; absolute and relative being.

2. *Ideal* being is any object in so far *as it is known*. It is also called 'intentional' or 'cognitional' being. It consists in the

presence to awareness which an object has in the mind when known. The mind is not purely passive in knowledge, but is actively engaged in the process and contributes its share to the production of the cognitional image. The ideal being is either sensible or intellectual.

3. *Logical* being is anything that has objective being *only in the mind*. There are two kinds: with or without a foundation in reality. Logical beings, which have a foundation in reality, are either negative, or privative, or relative.

READINGS

Coffey, P., Ch. I; Hugon, Ed., Tr. I, Qu. I, art. 1; McCormick, J. F., Ch. II.

Chapter IV

THE CONTRACTION OF BEING

THE VARIOUS kinds of being have been noted. They are widely diverse in nature and character. Since they all belong to the extension of 'being in general,' the vague concept of indeterminate 'being' must be narrowed down or contracted in its extension to these different classes. The *contraction of being* is the reduction or narrowing of the extension of 'being' to its inferiors by means of the addition of some element to the comprehension of 'being,' thereby including some definite beings and excluding others from this extension.

CONTRACTION BY LOGICAL COMPOSITION

'Being' is contracted to its inferiors, not by means of a physical or metaphysical composition, but by means of a *logical composition.*

By composition we mean the union of elements that are distinct from each other. If these elements are such that they are objectively different in idea and physically different as things, then their union is effected through a *physical* composition. If they are objectively different in idea, but really identical in their physical being as things, their union is effected through a *metaphysical* composition. And if these elements are neither objectively different in idea nor physically different as things, but merely different in the sense that the one idea contains implicitly and vaguely what the other expresses explicitly and determinately, their union is effected through a *logical* composition. The contraction of 'being' to its inferiors is made by means of a logical composition.

When we melt copper and zinc together, or when hydrogen and oxygen unite to form water, we have a physical composition. Here these realities are not only different in idea, but also as things. When the elements 'living body' and 'sentiency' are united together to form an 'animal,' we have a metaphysical composition. These elements are objectively different in idea, but in the animal as an existing reality they are not physically different as things; the very body of an animal which is 'living' is at the same time also 'sentient,' and 'sentiency' in the animal is an expression of its 'life.' When, however, we contract the idea 'being' to its inferiors 'substance' and 'accident,' we have only a *logical* composition, because these realities are neither altogether objectively different in idea nor physically different as things. This will be clearer from the following considerations.

When we discussed the mode of precision employed in abstracting the idea of 'being' from the essence of 'man,' we showed that the ideas of 'rational' and 'animal' are objectively different, because they are not mutually inclusive. The wider idea of 'animal' is contracted or narrowed down to its inferior 'man' by *adding* the idea 'rational' to the idea 'animal'; and the idea 'rational' is truly *foreign* and *extraneous* to the idea 'animal.' This, then, represents a metaphysical composition.

When we contract the idea of 'being' to its inferior ideas, like 'substance,' 'accident,' 'body,' 'animal,' 'man,' or to any other idea, does this also involve a metaphysical composition, such as exists between 'animal' and 'rational' in man? It does not. If it did, the element or idea *added* to 'being' would have to be objectively different from it and *positively excluded* from its content; it would have to be an element foreign and extraneous to 'being,' something not already contained in it. Now, what element could be added to 'being' which is not a 'being' in some form or other? The only element or idea that is *outside* the idea of 'being' is the idea of 'nothing'; but it must be evident that 'being' can make no composition with 'nothing,' because the latter can *add nothing positive* to the idea of 'being.'

Comparing, then, the idea of 'being' with that of 'substance' and 'accident' or any other idea, we find that the latter can add to 'being' nothing which would be objectively different from 'being,' nothing which would be new and extraneous to it. Whatever they contain of positive reality is merely an explicit and determinate *form of being* and is already contained in the idea of 'being in general' in an implicit and indeterminate manner. They are, therefore, neither physically different as things, nor objectively different in idea, from 'being' itself. And that is precisely the characteristic mark of a logical composition. Hence, the contraction of 'being' to its inferior members is effected, not through a physical or metaphysical, but through a *logical, composition.*

BEING IS NOT A TRUE GENUS

Nothing seems plainer than that 'being' should be the genus of 'substance' and 'accident,' because they form the natural divisions of 'being.' This can be seen from the following diagram:

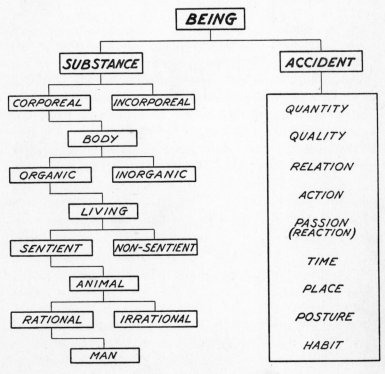

'Substance' and 'accident' certainly appear to be well-defined species under the genus of 'being.' But this is only apparently so. The reason why 'being' cannot be considered a true genus follows with necessity from what has just been said about the logical composition involved in the contraction of 'being' to its inferiors. A *species* is the result of the union between a *genus* and a *specific difference;* and the specific difference is an element new and extraneous to the content of the genus, something not contained in the genus in any way as a part of its comprehension. Unless, then, the content of the specific difference is something *new* and *extraneous* to the comprehension of the so-called genus, the latter is *not a true genus.* And that is the case with 'being' as applied to 'substance' and 'accident.'

The reason is obvious. One cannot find any specific difference *outside* the idea of 'being' which could make a *true difference* and thus constitute a true species, because any such difference would always be a 'being' in some form and on that account would already *be contained* in the idea of 'being.' 'Substance' is a being 'existing in itself,' and 'accident' is a being 'existing in another.' But 'existence,' whether 'in itself' or 'in other,' is already a modal form of 'being'; consequently, it is contained within the comprehension of 'being' in general and is nothing truly new and extraneous to 'being.' The only idea outside the comprehension of 'being' is the idea of 'nothing'; and that, of course, can never become a mark to distinguish one species from another. A specific difference *must* be a *positive element* of distinction between two species, so that the one is realized *with it* and the other *without it;* that is precisely what constitutes the difference between one species and another. 'Being,' then, is not a true genus for 'substance' and 'accident,' because we can find no specific difference outside its comprehension.

Since 'being' is no strict genus and since it includes every possible thing in the scale of reality, it is properly called *transcendental,* i.e., something which transcends or surpasses all classes or categories of determinate beings.

BEING IS AN ANALOGOUS IDEA

Three terms, depending upon their perfect or imperfect signification, can be considered in this connection: univocal, equivocal, and analogous. A *univocal* term is one which designates a number of things in an *identical sense.* Such things are of the same kind, so that the word used to name them has the same meaning throughout. The term 'dog,' as applied to mastiffs, bulldogs, terriers, poodles, etc., is a univocal term. The term 'metal,' used to designate gold, silver, copper, tin, etc., is also univocal. This is true of most terms signifying objects belonging to a certain class. An *equivocal term* is one which is used of diverse things, so that it has *entirely different meanings.* For instance, 'pen' as an instrument for writing and as an enclosure for animals; 'coach' as a vehicle and as an athletic director; 'page' as a leaf of a book and as an attendant at court. Here the identical word has entirely different meanings, as will be seen at a glance; it is, from this standpoint, the opposite of a univocal term.

An *analogous* term stands midway between these two: it is one which applies to *unlike things, partly for the same and partly for a different reason,* so that it is used in a meaning that is partly the same and partly different. There is always some fundamental relation present in such things, entitling the mind to designate them by the same term; hence, such a term is not equivocal. On the other hand, because of their partial unlikeness, the term is not used in a strictly identical sense, and so it is not univocal. That is why it is called analogous. Take the term 'healthy.' Man is termed 'healthy'; and since health is a condition affecting a living body, the term is applied here in an absolute sense. But we also say that a medicine is 'healthy,' because it causes health; a complexion is 'healthy,' because it is an indication of health; food is 'healthy,' because it preserves health; exercise is 'healthy,' because it promotes health: here the term is used in a relative sense, because the word 'healthy' can only be applied to them in relation to the health of a living body with which they have some connection. The meaning is not strictly identical nor is it entirely different; the things so designated are really unlike, but the fundamental relation to 'health' unites them in the same term and concept.

The term 'being,' as applied to its inferiors, e.g., to the infinite and the finite, to substance and accident, to the absolute and relative, etc., is manifestly *not equivocal*. It certainly does not apply to them like the term 'pen' to an instrument of writing and to an enclosure for animals. The objects designated here by the term 'pen' are totally different in meaning and have no common bond between them. But the infinite and the finite, the absolute and the relative, substance and accident, are 'beings' in the true meaning of the term; they contain a common element and are related by a common bond, namely by their mutual reference to existence, because all are 'existibles.'

The question now arises: Does not this common element 'existible' imply the selfsame meaning in these inferiors of 'being,' so that the term 'being' is applied to them in a *univocal* manner? At first glance one would think so. But an exact analysis of the conditions involved in univocal predication will show that 'being' is not applied to them in a strictly identical sense.

In order that a term be univocal in its application to its inferiors, two things are required: first, that there be *one thought-content* or comprehension corresponding to the one term, and this thought-content must really be *present in the inferiors;* second, that this one thought-content be present in all of them in a *strictly uniform manner.*

The first condition is undoubtedly verified in the application of 'being' to the infinite and the finite, to substance and accident, to the absolute and the relative, etc. 'Being,' in the sense of 'existible,' is truly found in them all. They exist; or at least they can exist. There is no intrinsic contradiction in any of these concepts as such, and that is sufficient to consider them at least as *possible beings*. They are, then, beings in the sense of something 'existible'; and in this sense the thought-content of 'being' is really found in them in a true manner.

But the second condition is not fully verified. When a thought-content is realized in a number of things in a *strictly uniform manner,* they are, so far as *this* element is concerned, *perfectly alike* and do not differ in this particular respect. If they differ nevertheless, this difference is due to some other element *added* to it and this element is added to it *from without* as something new and extraneous. For instance, 'animal' is a univocal term applied to man and brute. In so far as man and brute are 'animals,' i.e., 'sentient,' they do not differ among themselves. The distinguishing element 'rational,' the point in which they differ, is *not contained* in the concept of 'animal' at all and is added from without. This, however, is not true of 'being' as realized in its inferiors. 'Being,' of course, is found in every one of these concepts; but the element in which the 'infinite' differs from the 'finite' and 'substance' differs from 'accident,' etc., is not anything outside the concept of 'being' and added extrinsically to it, but *is itself also a 'being.'* Hence, 'being' is not only that in which they agree; it is also that in which they *differ* and as such, then, it is not found in them in a strictly uniform manner. Thus, the 'infinite' is a being that is of itself eternal, immutable, absolutely independent; the 'finite' is created, changeable, temporal, dependent on the infinite. 'Substance' is a being that exists in itself and does not need another to inhere in; 'accident' is something that cannot naturally exist in itself, but must always depend on its substantial support for existence. These are essentially different modes of 'being,' and thus 'being' is *not realized* in them in a *strictly uniform manner*. In consequence of this the term 'being' does not apply to them in an entirely identical meaning. And since a term, which applies to its inferiors in a manner and meaning partly the same and partly different, is called analogous, 'being' is an *analogous term.*

If we inspect the fundamental relation which forms the basis of the analogy here, we find that it is an *analogy of intrinsic attribution.* For this two conditions are demanded: the element common to the things designated by the same term must be present in them in a true and genuine sense, and not merely applied to them as a figure of speech; this element must be found in the one member in an independent and absolute sense, and in the other member relatively and with dependence on the first. Such is the nature of 'being' as applied to the infinite and the finite, to substance and accident, to the absolute and the relative. In all these the concept of 'being,' their common element, is present in a true and genuine sense, and not merely as a figure of speech; they are truly and genuinely *beings,* because they really are existible. But it is equally clear that the *infinite* (God) is 'being' in an absolute and independent manner, while the *finite* (creature) can have 'being' only in relation to, and with dependence on, the infinite (God). So, too, it is the *substance* which has 'being' primarily, while *accidents* can exist only in and with the substance. Similarly, the absolute is of its very nature something which is independent in its 'being,' while the *relative,* as its name indicates, is dependent on the absolute. We thus see that these dual members, although they are true beings, are such that 'being' is realized in them in a totally different manner, the second member having a relation of dependence on the first: the first can exist without the second, but the second cannot exist without the first. And this relation of dependence forms the basis for the analogy of *intrinsic attribution* between them, since that is what is meant by analogy of 'intrinsic attribution.'

Summing up, we find that 'being' is contracted to its inferiors, not by means of a physical or metaphysical composition, but by means of a *logical composition.* 'Being' is *not* a true *genus,* but an *analogous idea,* based on an analogy of intrinsic attribution. These distinctions may not seem very important, but they play a vital part in the controversy between theism and pantheism. If 'being' were a true genus, embracing as members God and the world, there would be danger of merging both in the higher reality of 'being in general'; and that would be pantheism. A confusion of this sort would indeed be disastrous in many ways. A clear-cut knowledge of 'being' will avoid this intellectual pitfall without much difficulty.

SUMMARY OF CHAPTER IV

By the *contraction of being* we understand the reduction or narrowing of its extension to its inferiors by the addition of some element to its comprehension or thought-content.

1. 'Being' is contracted to its inferiors, not by means of a physical or metaphysical composition, but by means of a *logical composition*. By a logical composition is meant the union of elements which are neither objectively different in idea nor physically different as things, but merely different in the sense that the one idea contains implicitly and vaguely what the other expresses explicitly and determinately. If we contract the idea 'being' to 'substance' and 'accident,' we find that whatever reality the latter contain is merely an explicit and determinate *form of being* and is already included in the idea of 'being in general' in an implicit and indeterminate manner. They are, therefore, neither objectively different in idea, nor physically different as things, from 'being' itself.

2. *Being is not a true genus.* 'Substance' and 'accident' are not true species under 'being' as their genus. A 'species' is the result of the union between a 'genus' and a 'specific difference'; and the specific difference is an element *new* and *extraneous* to the content of the genus. In order, then, that 'being' be a true genus, we must find a specific difference which would be extraneous to the concept of 'being' and be added to it in the species. But every such difference would itself be a 'being' of some kind, and then it would not be extraneous to 'being.'

The only thing outside 'being' is 'nothing,' and 'nothing' can make no difference between things.

3. *Being is an analogous idea.* A 'univocal' term is one that is applied to a number of things in an identical sense. An 'equivocal' term is one that is applied to a number of things in entirely different meanings. An 'analogous' term is one which applies to unlike things, partly for the same and partly for a different reason, so that it is used in a meaning partly the same and partly different.

The term 'being,' as applied to the infinite and the finite, to substance and accident, to the absolute and relative, is not equivocal, because these things are real beings. But neither is it applied to them univocally, because the thought-content of 'being' is *not* found in them in a *strictly uniform manner*. It is found in the infinite, in the substance, and in the absolute in a primary and independent sense, while it is found in the finite, in the accident, and in the relative in a secondary and dependent sense. 'Being' is thus an analogous term, based on an analogy of *intrinsic attribution.*

READINGS

Coffey, P., pp. 36–39; Rickaby, J., Bk. I, Ch. II; Hugon, Ed., Tr. I, Qu. I, art. 2; Urráburu, J. J., Disp. I, cp. III; Phillips, R. P., Vol. II, Part II, Ch. II.

CHAPTER V

THE SUPREME PRINCIPLES

SO FAR we have investigated 'being' with regard to its content, in order to have a clear idea of its meaning. Our idea of 'being' has been amplified by the enumeration of the main classes in which it can be realized; we have become acquainted in a general manner with real being, ideal being, and logical being. The concept of 'nothing' has also been examined, thereby setting off the positive content of 'being' against the negative content of 'nothing.' We have also seen how the idea of 'being' is contracted to its inferiors, to the infinite and the finite, to substance and accident, to the absolute and the relative. We must now turn our attention to the supreme principles of being.

THE NATURE OF A PRINCIPLE

A *principle,* generally speaking, is *that from which something else proceeds in any way whatever.* In order that something be a real principle, it is necessary: first, that the principle be *prior* to the reality which proceeds from it; secondly, that this priority be grounded in the things themselves on account of some *special connection.* This priority may be one of time, or of nature, or of origin.

A *priority of time* exists when the principle has an existence which precedes that of the reality which flows from it. Fire is prior in time to the boiling of the water which it causes; an inventor is prior in time to the machine he makes; an electric current is prior in time to the movement of the motor which it operates; the sun is prior in time to the light it emits. A *priority in nature* exists when the principle possesses a nature whose presence is necessary for the existence of something which proceeds from it, even though this nature be not prior in time. Thus, substances must be prior in nature to their own accidents, because the latter presuppose a substance as the subject in which they have their being. The substance of a body is prior in nature to the three-dimensional quantity which modifies the body; a rose is prior in nature to the color found in it; a man is prior in nature to the vital functions which exist in his being. These accidents are present at the same time as the substance, but they could not exist unless the nature of the substance were presupposed, because they proceed from it as from their natural principle. A *priority of origin* exists when the principle is neither prior in time nor in nature, but prior in origin, to the reality which proceeds from it. We have an example in the Blessed Trinity, as held in Christian theology. The Father is the principle of origin for the Son and is prior to Him in this sense, but this origin involves neither a priority of time nor of nature. Obviously, it is beyond the scope and possibility of philosophy either to prove or disprove this last type of priority.

The *special connection* between the principle and that which proceeds from it may belong either to the logical or to the ontological order. It will be a *logical* connection, when the truth of one statement depends upon the truth of another, from which it flows; this latter statement would then be a logical principle. For instance, the premises in an argumentation are the logical principle for the conclusion. It will be an *ontological* connection, when the entity of one thing depends on the entity of another; such a principle would be an entitative or ontological or metaphysical principle. The connection existing between effects and causes is ontological; thus, hydrogen and oxygen are the ontological principle of water, because water depends in its being on the entitative union of hydrogen and oxygen. While logical principles also interest the ontologist, his main concern is with ontological or metaphysical principles; and among these the supreme principles of being demand his particular attention.

By the *supreme principles of being* are understood those highest principles which are *immediately derived from the concept of 'being'*: the Principle of Identity, the Principle of Contradiction, the Principle of Excluded Middle, and the Principle of Sufficient Reason.

THE PRINCIPLE OF IDENTITY

The *Principle of Identity* rests immediately on the concept of 'being.' A 'being' is something 'that is.' It is evident, then, that 'a being is a being.' And since 'nothing' is that 'which is not,' it is also evident that 'a not-being is a not-being.' Here we simply compare 'being' with itself and 'not-being' with itself, and the truth of the judgments is intuitively clear to the mind without the need of any demonstration; the relation of self-identity expressed therein is objectively self-evident. The Principle of Identity is the natural formulation of this relation. It is formulated in different ways: *Whatever is, is; and whatever is not, is not: Everything is what it is: Everything is its own being: Being is being, and not-being is not-being.*

This principle may seem to be a mere tautology, as if it were stated that 'A man is a man' or 'A stone is a stone.' But the identity enunciated in the principle has a wider application than this. It applies with equal force and truth to the statements that 'A man is a living substance' and 'A stone is material.' Here, too, the mind affirms an identity *in this case* between 'man' and 'living substance' and between 'stone' and 'material'; and these are obviously not tautological statements. The Principle of Identity is thus exemplified in every affirmative judgment made by the mind and is valid in both the logical and ontological orders.

THE PRINCIPLE OF CONTRADICTION

This principle is based on a comparison of 'being' with 'not-being.' In comparing these two concepts, it is transparently clear to the mind that the one is not, and cannot be, the other.

They mutually exclude each other with an absolute necessity. 'Being' is simply 'being' and cannot be 'not-being,' otherwise 'being' would be 'nothing' and would not be 'being' at all. The same is true of 'nothing': it is 'not-being' and as such can never be 'being,' otherwise 'nothing' would not be 'nothing' but would be 'being.' In other words, something 'that is' can never, under any and all conditions, be something 'that is not.' And since these two concepts can never be united in the mind as identical, but must be universally and necessarily in opposition to each other as contradictories, this self-evident truth is expressed in the Principle of Contradiction: *It is impossible for a thing to be and not be at the same time: A thing cannot be and not be something at the same time.*

It must be borne in mind, however, that the phrase 'at the same time' has more than a temporal meaning. It means as much as: from the same standpoint, at the same time, in the same circumstances, under the same conditions, in the same respect. The statement could be true that 'It is possible for rain to fall and not to fall at the same time,' if we refer to different localities; but it could not be true about the selfsame rain in the selfsame locality. It is also true that 'A boy can be a man,' if we mean that he can be a man at a later period of his life; but a boy cannot be a man while he is still a boy. The principle, therefore, applies to things taken *in the same respect;* and then it will be obvious that they cannot both 'be' and 'not be' something at the same time.

The principle has *universal application.* It applies with equal validity to things temporal and eternal, to things finite and infinite. Thus, it is impossible for a man to walk and not to walk, to think and not to think, to live and not to live, to be a millionaire and not to be a millionaire, to own a car and not to own a car. It is impossible to be immortal and yet mortal, to be uncreated and yet produced, to have all perfection and yet lack entity, to be omniscient and yet be ignorant of something, to be omnipotent and yet be incapable of producing some possible being.

From this it must be clear that the identification of 'being' and 'nothing' on the part of *Hegel* is sheer absurdity. Consider this statement of his: "The distinction between Being and Nought is, in the first place, only implicit, and not yet actually made: they only *ought* to be distinguished. A distinction, of course, implies two things, and that one of them possesses an attribute which is not found in the other. Being, however, is an absolute absence of attributes, and so is Nought. Hence, the distinction between the two is only meant to be; it is quite a nominal distinction, which is at the same time no distinction. In all other cases of difference there is some common point which comprehends both things. Suppose, e.g., we speak of two different species: the genus forms a common ground for both. But in the case of mere Being and Nothing, distinction is without a bottom to stand upon: hence, there can be no distinction, both determinations being the same bottomlessness. . . . Nothing, if it is thus immediate and equal to itself, is also conversely the same as Being is. . . . In Being we have Nothing, and in Nothing Being. . . . In Becoming the Being which is one with Nothing, and the Nothing which is one with Being, are only vanishing factors; they are and they are not."[1] This may be good idealistic monism, but it is an absolute violation of the Principle of Contradiction and the destruction of the foundations of all knowledge, science, and philosophy.

THE PRINCIPLE OF EXCLUDED MIDDLE

This principle is also the result of a comparison between 'being' and 'not-being.' It is called the *Principle of Excluded Middle,* because the mind intuitively perceives that between 'being' and 'not-being' there is no middle or third thing which would be left, if both 'being' and 'not-being' were removed. Such a middle thing either 'is' or 'is not.' If it 'is,' then it is a 'being'; if it 'is not,' then it is a 'not-being.' Consequently, it

---

[1] *Logic,* tr. by W. Wallace (Clarendon Press, 1892), Vol. 2, §§ 87, 88, 89, pp. 162, 163, 167, 169.

will be either a 'being' or a 'not-being,' but not a middle thing *between* the two which is neither the one nor the other. If it is the one, it is not the other; and if it is not the one, it must be the other. It certainly cannot be both 'being' and 'not-being' at the same time, because that would be impossible in virtue of the Principle of Contradiction. This principle has also been formulated in a number of ways: *A thing either is or is not: Everything must either be or not be: Between 'being' and 'not-being' there is no middle or third thing possible.*

As in the case of the two foregoing principles, this principle rests immediately on the relation between 'being' and 'not-being.' It needs no demonstration to prove its truth, because a mere understanding of the concepts of 'being' and 'not-being' and of their relations to each other is sufficient to make it evident. If it is impossible for a thing to 'be' and 'not to be' at the same time, then such a thing must either 'be' or 'not be'; nothing could be simpler or truer. The Principle of Excluded Middle is thus seen to flow naturally and logically out of the Principle of Contradiction. If the latter is valid, the former must be valid also.

Like the foregoing principles, this principle applies *to all things* without exception, if it is a question of contradictory distinctions. No matter what point may be mentioned, it is always 'either — or.' God is either infinite or not infinite, either eternal or not eternal, either created or not created, either a person or not a person. This stone is either quartz or not quartz, either heavy or not heavy, either small or not small. This man is either white or not white, either an American or not an American, either old or not old, either sick or not sick. There can be no middle ground between these contradictories: a thing cannot be both, and it must be either the one or the other of the two.

THE PRINCIPLE OF SUFFICIENT REASON

Everything, in so far as it is a 'being,' has reality. Whatever reality a being has, it must have it either of and by itself or from and by another being; in the first case it has the *sufficient reason* for its reality in itself, and in the second case it has it in the other. This is so obvious that the mere statement suffices to show its truth. And if it has no reality, it is no being at all, and this is simply due to the fact that it has not received reality either of itself or from another being; in both cases it is a 'not-being' because it has *no sufficient reason* for its reality. If it could have reality nevertheless, it would have to receive it from 'nothing.' But 'nothing' has no reality itself and can, therefore, never give reality to anything. Consequently, were such a reality without a sufficient reason, it would both 'be' and 'not be' at the same time: it would 'be,' because that is the supposition; and it would also 'not be,' because, having no sufficient reason to account for its reality except 'nothing,' it could receive only that which 'nothing' could give, which is precisely nothing. But 'to be' and 'not to be' at the same time is a violation of the Principle of Contradiction; and that is an absurdity. Hence, if a being has reality, it must have it either of itself or from another, i.e., it must have a sufficient reason for itself: *Nothing is without a sufficient reason: Everything must have a sufficient reason for its being and existence.*

METAPHYSICAL AND LOGICAL PRINCIPLES

These metaphysical or ontological principles are called *First Principles,* because they follow immediately from the first and fundamental concept of 'being.' They are primarily metaphysical principles of *reality*. They have, however, also a *logical* character, and as such are the first and fundamental principles or *laws of thought*. This must be so. Ideas are mental representations of reality, of things. In order truly to represent things, they must conform to the reality they represent. Because things are what they are and are not what is different from themselves, we can judge and think that they are so. Reality is thus the standard and norm according to which the mind must regulate and formulate its judgments concerning reality. Just as reality itself must conform to the metaphysical laws of being, so all judgments must conform to these same laws. Consequently, the laws of being must also be the laws of thought; in other words, these supreme metaphysical laws are at the same time the supreme *logical* laws.

It must be possible, then, to translate these metaphysical laws of being into logical laws of thought. This is not a difficult task. The *Principle of Identity* will read: Whatever is true of a thing must be affirmed of it: Truth is always truth, and falsity always falsity. The *Principle of Contradiction* will be: Something cannot be both true and false at the same time: Contradictories cannot be true at the same time. The *Principle of Excluded Middle* can be expressed: Contradictory judgments must be either true or false. The *Principle of Sufficient Reason* can be stated as follows: There must be a sufficient reason for the truth or falsity of a judgment.

To say that these are the supreme metaphysical and logical principles, does not mean that all being and all truth are included in them in such a way that all particular beings and all particular truths derive their *origin* from them. Were this the case, it would be possible to deduce the existence of single beings and single truths from them; then a knowledge of these principles would enable the mind to acquire a knowledge of all being and all truth in their various determinate forms by means of *a gradual unfolding* and detailed *development* of these principles. But this cannot be done. These principles are based on the concept of 'being in general,' and the latter is the emptiest and most indeterminate of all ideas. 'Being in general' is a mental abstraction; as such, it *exists* nowhere as a *reality* which would possess in the richness and fullness of its existing entity all other existing beings and truths. As an *idea* 'being in general' includes all beings and all truths in its extension, but not as an existing reality. The supreme principles of being and thought, therefore, are *not productive* principles or *causes,* but *regulative norms* and *laws* to which the particular beings and truths must conform.

Particular beings and particular truths derive their origin from *sources outside* these principles. That the sun exists, is not due to these principles. But *if* and *when* it exists, then it must conform to these laws. If the sun exists, it is a sun, according to the Principle of Identity; it cannot be a sun and not a sun at the same time, according to the Principle of Contradiction; it must either be or not be a sun, according to the Principle of Excluded Middle; and it must have a sufficient reason for its reality and existence, according to the Principle of Sufficient Reason. And from a logical standpoint, it must be true that it is a sun; it cannot be true and false at the same time that it is a sun; it must be either true or false that it is a sun; and since the judgment about the sun agrees with its reality, there is a sufficient reason for the truth of this judgment. These principles themselves, however, *do not confer reality and existence* on the sun; nor do they enable us to know of the existence of the sun. And what has been said here about the sun, pertains to every other kind of being, whether it be the earth, a tree, a dog, a house, a desk, an apple, a man, or God. They do not owe their being to the First Principles; but, if they have being, their being and the truths concerning their being are regulated according to the laws inherent in these metaphysical and logical principles. Such, then, is the nature of these supreme metaphysical and logical principles.

THE MOST FUNDAMENTAL PRINCIPLE

The question has been raised among philosophers as to which of these supreme metaphysical and logical principles is the *most fundamental*.

That the Principles of Excluded Middle and of Sufficient Reason cannot be the most fundamental, should be clear from the foregoing exposition of these principles. They are without doubt a development of the Principle of Contradiction. It is only because a thing 'cannot be and not be something under the same respect,' that it follows with necessity that a thing must 'either be or not be' and that it 'must have a sufficient reason.' Their validity is thus clearly based on the Principle of Contradiction; they rest solidly on the validity of the latter as upon their primary principle.

It is not so easy to decide whether the Principle of Identity or the Principle of Contradiction is the most fundamental in the ontological and logical order. *Aristotle* and his followers, the scholastics, have always considered the Principle of Contradiction to be the more fundamental of the two. Their view of the matter held the ascendancy and remained practically unchallenged. In more recent times, *Gottfried W. Leibnitz* (1646–1716) advocated the opinion that the Principle of Identity was the first and foremost. In his first essay on Locke he expressed himself as follows: "My view is that nothing shall be taken as first principles but experiences and the axiom of identity or (what is the same thing) contradiction, which is primitive."[2] Later on, however, in his *New Essays,* he came out more definitely in favor of the priority of the Principle of Identity: "In the natural order the statement, that a thing is what it is, is prior to the statement that it is not another."[3] At first, this latter view of Leibnitz might seem to be the more logical. But on closer inspection, if we consider these principles from the standpoint of the certitude of human knowledge, we must say that the *Principle of Contradiction* is the most fundamental. As *D. Card. Mercier* states the situation: "That of Identity is first, i.e., the first in the order of the mind's analysis, or genetically first; but in the regressive order, when it is a question of the firm foundation of the certitude of our knowledge, the Principle of Contradiction is the last, the touchstone of all certitude."[4]

The reason is this. If we accept the Principle of Identity as a mere tautology, then, it is true, it is prior to the Principle

---

[2] *Sur l'Essay de l'entendement humain de Monsieur Locke,* at the beginning.

[3] *New Essays,* tr. by A. G. Langley (Macmillan, 1896), Bk. IV, Ch. 7, § 9, p. 470.

[4] *A Manual of Modern Scholastic Philosophy,* tr. by T. L. and S. A. Parker, 8 edit. (Kegan Paul, 1916), Vol. I, p. 474.

of Contradiction; but a tautology is no principle of being or thought. When, however, we wish to assert with strict certitude and necessity that 'whatever is, is,' we really intend to affirm that 'whatever is, is *necessarily* so' and cannot be otherwise. But this is tantamount to saying that a thing cannot be and not be something at the same time: and that is the *Principle of Contradiction*. When we, therefore, consider the practical import of the Principle of Identity, we find that it really coincides with the Principle of Contradiction. Taken for itself, the Principle of Identity is, according to *Tilmann Pesch,* "vague and indeterminate, so that it is rather the root and the imperfect germ of principles"[5] than a full-fledged principle itself. Consequently, the Principle of Contradiction is the *most fundamental* among the supreme principles of being and of thought.

We may even go a step farther and say that the Principle of Contradiction is the most fundamental *of all principles* of being and thought. The most basic idea involved in every thought and thought-process, in every substantial and accidental reality, is the idea of 'being.' This idea of 'being' is thus the first in the *logical* and *ontological* order. Hence, the principle immediately expressive of this idea in thought and reality must be the most basic and fundamental principle in the same order. But it is the Principle of Contradiction which does this, because it is constituted solely by the idea of 'being' as compared with its directly opposite idea of 'not-being.' This principle, therefore, is implicitly contained in every other principle and gives to them whatever they possess of certitude and stability; they stand and fall with the Principle of Contradiction.

With this we conclude our investigation into the concept of 'being in general' and the supreme principles which flow from it. These principles are the ultimate laws of all being and all thought. We must now direct our attention to an examination of the *primary determinations of being.*

---

[5] *Institutiones Logicales* (Herder, Friebourg, 1890), Vol. 3, n. 1230.

SUMMARY OF CHAPTER V

1. *The Nature of a Principle.* A principle is that from which something else proceeds in any way whatever. There must be *priority* of the principle relative to the reality which proceeds from it; and this priority may be one of 'time,' or of 'nature,' or of 'origin.' This priority must be grounded in the things themselves on account of some *special connection;* this connection will be 'logical,' when the truth of one statement depends upon the truth of another, or 'ontological,' when the entity of one thing depends on the entity of another.

2. *The supreme principles* of being are those highest principles which are immediately derived from the concept of 'being.' These are:

The Principle of Identity: Whatever is, is; and whatever is not, is not: Everything is what it is: Everything is its own being: Being is being, and not-being is not-being.

The Principle of Contradiction: It is impossible for a thing to be and not to be at the same time: A thing cannot be and not be something at the same time.

The Principle of Excluded Middle: A thing either is or is not: Everything must either be or not be: Between 'being' and 'not-being' there is no middle or third thing possible.

The Principle of Sufficient Reason: Nothing exists without a sufficient reason: Everything must have a sufficient reason for its being and existence.

3. *Metaphysical and Logical Principles.* The metaphysical or ontological principles just mentioned are also *logical* principles, i.e., they are laws of thought as well as laws of being. Reality is the standard according to which we must regulate and formulate our ideas and judgments; consequently, the metaphysical laws are at the same time logical laws. These principles, however, are not the productive principles or causes of things, but the *regulative norms* or laws to which the particular beings and truths must conform.

4. *The Most Fundamental Principle.* The Principles of Ex-

cluded Middle and Sufficient Reason are a development of the Principle of Contradiction; they are, therefore, not the most fundamental. The Principle of Identity really means that 'whatever is, is *necessarily* so' and cannot be otherwise; and that is equivalent to the Principle of Contradiction. Consequently, the latter is the most fundamental of the supreme principles of being and of thought.

The Principle of Contradiction is also the most fundamental *of all principles,* because it is constituted solely by the idea of 'being,' and the idea of 'being' is the most basic idea involved in everything in the logical and ontological order.

READINGS

Rickaby, J., Bk. I, Ch. II; Pesch, Tilmann, *Institutiones Logicales,* Vol. II, Pars. II, n. 1228–1249; Mercier, D. Card., pp. 473–475; Aristotle, *Metaph.,* IV.

Chapter VI

ACT AND POTENCY

SO FAR 'being' has been considered in its most general features. Certain kinds of being have been enumerated, but this was done more for the purpose of obtaining a better understanding of the concept of 'being' itself. 'Being in general,' as was noted, is characterized by extreme indeterminateness, signifying anything that is not nothing, anything that is existible. *Real* being, of course, is not as indeterminate as all this; it has a distinct and definite character of some sort. And it is this distinct and definite character of real being which we mean when we speak of the 'determinations' of being.

Among the manifold determinations of 'being,' we are mainly interested in those *primary determinations* which are *transcendental;* namely those which constitute the most fundamental distinctions of 'being in general' and go beyond all the ordinary classifications of beings as found among actual things. Such are the basic divisions of 'being' into act and potency, essence and existence, the necessary and contingent, the infinite and the finite.

CONCEPT OF ACT AND POTENCY

Strictly speaking, these terms cannot be defined. Act and potency are immediate divisions of 'being.' In order to be defined, 'being' would have to be their proximate genus in the definition; but 'being,' as was pointed out before, is not a strict and true genus. This must be borne in mind in the following explanations and discussions.

According to philosophical terminology an *act* (Lat., *actus*) means any entity of whatever kind and nature which perfects and determines a thing in its being. Thus, the term 'act' in-cludes the *power* or faculty as well as the *operations* of that power, because this power is a perfection for the thing which has it; it includes every *accidental* modification of a being, because every accident (e.g., color, heat, weight, shape, etc.) perfects the being in some way; it includes every *essential* entity, because nothing is more perfecting for a thing than its essence; it also includes *existence,* because existence is a per-fection for a being. Whatever a being *has* or *is* in a positive manner is an 'act' for it. Man's substantiality, materiality, life, sentiency, and rationality, are 'acts'; his quantity, size, shape, age, sex, color, health, are 'acts'; his powers of reason and of will, of locomotion, of digestion, of seeing, hearing, feeling, etc., all these are so many 'acts,' perfecting and determining his being in its respective order as 'man.' And so with all other beings. The term 'act,' therefore, has a specialized and technical meaning, much wider than its signification in ordi-nary language.

Potency (Lat., *potentia,* power) is *the capacity or aptitude for something.* It is the correlative term to 'act.' 'Potency' is always the capacity or aptitude in reference to something which a being is not or has not, but which it can be or can receive. Any being, in so far as it has not as yet received a certain 'act' or perfection, but is capable of receiving it, is said to be 'in potency' for this act. Hydrogen, for example, has the 'act' of hydrogen; and oxygen has the 'act' of oxygen: but both have the 'potency' of water; they are 'actually' hydrogen and oxygen, but 'potentially' water. Water, on the other hand, is 'actually' water; but it is 'potentially' hydrogen and oxygen, because it has the aptitude to be resolved into them. Common salt is 'actually' salt, but it is 'potentially' chlorine and sodium.

If we consider the *relation between 'act' and 'potency,'* we find that it is the relation of the completing to the incomplete, the determining to the determinable, the perfecting to the perfectible. Since these are relative terms, it is obvious that an entity may be a determination and perfection for a being in one way and thus be an act, and it may also be determinable and perfectible in itself and thus be a potency. The intellect, for example, is a positive perfection of the mind, and thus an 'act,' for man; but the intellect itself is perfected by the actual thinking process (which is an 'act' for the intellect), and it is, from this point of view, a 'potency.' Similarly, the power of locomotion is a perfection, an 'act,' for a resting dog; but the act of running is a perfection for this power of locomotion, and the power of locomotion is thus seen to be a 'potency' with regard to this act of running. An entity, therefore, can be both an 'act' and a 'potency,' when considered from different viewpoints; but never with reference to the same perfection under the same respect, because that would violate the Principle of Contradiction.

KINDS OF ACT

There are as many kinds of 'acts' as there are kinds of 'being,' because every being as such is a perfection. We must, then, make a division along general lines.

Essence, Existence, Property, Accident. The act or actuality of the *essence* is the act which perfects and determines a thing *in its species*. It is that constitutive element or principle in a thing which makes it to be just this particular kind of thing and no other. It is the 'act of essence' which makes a horse to be a horse and not a cat, a rose to be a rose and not a cucumber, a man to be a man and not an elephant, silver to be silver and not copper.

The act of *existence* is the act perfecting and determining a thing in such a manner that it is no longer a merely possible being, but is present in the real order. A hundred years ago we were merely possible beings; now we have the 'act of existence.'

The act of *property* is the act of perfecting and determining an essence in such a manner that the entity it gives to the being *flows necessarily from its nature, without being strictly essential*. The essence of man, for instance, consists in being a 'rational animal'; never, not even for a single moment, can he cease to be such without destroying his human nature. The power of speech, of using tools, of laughing, are not part of this essence, but they flow necessarily from his being as a rational animal. These powers demand a body, because speech and laughter and the use of tools are bodily operations; they also demand rationality, because only a thinking mind can express itself by means of speech, laughter, and the use of tools. Hence, only a 'rational animal' is capable of these operations. Since, however, they are only the results of his essence, rather than part of the essence itself, they are 'properties' of man and as such are an 'act of property' for him.

The act of *accident* is the act perfecting and determining a being in such a manner that the entity it gives does *not flow necessarily from the essence of the being.* Red hair, white skin, one's weight, height, shape, etc., are all 'accidental acts' of the body. Thoughts, emotions, states of consciousness, etc., are 'accidental acts' of the mind. All operations proceeding from powers or faculties belong to this class, whether they be animate or inanimate, such as motion, light, heat, electricity, gravitational attraction, and so on.[1]

Primary and Secondary Act. A *primary* act is one that is the *first in a series of acts,* so that it has another act proceeding or capable of proceeding from it. Thus, the nature or essence of a being is an 'act,' and so are its faculties and the operations of these faculties. There exists a natural hierarchy among them, because the operations proceed from the faculties, and the faculties proceed from the essence or nature; hence, since this essence or nature is the ultimate principle from which both faculties and operations proceed, it is a 'primary act' in reference to them. For the same reason the faculties or powers of a being are a 'primary act,' when compared to the operations which they perform. Man's rational nature, for instance, is the 'primary act' with reference to his intellect and thoughts;

---

[1] See *The Science of Correct Thinking,* by the author, for a more detailed elucidation of these terms, pp. 55–60.

and, in a more limited way, the intellect is the 'primary act' with reference to the thoughts.

A *secondary* act is one that *presupposes another act in a definite series,* so that it proceeds from a primary act. Every action and operation is a 'secondary act' with regard to the power or faculty from which it flows. Thought is a 'secondary act' flowing from the intellect as a 'primary act.' A boy who has the ability to whistle is, in so far, in possession of a 'primary act' or faculty; but when he practices his art and warbles a tune, he has the 'secondary act' of whistling.

Pure and Mixed Act. A *pure* act is one *without the least admixture of potentiality.* It is all actuality (act), all perfection, complete determination. Such a being can have no capabilities or aptitudes. There is nothing in such a being which could be considered determinable, perfectible: it is completely and absolutely determined, actualized, perfect. It lacks no entity nor can it receive an increase of entity, for the simple reason that it possesses all possible actuality. Of course, the Infinite Being alone is such a 'Pure Act.'

A *mixed* or *non-pure* act is one that in some form or other *has an admixture of potentiality.* Such a being does not possess its actuality always and all at once; its perfection is acquired gradually and successively, and it is subject to development and change. Whatever has faculties is such a 'mixed act,' because they are not always in operation. All creatural beings, inanimate as well as animate, belong to this class, because they are limited in essence and acquire and lose many determinations in the course of their existence.

KINDS OF POTENCY

Potency, or potentiality, as we have seen, is the capacity or aptitude for some act. There are two main kinds of potency: objective and subjective.

Objective Potency. By *objective* potency we understand *the capacity of a non-existent being for existence.* As this descriptive definition indicates, such a being has not as yet actual existence and is a non-being; there is, however, a possibility of its being brought into existence by some cause, and so it has a 'capacity for existence.' It is, therefore, not an absolute nothing. A hen, for instance, has laid a fertilized egg. The future chick is as yet non-existent; in as much, however, as the capability is there for the chick to be hatched later on, the chick is said to be 'in objective potency.' Sodium and chlorine are present in separate containers; salt is not yet an existing reality, but it has 'objective potency,' because the necessary elements are there for the production of salt.

Subjective Potency. Subjective or *real* potency is the *capacity of something existing for an act.* This potentiality may be such that it consists in a special power of *receiving* an 'act' from another being, or in a special power of *communicating* an 'act' to another: this gives rise to the distinction between 'receptive' and 'operative' potencies.

A *receptive* subjective potency is *the capacity for receiving an act.* A child's mind has the receptive potency of acquiring knowledge from a book or a teacher. Iron has the receptive potency of being magnetized. Water has the receptive potency of being heated to the boiling point or of being frozen to ice. This receptive potency will be *natural,* when it is a capacity for receiving an act in virtue of its natural powers. Such are the instances just mentioned. It will be an *obediential* receptive potency, when it is a capacity for receiving an act which transcends its natural faculties, provided this act be given to it by a superior power. Thus, a dead body cannot, in virtue of its own powers, come to life again; but it can receive life a second time, if God reanimates it: a dead body, therefore, has an 'obediential subjective potency' for renewed life.

An *operative* subjective potency is the *capacity for doing something;* it is the power of a thing to bring forth some act. Electricity is a power capable of producing mechanical motion, light, heat. Dynamite can effect violent explosive detonations. The mind can produce thoughts.

An operative subjective potency is either supernatural or

natural. It is *supernatural,* when it is the power to produce effects which transcend the capabilities of physical nature. Miracles, or acts involving a suspension of physical laws, can be performed only by a supernatural power. It is *natural,* when the effects produced are the result of an operative power inherent in the essence of a being and acting according to the laws of nature. That the eye sees, the ear hears, the mind thinks, the magnet attracts, the bird flies, the motor runs — all this is the effect of natural operative subjective potencies.

A natural operative potency may be passive or active. It is *passive,* when it presupposes its object and must be stimulated to activity by it; given the stimulation, however, the passive operative power becomes actively engaged in producing its proper effect. The eye, for instance, presupposes objects and light to stimulate it; it then produces vision through its own activity. Gasoline must be ignited in a motor cylinder; then its inherent forces explode and drive the pistons. A race horse must be led to the post and urged to race; but it does its own galloping. A potency will be an *active* natural operative potency, if it produces or prepares its own object. Thus, the vegetative powers first prepare the food in the digestive tract before assimilating the food into the tissues. Plants produce their own seeds. Bees produce their own wax for building cells and produce the honey for their own food.

POSSIBILITY, OR OBJECTIVE POTENCY

Possibility, or objective potency, as has been explained above, is the *capacity or aptitude of a being for existence.* A 'possible' being, then, is one that has an aptitude for receiving existence. *Impossibility* is the incapacity or inaptitude of a being for existence. An 'impossible' being is thus a being that has no aptitude for receiving existence. Possibility and impossibility are such important concepts in the philosophy of 'being,' that they deserve special treatment.

Many things we know to be 'possible' from the simple fact that we observe them as actually existing; if they were 'impossible,' they would not exist and we could not observe them. Trees, potatoes, vines, cows, giraffes, cats, iron, gold, buildings, automobiles, airplanes, men — all are seen to really exist and consequently are 'capable of existence.' We cannot observe 'impossible' things, because such things do not and cannot exist; but we know certain things to be impossible by way of conclusion from what we see existing and from self-evident first principles. We know what 2 and 3 mean, and in consequence of this we also know that their sum cannot possibly be 7 or 8. We understand the nature of circles and squares, and we perceive that 'square circles' are an impossibility. We have a clear perception of the essence of man as a 'rational animal,' and we are absolutely sure that a man without the power of reason cannot possibly exist.

What, then, is required and suffices, in order that a being be *adequately possible,* i.e., that it can really pass from a state of non-existence into a state of existence? Two things are essentially demanded and suffice.

The *first requirement* is that there be a *compatibility of the being's constitutive elements.* These elements must not be mutually exclusive in any way, not antagonistic, incompatible, repugnant. If one element denies and removes as much as the other posits, it is obvious that such elements mutually remove each other; the result would really amount to a non-being, and a non-being cannot exist. Take a 'square circle.' A circle is a geometrical figure that consists entirely of a curved line; the curved line eliminates all straight lines in the thing. A square, on the other hand, consists essentially of four straight lines of equal length and joined at their ends to make one figure; the straight lines thus eliminate any curved line. Hence, a 'square circle' would be a figure of straight lines, since it is 'square' (and that removes the curved line), and it would also be at the same time a figure consisting of a curved line, since it is a 'circle' (and that removes the straight lines); the final result would be that there are neither straight nor curved lines, and so nothing would be left that is capable of existence.

If the straight lines alone remained, we would have a 'square,' but not a 'circle,' and if the curved line alone remained, we would have a 'circle,' but not a 'square'; in neither case would there be a 'square circle' as originally supposed. Due to the incompatibility of the elements involved in a 'square circle,' it is an impossible thing.

It is a different matter entirely, when we speak of a 'mountain of gold,' or a 'crystal palace,' or an 'eagle-headed lion,' or a 'winged horse,' or a 'beanstalk that reaches to the clouds,' and similar fanciful objects. Though such objects, as a matter of fact, do not exist, there is no real impossibility about them. Gold and crystal could exist in such quantities. A lion could have a head shaped like an eagle. A horse could exist with wings. A beanstalk could, absolutely speaking, grow so tall. These objects contain *no contradiction in terms,* and it is only a thing that contains a contradiction in its constitutive elements that is intrinsically impossible and therefore incapable of existence.

In so far, then, as a thing has a compatibility of its constitutive elements, it is said to possess *intrinsic (metaphysical, absolute, logical) possibility.* That is the first requirement for a 'possible' being.

The *second requirement* for a 'possible' being is that there exist *an efficient cause* capable of communicating existence to the possible being. No being can bring itself from non-existence to existence, nor can it receive existence from 'nothing,' as will be shown when the Principle of Causality is under discussion; hence, a being can be capable of existence (i.e., be possible) only if some other being is capable of producing it. Naturally, though, a thing may be capable of receiving existence through production by one cause, while not being capable of being produced by a cause possessing less power. Something may thus be impossible for a child, while it is quite possible for a man. Again, many things, i.e., miracles, are impossible to man with his natural powers, but are possible for the Supreme Being. There must be a proportion between effect and cause: a cannon can obviously do more than a popgun.

ENTITY AND KINDS OF POSSIBLES

It may seem odd to speak of the *entity of a possible being.* From the standpoint of actual existence, the possibles are clearly nothing, since they are as such non-existent. It would be wrong, nevertheless, to identify them absolutely with 'nothing.' For one thing, the possibles are *capable* of existence; 'nothing' is absolutely incapable of existence. Then, too, the possibles have a *positive thought-content* (e.g., a 'mountain of gold,' a 'crystal palace'); 'nothing' has no content whatever and can be known only through a negation of being. Finally, the possibles differ among themselves by means of *objectively different concepts* (e.g., there is a real difference between a 'mountain of gold' and a 'crystal palace'); but between 'nothing' and 'nothing' there is no difference. The possibles are, therefore, real, though not actual; 'nothing,' however, is neither real nor actual. The possibles thus possess a *positive metaphysical entity,* but not any kind of physical actual entity.

As for the *various kinds of possibility,* we distinguish between intrinsic and extrinsic possibility.

Intrinsic (metaphysical, absolute, logical) possibility is the capacity or aptitude of a being for existence, due to the compatibility or *non-contradiction of its constitutive elements.* There must be no contradiction in terms, no contradiction in the thought-content or comprehension of its idea. A large circle is intrinsically possible, but a square circle is not. A winged horse is intrinsically possible, but a bodyless horse is not, because, being an animal, it must be a corporeal substance. A stick a million miles long is intrinsically possible, but a stick with only one end is not, because it would be finite and infinite in length. The latter alternatives all contain a contradiction in terms.

Extrinsic (relative) possibility is the capacity of a being for existence *in virtue of the power of an efficient cause capable of producing it.* Next year's automobiles are extrinsically possible, because the men and machines are in existence to make them. For the same reason houses, clothes, shoes, tools, railways, dirigibles, guns, boats, motors, books, and similar things, are extrinsically possible. But it would be extrinsically impossible for a man to lift a five-ton truck with his hands alone, to run a mile a minute, to jump fifty feet into the air, to make a tree or a bird. Extrinsic possibility always presupposes intrinsic possibility.

Extrinsic possibility may be twofold: physical and moral. *Physical* possibility is the possibility due to the powers of a thing *acting according to the laws of nature.* For instance, a heavy charge of electricity in opposite clouds is physically capable of producing a flash of lightning. A normal man possesses the physical possibility of standing without support for five minutes; it may be physically impossible for a sick man to do the same. Other instances of physical possibility and impossibility are given in the preceding paragraph.

Moral possibility is the possibility of free agents to do something *without grave difficulty.* Where a grave difficulty is present, an action is said to be 'morally impossible,' although it may still be physically possible. It would be a serious inconvenience and therefore a moral impossibility for a man with pneumonia to perform hard labor. It is morally possible for a man of perfect health to walk five miles over good roads and in good weather for the sake of signing a contract that will net him a pretty sum of money; but it would be morally impossible for a child to walk a mile to school, when the temperature is 30° below zero.

Comparing these various kinds of possibility with one another, we arrive at the following general principles or *laws of possibility:*

Moral possibility always includes physical and metaphysical possibility; physical possibility includes metaphysical. But what is metaphysically possible need not for that reason be physically or morally possible; and what is physically possible need not be morally possible.

Metaphysical impossibility excludes physical and moral possibility; and physical impossibility excludes moral possibility. But what is morally impossible, need not for that reason be physically impossible; and what is physically impossible need not be metaphysically impossible.

A perusal of the examples given above will show the truth of these conclusions. The greatest number of possibles is found among things that are metaphysically possible, and the smallest number among those that are morally possible. Reversely, the greatest number of impossibles can be found among those that are morally impossible, and the smallest number among those that are metaphysically impossible.

Having seen the immediate reason or ground why things are said to be possible or impossible, it is but natural to ask ourselves, What is the *ultimate ground* of the possibility of things? This question reaches down into the very root of all 'being' and deserves special attention.

SUMMARY OF CHAPTER VI

The *primary determinations* of 'being' are transcendental, i.e., they constitute the most fundamental distinctions of 'being' in general and go beyond the classifications of beings as found among the ordinary things. One such primary determination of 'being' is *act* and *potency*.

1. *Act* is *any entity perfecting and determining a thing in its respective order of being.* This includes all operations, all powers or faculties, all accidental modifications, essence, and existence, of things: whatever a being has or is.

Potency is the *capacity or aptitude for something.* The relation between act and potency is the relation of the completing to the incomplete, of the perfecting to the perfectible, of the determining to the determinable.

2. *Kinds of Act.* There are 'acts' of essence, existence, prop-

erty, and accident; primary and secondary; pure and non-pure or mixed.

Kinds of Potency. We distinguish between *objective* potency, which is the capacity of a non-existent being for existence, and *subjective* potency, which is the capacity of an existing being for an act. Subjective potency may be 'receptive' or 'operative.' A receptive potency may be either 'natural' or 'obediential'; an operative potency may be either 'supernatural' or 'natural'; a natural operative potency may be either 'passive' or 'active.'

3. *Possibility, or Objective Potency.* In order that a being be *adequately* possible, it is required and suffices that there be a compatibility of its constitutive elements and that there exist an efficient cause capable of conferring existence upon it. The compatibility or non-contradiction of these constitutive elements gives to a being *intrinsic* (metaphysical, absolute, logical) possibility; and the existence of a capable efficient cause gives to a being *extrinsic* (relative) possibility.

4. *Entity and Kinds of Possibles.* Though the possibles do not exist, they are not absolutely identical with 'nothing': possibles can exist, while 'nothing' can never exist; the possibles have a positive thought-content, while 'nothing' is a mere negation; the possibles differ among themselves, while between 'nothing' and 'nothing' there is no difference.

Kinds of Possibility. The main kinds are *intrinsic* and *extrinsic*. Extrinsic possibility is either 'physical' or 'moral.' *Impossibility* is the reverse of 'possibility,' and there are as many kinds of impossibility as there are kinds of possibility.

READINGS

Coffey, P., Ch. II; Hugon, Ed., Tr. I, Qu. II, art. 1 et 2; Aristotle, *Metaphysics*, V, IX; St. Thomas, Comment. in IX *Metaph.*, in II, III, VII et VIII Phys.; *De Ente Et Essentia;* Urráburu, J. J., Disp. III, Cp. II; Phillips, R. P., Ch. IV; McCormick, J. F., Ch. IV, pp. 47–51.

Chapter VII

ULTIMATE GROUND OF POSSIBILITY

THINGS ARE possible beings when they have a capacity for existence. For a thing to be possible, two conditions must be present: the elements constituting its being must be compatible (non-contradictory), and that is 'intrinsic' possibility; and there must exist an efficient cause with sufficient power to bring the possible thing from non-existence into existence, and that is 'extrinsic' possibility. Extrinsic possibility presupposes intrinsic possibility; for no efficient cause can produce a thing, if the constitutive elements of this being are contradictory and cannot be realized together. The compatibility of the elements is thus an *absolute* condition; without it a thing is metaphysically and absolutely impossible. The existence of an adequate efficient cause is a *relative* condition; one sort of efficient cause may not have enough power to produce the thing in question, but a higher and more powerful cause might be able to produce it. In the verification of these two conditions we have the immediate or *proximate ground* of possibility.

At present we are concerned with the deeper problem of the final or *ultimate ground* of possibility. It is not a question now whether this or that thing has a compatibility of its constitutive elements, or whether this or that efficient cause can produce this or that particular thing. It is rather the question: Why have the possibles any intrinsic and extrinsic possibility *at all?* Why are constitutive elements *ultimately* compatible or incompatible, so that some things are intrinsically possible, while others are intrinsically impossible? What is the ultimate foundation for extrinsic possibility, not only for a particular possible being, but for *each and every possible reality,* whether it ever becomes existent or not? Even the existing realities are possible, otherwise they could never have received existence. The question, therefore, involves the ultimate ground of *all possibility,* independent of actual existence as present or absent.

We will first consider the ultimate ground for extrinsic possibility, and then that for intrinsic possibility.

ULTIMATE EXTRINSIC POSSIBILITY

We may as well state, without further ado, that the ultimate ground or foundation of all possibility is found in the Supreme Being, in the *nature of God.* No philosophic proofs for God's existence and His infinite perfection will here be adduced. It would take us too far afield.[1] In connection with the present problem God's existence and infinite perfection must be assumed as validly demonstrated. Granted, then, the existence and infinite perfection of God's nature, we are prepared to prove that the ultimate ground for all extrinsic possibility is found in the *omnipotence* of God, guided by His infinitely perfect *intelligence.*

In stating this thesis, we do not intend to affirm that God's omnipotence is the sole efficient cause, thereby denying the efficient causality of creatural beings. Creatural beings are also efficient causes. They possess productive powers and do actually produce things by means of these powers; as such they are the proximate ground for the extrinsic possibility of the things they produce. However, a moment's reflection should convince us that they are not the ultimate ground for this possibility. Finite causes do not and cannot produce the *total reality* of their effects, so that they bring the complete being from non-existence to existence. That would be creation, and finite beings *cannot create;* they merely *change* one kind of being into another kind of being. The forces of nature never produce the *matter* of which things consist; matter is always

---

[1] These proofs will be given later in theodicy, in considerable length and detail.

presupposed in every kind of creatural activity and causality. This 'matter' must also be accounted for when there is question of the ultimate ground of the extrinsic possibility of the things which creatural beings produce.

Similarly, finite beings produce things through the mediation of their operative powers, faculties, energies. The energies of nature can be transformed from one kind into another, as when heat is transformed into mechanical motion and electricity into light. But here again, it is a question of accounting for the extrinsic possibility of this creatural *energy*. Though an existent reality, it also is limited and contingent in its very nature, and we are therefore compelled to look for the ultimate ground of its own possibility. Matter and energy can no more produce themselves than any other thing can produce itself; consequently, they also demand an ultimate ground *outside themselves* for their existence. They belong to the class of beings which we call the 'possibles' and as such are not self-explanatory.

Finally, we must admit that there are far more things of the same kind which *do not exist* than those which do. There could be more men, animals, plants, metals, elements, protons, electrons, etc., than those which actually exist; there could also be more electricity, heat, magnetism, light, mechanical motion, etc., than that which is actually present in our existing universe. These things, though they do not actually exist, are possible; they *could exist,* taken absolutely and by themselves, even though there are no existing causes in the universe which could create them and thus bring them from non-existence to existence. Since the present causes in our universe cannot give them existence, although they are possible, the ultimate ground of their extrinsic possibility does not lie in the actual universe but in something *outside the universe.* For we must bear in mind that the question before us involves *all possibles,* whether actually existing or not. Hence, when it is a question of the 'ultimate' ground of all extrinsic possibility, i.e., when we look for the *ultimate efficient cause* which could bring *all possible beings* into existence, this power can only be found in a being which is outside and beyond all beings of limited power and causality.

While the number of creatural beings in the actual universe is limited, there is no limit to the number of non-existing possible beings which are capable of existing, provided there be a cause sufficiently powerful to produce them. It must be obvious, however, that only a *positively infinite power* is capable of producing the *negatively infinite number of possible beings*. The reason is clear. Since all creatural beings without exception, whether existent or non-existent, demand an 'ultimate' ground for their extrinsic possibility, the efficient cause which can give them existence must be an *existent cause* and it must be completely *outside the class* of creatural beings. If it were not an 'existent cause,' it could not give existence to the possibles; and if it were not 'outside the creatural class,' it would itself belong to the possibles and as such would again demand an 'ultimate' ground for its own possibility. But such an existent cause which is outside the creatural class and which possesses a positively infinite power of causality, is the Infinite Being, God. The causality of God, however, resides in His *omnipotence*. Hence, it is the omnipotence of God which is the ultimate ground of all extrinsic possibility.

All extrinsic possibility is thus seen to be ultimately grounded in God's omnipotence. But not in His omnipotence alone. The infinite *intelligence* of God also has an essential part in the possibility of things. If His intelligence did not direct and guide His omnipotence, this omnipotence would act *blindly* in its productive activity. But that is absurd. God, the infinitely perfect being, cannot act blindly and unintelligently in any of His operations: intelligence is a prerequisite condition for His omnipotence to act. Of course, it is the omnipotent *power* of God which exerts *causality,* and not His intelligence; that is why we do not place the ultimate ground of extrinsic possibility in His intelligence. Nevertheless, the possible beings must be 'known' before they can become the object of His omnipotent causal action; hence, His omnipotence must be directed and guided by His intelligence, in order that things can have extrinsic possibility.

And thus we see that the ultimate ground or foundation for all extrinsic possibility is found in the omnipotence of God, guided by His infinite perfect intelligence.

ULTIMATE INTRINSIC POSSIBILITY

In order that beings be truly 'possible,' they must also be *intrinsically* or metaphysically possible. That is to say, their constitutive elements must be *non-contradictory,* mutually compatible. This raises the vital question: What is the ultimate reason and ground why some constitutive elements are compatible, thereby making a being intrinsically possible, while other elements are incompatible so that a being is intrinsically impossible? In answer to this question we propose to prove that *God* is the ultimate ground of all intrinsic possibility in things. More specifically, it is not God's omnipotence, nor His will, nor His intelligence, but His infinitely perfect *essence,* which is this ultimate ground.

God is the *ultimate* ground of all intrinsic possibility in the possible beings.

This must be so. We have just shown that God is the ultimate ground of 'extrinsic' possibility. But 'extrinsic' possibility has its foundation in 'intrinsic' possibility. This 'intrinsic' possibility of things, then, must also have its ultimate ground *outside* the entire class of possibles; because, being only 'possible,' they themselves cannot give to themselves constitutive elements which would be either compatible or incompatible. Consider the vast amount of 'possible' beings that do not exist and never will exist. As 'mere possibles' they are entitatively nothing. They could, however, absolutely speaking, receive existence, due to the omnipotence of God and the compatibility of the constitutive elements of their essence. If the ultimate ground for this compatibility or incompatibility were found in them, they themselves would be the cause, or reason, or principle, why some things are intrinsically possible and others intrinsically impossible. But an 'entitative nothing' cannot be the cause, or reason, or principle, of anything. The possibles are *subject* to the law of intrinsic possibility, regarding both their essence and their existence, and as such must *conform* to this law in order to be 'possible' at all. They cannot, then, be the cause, or reason, or principle, of this law. Consequently, there must exist some being outside the entire class of possible beings, which is the ultimate ground of their intrinsic possibility. That being, of course, is God.

If God were not this ultimate ground, and if this ultimate ground were in the creatural things themselves, it would mean that God's omnipotence would be *dependent on His creatures* for the exercise of its causality. Even God's omnipotence, as we will see shortly, cannot produce an 'impossible' thing. If the reason for this does not lie in Himself, but in the creatures, these creatures would *restrict His omnipotence* in a definite manner. But that is an absurdity. Creatures cannot restrict the power of omnipotence. Omnipotence, thus dependent and restricted by outside beings, would *not be infinite* in its perfection and would, as such, not be omnipotence at all. Consequently, to affirm that the ultimate ground of intrinsic possibility rests in the possibles themselves and not in God, would be a virtual denial of God's omnipotence and of God Himself. We must conclude, therefore, that this ultimate ground exists in God.

God's *omnipotence* is *not* this ultimate ground.

Some philosophers, among them *William of Ockham*[2] (about 1280–1349), defended the doctrine that intrinsic possibility depends ultimately on God's power. It is true that, because things are intrinsically possible, God's power can produce them. But we cannot reverse the statement and say that things are intrinsically possible *because* God's power can produce them. This statement seems innocent enough. However,

---

[2] Comment. in 1. *1 sent.* dist. 43 q. 2.

consider what it implies. Why would things be intrinsically possible, i.e., why are their constitutive elements compatible and non-contradictory? Because God's omnipotence can produce them. And why are other things intrinsically impossible, i.e., why are their elements incompatible and contradictory? The only answer can be, *because* God's omnipotence *cannot* produce them. The ultimate ground for intrinsic impossibility would thus be the *lack of power* in God. If God had more power, the impossibles would also be intrinsically possible. But that is patently false.

God possesses power in an infinite degree; therefore, no things should be intrinsically impossible, if it were merely a question of God's power. In that case it should be within God's power to produce a being which is finite and infinite at the same time, which exists and does not exist at the same time, which is rational and irrational at the same time, which is living and dead at the same time. But to make an assertion like this, means to invalidate the Principle of Contradiction and that means to destroy the foundation of all being and knowledge: skepticism must follow such a view.

Consequently, if we accept God's omnipotence as the ultimate ground for intrinsic possibility and impossibility, we face the following dilemma: either God *lacks power,* because He cannot produce certain things, and that is why they are impossible; or He can *produce contradictory beings,* because He is truly omnipotent, and then there are no impossible beings at all. In the first alternative we deny God's omnipotence and thereby God Himself, and in the second we deny the validity of the Principle of Contradiction and thereby destroy the foundation of all being and knowledge. Both admissions are fatal. We must, therefore, conclude that the ultimate ground of the intrinsic possibility and impossibility of things is not due to God's omnipotence.

God's *will* is *not* this ultimate ground.

It has been maintained that the fundamental reason, why some things are intrinsically possible and others intrinsically impossible, is due to the fact that God freely willed that some constitutive elements shall be compatible and others incompatible. He could just as well decide that what is now impossible shall be possible and what is now possible shall be impossible. *René Descartes* (1596–1650), for instance, affirmed that God did not will that the three angles of a triangle should be equal to two right angles because He knows that they could not be otherwise; on the contrary, this is so, and it cannot be otherwise, because He willed that these angles be necessarily equal to two right angles. In a similar manner, $1 + 2 = 3$, because God wills it to be this way; but if He had willed it to be different, the sum of $1 + 2$ could equal any other number.[3] In other words, intrinsic possibility and impossibility has its ultimate foundation solely in the free will of God. God, of course, will not change His decision, and all things thus remain without confusion as He has willed them from eternity.

Such a view, however, has *disastrous consequences*. It is true that possible things can receive existence, and thus become actual, only if God freely decides to give them existence, for without His will no creatural thing can exist. But it is a totally different matter to assert that on that account His free will can change the contradictory elements of an intrinsically impossible thing into non-contradictory elements. Consider the results of such a view. If God willed, He could create a man who would be God and, though God, would be only a plant, and this human-divine plant could be devoid of all life and still be omniscient and more than omniscient. If God willed, He could make a being which could be more powerful than His own omnipotence and at the same time could be absolutely inert, inactive, and powerless. A doctrine which involves absurdities such as these refutes itself.

God's *intelligence* is *not* this ultimate ground.

If the intelligence of God were the ultimate ground for

---

[3] In his *Resp. ad Sex. Object.*, n. 6 et 8.

the intrinsic possibility of things, it would mean that the constitutive elements in the essence of things would be compatible and non-contradictory, *because* they are *known* by God; God's intelligent knowing would then be the real reason why the elements of the possibles are non-contradictory and why the elements of the impossibles are contradictory. While this view comes closer to the true solution of the possibles than the others, it is not the final answer.

Certainly, if God's intelligence cannot think of the constitutive elements of a thing as being compatible, then such a thing is impossible; and if He can think of them as compatible, the thing is truly possible. But that does not necessarily imply that God's intelligence *confers* compatibility or incompatibility upon these elements. As a matter of fact and principle, 'being' is *logically prior* to 'thought,' because thought, to be true, must conform to the thing thought of. Thought logically presupposes the thing which is the object of thought; and that, in this case, is the 'possible' being.

Intelligence, through its act of knowledge, does *not make* the object *intelligible*. Rather, intelligence can know a thing only because this thing possesses intelligibility *in itself*, i.e., because it is a 'being' whose essence is constituted of elements that are compatible and for that reason has a *positive content* which can become an object of thought. Intelligence merely perceives and recognizes this compatibility or incompatibility of the essential elements as something which is present and then acknowledges the fact that the thing is 'possible' or 'impossible.' Such is the nature of knowledge and intelligence. From this it will be seen that intelligence, in thinking of a thing, presupposes its intelligibility; and the intelligibility of a thing presupposes the compatibility of the elements of its essence. Consequently, intelligence does not really make a thing to be 'possible,' and God's intelligence thus cannot be the *ultimate* ground of possibility.

God's essence is the ultimate ground of intrinsic possibility. This follows as a necessary conclusion from what already

has been proved. God must be the ultimate ground for all
possibility. But neither His omnipotence, nor His will, nor
His intelligence, is the ultimate reason why some constitutive
elements are compatible and others incompatible in the essence
of things, so that the latter are possible or impossible. The
ultimate ground for this must lie, then, in some reality in
God which is logically prior to His omnipotence and will and
intelligence. This reality, however, can only be His essence.
Therefore, His essence is the ultimate ground of all intrinsic
possibility.

A possible thing is fundamentally a 'being,' an 'essence,'
while an impossible thing is fundamentally a 'non-being,' a
'non-essence.' Now, 'being' ('essence') cannot have its ultimate
ground in anything but 'being' ('essence'), because 'being' can
proceed only from 'being.' Consequently, God's *being* or
essence is the ultimate ground for the intrinsic possibility of
things. Because God possesses 'being' to the fullness of infinite
perfection, other things can obtain 'being' from Him, in a
limited and participated degree. This does not mean that they
emanate from God's essence in any way, but that they can be
creatural imitations which He can *produce*. In as much, then,
as creatures can be made by God in imitation of His own
'being' and 'essence,' they are capable of receiving existence
from His omnipotence, through an act of His will, guided by
His intelligence; and in so far, and *only* in so far, are they
'possible.' On the other hand, a 'non-being,' a 'non-essence,' a
'nothing,' is the antithesis of God's being and essence and as
such can be no imitation of Him; for that reason it is incapable
of receiving existence from Him, that is, it is 'impossible.'
And this also explains why the *possibles are intelligible,* while
the impossibles are unintelligible. The former, since they imitate the infinite essence of God, possess constitutive elements
in their essence which are compatible and therefore conceivable. The opposite is the case with the impossibles, and that is
the reason why we can only think of them as negations of

'being,' as things that involve a contradiction in their very idea; the impossibles are inconceivable.

God's essence, then, is the ultimate ground for all intrinsic possibility, just as His omnipotence, guided by His intelligence, is the ultimate ground for all extrinsic possibility.

We now also understand why the *proximate* ground for intrinsic and extrinsic possibility resides in the possible things *themselves*. Because a possible thing possesses compatible constitutive elements in its own essence, it is 'intrinsically' possible in itself; but it possesses such elements only because it is a finite copy of the compatible essence of God. Similarly, because there exists a finite cause which has the requisite power to produce the possible thing, this latter being is 'extrinsically' possible; but the finite cause has the power of causality only because it is a finite copy of the infinite causality of God's omnipotence.

This also explains why a thing is intrinsically or metaphysically impossible when *our* concept of such a thing involves a *contradictory thought-content*. Our concepts, of course, do not influence the reality of things, so as to make them either possible or impossible. But God's essence is the ultimate ground of all *being and thought,* the ultimate foundation for all *ontological and logical laws.* Our concepts copy reality, and the laws of our thought follow the laws of being. Consequently, just as there can be no contradiction in the 'being' of things without them being thereby intrinsically and metaphysically impossible, so there can be no contradiction in our 'concept' of things without them being thereby intrinsically and metaphysically impossible: our concepts of things imitate God's concepts of things, no matter how inadequately, just as the being of things imitates the being of God, no matter how inadequately. If, then, our concept of a thing involves a real contradiction, this contradiction will also exist for God's intelligence, because the thing is in contradiction to His own essence and as such must be intrinsically and metaphysically impossible *in itself:* God, therefore, could never make it either extrinsically or intrinsically possible without contradicting His own intelligence and essence.

We thus see the inner nature of possibility and impossibility. Being and thought, actuality and potentiality, possibility and conceivability — all have their root, their foundation, their final reason, their ultimate ground, in the infinite fullness and richness of God's own being and essence.

SUMMARY OF CHAPTER VII

The problem before us is the *ultimate ground* of all 'extrinsic' and 'intrinsic' possibility.

1. *Ultimate Extrinsic Possibility.* Finite or creatural beings possess real causality, but they do not produce the *total reality* of their effects: 'matter' and 'energy' are always presupposed as existing; their causality can only change things from one kind of being to another. But 'matter' and 'energy' must also be accounted for, when it is a question of the ultimate ground of all extrinsic possibility, because they also belong to the class of 'possibles.' Besides, there are far more possible beings which never receive existence than those which become existent. Since the finite causes of the present universe cannot give them existence, the ultimate ground for their possibility must lie *outside* the universe — in God. But it is God's *omnipotence* which is the principle of His causality. Consequently, God's omnipotence is the ultimate efficient cause which makes all possible things capable of receiving existence. God's omnipotence, however, cannot work blindly, but must be guided by His *intelligence.* Hence, God's omnipotence, guided by His intelligence, is the ultimate ground of all extrinsic possibility.

2. *Ultimate Intrinsic Possibility.* The reason why the constitutive elements of some things are compatible and those of other things incompatible, is found in God. This reason cannot lie in the things themselves, because both the 'possibles' and the 'impossibles' are as such 'entitatively nothing,' and thus they cannot be the reason for the compatibility or incompati-

bility of their elements. This reason must, then, be found in a being *outside* the whole class of 'possibles' and 'impossibles.' That being is *God*.

But God's *omnipotence* is not this ultimate ground. If it were, then the only reason why certain things are 'impossible' would be because He lacks the power to produce them; that is a virtual denial of His omnipotence.

Neither is God's *will* this ultimate ground. If this compatibility or incompatibility were the result of His will, then, provided He willed it, the 'impossibles' could become 'possible.' But this leads to absurd consequences, since He could then produce 'beings' which would also be 'non-beings' at the same time.

Neither is God's *intelligence* this ultimate ground. Things would be 'possible,' *because* He thinks them, and 'impossible,' *because* He does not or cannot think them. But the 'object' is always logically prior to the 'thought'; intelligence presupposes its object and merely recognizes the fact of compatibility or incompatibility.

God's *essence is the ultimate ground* of intrinsic possibility. That must be the ultimate ground in God which is logically prior to His omnipotence, will, and intelligence; but that is His *essence*. Besides, things are 'possible,' because they are a 'being'; things are 'impossible,' because they are a 'nothing.' And since 'being' can only be grounded in 'being,' God's infinite essence must be the ultimate ground for the essence of the possible things. Things are, therefore, intrinsically possible, because their being is in some way an imitation of God's infinite essence.

READINGS

Coffey, P., 1, pp. 95–100; Rickaby, J., Bk. I, Ch. V; Hugon, Ed., Tr. I, Qu. III, art. 2; Lehmen, Alfons, *Lehrbuch der Philosophie,* Vol. I, Ontologie, I Abh., 2 Ab., 3 Kap.; Mercier, D. Card., pp. 422–426; McCormick, J. F., Ch. IV, pp. 51–56.

Chapter VIII

CHANGE AND *MOTUS*

GOD, THE infinite being, is Pure Act, Absolute Actuality. He is the most real being (*ens realissimum*), without any admixture of potentiality. In Him there is, and can be, no 'becoming' of any kind, because He possesses the fullness of being all at once and always. Whatever He is, He is from eternity and in an infinite degree of perfection. Such is our idea of God. How far this idea is justifiable before philosophic reason, will be seen in theodicy, a separate department of philosophy.

Creatural beings are a compound of potency and act. They do not possess their complete being all at once and always. Even when they have existence, they are perfectible, determinable, actualizable, to a greater or less degree; as such they continually pass *from potency to act*. There is a constant 'becoming' in them and an uninterrupted *change*. This metaphysical notion of 'change' will now claim our attention.

THE CONCEPT OF CHANGE

We acquire the concept of 'change' from our daily experience. We sleep and wake; we labor and become fatigued; we are glad and then grieved; we are healthy and then ill; we are conscious and afterwards grow unconscious; we are young and vigorous and then become old and feeble; we live and die. And we observe similar happenings in the various beings in our environment. All things, we are convinced, undergo changes in some way. Plants and animals come into existence, develop, mature, and decay. The seasons change, and so do the physical bodies, the elements, the earth, and the stars.

The *Eleatics* (6 and 5 cent. B.C.) denied the fact of change and considered it an illusion: there is but one reality and that is absolutely unchanging and unchangeable. *Heraclitus* (born about 530 B.C.) went to the opposite extreme. He maintained that there is no permanent reality at all: nothing 'is,' everything is in a state of continuous change or 'becoming' (πάντα ρεῖ). The truth lies in the middle. Things change; but there is an underlying, relatively permanent subject in which the change takes place.

What is change? *Change is the transition from one positive state of being to another.* There are three *conditions* required for a true and strict change or mutation: (1) A positive *starting-point* (*terminus a quo*, term from which). A thing can be said to 'change' only when it already exists and has a definite, positive state of being to begin with. It must be an actual being, with a potency for some new state or act. (2) A positive goal or *ending-point* (*terminus ad quem*, term toward which). Just as the changing thing begins as a reality in a positive state of being and not in a state of nothingness, so it must also end as a reality in a positive state of being and not in a state of nothingness. It must end as an actual being, with a newly acquired state or act. (3) A *real transition* from one positive state of being into another positive state of being. The changing thing must really pass from a state of potency to act, so that it is a different sort of being in some way after the change has taken place.

Examples will make these points clearer. Let us take a piece of ice and proceed to melt it over a fire. The *solid* state of the ice is evidently a positive state of being for the water. The result aimed at as an ending-point of the process of melting is the *liquid* state of the water, and that is also a positive state of being for the water. The process of 'melting' is the 'transition': the water passes from a solid state (starting-point, *terminus a quo*) over into a liquid state (ending-point, *terminus ad quem*). The water has 'changed.'

If any of these three conditions be missing, the change is

not a *strict change;* but it may be called a 'change' in a *wider* and *improper* sense.

Sometimes the 'starting-point' is not a positive state of being, but a state of non-existence: we would then have the production of a thing from 'nothing,' and that would be *creation.* The notion of 'creation' is so common in the discourse of men, that this fact alone warrants its introduction here. At any rate, the notion of 'creation' represents an *intrinsic change* in an *improper* sense of the term.

Again, it may be that the 'ending-point' is not a positive state of being, but rather a state of non-existence: the result would be, not a strict change, but *annihilation.* If God were to destroy the world absolutely, so that not a vestige of it remained in existence, it would be annihilated. This is also called an *intrinsic change* in an *improper* sense.

The third kind of a change in a wider or improper sense would be, if there were *no real transition* on the part of the being that is said to change. An example: I walk through the rooms of an art gallery and look at the pictures. As I turn my gaze upon them, each one changes from a 'not-looked-at' picture to a 'looked-at' picture. Does a real change occur thereby in the picture itself? Evidently not; nothing has happened to the picture itself through the mere fact of my looking at it, so that it would now have acquired a new act or state of being. I am the one who undergoes a real change through the act of sight, but the picture remains just what it was before. Another example. Unknown to me, a distant relative has died. I have lost a relationship, and in that sense I can be said to have 'changed.' But the only one who really changed is my relative who died; so far as I am personally concerned, no real change has occurred in me. Such instances represent an external or *extrinsic change* in an *improper* or wider sense.

We thus notice that the term 'change' is not always used in a uniform meaning. In a strict sense, the notion of change involves a positive starting-point, a positive ending-point, and a real transition from one positive state to another.

KINDS OF STRICT CHANGE

A strict intrinsic change or mutation may appear in any of the following ways:

Generation and Corruption. Generation and corruption are two different aspects of one and the same change: it is the transition of a being from one kind of *substantial entity* into another kind of substantial entity. The difference between generation and corruption is this: the substantial change which makes the one substance cease to be is called 'corruption'; and the same substantial change which, by means of the corruption of this first substance, brings the new substance into being is called 'generation.' The new substance is always generated through the corruption of the old substance; the old substance ceases to be in order to give place to the new. There are not two changes involved in this process, but a single substantial change which corrupts the one while it generates the other. Hence, the axiom: the generation of one substance involves corruption of another. We observe this kind of change in the life and death of plants and animals. The chemical elements are assimilated in nutrition and become parts of living tissue and living function, partaking of the life of the plant or animal; but when the plant or animal dies, they again change from living substances to inanimate chemical elements. Every substantial change thus involves generation and corruption.

Augmentation and Diminution. This change is the transition of a being from one *quantitative* state to another. If the being increases in quantity, it is 'augmentation'; if it decreases in quantity, it is 'diminution.' This is a common occurrence among corporeal beings. A boy grows in stature in the course of youth; an acorn develops into a stately oak; the muscles grow weaker in severe illness; light fades when the voltage of electricity drops in the filament of a bulb.

Alteration. It is the transition of a being from one *qualitative* state to another. The skin becomes tanned, when exposed to the sun in summer; iron glows, if heated to a high degree of temperature; water vaporizes to steam at $+ 212°$ F.

Local Motion. It is the change which occurs in the transition of a thing from one *place* to another. A train travels from Chicago to New York; a lady walks from her house to the store; a boy runs through the park; a ball is thrown through a window.

If we compare these various kinds of strict changes, we notice that generation and corruption are *substantial* changes, while the others only change the accidental condition of a being and are, therefore, *accidental* changes. A thing changes from one substance to another in an instant (for instance, from non-living to living, from life to death); a substantial change is, therefore, an *instantaneous change.* On the other hand, augmentation and diminution, alteration, and local motion, are in their nature changes that progress in steps and stages, gradually and successively; for this reason they are *successive* changes.

Closely related to the notion of 'change' is the notion of *'motus'* or *'movement.'* It represents one of the most important phenomena of nature and deserves special attention.

MOTUS

The idea of *'motus'* has an honorable history. It dates back to the earlier days of Greek philosophic thought. *Aristotle* analyzed and developed it and fixed its meaning in a philosophic sense. Christian thinkers, especially the medieval *scholastics,* took it over and gave it considerable treatment, especially in their discussions on the existence and activity of the Supreme Being.

The term *'motus'* (Lat., *motus,* Gr., κίνησις, movement), in the technical meaning which it has acquired in ontology, cannot be adequately rendered into English. 'Motion' and 'movement' are derivatives of the Latin word *motus,* but their meaning is more restricted. 'Motion' is used for local change, change of position regarding place and space. 'Movement,' though broader in connotation than 'motion,' has not the philosophic width and depth of the term *motus,* as we shall see. The latter term, *motus,* is taken from the obvious case of local change and then broadened in meaning to apply to other activities of somewhat similar nature, even to vital and intellectual activities. The best thing to do under the circumstances is to specify the meaning of *motus* and use this Latin form, employing the English term 'movement' as an alternative.

Motus agrees partly in meaning with a number of concepts which we have discussed so far, such as 'act' (Lat., *actus,* Gr., ἐντελέχεια, ἐνέργεια), 'potency' (Lat., *potentia,* Gr., δύναμις), 'change' (Lat., *mutatio,* Gr., μεταβολή), 'motion' or 'movement' (Lat., *motio,* Gr., κίνησις); yet it differs in some respects from them all. This will be clear from the following explanations.

In its *widest* sense the term *motus* means *any activity* whatsoever, whether or not it involves a transition from potency to act. All creatural activity contains a transition from potency to act; but God's activity does not, because in Him there is no potentiality of any kind. Both kinds, whether divine or creatural, are called *motus* in this sense. Thus, God's thinking, willing, living, loving, creating, etc., are eternally present 'acts' without any admixture of potency. Living, thinking, knowing, running, eating, producing, seeing, feeling, etc., or any activity of pure spirits, men, brutes, plants, or inanimate things, take place by means of a transition from potency to act; they become 'actualized' through their activities. All these activities, whether of God or of creature, are *motus* in this widest use of the term.

In a somewhat narrower, though still in a *wide* sense, *motus* means any activity involving a transition *from potency to act.* This qualification excludes God's activities, but it still includes all creatural activity. Therefore, all activities of pure spirits, men, brutes, plants, and inanimate things, belong to this class.

In a *stricter* sense *motus* means any activity involving a transition from potency to act *in a corporeal being,* whether it be an instantaneous (substantial) or a successive (accidental) change. This class excludes the activities of pure spirits, because they are incorporeal, but it still includes the activities of men, brutes, plants, and inanimate bodies. To this class we thus refer the production and death of man, brute, and plant; any chemical change of substance. These are instances of a substantial change. As examples of accidental changes belonging to this class of *motus,* the following physical activities are characteristic: heating, freezing, illuminating, magnetizing, electrifying, etc.; running, walking, sleeping, eating, etc.; seeing, hearing, feeling, tasting, digesting, etc.

In a *strict and proper* sense *motus* is any activity involving the transition from potency to act in a corporeal being *through successive stages,* i.e., it is a successive change in a body. This, therefore, excludes all bodily changes of an instantaneous character, namely, generation and corruption; such would be the origin and death of living bodies and every substantial chemical change. On the other hand, it includes every kind of quantitative augmentation and diminution, qualitative alteration, and local change *in a body.* Examples are: growing physically larger or becoming smaller; heat and cold, strength and weakness; color, pain, pleasure; riding, jumping, rolling, etc.

ARISTOTLE'S DEFINITION OF MOTUS

Aristotle defined *motus* or successive change in the following manner: *the act of a being in potency while still in potency;* or, the actuality of that which is potential, in so far as it is a thing that is potential.[1] This definition may seem

---

[1] Διῃρημένου δὲ καθ᾽ ἕκαστον γένος τοῦ μὲν ἐντελεχείᾳ τοῦ δὲ δυνάμει, ἡ τοῦ δυνάμει ὄντος ἐντελέχεια, ἡ τοιοῦτον, κίνησίς ἐστιν· "Reverting, therefore, to the universal distinction already established between 'being-at-the-goal' in actuality and being in potentiality 'such-as-is-capable-of-attaining-the-goal,' we can now define motion or change as the progress of the realizing of a potentiality, *qua* potentiality." *Physics,* Bk. 3, Ch. 1, 201 a, tr. by P. H. Wicksteed and F. M. Cornford (Harvard U. Press), pp. 194, 195. See also *Metaph.,* Bk. 10, ch. 9, 1065 b.

obscure, but, like all of Aristotle's definitions, it possesses a marvelous compactness and philosophic precision. Perhaps the best way to reach Aristotle's meaning will be to take an ordinary instance of local movement.

A train is about to travel from Chicago to New York and stands ready in the terminal. Here are the elements of its *motus* or movement: the starting-point (*terminus a quo*) is the station in Chicago; the goal or ending-point (*terminus ad quem*) is the station in New York; the passage or transition is the entire trip from the station in Chicago to the station in New York. Wherein does the change, movement, *motus*, consist? As long as the train stands in the station in Chicago (starting-point) it is not yet in motion. When it stands in the station in New York (goal, ending-point), it is no longer in motion. Both these terminal points mean rest, not motion. Motion begins, when it leaves the station in Chicago, and lasts until it has come to rest in the station in New York. The complete 'act' to be acquired is its *arrival* at the station in New York, and it will always be *in potency* for this act until it arrives there. While it stands at the starting-point (Chicago), it is in *complete potency* for this act; and when it has arrived at its goal or ending-point (New York), it is in *complete act*. While traveling along the rails, the train partly realizes its act, because it is on the way, and it realizes its act more and more until it has its complete act on arriving in New York. But because its act is but partly realized while 'on the way,' it is always still partly 'in potency,' because its act must be realized further; and it must continue to pass from potency to act, until it finally arrives at its destination. Hence, the entire trip is a *partial act* which will be fully realized in the *complete* act at the arrival of the train in New York; and the train is always *in potency* toward this complete act as long as it is on the way: its *motus* is thus seen to be the act of a being in potency while still in potency. In other words: it is the actuality of a partly realized potency while still only partly realized and tending toward complete realization.

As will be observed from this explanation, Aristotle's definition, though technical, displays a very keen and profound understanding of the essential elements of *motus,* as exemplified in local motion. The definition, of course, is not restricted to local motion. It applies with equal precision to *any successive change* or transition from potency to act, as long as the activity in question takes place in stages, so that there is a gradual realization of the complete 'act' striven for. Whenever a change is instantaneous, *motus* or movement, as just defined, does not occur; but it may occur in the *preparation* for this instantaneous change. In every case of *motus,* therefore, there is the following sequence: Before the thing 'moves,' it is in potency for both the *motus* and the final actuality to be acquired by it; when it begins to be 'moved,' it is no longer in potency for the *motus,* but has already acquired it as an intermediary act; while 'moving,' it still remains in potency for the final and complete actuality to be acquired at the ending-point of its *motus;* when it has acquired its final and complete act, *motus* ceases, and the thing comes to rest as completely realized. If we desire to use the term in a wider sense, we may do so; but then we must define our term accordingly.

Our concept of *motus* will receive further clarification, when we consider the various classes into which it can be divided.

KINDS OF MOTUS

As there are naturally many kinds of acts or actualities which can be acquired by objects in the universe, so there must be different kinds of *motus* or transitional ways of acquiring them. We thus distinguish:

Immanent or Vital Activity. It is the activity through which a living being perfects itself and makes *itself the goal* for the acquired actuality or perfection. Such an activity does not tend to leave the agent, in order to actualize a being distinct from itself; rather, it begins and terminates in the agent itself, so that it is also the passive recipient of the perfection acquired through its activity. Nutrition, for example, is an immanent activity. This function assimilates foodstuffs, so as to build and strengthen the very body in which it resides and remains (Lat., *immanere, manere in,* to remain in) and has its being. Plant, animal, and human bodies have immanent action; they are the term or goal of their own function; they move and actuate themselves. Thus, too, the various sense-perceptions, thought-processes, will-acts, emotions, etc., are immanent activities.

Transient, or Transeunt, or Transitive Activity. It is the activity which tends to *change another object,* distinct from the agent, thereby making this other object the term or goal of the acquired actuality. Here the agent and recipient are two distinct beings. The agent influences and modifies the recipient, while the recipient is thereby influenced and modified; the agent has the producing action, while the recipient receives the produced effect. Thus, a hot radiator sends heat in all directions, raising the temperature of the surrounding atmosphere; the steam in the boiler of a locomotive drives the wheels which propel the train along the tracks. Since the changes produced in bodies may be of a varying character, we distinguish between three kinds of transient activity: mechanical, physical, and chemical.

Mechanical action is the active tendency of a body to change the *local position* of another body. Cases in point: swinging a baseball bat, throwing a stone, pushing a cart, drilling a well, digging a trench, closing a window, etc. *Physical action* is the active tendency of a body to change the *qualities* of another body without changing its substance and nature. For example: heating a body, freezing water, tempering steel, painting a picture, magnetizing a needle, illuminating a room, etc. *Chemical action* is the active tendency of a body to *change the nature* of another body by combining elements into a compound, or dissolving a compound into its elements, or changing one compound into another. For instance: the chemical action which combines hydrogen and oxygen into water; the electrolytic action which dissolves water into hydrogen and oxygen; the radioactive change of uranium into radium.

In all these kinds of activities we find Aristotle's definition verified, namely, "that movement (*motus*) is a realization, but an incompleted one; because a potentiality, as long as it is such, is by its nature uncompleted, and therefore its actual functioning — which motion is — must stop short of the completion: on the attainment of the end, the motion toward it no longer exists, but is merged in the reality."[2] It is always the case of the act of a being in potency while still in potency: *actus entis in potentia quatenus in potentia.*

SUMMARY OF CHAPTER VIII

The transition from potency to act in finite beings is effected by means of 'change.'

1. *The Concept of Change.* Change is the transition from one positive state of being to another. Three *conditions* are required for this: a positive starting-point; a positive ending-point; and a real transition from the one to the other. If any of these three conditions be missing, we have 'change' in a wider and improper sense: such are creation, annihilation, and extrinsic change.

2. *Kinds of Strict Change.* 'Generation' and 'corruption' are the transition of a being from one kind of substantial entity into another kind of substantial entity. 'Augmentation' and 'diminution' are quantitative changes, while 'alteration' is a qualitative change. 'Local motion' is the transition from one place to another.

3. *Motus.* In its *widest* sense, *motus* means any activity whatsoever, whether divine or creatural. In a *wide* sense, it is any activity involving the transition from potency to act; this excludes God's activities. In a *stricter* sense, it is any activity involving a transition from potency to act in a corporeal being; this excludes the activities of pure spirits. In a *strict and proper*

---

[2] Aristotle, *Physics*, Bk. 3, Ch. 2, 201 b. Translated by P. H. Wicksteed and F. M. Cornford (Harvard U. Press, 1929).

sense, it is any activity involving the transition from potency to act in a corporeal being in successive stages.

4. *Aristotle's Definition.* He defines *motus* as the act of a being in potency while still in potency; the actuality of that which is potential, in so far as it is a thing that is potential.

5. *Kinds of Motus.* 'Immanent' or 'vital' action is that through which a living being perfects itself and makes itself the goal for the acquired actuality. 'Transient,' 'transeunt,' or 'transitive' action is the activity which tends to change another object, distinct from the agent. This transient action is 'mechanical,' when it is an active tendency to change the local position of another body; it is 'physical' action, when it tends to change the qualities of another body; it is 'chemical' action, when it tends to change the nature of another body.

READINGS

Coffey, P., pp. 61, 62; Mercier, D. Card., pp. 506–510; Pesch, Tilmann, n. 1317–1329; St. Thomas, *Summa Theologica,* I, q. 9, a. 2; McCormick, J. F., Ch. IV, pp. 56–59; Aristotle, *Metaph.,* III, IV; *Physics,* V–VIII.

CHAPTER IX

THE PRINCIPLE OF CHANGE

CHANGE AND becoming are universal occurrences in nature. Finite things, as the name indicates, have only limited being. As such they are always in potency for further actualization and determination. The terms 'change' and 'becoming' are not identical in meaning. Every 'change' is a form of 'becoming,' but not *vice versa*. According to strict terminology, 'change' is the transition from one positive state of being to another positive state of being; 'becoming' is any transition from potency to act, even if it be from non-existence to existence. 'Becoming' is, therefore, in itself, a wider term than 'change.' These terms, however, are often employed to mean simply a transition from potency to act, and it is in this latter meaning that they must be taken when we speak of the Principle of Change.

STATE OF THE QUESTION

The importance of this principle, from a philosophic standpoint, can hardly be overestimated. It reaches down into the very depths of thought and being, and thus deserves a careful study. Resting directly on the Principles of Contradiction and Sufficient Reason, the Principle of Change is nothing more than the application of these two primary principles to the processes of becoming and change as observed throughout the realm of nature. This Principle of Change is usually formulated: *'Quidquid movetur, ab alio movetur; whatever changes, is changed by another.'*

'Change' here means the transition from potency to act, and it makes no difference whether this transition is a transition from non-existence to existence or from one positive state of being to another positive state of being: the principle or law applies with equal validity to both kinds of becoming. In the first case, the transition from non-existence to existence involves the production of the whole entity of the being from nothingness. In the second case, it involves the transition of an existing thing to a different kind of being; this sort of change presupposes an underlying subject in which the change takes place.

When a concrete, positive being undergoes a change, there is always an underlying potential reality, called the *subject* or *matter,* in which the change occurs, and a perfection or actuality, called the *form,* which is either gained or lost; and this change always ends in a new positive state of being for the subject, because it is now something that it was not before. In all such cases of change, as *Aristotle* points out, "whether of quantity or quality or relation or time or place, it is obvious that there must be some underlying subject which undergoes the change."[1] And he mentions the following methods in which change may take place: "(1) Change of shape, as with the statue made of bronze, or (2) additions, as in things that grow, or (3) subtractions, as when a block of marble is chipped into a Hermes, or (4) combination, as in building a house, or (5) such modifications as effect the properties of the material itself."[2]

The Principle of Change, as enunciated, has this specific meaning: Nothing ever passes from receptive potency to act except under the influence of another being which is already in act. Or, to put it in a different way: No being can bring itself from receptive potency to act. 'Act' must be understood here in its philosophic sense as any entity determining or perfecting a thing in its being.

In testing this principle and giving its proof, we may appeal

---

[1] *Physics,* Bk. I, Ch. 7, 190 a., tr. by P. H. Wicksteed and F. M. Cornford (Harvard U. Press, 1929), pp. 75–77.

[2] *Loc. cit.,* p. 77.

either to *experience* or to the *analysis* of the elements contained
in the principle.

PROOF FROM EXPERIENCE

Physical science subscribes to this axiom of philosophy with
regard to *mechanical motion*. *Newton* (1642–1727) gave scientific expression to it in the first two of his famous laws of
motion: "(1) Every body tends to persevere in its state of rest
or of uniform motion in a straight line, unless it is acted on
by an impressed force; (2) change of momentum is propor-
tional to the impressed force and takes place in the direction
of the straight line in which the force acts." These laws express plainly the universal fact that *inertia* governs the entire
inanimate world and that nothing will ever pass from a state
of rest (which is a state of potency) to a state of motion (which
is a state of actuality, and newly acquired), without it being
brought into motion through the activation of some other
body already in act. A body in motion, after having been
brought into motion, cannot even change its own motion;
this change must come through the influence of some other
outside force. This clearly shows that, concerning mechanical
motion at least, the Principle of Change is true: Whatever
changes, is changed by another.

Science treats of *potential* and *kinetic energy*. Potential
energy is energy of *position,* as we observe it in lifted weights,
coiled or stretched springs, compressed gases, chemical com-
binations (e.g., explosives), storage batteries, etc. Kinetic
energy is energy of *motion,* as we see it in a falling pile driver,
a ticking watch, a discharging rifle, a burning flashlight, etc.
Potential energy can be transformed into kinetic, and kinetic
energy into potential. But it always necessitates an outside
force to make potential energy active; of itself potential energy
will *always remain potential,* and it will never be transformed
into kinetic energy without some other transforming agency.
An example or two from nature will elucidate this.

A punch press in a factory is punching holes into a steel

plate. The punch die is worked by the machine, the machine by the belt, the belt by the shaft, the shaft by the flywheel, the flywheel by the crank arm attached to the piston rod, the piston rod by the steam, the steam by the heat; the heat is generated by the combustion of the coal, the coal obtains its potential energy from the sun, the sun obtains it from the stored-up energy of its atoms; and the atoms — ?

Inertia is a universal attribute of matter. Things tend to assume a stable equilibrium and to remain therein. They possess the potency of becoming something; but in order to change, they require the active agency of another thing. We can trace this process back to the primary and elemental forces of nature, such as gravitational and sub-atomic energy, which supply the dynamic activities of physical bodies. Whether these agencies are kinetic transformations of deeper potential energies, science cannot say, for they lie beyond the ken of human observation. But so far as experiment and observation reach, we see that potential beings must be actualized by beings which are already in act. Hence, whatever changes, is changed by another.

PROOF FROM REASON

If we subject the Principle of Change to an analysis of its constituent factors, we will see that it is a principle which is *universally and necessarily true*. To state it again: No being can pass from receptive potency to act except under the influence of another being which is already in act; no being can bring itself from receptive potency to act; whatever changes, is changed by another.

This must be so. For one thing, every act or perfection thus acquired is a *new perfection or reality* for the being which was first only in receptive potency for it. Every 'act,' in contradistinction to receptive 'potency,' means some positive reality or entity modifying the thing; the thing *changes* thereby; it *acquires* something; it is now *different* from what it was before the change; it is in a *new state*. It is impossible that the thing changed be the same after the transition from potency to act as it was before: because 'change' means to pass from one state *to another*. Hence, through this change an act is acquired which is some new positive reality or entity.

It is evident that this new actuality acquired by the potential being demands a *sufficient and adequate reason* for its arrival: there can be nothing without a sufficient reason. This is an absolute requirement, based, as we have seen, on the Principle of Contradiction. In virtue of this requirement, the newly acquired actuality must be accounted for down to the last vestige. In so far as a thing is without sufficient reason, it has no being at all and cannot exist. Hence, when a being passes from potency to act, this act is something in the order of reality, and the being acquires it through the process of its change, and there must be a full and adequate reason for its presence after the change.

It must also be evident that the potential being, passing from potency to act in the change, *did not possess this act before the change*. When is a being 'in potency'? When it has the 'capacity for something.' In such a state it certainly cannot possess this act already; otherwise it could no longer be 'in potency' for it, i.e., it could no longer be able to pass from a state of potency *to obtain it*. 'Potency' means a state of passivity, of receptivity, of possibility. It means the absence of a certain actuality, but it means at the same time the aptitude and possibility of *receiving* it. However, it receives it precisely by means of its transition from potency to act, by means of the *change*. But if it receives it by means of this transition and change, it could not possibly have had it before the transition and change. Otherwise an open contradiction is stated: the being *had* this particular actuality *before* the transition and at the same time it *did not have it*. It had it before the transition from potency, because that is here assumed and claimed; and at the same time it also did not have it before the transition from potency, because it really acquired this actuality only by having passed from potency to act in order to obtain it. Hence, the thing passing from potency to act could not have possessed the actuality before the change, since the opposite assumption is *contradictory*.

So far it has been established that every actuality acquired through change is a new reality or perfection; its presence after the change demands a sufficient and adequate reason; it was not possessed as such by the potential being before the change, but was acquired by means of the change. Going a step farther, we must see that the being which passes from potency to act *cannot give this act to itself*. This means that the potential being cannot itself be the complete and adequate principle for the newly acquired actuality: It cannot 'move' or change itself.

Under the conditions as given, the potential being is incapable of giving this actuality to itself. The reason is extremely simple: *no being can give what it does not have*. No being can acquire the identical thing that it already possesses; and no being can give, either to itself or to another, something which is not in its possession: if it already has it, it can no longer acquire it; and if it lacks it, it cannot give it to itself or to another. It follows then, that, while a being is in potency for an act, it is without it. A potency *minus* the act, however, is certainly less perfect than the potency *plus* the act. The act, consequently, is a plus-amount over and beyond the potency as such, *something superadded* to it.

Now, there are only three conceivable possibilities to account for this new reality: it can come either from the potential being itself, or from some actual being, or from nothing. Consider these cases. The *potential* being itself cannot give the new reality to itself, as has just been pointed out, because no one can give what it does not have; it is, then, no sufficient reason for it. On the same grounds, *'nothing'* cannot be a sufficient reason for the appearance of the newly acquired actuality, because 'nothing' possesses nothing and thus can give nothing to the potential being. Therefore, the potential being, in acquiring a new actuality through the transition from po-

tency to act, can receive it *only from some other actual being.*
Here, then, we have a truly sufficient reason: this other being
exists; it possesses the actuality and communicates it to the
potential being by 'moving' or 'changing' it, by making it
pass from potency to act. That alone is a satisfactory explanation and does no violence to reason.

From all this we must derive the necessary conclusion:
*Whatever passes from receptive potency to act does so under
the influence of some other being already in act.*

THOMISM AND THE PRINCIPLE OF CHANGE

The Principle of Change, as enunciated above, refers to a
receptive potency. All scholastics are in agreement as to the
validity of the principle in this respect. There are, however,
also *operative potencies* (faculties, powers); these, apparently
at least, are capable of performing operations *spontaneously,*
without the necessity of being activated by other agencies.

Given the proper conditions, the mere proximity of certain
chemical elements is sufficient to bring about an interaction
between them, resulting in a chemical compound endowed
with properties quite distinct from those of the constituent
elements. A change has undoubtedly occurred, but this change
is due, to all appearances, to the elements themselves, and not
to the influence of any other agency. Radioactive elements are
particularly remarkable in their change. Irrespective of their
surroundings, they undergo transmutations which are spontaneous in character, and no known physical or chemical
agency can hasten or retard these transmutations which take
place within these elements themselves. They certainly seem
to 'change themselves,' due to their own intrinsic operative
potencies.

When we turn to the investigation of living beings, *organisms,* the facts become even more obvious. Plants, brutes, and
men, it appears evident, possess *spontaneity of action, self-
movement.* The operations of vegetation, sentiency, and ra-

tional life are *immanent* actions, proceeding from the organism itself and perfecting it in its being.

This does not mean that organisms are not *influenced* by outside agencies; the opposite is true. The seeds of plants, in order to begin development, need the stimulation of soil, moisture, and warmth. The assimilative powers need the stimulation of foodstuffs in order to become active. The leaves need the stimulation of light for the production of chlorophyl, starch, etc. In animals the senses require the presence of definite stimuli before sensation can take place. The central sense, imagination, instinct, and sense-memory must be aroused into activity by the action of the peripheral organs of perception. The intellect of man requires the presentation of an object to stimulate it into activity. The appetency of the brute and the will of man also need an object to exercise their function. In some way, therefore, these operative faculties require an outside agency in order to pass from potency to act.

Nevertheless, in all these instances, the presence of these stimulations and objects seem to be more in the nature of a *condition for self-activity* than a changing agency as such. We cannot, of course, deny the existence of activity in creatural beings, whether it be transient activity in inorganic beings or immanent activity in organic beings; such a denial would lead to the false theory of occasionalism. It seems equally obvious, too, that such beings are *spontaneously active* and pass from the potency of their faculties to the act of their operations by their *own agency,* and not through the agency of another being: they 'move' or 'change' themselves.

Because of these considerations, many scholastic philosophers restrict the Principle of Change to the *receptive* potencies; the *operative* potencies are outside the scope of this principle and are not affected by it. *Thomistic* scholastics, however, claim that the Principle of Change applies with equal force and rigor to *receptive and operative* potencies alike. The school of Thomism defends the view that 'nothing ever passes from potency, whether receptive or operative, to act except under the influence of another being which is already in act'; 'no being, under any conditions, can reduce itself from potency to act,' and this applies, therefore, also to the operative potency.

According to the view of modern Thomism, an *antecedent physical influence, or physical premotion (praemotio physica)*, is required in order that the faculty of a creature can pass from potentiality to actuality. It is only in virtue of this antecedent physical influence that the faculty is immediately capable of operation. This influence is supplied by God to all creatural activity.

On what grounds do the Thomists base their contention that the Principle of Change also applies to the 'operative' potencies? On the grounds that the Principle of Sufficient Reason absolutely demands their inclusion in the Principle of Change. There is, they say, no essential difference between a 'receptive' and an 'operative' potency, when it is a question of passing into act. An operative potency, such as intellect and will, is certainly *perfected* by its operation. By means of this operation, which is an 'act,' the faculty now possesses a perfection which was not present before; it is something superadded to the faculty, a plus-amount newly acquired. Since the faculty did not possess it before, it could not give it to itself; only an outside agency can, then, be adequate cause of this new perfection. The faculty itself as a 'potency' cannot be the sufficient reason for the acquisition of the new perfection contained in the operation as an 'act.' Hence, it cannot reduce itself from potentiality to actuality, and the Principle of Change applies to the 'operative' potency with the same rigor as it applies to the 'receptive' potency. In other words, the Principle of Change is a universal principle without exception. And because of this, a physical premotion on the part of God is necessary in order that the operative potency or faculty can become active.

Those who disagree with the thomistic view in this matter fail to see the stringency of their argument. Especially, the theory of this physical premotion seems to them to be inadequate. They point out that such an influence only places the faculty in *immediate preparation* for the operation that is to follow; it does not communicate the actual operation itself, but makes the faculty 'capable' of action. But in that case, the faculty still must pass from potency to act; and that would be contrary to the Principle of Change, as interpreted by the Thomists. Then why should it not be possible for the Creator to endow the creatural being with a complete faculty capable of action without the antecedent physical influence? The latter seems altogether superfluous under the circumstances and incapable of performing the function ascribed to it by the Thomists. And if the Thomists were to assert that it is precisely this physical premotion which reduces the faculty from potency to act, then it would seem that the faculty is no longer an 'operative,' but purely a 'receptive,' faculty and as such has no operation of its own. But is that not tantamount to a denial of all creatural activity?

On their part, the opponents of Thomism have the difficulty of explaining the presence of the 'new perfection' of the operation as an 'act' perfecting the faculty. We must uphold the Principle of Sufficient Reason; all admit that. On the other hand, it seems obvious that creatural beings are truly active in virtue of the intrinsic powers with which they have been endowed by the Creator. If the operative power needs an outside agency (a physical premotion) to reduce it from potency to act, then the same situation applies to this agency; it is also a creatural power and needs another agency to reduce it to act. But this involves either an infinite regress, or we must end the series by stating that God is the direct agent of all creatural activity; that, however, would be occasionalism, denying true activity to creatures, and this agrees neither with experience nor with the principles of sound philosophy.

How can we harmonize this view with the Principle of Sufficient Reason? The opponents of Thomism make a distinction between the *virtual act* and the *formal act*. The 'perfection' of the operation is precontained in the faculty as an effect in its equivalent cause. The 'change' which takes place, when a faculty passes from potency to act in its operation, is not a change in this perfection itself, but in the perfection's *manner of being:* from being a *virtual* act it changes to a *formal* act. The perfection of the operation as an 'act' is not contained 'formally' in the faculty; all are in agreement on this point. However, if this perfection of the operation were not precontained at least 'virtually' in the faculty, then the faculty would not be an 'operative' potency at all, but merely a 'receptive' potency; then we should drop the concept of an 'operative' potency entirely and deny the possibility of true creatural activity. Hence, in order to safeguard the Principle of Sufficient Reason and the natural activity of creatural beings, we must maintain the presence of the *perfection* of the operation as 'act' in the faculty as 'potency'; the change, then, which takes place in the passage from potency to act is the change of the virtual act to the formal act. In this view, therefore, the Principle of Change applies strictly to the 'receptive' potencies, but not to the 'operative' potencies.

In a more limited way, and in a wider sense, the Principle of Change can also be said to apply to the *operative* potencies. This is done, for instance, by *Sylvester Maurus:* "The opponents seem to have understood this principle *negatively* as if the sense were that nothing is moved by itself; and against this they have instanced the actions of animals and other beings which move themselves. However, the sense of the principle is *affirmative* in intent. No one denies the something can move itself, concurring *partially* to its own movement: but we assert that no being can move itself *totally* and as *with perfect self-sufficiency:* it must be moved by another so that it can move itself. It will be manifest to anyone giving due consideration to these terms, that everything which is moved, that is to say, everything which is changed intrinsically, now possessing some entity and now lacking it, is not its own *total cause* of possessing or lacking it, but must be moved by another being which forces it, or entices it, or attracts it, or perfects it. Consequently, even the free will, being a created and mutable reality, though it is primarily the cause of changing itself, cannot change itself except in so far as it is moved to change itself through some object which attracts or entices it."[3]

The arguments of the Thomists and their opponents, as outlined above, are based on fundamentally different views concerning the nature of an operative potency. The reader must decide which view he considers to be more consonant with fact and principle.

COROLLARIES

From the above explanations a few simple *principles* concerning act and potency are clearly seen to flow.

In so far as a thing is in act, it is perfect. An act is an entity determining and perfecting a thing in its respective order. An act is the realization of a certain power, the natural complement of a potency. Thus, the intellect is a faculty, a power; its natural purpose is to understand, and thought is its act, its actualization. It is evidently more perfect actually to think than merely to be able to think. Similarly, sight as a power or faculty is but the capacity for seeing; actual seeing, or vision, is the act or determination of sight as a faculty, and it is more perfect to have actual sight than only capacity for it. Potency is the mere capacity for something, and an act is the perfection, the realization, of this capacity. From the reverse standpoint, then, the following principle is equally true: *In so far as a thing is in potency, it is imperfect.*

What, then, must be the most perfect being? A being that is purest actuality, one without the slightest potentiality, one which (who) has being to the utmost degree possible, intensively and extensively — God. And what is the most imperfect being? The one with most potentiality. Spiritual beings are

---

[3] *Quaest. phil.*, 1. 4 *de ente immat.*, q. 8. (Italics mine — Author.)

more perfect than material things, because they come nearer to the actuality of God, who is the Supreme Spirit. The most imperfect being must, therefore, be found in the material order, and in this order 'primal matter' is the most imperfect. More will be said of 'matter' and 'form' in cosmology.

In so far as a thing is in act, it is a principle of activity. A thing is a principle of activity, when it influences another; it influences another, when it changes it; it changes it, when it communicates some new state of being to it; and in order to communicate a new state or actuality to this other thing, it must itself first possess the actuality; but to possess an actuality means to be 'in act': consequently, a thing is a principle of activity in so far as it is in act. Reversely, then, *a thing is passive in so far as it is in potency.* This should be clear. A thing is in potency in as much as it has a capacity for an act; this presupposes the absence of the actuality and the possibility of receiving it; the more actuality it lacks, however, the more it can receive; but to be able to receive means to be 'passive'; hence, in so far as a thing is in potency, it is passive.

From the act one can validly conclude to the operative potency. The sense is: from the fact that a thing actually performs a certain activity, one can rightly conclude that it has the 'power' to perform it. The act flows out of the operative faculty or power, and the presence of an act or activity presupposes the power of faculty as source. The power is the cause for the act as effect, and every effect demands the existence of a corresponding cause. Hence the principle. From the fact, e.g., of a supra-material and spiritual operation, even of only a single one, we can legitimately conclude to the presence of an underlying supra-material and spiritual mind. Reversely, we must say: *From the operative potency one cannot validly conclude to the act.* From the mere fact that something is potential or possible, we cannot infer that it is or will be actual. It is possible that all men may die tomorrow; but from this we cannot conclude that they actually will die tomorrow. Scientists have the potency to discover an entirely new principle of aeronautics this month; but from that we cannot draw t inference that they actually will discover it within that time. We cannot make a valid conclusion from potency to act, because a potency may remain a mere potency, and no one can state definitely whether or when it will pass into act.

In the real order, act (actual being) must precede potency (potential being). This follows with necessity from the general Principle of Change. Nothing can move itself from potency to act; whatever becomes or changes, must be moved from potency to act by another being already in act. Consequently, if the first being were a potential being only, it could never of itself make the transition to actuality; and if there were no actual being *prior* to it, moving the potential being to actuality, the potential being would remain in a state of potentiality forever. Since the potential being cannot actualize itself, it makes no difference whether it have a beginning in time or be from eternity: its actualization intrinsically demands the priority of an actual being, in order to account for the act which it receives in its becoming or change. The opposite supposition would involve a contradiction.

APPLICATION OF THE PRINCIPLE

When we consider the nature of the beings which comprise the universe, we observe that they are subject to a continuous process of change. Each single entity in the universe is limited in the amount of its active energy, and this energy is gradually consumed in moving potential beings from potency to act. Every action entails reaction, and the agent is changed in the very operation of changing another. This is a universal law. All observable beings, therefore, undergo change in some manner, and by this very fact of changing they manifest themselves to consist, at least in part, of potentiality. And since the sum of all beings in the universe is the universe, the universe itself is essentially potential in many respects. According to the Principle of Change, then, the existing universe essentially requires, *outside* itself and *prior* to itself, an actual being or beings to account for the actuality contained in the universe. The multiplicity of beings in the universe might lead us to the conclusion that there must also exist a plurality of actual beings outside the universe and prior to it. However, if it can be shown that the world is really a *uni*verse and not a *pluri*verse (to employ an unusual term), this line of thought would lead to *one* being as the actuality postulated by the facts under consideration. That the world is really a 'universe' seems quite clear. Astrophysics has established the fact that the stars and the earth consist of the same chemical elements and are governed by the same mechanical, chemical, and physical laws throughout; the world is a *co-ordinated system,* a totality of beings united together into a real *universe, a cosmos.* Since this involves a unified plan of construction and of activity, the changes and developments in the universe point very definitely to *One Being* as the agent responsible for the actuality acquired anywhere throughout the vast expanse of the present cosmos as we know it. And since an infinite regress in potential beings is impossible, and since even an infinite series of potential beings would demand an actual being outside the series itself, there must actually exist a *Prime Mover Unmoved* possessing complete actuality without any admixture of potentiality. If this Prime Mover again had any potentiality, this would also presuppose another actual Being preceding it, and so on backward, until we arrive at the First Being who is the real Prime Mover Unmoved, capable of conferring actuality on *all* potential beings without exception by assisting them in their transition from potency to act. These secondary beings can be active only in co-operation with the Prime Mover.

There must, then, exist in the real order a Being who is *Pure Actuality.* We call this Being *God.* God, therefore, is not a mere abstraction, something like 'being in general,' devoid of all real content, but *Supreme Reality and Power.* He is in all truth the First Principle of thought and being, and as such

He is, if we understand the term in its fullest and richest meaning, the *Absolute.*

Furthermore, the implications of the Principle of Change show the futility of the attempt of *Hegel* to deduce all things through the *logical evolution* of the concept of 'being.' The concept of 'being,' with which Hegel begins, is not the concept of God as Pure Actuality; it is the concept of 'being in general,' so empty of all real content that he considers it absolutely void and equal to 'nothing.' As he himself states: "Being is not a particular or definite thought, and hence, being quite indeterminate, is a thought not to be distinguished from Nothing."[4] But 'being' does not remain in this indeterminate condition; it 'becomes,' and through this becoming it evolves into all determinate being, into nature and spirit and eventually into the Absolute. "Becoming is the first concrete thought, and therefore the first notion: whereas Being and Nothing are empty abstractions."[5]

This 'becoming' then gives rise, according to Hegel, to 'determinate being' in the following interesting process of logical evolution: "Even our ordinary conception of Becoming implies that somewhat [something] comes out of it, and that Becoming therefore has a result. . . . Becoming always contains Being and Nothing in such a way that these two are always changing into each other, and reciprocally cancel each other. Thus Becoming stands before us in utter restlessness — unable, however, to maintain itself in this abstract restlessness: for since Being and Nothing vanish in Becoming (and that is the very notion of Becoming), the latter must vanish. . . . The result of this process, however, is not empty Nothing, but Being identical with the negation — what we call Being Determinate (being then and there): the primary import of which evidently is that it *has become.*"[6]

---

[4] *Loc. cit.,* § 87, p. 163.
[5] *Loc. cit.,* § 88, p. 167.
[6] *Loc. cit.,* § 89, p. 170.

In evaluating Hegel's views, as given above, we must remember that he was actuated by the purpose, laudable in itself, of effecting a *supreme synthesis*. But in this endeavor he was misled into attempting to synthesize 'thought' and 'thing' into the ultimate ground of 'being in general,' of abstract and indeterminate being; he thereby hoped to harmonize not only the conflicting elements of 'being,' but also the contradictions or antinomies of 'thought.' Hence his contention that all 'being' is thought 'realized' and all *becoming is a logical development*. He therefore begins with the *idea* of 'being'; and since this idea is also the *reality* of 'being,' it actually develops itself from indeterminateness to determinateness ('determinate being') by means of an *eternal logical process* of internal evolution. At first 'being' is so indeterminate that it is equivalent to 'nothing,' but through this process of logical 'becoming' it gradually unfolds itself into every kind of determinate being: it is a process of *self-actualization*.

This, however, is an *essential error* in Hegel's idealistic monism, because it is in contradiction to the Principle of Change (Becoming), as shown above. From both a logical and ontological viewpoint, Hegel's 'Being' is incapable of evolving in this manner. As a *logical* entity, his 'Being' is abstract, indeterminate, empty of content, equivalent to 'Nothing.' Since it contains nothing, nothing can arise out of it; hence, 'determinate being' can never be deduced from it. As an *ontological* entity (supposing it to be such), it is devoid of all actuality and therefore purely potential. This 'Being' does not contain all actuality in itself like coins in a purse or peas in a pod; it is rather, according to Hegel's own statement, "empty Nothing."[7] Consequently, this 'Being' must be pure *potentiality*. It develops into all determinate being, not through some *other* being distinct from itself (for how can there be any being outside the whole class of 'being'?), but by means of the intrinsic *self-actualization* of its potentiality. But this is unintelligible and impossible. Since 'Being' con-

---

[7] *Loc. cit.,* § 88, n. 5, p. 167.

tains no actuality, it cannot give any actuality to itself, because no one can give what one does not possess. And this 'Being' cannot receive it from another being, because outside the totality of 'Being' there is only 'Nothing,' and 'Nothing' has nothing to give. If, then, Hegel's contention were correct that the origin of all things comes from indeterminate 'Being,' which is equivalent to 'Nothing,' no determinate beings could ever come into existence. But the *universe is here*. Hence, it did not originate from this abstract, empty 'Being,' and Hegel's monism must be rejected as inadequate and false.

Finally, the Principle of Change shows conclusively that no theory of complete *evolution,* whether mechanistic or vitalistic, can fully explain the origin and development of living beings and of the world at large. The very idea of evolution involves change and development. It means the unfolding of forces in the direction of beings possessing more complicated structures and *higher forms* of organization from a more or less primitive and amorphous state. This implies a movement of an upward trend, with a constant and gradual acquisition of *higher perfection;* it is a transition from potency to act on a world-wide scale, an *actualization* which becomes more complete in the course of the ages. Such an evolution, however, if it took place, could never occur in virtue of the inherent forces of nature alone. There must be an actual Being outside this whole process of evolution, to activate these forces and give them direction toward higher actuality: whatever changes, is changed by another.

It makes little difference whether we accept mere matter and force as the moving principle of evolution, as the materialists do; or whether we claim that all matter is endowed with psychic activity, as the panpsychists do; or whether we postulate some 'mind stuff,' which later develops into mind and matter, as the neutralists do; or whether we attribute evolution to a general vital impulse (*élan vital*), as Henri Bergson and his followers do; or whether we assume a *nisus* as the driving power of evolving new and unpredictable qualities, as the advocates of 'emergent evolution' do; or whether we take 'space-time' as the matrix of all evolving reality, as S. Alexander and some relativitists do: evolution in every form starts with potentiality and progresses toward actuality. Even though evolution should be proved to be a fact, the Principle of Change would still necessitate the *prior existence of a Prime Mover* to account for the presence of evolution in the universe. Any other supposition would leave the entire process without a sufficient reason to explain the change and as such would involve a contradiction.

Such, then, is the Principle of Change (Becoming) in its nature and in its consequences. No being, subject to change, can escape its influence. It applies with equal force to things in the material and in the spiritual order of being. As a metaphysical principle, it will be noted, it is linked very closely with the ultimate foundation of possibility.

SUMMARY OF CHAPTER IX

The term 'becoming' means the transition from potency to act; 'change,' in the strict sense, means the transition from one positive state of being to another. But here we take 'change' in the wider sense of 'becoming,' when discussing the Principle of Change.

1. *State of the Question.* The Principle of Change reads: Whatever changes, is changed by another; or, nothing ever passes from receptive potency to act except under the influence of another being already in act; or, no being can bring itself from receptive potency to act. In every change the result is the acquisition of a *new state* of being.

2. *Proof from Experience.* Physical science acknowledges this principle regarding *mechanical motion,* as can be seen from Newton's laws of motion. The principle of *potential* and *kinetic* energy also shows that potential energy cannot become kinetic except under the influence of the active agency of kinetic energy, because *inertia* is a universal attribute of all matter. Even the *vital powers* of organisms cannot become

active unless stimulated into activity by other agencies; at least they are not the *total* cause of their self-movement.

3. *Proof from Reason.* Every act acquired through change is a *new* perfection or reality; this new reality demands a *sufficient* and adequate reason; this sufficient reason does not lie in the potential being, because it does *not possess* it before the change; since this new reality is something superadded to it, it can only receive it from another being already in act. Hence, no being can pass from receptive potency to act, except under the influence of another being already in act.

Thomistic scholastics apply the Principle of Change in all its rigor also to 'operative' potencies and postulate a physical premotion to assist a creatural faculty in its passage from potency to act; this influence is supplied by God. Other scholastics oppose this view on the grounds that such a physical premotion, as described, would destroy all genuine creatural activity and lead to occasionalism; they maintain that the perfection of the act is contained 'virtually' in the faculty, and the change consists in the virtual act becoming a 'formal' act.

4. *Corollaries.* In so far as a being is in act, it is perfect; and in so far as a being is in potency, it is imperfect. In so far as a being is in act, it is a principle of activity; in so far as a being is in potency, it is passive. From the act we can validly conclude to the operative potency; but from the operative potency we cannot conclude to the act. In the real order, act (actual being) must precede potency (potential being).

5. *Application.* Since all beings in the universe undergo change, the universe itself is essentially potential in many respects. And since the world is really a *uni*verse, not a *pluri*verse, it demands a Prime Mover Unmoved, who is Pure Actuality and as such necessary to assist all beings in their transition from potency to act.

Hegel's monism is thus seen to be impossible. He attempts to deduce all beings from the idea of 'being in general.' Since 'being in general' is entirely potential, its self-actualization into 'determinate being' is contrary to the Principle of Change.

Even if the present universe were the result of *evolution* in some form, a Prime Mover would be required. The very fact of an evolution from a primitive state to a condition of higher organization and perfection involves the transition from potentiality to actuality; this process of change demands an existing Actual Being prior to it, giving it direction and actuality.

READINGS

Coffey, P., pp. 62–67; Mercier, D. Card., pp. 509–511; Fuetscher, Lorenz, *Akt und Potenz*, pp. 311–337; Suarez, *Disp. Met.* 29, s. 1, n. 7; St. Thomas, I, q. 2, a. 3; McCormick, J. F., Ch. IV, pp. 59, 60; Aristotle, *Physics,* VII, VIII.

CHAPTER X

ESSENCE AND EXISTENCE

ESSENCE AND existence are closely related to possible and actual being, and as such also to potency and act. A possible being is one which has a capacity for existence, without having come into existence. An actual being is one which has existence, its capacity for existence having been realized. Existence is an act, a determination, a perfection. A 'possible' being is in potency for the existential act, while an 'actual' being is in possession of the existential act. A possible being can exist, and an actual being does exist. A deep and subtle problem lies at the root of essence and existence; hence, an examination of these fundamental realities will not be amiss.

ESSENCE

To arrive at the knowledge of the essence of a thing is a very difficult task, and it is seldom adequately accomplished. Psychology shows that the natural and proper object of knowledge for the human mind is the material thing, the 'sensible.' The channels through which the material thing reaches the mind are the bodily senses — sight, hearing, touch, and so forth. The senses perceive only the accidental properties of things. We cannot perceive the essence of things with our senses; we can only *infer* the essence from the accidental properties by means of our intellect. We must analyze all our knowledge of a being, until we arrive at those elements which are absolutely required and which absolutely suffice to make that being to be just what it is, distinct from any other similar or dissimilar thing. These elements are its essential notes, its essence.

Hence, *essence* is defined as *that through which a being is just what it is* (*id quo res est id quod est*).

What, for instance, is the essence of man? That which makes him to be simply and positively a 'man,' and not a brute beast or a plant or an inanimate object or anything else. 'Animality' and 'rationality' are found in every individual 'man' and distinguish him from every other being in nature. His animality places him in the genus of 'animal,' and his rationality is the specific difference which places him in the species of 'man' as such. It will thus be seen that the definition of a being according to *proximate genus* and *specific difference* is equivalent to designating the *essence* of a being. For this reason *St. Thomas Aquinas* defines essence as "that through which a being is placed in its proper genus or species and which we signify by means of a definition indicating what a thing is."[1]

Every being consists of essentials and non-essentials, when found in the natural order of the universe. Whatever is present in a thing is 'being'; not 'being' in the wide and abstract sense of 'being in general,' but rather definite degrees and determinations of entity in a *concrete* manner. A man, as he actually exists, is not merely some indefinite and indeterminate being; he is a concrete being which consists of a definite amount of corporeal, living, sentient, rational substance and which has definite size, weight, shape, color, sex, and all those manifold powers of operation that we observe in our lives. And for all this complex amount of entity there must be a common source and fountainhead of being and operation. This source we appropriately designate the thing's *essence* (Lat., *esse,* to be; *essentia,* being), because it is the ultimate principle in the thing from which it derives whatever it possesses in the line of 'being' in any form.

Philosophers express the essence in various terms, depending on a difference of viewpoint. The essence of a thing is

[1] *De ente et essentia,* c. 1: *"Illud per quod res constituitur in proprio genere vel specie, et quod significamus per definitionem indicantem, quid est res."*

sometimes called *nature*. Out of the essence as out of a matrix all being of a thing is, so to say, born (Lat., *nascor,* to be born; *natus,* born; *natura,* nature); the elements of a thing, which constitute its being, have existence only in so far as they flow (are born) from the essence. Specifically, 'nature' is an essence considered as the ultimate principle of operations in a being. Man, for example, increases in weight and size, digests food, feels pain, thinks, and wills; but all these operations flow from his essence as a 'rational animal' as from their ultimate principle.

The essence of a thing is also called *quiddity* (whatness). This term is derived from the Latin word *quidditas,* which is a technical noun made from *quid* (what). The reason is obvious. When we desire to know what a particular thing really is, we ask the question 'What is it?' And in answer to this question we obtain a knowledge of its 'whatness'; because, in being told what it is that makes this thing to be just this being and not another, we find out its essential elements (essence) in the definition given.

Oftentimes, too, the essence of a thing is designated as its *substance*. Every creatural being is a combination of 'substance' and 'accidents.' This pair of concepts will receive special treatment later; for the present it will suffice to show why the term 'substance' is used for the term 'essence.' The substance supports the accidents in their being and existence. Iron, for example, has many qualities and properties, like weight, extension, solidity, fusion point, color, etc., but these accidental determinations cannot exist except in the body of the iron; the body or 'substance' of iron is thus seen to be the principle from which such accidents flow and in which they have their being. Hence, the substance is the primary reality in a thing, while the accidents are only secondary realities in it. However, the primary reality in any being is its essence; and that is the reason why the 'essence' of a thing is often called its 'substance.'

The designation of essence as 'substance' can, however, be

ambiguous and lead to confusion of thought. We have seen that 'essence' is defined as that which makes a being to be what it is. Accidents, too, are beings, things, realities; and as such they contain within themselves elements which make them to be what they are: weight to be weight, extension to be extension, thought to be thought, motion to be motion, and so forth. Each accident has an 'essence,' taken by itself, which makes it to be just this sort of accident as distinct from every other. When, however, we look for the essence of any concrete *individual,* considered as a substance endowed with certain accidents, then, of course, it is the 'substance' of this individual which constitutes its essence. Generally speaking, therefore, it is correct to say that the essence of a thing is its substance. The context of the discussion will reveal whether the term 'essence' applies also to accidents.

CLASSIFICATION OF ESSENCE

There are two main kinds of essence, because we can view essence from two fundamentally different standpoints: from the standpoint of its *concrete* existence in the physical world, and from the standpoint of its *abstract* conception by the mind in thought. Correspondingly, we speak of physical and metaphysical essences.

Physical essence is an essence as it exists *concretely in nature,* independent of the mind's thinking. Such an essence is taken objectively, and thereby we mean the sum of those fundamental elements which, in the natural order of the world, constitute the object's innermost being, no matter how our mind may conceive them in its thoughts. Man, for instance, consists of two essential principles in his physical nature, namely, body and soul. The same is true of animals and plants; they, too, consist of a body and a life-giving principle. These various classes of living beings are composed of the same chemical materials (matter) as the determinable element of their physical being; that plants and brutes and men differ so greatly among themselves is due to their determining life principle (form, soul) which uses this common material according to the needs of its specific nature. These elements or principles constitute the essence of a thing in the *concrete physical* order, irrespective of any mind that may contemplate them, and hence such an essence is called a 'physical' essence.

If such a physical essence is simple, i.e., constituted by a single substantial principle, and not by two or more substantial part-principles, it is a *simple* physical essence. God's essence and that of pure spirits are one in nature and not compounded by two or more substantial parts. But if this essence is composite, i.e., if it consists of two or more substantial part-principles (like body and soul), which together constitute one complete nature, it is a *composite* physical essence.

Metaphysical essence is the sum of the various *grades of being which constitute a thing in the abstract concepts of the mind.* Here we do not consider an object as it exists concretely in the physical world, but according to the manner in which it is conceived by the mind. An example will clarify this. In the physical order of existence, man is a compound of body and soul; notwithstanding this composition, he is a single being or essence. When the mind conceives man as a 'corporeal, living, sentient, rational substance,' the mind is fully aware of the fact that he does not consist of one physical part which is his 'substance,' and of a second physical part which is his 'body,' and of a third physical part which is his 'vegetant life,' and of a fourth physical part which is his 'sentiency,' and of a fifth and final physical part which is his 'rationality.' Man is a substance, and this substance is at one and the same time corporeal and living and sentient and rational — one reality expressed in five objectively different concepts, like a set of photographs taken of the same person from five different angles. The five concepts, taken alone by themselves, give but a partial and inadequate idea of the one essence; taken together, however, they supplement each other and give a correct and complete idea of man's essence. The mind must represent the one reality by means of five objectively different concepts, because it is incapable of expressing it in a single all-comprehensive concept.[2]

Such parts of an essence which are the 'grades of being' of one concrete nature (in reality identical and inseparable, but distinct and separable in thought) are called *metaphysical parts;* and the essence which is conceived by the mind as consisting of such metaphysical grades of being is called the *metaphysical* essence of the thing. Needless to say, it is possible to express a number of such metaphysical grades of being by means of a single term. A corporeal substance is termed a 'body'; a living corporeal substance is termed a 'plant.' A sentient, living, corporeal substance is termed an 'animal.' A rational, sentient, living corporeal substance is termed a 'man'; and a man is often termed a 'rational animal.' A glance shows us that this latter mode of expression is the definition of man according to his proximate genus and specific difference. Whichever way we express the essence of a thing, whether by an enumeration of the single grades of being or by a definition according to the proximate genus and specific difference, in either case we express the *metaphysical* essence of that thing.[3]

PROPERTIES OF METAPHYSICAL ESSENCES

Metaphysical essences possess a number of properties: they are immutable, indivisible, necessary, and eternal.

Essences are immutable. The sense is: no constitutive element can be subtracted from, or added to, an essence without destroying the essence itself; any essence will cease to be that particular essence, if an element is added to it or subtracted from it. An essence is that which makes a thing to be what it is. To add another essential element to such an essence, or to take an essential element away from it, would mean that the thing would no longer be what it is. For a man to be a 'rational animal,' is his whole essence; that makes man to be precisely a 'man.' If 'rationality' were removed from the con-

---

[2] See the author's *Science of Correct Thinking,* p. 80 ff.

[3] For a more detailed explanation of the terms 'genus,' 'species,' and 'specific difference,' see the author's *Science of Correct Thinking,* p. 55 ff.

cept of man, only 'animality' would remain; but 'animality' alone does not constitute man's essence, and man would no longer be 'man.' Similarly, we cannot add any constitutive elements to an essence. A brute's essence is a sentient, living, corporeal substance; it does not possess 'rationality.' If we add 'rationality' to the brute's essence, it would be a 'rational animal'; thereby it would cease to be a brute and would now be a man. A man's essence, however, is always that of a 'rational animal,' and a brute's always that of a 'non-rational animal': they cannot be changed without ceasing to be what they are. Hence, metaphysical essences are immutable.

Essences are indivisible. A metaphysical essence, as we have seen, may consist of a number of grades of being. These grades of being, however, are not separable physical parts or entities; on the contrary, they are inseparably fused together into a single, identical substance. Hence, it is impossible to divide them. Were it possible to divide them, they would be separable one from the other. Since essences are immutable, such a separation and division cannot take place without destroying the essence itself. For the same reason no essences are present in unequal amounts or degrees in individuals of the same class. Thus, all men have 'humanity' in the same degree; no individual is 'more man' than another: human nature and human essence is everywhere alike. The same is true of any other kind of being belonging to a definite class, such as lions, eagles, roses, trees, gold, radium, carbon, and the like.

Essences are necessary. This, of course, does not apply to essences in so far as they are found in the actual order of existence as physical things; as such they are clearly perceived to begin and to cease to exist. Individual men, brutes, and plants, for example, live and die; they have no necessary existence. Necessity, as applied to metaphysical essences, means that they must consist of their respective constitutive elements and of no other. Man's essence, for instance, must be that of a 'rational animal,' and it can never be anything else. Did the fact that man is a 'rational animal' ever have a beginning, or can it ever change? Evidently not. Under no circumstances or conditions can man be anything but a 'rational animal'; if he is not that, he is some other being, but he is not a 'man.' Hence, the content of metaphysical essences is a necessary content.

Essences are eternal. This follows from the foregoing. All that is meant by this is that the elements of an essence must be considered as constitutive of that particular essence, without regard to past, present, or future. That the essence of 'man' consists in his being a 'rational animal' is something which has always been true, is true now, and will remain true forever. Man is simply such an essence, and he can be nothing else. In the idea of God man is just that; and since His ideas are eternal in their content, it is necessarily and therefore eternally true that man is a 'rational animal.' And what is true of man's essence, is also true of every other essence. Metaphysical essences are independent of time.

The unwary mind may become confused in this application of the idea of eternity to essences. It might think that somehow these metaphysical essences exist and possess an eternity of 'existence.' Nothing is farther from the truth. So far as *actual existence* is concerned, they are nothing. Only God is immutable, indivisible, necessary, and eternal in actual existence. An explanation of 'eternity' will elucidate this.

Eternity is duration without beginning, end, or change. It may be positive or negative. *Positive* eternity is a duration without beginning, end, or change in existence. This is 'real,' when it refers to actual existence; or 'ideal,' when it refers to possible existence. *Negative* eternity is the indifference of a thing toward existing in a determinate portion of time. Thus, we exist at this very moment; but there is no reason why God could not have called us into being at any other time in the past or future: we would simply exist then, and not now. From the above it will be clear that abstract, metaphysical essences possess an ideal and negative, but not a real, positive eternity.

To sum up: metaphysical essences, considered absolutely, as

abstractly conceived by the mind according to their constitutive elements, have a content which is immutably, indivisibly, necessarily, and eternally the same. Physical essences, however, when actually existing in the physical universe, have no immutable, indivisible, necessary, and eternal existence; this will become more clear after an examination of the character of existence.

EXISTENCE

The essences, as just treated, were considered as abstract, metaphysical essences; they were not considered as they are found in actual existence. What is 'existence'? This is a primary and fundamental reality which cannot be adequately defined, but only known and recognized as the reality it is. Only those realities can be adequately defined, as logic shows, for which we can adduce a proximate genus and a specific difference. This, however, is not possible for a reality like 'existence.' The only proximate genus that could be used in its definition would be the idea of 'being'; but 'being,' as has already been observed, is no genus in the strict sense of the term. 'Being' can be applied only in an analogous meaning to its inferiors. The best that can be done, therefore, is to obtain a fairly accurate concept of existence by means of a description of its characteristics.

As long as an essence is contained merely as a thought-content in a mind ('intrinsic' possibility) and contained potentially in the producing power of its cause ('extrinsic' possibility), it is still non-existent. When, however, through the agency of the producing cause, such an essence ceases to be merely in a mind as a 'thought-of' essence and in its cause as a 'possible' essence, it is said to *exist.* A cause, producing an essence in this manner, gives it 'existence.' *Existence, then, is that state of a being in virtue of which it is present as an actuality, and not merely as a possibility, distinct from the mind and, if it be a produced being, distinct from its producing cause.*

When a thing 'exists,' it is a part of the visible or invisible world of beings. Hydrogen and oxygen, when not united, exist as hydrogen and oxygen and are only potentially water; but when united, water exists, and hydrogen and oxygen are only potentially there. A thousand years ago none of us actually existed; we were, however, potential beings in our forebears and in the creative power of God. Now we are conscious of our own identity as apart from the causes which produced us; we are, therefore, conscious of our 'existence.' It is thus far easier to point out existing things and recognize 'existence' concretely in this way, than it is to explain 'existence as such' in words.

The concepts of 'essence' and 'existence' are closely related, especially in an actually existing being. The attempt to specify the exact character of the distinction between the two has been the occasion for one of the most protracted controversies in philosophy.

THE PROBLEM OF ESSENCE AND EXISTENCE

It is obvious that there is a distinction between 'essence' and 'existence,' when we speak of creatural beings. In them their essence *receives* existence, because they obtain existence through the agency of their producing causes. Their essence is not the ultimate ground of their own existence. If it were, they would have existence in virtue of their particular essence, and then, their essence as such being eternally what it is, they would of necessity possess an eternal existence. That, however, is not, as a matter of observed fact, the case: things begin to exist and cease to exist. Only in God is the essence the ultimate and full ground of His existence. God's essence, being infinitely perfect, includes existence. In Him essence and existence are absolutely identical. Hence, He possesses an immutable, indivisible, necessary, and eternal existence in reality. God simply *is*. In Him there is no potentiality of any kind; He is Pure Act. That cannot be said of finite, creatural beings;

they are a mixture of act and potentiality. In their case, existence is to their essence like a determining act to a determinable potency.

Just *what* and *how great* is the *distinction* between 'essence' and 'existence' in an actually existing finite thing? That is the problem. The point at issue is this: Is the distinction between the essence and existence in an actually existing object a *real* or only a *virtual* distinction? First of all, therefore, it will be necessary to understand when a distinction is 'real' and when it is only 'virtual.' The subject of distinctions in their various forms will receive a fuller treatment later; at present, it will be sufficient to restrict our explanation to the two forms of distinction just mentioned, because they are the ones which are involved in this problem.

Objects are *really* distinct, when they are distinct from each other in *entity* and in *concept*. Not only are their respective concepts (definition and comprehension, thought-content) different, so that the concept of the one does not include that of the other, but they are also different in their entity, independent of any mind and its thinking. The mind does not make the distinction here, but merely recognizes the difference which was present in the objects before ever the mind directed its attention to them.

Things are *virtually* distinct, when they are distinct from each other in *concept,* but *not in entity*. They are distinct in concept (definition and comprehension, thought-content), so that the concept of the one does not signify the same content as that of the other; but they are not different in their entity as they are found *in nature*. In nature there exists but one reality, and the mind makes two or more distinct concepts of them.

There is a real distinction between an essence in the 'possible' order and the same essence in the 'actual (existing)' order; because, so long as it is merely possible it is actually nothing, while in the actual order it is a real being among physically existing things. There is no problem here. But, taking an object as it is present here and now *in the actual order of physically existing things,* as it stands here and now *outside the mind and outside all producing causes,* is there a *real* or only a *virtual* distinction between an essence and its existential act (existence)? In other words: Are essence and existence in an actually existing being *entitatively two realities;* or are they at bottom identical and only *one reality in nature,* but with two *distinct concepts* in the mind? That is the crux of the problem.

The controversy regarding the real or virtual distinction between essence and existence in an actually existing being has held the attention of philosophers, especially among the scholastics, from the Middle Ages to the present day. Men of great caliber, celebrated for the depth and acumen of their insight into philosophic matters, have sought with great eagerness to find a solution for this vexing question; but no one has been able to bring forth arguments which would definitely settle the problems to the satisfaction of all.

There is a very great difficulty in the subject matter itself, since it revolves around two of the most fundamental concepts of the human mind — essence and existence. These two concepts lie so close to the borderland of 'possible' and 'actual' existence, and the line of demarcation separating them is so fine, that the unhappy controversialist may unwittingly lapse into a begging of the question. In fact, authors have frequently charged each other with this illogical procedure; the recriminations are mutual.

The philosophers of the *Thomistic School* defend the real distinction between essence and existence; it is a cardinal doctrine of their system. A number of scholastics, though not Thomists, follow them in this. Others follow *Suarez* and defend a virtual distinction between essence and existence. There are great authorities in either camp. To do justice to both sides would require extensive quotations, and it is doubtful whether the beginner in philosophy would derive much benefit from these conflicting views. It must therefore suffice here to merely mention the problem.[4]

SUMMARY OF CHAPTER X

Essence and *existence* are a main division of 'being in general.'

1. *Essence.* It is that in virtue of which a being is just what it is. The definition of a being according to its proximate genus and specific difference gives its essence. It is the ultimate principle in a thing from which it derives whatever it possesses in the line of 'being' in any form. It is also called 'nature,' 'quiddity,' 'substance.'

2. *Classification of Essence.* Essence is either physical or metaphysical. *Physical* essence is an essence as it exists concretely in nature, independent of the mind's thinking. It is 'simple,' if it is constituted by a single substantial principle; it is 'composite,' if it consists of two or more substantial part-principles which together constitute one complete nature. *Metaphysical* essence is the sum of the various grades of being which constitute a thing in the abstract concepts of the mind. These 'grades of being' in a concrete nature are in reality identical and separable only in thought.

3. *Properties of Metaphysical Essences.* Essences, taken metaphysically, are immutable, indivisible, necessary, and

---

[4] The interested student will find the main points of the discussion elucidated in any standard work on scholastic philosophy. The following selected list of works may be consulted with profit: Gredt, *Elementa philos.* II; Remer-Geny, *Ontol.;* Frick, *Ontol.;* Donat, *Ontol.;* Mercier, *Métaphysique Générale, A Manual of Modern Scholastic Philosophy;* Garrigou-Lagrange, *Acta primi congressus thom. internat.;* Hugon, *Metaph., Les vingt-quattre theses thomistes;* Coffey, *Ontology;* Schiffini, *Principia philos.;* T. Pesch, *Institut. logic.;* Mauri, *Lectiones philos. schol.;* De Maria, *Philosophia peripatetico-scholastica;* Stöckl, *Lehrbuch der Philosophie;* Liberatori, *Institut. philos.;* Sanseverino, *Phil. Chr. Compendium;* Del Prado, *De veritate fundam.;* Zigliara, *Summa phil., Ontol.;* Lehmen, *Lehrbuch der Philosophie;* Fuetscher, *Akt und Potenz;* Balmes, *Fundamental Philosophy;* Mattiussi, *Le XXIV tesi della filosofia di S. Tommaso d'Aquino;* Grandclaude, *Breviar, phil. Metaph. Gen.;* Suarez, *Disp. Metaph.,* 5, 31.

eternal. This does not apply to physical essences in their actual existence. Only God's existence has these properties in the actual order.

4. *Existence.* The term does not admit of a strict definition, because existence is a primary reality and concept. It is opposed to mere 'possibility.' It can be described as that state of a being in virtue of which it is present as an actuality, and not merely as a possibility, distinct from the mind and, if it be a produced thing, distinct from its producing causes.

5. *Problem of Essence and Existence.* The problem is this: Is the distinction between the essence and existence in an actually existing object a *real* or only a *virtual* distinction? Objects are 'really' distinct, when they are distinct from each other in entity and in concept; they are 'virtually' distinct, when they are distinct from each other in concept, but not in entity. Hence: Are essence and existence in an actually existing being *entitatively two realities;* or are they at bottom identical and only *one reality in nature,* but with *two distinct concepts* in the mind?

READINGS

Coffey, P., Ch. III; Rickaby, J., Bk. I, Ch. III; Hugon, Ed., Tr. I, Qu. III, art. 3 and 4; Baschab, C. R., Ch. XXII; Phillips, R. P., Ch. V; Mercier, D. Card., *Ontologie,* n. 16 ff., *Manual,* pp. 434–439; Mc-Cormick, J. F., Ch. III, pp. 36–39 and 39–42; Fuetscher, L., Kap. V–X; Aristotle, *Metaph.,* V.

PART II
THE TRANSCENDENTAL ATTRIBUTES
OF BEING

Chapter XI

BEING AND ONENESS

THE TRANSCENDENTAL attributes of being are often styled 'properties.' In the strict sense of the term, a 'property' is some attribute which is not a direct part of an essence itself, but which flows necessarily from an essence integrally constituted. As such, it must be a positive entity, different from the essence itself. Applying this to the concept of 'being in general,' it is evident that, in the strict sense, there can be no such properties of 'being in general'; because a property that would be different from 'being' would have to be a non-being, and a non-being cannot be an attribute of anything. An attribute that flows necessarily from being must itself be a 'being' and therefore must already be contained in the concept of 'being in general.' However, in a wider use of the word we speak of the properties of being. We call them 'properties,' because they resemble the properties taken in the strict acceptation of the term. Bearing this in mind, the *transcendental properties or attributes* of being in general are defined as certain *supreme modes or attributes necessarily connected with every being, which are different phases of the same fundamental being, but are not explicitly contained in its concept as such*. They are called 'transcendental' in as much as they are not confined to any particular category or classification of being, but are found in all, affecting each and every conceivable being: they 'transcend,' or 'go beyond and over,' all categories.

There are six transcendental concepts: *being, thing, something, one, true, good (ens, res, aliquid, unum, verum, bonum)*. But of these 'being,' 'thing (reality),' and 'something' are synonymous; there is no real difference of meaning between them, since all merely signify the opposite of non-entity. A glance at 'one,' 'true,' and 'good,' however, shows that these mean something different in their comprehension, when compared to each other, even though they are identical with the more fundamental concept of 'being.' These, then, *oneness, truth,* and *goodness,* are the transcendental properties or attributes of being.

In the previous chapters our investigation has considered 'being' only in its concept and in its primary determinations. We must now consider it more in its *relations*. If we consider a being in relation to its constitution, it is 'one.' If we consider it in its relation to another, it may be taken in relation to a knowing intellect, and this adds to it the mode of being 'true'; or it may be taken in relation to an appetitive power, and this adds to it the mode of being 'good.' These three transcendental properties or attributes will be investigated in this order.

THE CONCEPT OF UNITY

When is a being 'one'? Oneness or unity necessarily implies the idea of indivision within a being's own reality. Hence, a being is said to be 'one' when it is *undivided in itself*. This is the most fundamental idea underlying the concept of 'one' and 'unity.' There is no need of comparing a thing with another, in order to speak of its 'oneness'; a thing would be 'one' even if no other being were in existence or possible. God, for example, existed from eternity; He, therefore, had oneness or unity in His own being, irrespective of the fact that He existed alone and no creatural beings co-existed from eternity with Him.

Usually, however, philosophers add another element to this definition, namely, that a being be *divided from other things*. It will readily be observed, though, that this latter is secondary and flows from the first: because a thing is undivided in itself, it will also be divided from all others. Since a thing, according to the Principle of Identity, is what it is, it must primarily be undivided in itself; then, since the thing, according to the Principle of Contradiction, cannot simultaneously be both itself and not itself, it must secondarily be divided from every other. From this it follows that a 'part' of a thing cannot be considered, with respect to some other part of that thing, as being truly one, because it is not actually divided from the other part; a part is united with the other part or parts, to form the unity or oneness of the whole: the whole is one, not the part. On the other hand, a 'compound' would truly be one, because the component parts are not actually divided: the whole has indivision in itself, notwithstanding its composition, and as such it possesses unity or oneness.

Viewed in this light, every being is one, and oneness is a transcendental property of being. *Transcendental unity* can, therefore, be defined as that *mode or attribute of a being in virtue of which a being is undivided in itself (and divided from every other being)*.

From this transcendental unity or oneness we must distinguish *predicamental unity* or oneness. We speak here of the unit or units of numbers. It is called 'predicamental,' because number belongs to the predicament or category of 'quantity.' Predicamental unity or oneness is the same as *mathematical* or *numerical* unity, or oneness, and it is defined as a unit considered as a standard for measuring mathematical or numerical quantity. In the metric system the millimeter, centimeter, meter, kilometer, etc., are mathematical units; in the English system we have the inch, the yard, the rod, the mile. Thus, too, the gram, the liter, the pint, the gallon, the ounce, the pound, the ton, etc., are all mathematical units of measurement. Such units differ with different peoples and with different scientific requirements.

CLASSIFICATION OF UNITY

Beings are said to be 'one,' either because there is unity in them as *things,* independent of the thinking mind which contemplates them (*real* unity), or because the mind conceives them as possessing unity as a *class,* although in nature they are not actually one (*logical* unity).

Real Unity. Real unity is the *indivision of a thing in its entity,* independent of our mode of thinking. Such a thing would be undivided in itself and consequently 'one,' even if there were no mind in existence to contemplate it. Thus each object in the world, as it exists for itself, is one: a man, a dog, a bird, a plant, a stone, a star, a proton, an electron. Real unity may be simple or compound.

Real unity is a *unity of simplicity,* or a thing is said to be simple in its unity, when its indivision is such that the thing does *not consist of any parts* into which it could be divided; such a thing is actually undivided and potentially indivisible. A case in point is the soul of man; it is a spiritual being which does not consist of any parts and as such is one and indivisible. The same is true of the essence of God and of pure spirits.

Real unity is a *unity of composition,* or a thing is said to be composite in its unity, when it is a *whole not actually divided into the real parts of which it consists.* A being of this kind has parts within itself, but these parts are so united that they form a unit, a whole, a totality. Man's body, for instance, is composed of head, trunk, and extremities, and each of these consists of various minor parts; but they are not actually separated from one another, so that they would be mutually independent: they form an organism, and an organism is a whole or unit.

If the parts of a composite whole are substantial parts constituting a single nature, there is a *substantial* unity. Man is a single nature, consisting of body and soul. All brutes and plants are composed of a substantial material principle (matter) and a substantial life-giving principle (soul). According to the hylomorphic theory of Aristotle and the scholastics, even inanimate beings consist of two part-substances, matter and form. If the parts of a composite whole are united because of something accidental, there is an *accidental* unity. There are three possibilities. Two or more substances may be united in an accidental bond; for example, two horses pulling a wagon, a piece of iron attracted by a magnet, the planets and the sun in the solar system. A substance may be united with accidents; for example, the union between the human body and its weight, energy, heat, color. An accident may be united with another accident; for example, the union between the accident of bodily extension in a stone and its modal accident of shape or size.

The unity of composition may also be metaphysical, physical, or moral. This unity will be *metaphysical,* if the whole consists of grades of being as metaphysical parts, united through mutual compatibility; for example, the metaphysical parts of man's concrete nature are rationality, animality, vegetancy, materiality, and substantiality. It will be *physical,* if the unity of the parts of a whole is effected through the influence of the physical forces of nature; for example, the unity of electrons and protons forming an atom, of various atoms forming a body. It will be *moral,* if the unity of the various parts of the whole is the result of free-acting agencies; for example, the unity which exists among human societies, governments, firms, armies, families.

Again, if the unity of composition is brought about by means of an inherent tendency of the forces of nature, the result will be a *natural* unity. For example, body and soul in man; feathers, wings, legs, and the other parts of a bird; roots, stem, leaves, flowers, and fruit in a watermelon plant; hydrogen and oxygen in the formation of water. But if the parts have no natural tendency to form a whole and do so only because an outside intelligence arranges them into a unit, such a unity is *artificial.* Thus, a house, a cap, a watch, an automobile, a ship, a gun, a desk, a book, etc., are artificial units.

In all these cases there is a 'real' unity, a unity of things as things, independent of the mind contemplating them; they have and retain their unity, even though no mind adverts to them.

Logical Unity. This form of unity is entirely dependent on the activity of the mind, and for that reason it is not found in the things of nature as such. Logical unity is the result of a thought process of man's intellect and is due to its generalizing and classifying tendency. The mind groups a number of things, actually divided and separated in nature, into a *class* on the basis of some similarity existing among them and in this manner unites them into a *conceptual whole.*

Any point of similarity may be taken by the mind as the basis for such a class-idea. Thus, between a human being in America and another in Africa and a third in China there is no possible real unity; they are really separated and divided. And the same fact applies to all human beings, dead or alive, present or past or future. Nevertheless, they all possess the essential similarity of a common human nature — they are 'rational animals.' The mind grasps this similar element in them all and expresses it in a universal idea, the unified concept 'man.' The concept 'man,' therefore, is a conceptual whole, of which the individual men are considered by the mind as being logical parts.

In this manner the mind develops its universal ideas or class-ideas as conceptual wholes, of which the subclasses or individuals are the logical parts. All universal ideas possess this character. Scientific classifications fall under this head. Beginning with the individuals, they build up class after class, until they cover the entire field in one supreme, all-embracing class. Hence, *logical unity* is defined as the *indivision of a universal idea (class) considered as a whole of which the inferiors are the parts.*

CONVERTIBILITY OF BEING AND UNITY

When it is stated that being and unity are convertible, the meaning is: *Every being is one or a unit, and everything that is one or a unit is a being.* A brief consideration of the concepts of 'being' and 'one' will show the truth and necessity of this statement.

Every being, of whatever kind and character, is either *simple* or *compound* in its nature. This is clear from the definition of these terms: a thing is 'compound,' when it consists of parts; and it is 'simple,' when it does not consist of parts. These terms are contradictory in meaning, and between contradictories there is no middle; hence, according to the Principle of Excluded Middle, every being must be either simple or compound. Whatever is 'simple' is undivided actually as well as potentially, because it has no parts into which it can be divided; consequently, a simple being is undivided in itself and therefore a unit or one. Whatever is a 'compound' is a compound only in so far and only so long as its parts are united and are not actually divided, because that is what is understood by the term 'compound'; consequently, a compound being is undivided in itself and therefore a unit or one. From this it is evident that the being of every thing, whether simple or compound, is characterized by *indivision;* in other words, every being is a unit or one.

That everything which is a unit or one is also a being, is evident. To be a 'unit' or 'one' means to have the unity of simplicity or the unity of composition. That, however, presupposes that *some thing* has this unity of simplicity or this unity of composition. The concept of the 'unity of composition' necessarily involves the concept of a *reality consisting of parts,* and these parts must be real in the whole; otherwise they would be nothing, and nothing cannot be distinguished into parts. For the same reason the 'unity of simplicity' necessarily implies the concept of a *reality consisting of no parts;* if the simple unit were not a reality (being), it would be nothing, and nothing cannot be a unit of any kind, whether simple or compound. Hence, only a being can be a unit or one. From this it follows that 'being' and 'one' are convertible, because they are *identical;* every being is a unit, and every unit is a being.

Regarding this question, it is well to remember that we are not speaking of *beings,* but of a *being.* We do not deny the plurality of beings in this world, nor do we assert that all beings together form a single being. It is merely a question whether an *individual being* is a unit *in itself*. Concerning a 'simple' being, the matter is easily solved: since it has no parts, it is naturally undivided in itself, and therefore a unit or one. It is in connection with a 'compound' being that the question of unity can be raised. It consists of parts. Should a being consisting of parts really be considered as 'one,' as a 'unit'? Do not these parts imply a plurality, so that we should speak of 'beings' rather than of a 'being'? It is obvious that the parts of a compound, if actually separated and divided, no longer form a 'compound' at all; each separated and divided part becomes a being of its own, and thus actual division entails plurality. But if they are not actually separated and divided, they are not actually 'beings' either, since in their mutual union they form a unitary 'being.' Now, it is precisely when they are not actually separated and divided, that they form a 'compound.' Hence, so long as a thing is really a compound, it is not a plurality of beings, but *one single being*.

BEING AND INDIVIDUALITY

The unity of being, considered so far, is the unity proper to *all being,* whether possible or actual, abstract or concrete. A 'man,' for instance, is a unit, whether we consider him merely as a possible being who can exist, or as an actual being who does exist, whether we consider his nature in the abstract as a 'rational animal,' or as a concrete reality in the physical world of things: he is considered in all cases to be a compound being consisting of parts which form a complete and unitary nature. And what is true here of man, is true of every other being mentionable or conceivable.

There is, however, a special kind of transcendental unity which is called the *unity of individuality* or the *unity of an individual;* it is defined as the unity of a being which is *one in itself and non-multipliable.* An individual, therefore, is an existing unit of being, incapable of being multiplied; in other words, an individual is 'one' in such a manner that it cannot be divided, so that each member resulting from the division would be the same as the original undivided individual.

The concept of the 'individual' is thus seen to be in opposition to the concept of the 'universal.' The universal is conceived by the mind as a nature common-to-one-and-many; it is capable of being realized in any number of individuals of that class. As a class-nature it is conceived as a (logical, or conceptual) unit; since, however, it is communicable to many, it is multipliable. The individual nature, on the other hand, is conceived as being one for itself alone, so that it is incommunicable to others; there may be any number of individual natures of a certain type and class (e.g., men), but they are *not the same, identical* nature. The individual nature, as an existing individual, since it is not communicable to many, is thus conceived as non-multipliable.

Is this idea of the 'individual' justified? Why should it be impossible for a being to exist concretely in the physical world as a 'universal'? And why must a being, if it exist, exist only as an *'individual'*? For the following reason:

The universality of a universal idea involves the concept of a nature or essence which applies to a *class* as a whole and to *every member* of that class; it is applicable to one-and-many. Take the universal idea 'man.' It represents a nature or essence ('rational animal') which applies to the whole class of men taken together, as when we state 'Man is mortal'; here we mean that the whole class of men as a class is mortal. But the universal idea 'man' also represents the same nature or essence as applied to each single member of the class of men, as when we state 'Peter is mortal, Napoleon is mortal, Margaret is mortal'; and here we mean that each man is mortal, taken singly and individually. The universal, therefore, is applicable to one-and-many; it is (conceptually) one, but also many. Hence, if the universal could exist *as a universal,* it would exist as 'one' and as 'many' *simultaneously.* That, however, involves a contradiction. As 'one' it would be a unit; as 'many' it would be a plurality: it would exist as a unit and as a plurality simultaneously — an obvious contradiction. It must exist either as a unit or as a plurality; it cannot be both. But we have just seen that every being is one, and oneness excludes plurality. Every being, therefore, if it exist, must be one and singular, not universal and plural. Consequently, no being can exist as a universal, but *only as an individual*.

THE PRINCIPLE OF ABSOLUTE INDIVIDUATION

Every being which exists must exist as an individual being. As such, the individual nature or essence is not communicable to others, but is absolutely restricted to this one individual, e.g., to Peter or Napoleon or Socrates. Individuality, in a philosophic sense, is therefore that state of an existing being in virtue of which it is one in itself and non-multipliable. This raises an important question: What is the *principle of individuation* which makes an existing being to be an individual, so that its nature or essence is incommunicable to others and is restricted to this one? We can distinguish between an extrinsic and an intrinsic principle of individuation for a being. The 'extrinsic' principle is the cause which gives an individual being its existence. That, of course, is the efficient cause, either God or creature; and with that we are not concerned here. The 'intrinsic' principle of individuation is the ground or reason (principle) in the being itself which *gives individuality* to the being so that it is one in itself and non-multipliable into many. In other words, what is it in the being itself that makes it to be 'this' particular individual (*haecceitas,* 'thisness') ? Since this question refers to the single individual, taken absolutely and without any relation to others, this intrinsic principle is called the *principle of absolute individuation,* i.e., the intrinsic principle which gives the unity of individuality to an existing being.

In order to understand the problem rightly, we must compare the 'individual nature' of a being with its 'specific nature.' The specific nature of a being is the result of the union of its proximate genus and specific difference. For instance, the specific nature of man consists of the proximate genus 'animal' and the specific difference 'rational'; the union of the two constitutes the specific nature (species) of man, for 'man' is a 'rational animal.' This specific nature is, of course, alike in all men, because all men possess the nature or essence of a rational animal. From this standpoint alone there would be no difference in the concept of one man and another. In an existing man, however, this general 'specific human nature' becomes an 'individual human nature,' and this is done through the union of the 'specific nature' with 'individuality'; Napoleon, through his individuality, is not merely *a man,* but *this man Napoleon.* In this manner the general 'specific nature' becomes *individuated* in an existing individual by means of a union between it and 'individuality.'

Hence, the question: What is the principle of absolute individuation which makes an individual to be an individual? Is 'individuality' a reality *really distinct* from the reality of the 'specific nature or essence,' united as physical entities in a *physical union?* In this case, the principle of absolute individuation would be the entity of the 'individuality' as such, and not the nature or essence at all. Or, are the 'specific nature' and the 'individuality' in an existing individual *entitatively identical,* with merely a distinction in thought between them, so that they form a *metaphysical union?* In that case, the (formal) principle of absolute individuation would be the entity of the 'individual nature or essence' itself, and there would be only a virtual distinction between 'individuality' and 'specific nature' in an individual. The latter view is correct, and that will now be demonstrated.

If we maintain a *real distinction* in an existing nature between its 'specific nature' and its 'individuality,' we must maintain that the 'individual nature' results from a physical composition of these two entities, so that the 'specific nature,' when it exists, cannot become individuated (i.e., become an 'individual nature') except through the reality of this 'individuality.' But this 'specific nature,' *in itself,* must be either a *uni-*

versal or an *individual* nature. If it is universal, then a universal nature would exist as a universal; the 'individuality,' being distinct in its entity from the entity of this 'specific nature,' is merely superadded or united to it and cannot change it. As was shown before, however, a universal nature cannot exist in the physical order of things as a universal. Therefore, the specific nature must come into existence as an 'individual nature.' But if it comes into existence as an 'individual nature' the entity of 'individuality' is entirely superfluous and can no longer make it individual, because it is already an 'individual nature' *in itself* when it comes into existence. Consequently, the 'thisness' or 'individuality' of an existing nature is not really, but only mentally, distinct from the existing nature itself, and the principle of absolute individuation in an existing individual is the *nature* or *essence* itself. In other words, every specific nature, by the mere fact that it exists, thereby becomes an *individuated* (individual) nature. 'Individuality,' therefore, is not an entity added or united to the nature, but solely a manner of existence for it.

The distinction, then, between the 'specific nature' and the 'individuality' or 'thisness' of an existing individual is a mental or *logical distinction,* i.e., there is no distinction between them as 'things,' but there is a distinction between them in their 'concepts.' That they are distinct in concept, is obvious, because we define them differently; we certainly do not mean the same thing when we speak of the 'nature' and of the 'individuality' of an individual. The question then arises: Is there a ground or reason or *foundation* in the individuals for making this distinction in concepts? There is. 'Individuality,' as such, is the same in kind for all existing beings; it is simply conceived as that which makes a specific nature to become individuated in this particular individual. But there is a great variety of specific natures among existing beings (e.g., men, plants, animals, inanimate things, etc.), each of which is individuated in a large number of existing individuals, while a still larger number is merely possible and therefore not actually individuated at all. Here we have the ground, the reason, the *foundation in the things* themselves for our making a mental or logical distinction between the 'nature' and the 'individuality' in them. Now, when there is an identity of thing, but a distinction in concept, with a foundation in the thing for making this distinction, this distinction is not real, nor purely mental, but virtual. In an existing individual, therefore, there is a *virtual distinction* between the nature and its individuality.

The Scotists, followers of Duns Scotus, claim that this distinction is a 'formal distinction on the part of the nature of the thing.' In the next chapter we will discuss this formal distinction, and there it will be shown to be invalid.

THE PRINCIPLE OF RELATIVE INDIVIDUATION

In the foregoing problem an individual nature was considered in and for itself, and the problem consisted in determining the principle of absolute determination for this single individual as such. In the present problem the individuals of a certain species, as they exist in the world of real beings, are taken in relation to each other, and the problem consists in seeking to determine the principle of individuation in virtue of which it is possible to have *a number of individuals of the same species*. To express the problem in a more concrete manner: What is the principle which individuates a specific nature, for example 'man,' into a number of individual natures or individuals, like Peter, Paul, Napoleon, etc., so that it is possible to have more than one individual of that species? This principle is called the *principle of relative individuation*. A solution of the problem has been attempted along two lines.

St. Thomas Aquinas and in general the scholastics follow the view of Aristotle and consider the principle of relative individuation to be *matter affected by dimensive quantity*. They reason as follows: Since it is a question of the plurality of individuals in the same species, the principle of individuation must be a principle of plurality. Plurality implies division and divisibility. The ground or principle of divisibility will, therefore, also be the ground or principle of plurality. Consequently, the ground or principle of relative individuation must be that ground or principle of divisibility which enables a specific nature to be multiplied into a plurality of individual natures. Now, in the physical order, the ground or principle of divisibility lies in *matter* as affected by dimensive quantity (*materia sub dimensionibus signata*), because matter alone, with its threefold dimensions, is *of itself divisible* in such a manner that a plurality of individuals can arise through its division. When a portion of matter is separated from another, due to a division of its dimensive quantity, a plurality is effected in it which gives rise to a plurality of individual beings of the same species.

This is observed in *inorganic* beings. A piece of gold can be divided into a number of individuals of the same species of gold by a simple division of its quantity. In *organic* beings a new individual arises through a variety of processes, but they are all effected through a division of the quantity of matter. Whether the generation of new individuals takes place through fission or budding, by means of spores or seed, it always happens through the division and separation of a portion of matter affected by quantity in its threefold dimensions. Quantified matter, then, is the principle of relative individuation.[1]

Such is the solution of St. Thomas and his followers. The theory explains the individuality and plurality of *corporeal* beings, as we know them to exist in this physical world. It also explains the plurality of individual human *souls*. Souls, though spiritual in nature, are essentially ordered toward union with a certain amount of quantified matter, so as to form with it a body; man is naturally a compound of soul and matter, and the soul is not a pure spirit. This ordination toward union with matter, since it is a natural exigency of the soul, can never be lost. Hence, even after death a disembodied soul will

---

[1] See St. Thomas Aquinas, *Summa theol.*, 3, q. 77, a. 2; *Contra Gentiles*, c. 65; *De Veritate*, q. 2, art. 6. T. Pesch, *Institutiones Logicales*, n. 1285. D. Mercier, *Ontologie*, §§ 36–42. Coffey, P., *Ontology*, n. 32, pp. 128 f.

retain its separate individuality with respect to other souls. However, it also follows as a logical consequence of this theory that *pure spirits* cannot be multiplied as individuals in the same species. They do not consist of matter, nor have they a natural ordination toward union with matter. For this reason a plurality of individual pure spirits, belonging to the same species, is impossible, because 'quantified matter' is the principle of relative individuation. The result of this theory would be that each single pure spirit represents a distinct species. Of course, the human mind, in its condition of embodiment on earth, has no way of either directly proving or disproving this contention. In virtue of its own observation it cannot know whether or not pure spirits are represented by a number of individuals within the same species; in fact, it is questionable whether the human mind, with the natural light of reason alone, can prove even the existence of pure spirits. But there certainly seems to be no contradiction in the *idea* of a plurality of individual pure spirits within the same species. To deny such a plurality of individuals, then, as this theory does, would rather seem to be a weakness of this theory which places the principle of relative individuation in quantified matter.

For this reason, *Suarez*,[2] and others with him, offer a different solution of the problem. According to them, the principle of relative individuation lies in the *contingency* and *finiteness* of creatural beings. God, because He is infinitely perfect, subsistent in virtue of His own essence, possesses the unity not only of individuality, but also of unicity: there can be but one God. With creatural beings the situation is radically different; since they are contingent and finite both in essence and existence, they are multipliable into any number of individuals of the same species. Here is the reason.

The possibility of any creatural being to acquire existence is derived from the *imitability* of God's infinite essence. Because God is imitable by created essences, His omnipotence can create

---

[2] *Metaph. disp.* 5, sect. 3, n. 17. See also Lehmen, *Lehrbuch der Philosophie*, p. 381.

them. That, as was shown before, is the ultimate foundation of their possibility. Since, however, His essence is infinitely perfect, it is infinitely imitable, both *intensively* and *extensively;* if this were not so, it would not be infinitely perfect in itself. That His imitability be infinite 'intensively,' means that His essence can be imitated by all kinds or *species* of being without number; and that it be infinite 'extensively,' means that each kind or species of being can be represented by *individuals* without number. The actual number of such imitations will, of course, never exhaust the possibility of the imitability of God's essence, for the very reason that God's essence is actually infinite as an existing reality. Consequently, no creatural being can ever be so perfect in essence or existence that other individuals of the same species would not be possible. As a result of this, any number of individuals of the same species can receive existence through the omnipotence of God. And this is true both of pure spirits and of corporeal beings; there is no difference between them in this respect, because both classes are contingent and finite. To say that the various species of pure spirits could not be represented by a number of individuals, would seem to be tantamount to placing a limitation on the imitability, and thereby also on the perfection, of God. The principle of relative individuation, therefore, lies in the contingency and finiteness of creatural beings.

These are some of the problems which arise from the transcendental attribute of being as 'one.' They may not have much practical value, but they give us a better understanding of the ultimate metaphysical constitution of things, and that is always something worth knowing.

SUMMARY OF CHAPTER XI

Transcendental properties or attributes of being in general are the supreme modes or attributes necessarily connected with every being, which are different phases of the same fundamental being, but are not explicitly contained in its concept as such. Such are the attributes of *one, true,* and *good.*

1. *The Concept of Unity*. Something is 'one' which is *undivided in itself* and divided from every other being. This transcendental oneness or unity must be distinguished from 'predicamental unity,' which is the unity of a quantitative being considered as a standard for measuring quantity.

2. *Classification of Unity*. Unity will be either real or logical.

Real unity is the indivision of a thing in its *entity*, independent of our mode of thinking. It is a unity of *simplicity*, when the indivision is such that the thing does not consist of any parts into which it could be divided. It is a unity of *composition*, when the thing is a whole not actually divided into the real parts of which it consists. If the compound (whole) consists of substantial parts, it is a 'substantial' unity; if the parts are united together because of something accidental, it is an 'accidental' unity. The unity of composition may also be metaphysical, physical, or moral, depending upon the fact whether the uniting bond is metaphysical, physical, or moral; it may also be a natural or artificial unity.

Logical unity is the indivision of a *universal idea* (class) considered as a conceptual whole of which the inferiors are the parts. In this sort of unity the things are actually divided from each other, independent of the mind, and form no real unity; but the mind unites them into a class-idea or conceptual whole, due to some common element in which they are similar.

3. *Convertibility of Being and Unity*. This means that every 'being' is 'one,' and everything that is 'one' is a 'being.' Every being has unity, either of simplicity or of compostion. Everything that is 'one,' is a 'being.' If it were no being, it would be 'nothing' and 'nothing' can have no unity either of simplicity or of composition.

4. *Being and Individuality*. Individuality is a kind of transcendental unity, in virtue of which a being is *one in itself and non-multipliable*. The individual is opposed to the universal or class. The 'universal' represents a nature common-to-one-and-many; it applies to the class as a whole and to every member

of that class. If a universal could exist as a universal, it would exist as 'one' and as 'many' simultaneously; but that is impossible: consequently, a being can *only exist as an individual*, not as a universal.

5. *The Principle of Absolute Individuation.* By this is meant the intrinsic principle which gives the unity of individuality to an existing being. There is only a *virtual* distinction between the 'specific nature' and the 'individuality' in an existing being, because the 'specific nature' cannot exist as a universal, but only as an individual nature.

6. *The Principle of Relative Individuation.* The problem is: What is the principle of individuation in virtue of which it is possible to have a number of individuals of the same species? *St. Thomas Aquinas* and others consider this principle to be matter affected by dimensive quantity. *Suarez* and others consider it to lie in the contingency and finiteness of creatural beings.

READINGS

Coffey, P., Ch. IV; Rickaby, J., Bk. I, Ch. IV; Hugon, Ed., Tr. II, Qu. I, art. 1 et 2; Aristotle, *Metaph.,* IV, V, X; St. Thomas, 1. 7 et 8 in V *Metaph.,* et 1. 4 in X *Metaph.; Summa Th.,* I, q. 11, a. 1; Urráburu, J. J., Disp. II, cp. II; Mercier, D. Card., pp. 446–459; McCormick, J. F., Ch. V, pp. 65–72.

Chapter XII

IDENTITY AND DISTINCTION

UNITY OR oneness is a transcendental attribute of being. Every being is one or a unit, and everything that is one or a unit is a being: 'being' and 'one' are convertible. As things they are identical, but as concepts there is a distinction between them.

The terms 'identity' and 'distinction' play an important role in philosophy. The terms, however, have a variety of meanings, and their indiscriminate use frequently gives rise to confusion of thought. It will be necessary, therefore, to give a somewhat detailed exposition of both terms. In its fundamental meaning, *identity* is a *sameness between concepts or things; distinction* is the *absence of sameness between concepts or things.*

'Things' are real beings, and as such have an entity independent of the mind's thinking process. 'Concepts,' on the other hand, are the result of the mind's activity, and as such have only a mental or logical entity. We, therefore, speak of a real or logical identity, and also of a real or logical distinction.

REAL IDENTITY

Real identity is the sameness (oneness) of things in themselves. A distinction between them may be made in the concepts of the mind. For instance, we speak of man as a 'being' and as a 'substance.' Mentally we make a distinction between these two; but as things they are identical: man's being is his substance, and his substance is his being. Hence, there is a real identity between being and substance in man, notwithstanding the distinction between their concepts made by the mind.

A real identity is a *metaphysical* identity, when a being is one with itself so that it *can absolutely not change in any manner*. Since God is infinitely perfect, He possesses all being and perfection without regard to past, present, or future. If He could gain or lose any degree of being or perfection, He would not be infinitely perfect. He must, therefore, possess His infinite perfection from all eternity and keep it through all eternity; and this means, that He can absolutely not change in any manner. God, then, is metaphysically identical with Himself, beyond and above all change.

A real identity is a *physical* identity, when a being is one with itself so that it *does not change in its essential reality,* although it can change in its accidental realities. Thus, the human soul, as will be shown in psychology, is spiritual in nature. It has the unity of simplicity, being devoid of any substantial parts into which it could be divided. A simple being of this kind can be annihilated, but it cannot undergo any change in its essence. It can, however, undergo an alteration in its accidental realities. Every thought, for instance, involves the transition from the potentiality of thinking to the actuality of thinking, and that is an accidental change. Such a being, therefore, is physically identical in its essence.

A real identity is a *moral* identity, when a being is one with itself so that the *change which takes place in its essential being is successive and gradual;* although it undergoes a change, this change is such that, in the common estimation of men, it still remains the same. Due to this change, none of the original parts may possibly be left after a lapse of time; however, these original parts have been supplanted by new material, so that the fundamental structure or organization has remained intact throughout the entire process of change. A case in point is the human body. The vital functions are continually tearing down old material and replacing it with new material; but this change is so gradual and imperceptible that the general structure of the body remains fundamentally the same to the end of life. This is true of every organism, as long as it lives. So, too, a society or government or nation may retain its moral identity for a hundred or a thousand years and longer. After a few generations not a single original member will be living; nevertheless, the society or government or nation will continue to preserve its moral identity, because the organization has not been dissolved, but has retained its structure intact through the successive and gradual assimilation of new members.

LOGICAL IDENTITY

Logical identity is the *sameness (oneness) of things based upon the same concept of the mind*. Logically identical things are not one in reality; they are a plurality of things, each of which is not entitatively the same as the other. They agree, however, in some similar element, and on account of this similarity the mind groups them into one concept and considers them *identical in this respect*. Such things, therefore, are really distinct, but conceptually the same. The similarity existing between such things will lie either in their essence or in their accidents; correspondingly, logical identity will be either an essential or an accidental identity.

An *essential* logical identity is the logical identity of things based upon the *similarity of their essence*. Peter, Paul, Napoleon, and all human beings agree in this that they possess a similar human essence; as 'men,' therefore, they are logically identical in their essence. Men, brutes, plants, and inanimate things are essentially similar to each other in so far as they are 'corporeal'; they are, therefore, conceived by the mind as possessing an essential logical identity. If the essence expressed in the concept represents the genus, so that the things are similar in their 'generic essence,' we have a *generic* identity; thus, men and lions are generically identical, because they possess a similar generic essence, namely 'animality.' If the essence, in which they are similar, is the 'specific essence' or species, we have a *specific* identity; for example, Peter and Paul and Napoleon are specifically identical, since they are alike in their species, namely 'humanity.'

An *accidental* logical identity is the logical identity of things based upon the *similarity of their accidents*. Any accident may be taken as the point of comparison between things, and a conceptual identity will thereby be established between them. If the accident, in which things are similar, is a quality, it will be a *qualitative* logical identity. Thus, snow, milk, sugar, and clouds are qualitatively identical so far as 'white color' is concerned. A toothache, rheumatism, and neuritis, from the standpoint of 'pain,' are qualitatively identical. If this accidental identity is based on similarity in quantity, it will be a *quantitative* logical identity. For instance, two men, each weighing one hundred and fifty pounds, or each having a height of five feet and ten inches, are quantitatively identical.

REAL DISTINCTION

Identity is the sameness between concepts or things; distinction is the absence of identity or sameness between concepts or things. And just as there is a real and logical identity, so there is also a real and a logical distinction.

Real distinction is the absence of sameness between *things different in their reality,* independent of the mind's consideration. The entity of the one is not the entity of the other, even though they be parts of the same totality. A tree and a house are really distinct, because the reality of the tree is different from the reality of the house. The various leaves and branches of a tree are really distinct among themselves, although they are parts of the same tree; and the foundation stones, the bricks, the boards, and the plaster are really distinct with respect to each other, even though they belong to the house as a whole. A real distinction may be either a 'major' or a 'minor' real distinction.

A distinction is a *major* real distinction, when there is an absence of identity between thing and thing to such an extent that they are distinct from each other *as entities*. Hence, if two or more beings are actually separate, and each exists for itself, they are really distinct beings, with a major real distinction between them; for example, stars, plants, animals, men, metals, buildings, and in general all the individual objects we perceive in the physical world. Again, entities may actually be united in a single being, but so long as they could exist separately, if they were actually divided, they are really distinct among themselves with a major real distinction; for example, the distinction between two substantial or integral parts of the same substance, like apple and apple tree, the branch and its leaves, the right and left side of a stone, the paws and legs of an animal, body and soul in man. So, too, the distinction between a substance and its accidents is a major distinction, if the accident confers a positive entity upon the substance in which it inheres; for example, a corporeal substance and its quantity. Finally, a major distinction exists between accidents, when the entity of each is of a different order; for example, quantity and quality, thinking and willing, warmth and seeing.

A distinction is a *minor* real distinction, when there is an absence of identity between a *thing and its mode*. A 'mode' is the actual determination of a being which is indifferent toward this or that determination, but without the mode adding a new entity to it through the modification. It is of such a nature that it confers no new entity upon its subject and is distinguished from 'nothing' through and in its subject only; the subject can exist without a particular mode, but the mode cannot exist outside the subject which it modifies. A 'mode' is more than a mere logical being (*ens rationis*), and as such is more than a fabrication of the mind; it really affects the subject, independent of the mind, by determining the indifferent subject to a definite manner of being or existence.

Perhaps an example or two will clarify our concept of a 'mode.' Place a coin on the table, with its face downward; and then reverse it, with its face upward. There is a real difference of position here, and it really affects the coin, independent of all thought; but the different positions add no new entity to the coin as such. You cannot separate this position of the coin from the coin itself; the coin is indifferent to various positions, but each position gives a definite 'mode' to the coin. Or, take a lump of modeling clay and shape it, first into a sphere, and then into a cube. This shaping merely shifts the outer limits or boundaries of the quantity of the clay, without adding any new entity to the quantity itself; the shape (sphere, cube, cone, etc.) is nothing but a 'mode' of the quantity (extension) of a body, in as much as it gives determination to this quantity which, of itself, is indifferent to various shapes. These shapes, though, are distinct, because they differ among themselves and actually modify the subject. Again, take curved motion and straight motion. The curvedness and straightness of the motion are not entitatively different from the motion itself; but they are 'modes' of motion, which imply a difference of direction in the motion, giving this motion a definite determination. Such modes, therefore, are distinct from their subjects with a *minor* real distinction.

Besides a major and minor real distinction we also have an adequate and an inadequate real distinction. A real distinction will be *adequate,* when things are distinct *in their total being.* Such is the distinction between George Washington and Napoleon, between a book and a table, between one piece of gold and another, between two apples or pears or oranges, etc. A real distinction will be *inadequate,* when the things are distinct *as part and whole.* The whole thing is always really distinct from any one of its constituent parts, otherwise the part would be the whole and the whole would be only a part; the whole is the sum of all the parts taken together and cannot be identified with only one of the parts to the exclusion of the others. The whole, however, is *partly identified* with each of its constituent parts; there is, consequently, an inadequate distinction between them. Such is the distinction between a block of ice and its lower (or upper) half, between a dog and its tail, between a plant and its roots, between a house and its roof, between a man and his head, between a pipe and its bowl, etc.

We also speak of a positive and a negative real distinction.

It is a *positive* real distinction, if the distinct things are *real* (*positive*) *entities* and differ in their entities. For instance, a tree and a stone, a pen and its ink, two books, two elephants, two magazines, two men. It is a *negative* real distinction, if there is *a non-entity* either on one side or on both sides of the distinction. On one side: life and death, sight and blindness, health and illness, light and darkness, etc. On both sides: death and blindness, dumbness and deafness, illness and darkness, etc. It may be questioned how it is possible to have a real distinction between non-entities, since they are physically 'nothing.' The fact is that such non-entities are the absence or privation of *definite beings;* since these definite beings are really distinct from each other, their opposites are also really distinct from each other.

Signs of Real Distinction. Bi-lateral or uni-lateral preservation in existence after separation; for example, an apple and the tree on which it is growing, a lump of clay and its 'squareness' of shape. The *procession* of the one from the other as from its real principle; for example, light and the sun, child and parent, flower and plant. *Contrariety of concepts,* so that the concepts imply incompatible elements; for example, matter and spirit, man and brute, substance and accident.

LOGICAL DISTINCTION

Our experience shows us that the things in nature do not form one single reality. They are a plurality, a multitude of beings. They are different entities, and as such are distinct in thought and thing; there is a real distinction between them. It is equally true, however, that we often have different concepts of things that are really one in nature; they differ in thought, but not in the thing. Such a distinction is called *a logical* or *mental distinction,* and it is defined as the *absence of sameness between concepts of the same reality*. In making this distinction between concepts of the same thing, there is either a reason in the thing itself for making it, or the reason for making it is only in the mind. Correspondingly we have a 'virtual' or a 'purely mental' distinction.

A *purely mental distinction* (*distinctio rationis ratiocinantis*) is the distinction between different concepts of one and the same reality, *without a foundation* in the *object* itself for making the distinction. The distinction is due solely to the distinguishing power of the mind itself (*ratio ratiocinans*). The content of the different concepts is identical, the meaning is the same; the difference between them lies merely in the difference of the manner of their representation. There are a few general types of this purely mental distinction.

Such are terms and ideas which are more or less *synonymous* in meaning. Examples of this type are: a ton and two thousand pounds; the sky, the heavens, the firmament, the welkin; the sun and the day star; Christ and the founder of Christianity; six and half a dozen. Each concept in its respective group represents the same reality, but in a somewhat different manner. Another type is that of *definitions* and of the *things defined*. Cases in point are: man and rational animal; plant and non-sentient organism; clock and mechanism for measuring time; intellect and rational faculty of thought; water and compound of two atoms of hydrogen and one atom of oxygen per molecule. The concept expressed as the definition is clearer than that of the thing defined, but they evidently mean the same thing. Another type is found in certain *transcendental ideas*, namely 'being,' 'thing or reality,' and 'something' (*ens, res, aliquid*). The mind here makes a distinction between these concepts, but they are all really identical in meaning with respect to the object for which they stand. In all these types and instances there is a purely mental distinction between the different concepts of the thing, because there is no foundation or reason or basis in the thing itself for making these distinct concepts of it.

A *virtual distinction* (*distinctio virtualis, distinctio rationis ratiocinatae, distinctio rationis cum fundamento in re*) is the distinction between different concepts of one and the same reality, *with a foundation* in the *object* itself for making the distinction. Here the distinction is not due solely to the distinguishing power of the mind; the mind is induced to make the distinction because of the nature of the object itself, and the object, as it were, forces the mind to make the distinction (*ratio ratiocinata*). The limited power of the mind is incapable of expressing the whole reality of the object in one adequate concept and for that reason expresses it in a number of concepts, each of which expresses a phase of the one reality; the concepts are, therefore, not identical in meaning, when compared to one another, but they all refer to the same reality taken as it is in itself. This will become clearer when we consider the two kinds of virtual distinction, based upon the two kinds of 'foundations' which are possible: they are the virtual distinctions with a *perfect* and with an *imperfect* foundation in the thing.

The virtual distinction with a *perfect foundation* in the thing is the virtual distinction in which the concepts are so distinct in comparison to each other, although they apply to the same reality, that they are *objectively different in content*. They are so distinct that the concepts are not mutually inclusive, but each has a definition different from that of the other. The concept of man's essence is made up of these five distinct and objectively different concepts: 'rationality, animality, life, body, substance.' These concepts, however, as has been mentioned before, do not represent five distinct and entitatively different *realities* in man. If they did, a preposterous result would ensue for man. His 'substance' would be really distinct from his 'corporality'; these two would be really distinct from his 'organism' or 'life'; these three would be really distinct from his 'animality'; and these four would be really distinct from his 'rationality.' Man would then be a five-part being. That, however, is not the case: man is one being, *a single substance;* and this substance is a single reality which is bodily, living, sentient, and rational at the same time. Man is not a 'substance'.

with one part of his being, a 'body' with another, an 'organism' with another, an 'animal' with another, and finally a 'rational being' with another: he is all these things at once and *as one*.

So far we have seen that we have five objectively different concepts for one and the same reality. Is this a purely arbitrary distinction on the part of the mind, without a foundation in the nature of man himself? On the contrary, man's *nature* contains the *foundation* or reason or basis because of which the mind makes these objectively different concepts of the one reality of man. These concepts represent *grades of being* which, though really only a single essence in man, are rightly distinguished from one another, because they can be, and actually are, *separately realized in other beings*. Pure spirits, for instance, are *'substances,'* but not bodily substances; here we see one grade of being, as found in man, separately realized. Chemical elements and compounds are substances, but they are *'bodily* substances'; here we see two grades of being of man separately realized. Plants are bodily substances, but they are *'living,* bodily substances'; here we see three of man's grades of being separately realized. Brutes are living bodily substances, but they are *'sentient,* living, bodily substances'; here we see four of the five grades of being present in man separately realized. Man himself is a sentient, living, bodily substance, but he is a *'rational,* sentient, living, bodily substance,' with an additional essential element of his own, namely 'rationality.' Each grade of being thus gives rise to a different type, when added to the other or others; in man, however, we find all five united into a single substantial reality. Here, in the very nature of man, we have the reason or basis or *foundation* for making a distinction of five different concepts concerning his one essence.

To sum up: When the mind forms objectively different concepts of the same reality, and these concepts have as their foundation the fact that they can be separately realized in nature in different kinds of being (though in this individual kind of being under consideration they stand for one reality only), then we have a *virtual* distinction with a *perfect foundation* in the thing.

Man's essence was chosen as a typical example, because we are fairly familiar with it. But cases of such virtual distinctions are found in all creatural beings, whenever we distinguish between the various *metaphysical grades* of their essence. Virtualists also contend that the distinction between *essence* and *existence* in an actually existing being is only a virtual, not a real, distinction. A case in point, too, is the distinction which we make between the concepts of the *soul* in man, when we speak of it as a 'vegetant' soul, a 'sentient' soul, and a 'rational' soul. The soul is the life-giving principle in an organism. A plant demands a soul for its vegetant functions; a brute demands a sentient soul for its sentient functions; man's rational operations demand a rational soul. Since man has the triple vital functions of vegetancy, sentiency, and rational thought, we speak of a vegetant and sentient and rational soul in man. There are, however, not three souls in man; he has *one soul* which performs these triple functions. Since, though, we have a foundation or reason in the nature of the soul itself for making a distinction, the distinction we make in man between a vegetant, sentient, and rational soul is a virtual distinction with a perfect foundation.

Besides a virtual distinction with a perfect foundation in the thing we have a *virtual* distinction with an *imperfect foundation* in the thing. It is the virtual distinction in which the different concepts of the one reality are distinct in such a manner that they are not mutually exclusive but rather *include each other implicitly*. It will be manifest that, since the one contains the other implicitly, they can never be realized separately, because the one cannot be present without the other. The reason, however, why the mind makes a distinction between them lies in the object itself. There is thus a *foundation in the thing,* but is not as adequate a foundation as the one of the virtual distinction with a perfect foundation. Examples will clarify the meaning of this.

Such a distinction exists between the concept of *'being'* and its inferiors. In man, for instance, there is no complete and perfect difference between 'being' and 'substance,' 'being' and 'body,' 'being' and 'life,' 'being' and 'sentiency,' 'being' and 'rationality.' By the concept 'being' we mean anything that is 'not nothing.' But that includes absolutely everything conceivable; consequently, 'being' includes within itself implicitly also substance, body, life, sentiency, and rationality. Similarly, these various concepts include implicitly the concept of 'being' within themselves, because their reality is a form of being. Hence, the distinction between 'being' and any particular kind of being is based upon an imperfect foundation.

We have another instance of this sort of distinction in the *attributes of God.* God's wisdom, mercy, power, intelligence, etc., are virtually distinct with an imperfect foundation. This is due to the *infinite* perfection of God's nature. In themselves the concepts of wisdom, mercy, power, intelligence, etc., are objectively different and can be separately realized: this is seen in creatures. When, however, it is a question of *infinitely perfect attributes,* they cannot be separately realized. If infinite wisdom and infinite power could be separately realized, it would mean that each would not include the other; but by that very fact neither of them would really be 'infinite,' because each would lack the perfection contained in the other. Each attribute of God is really identical with the other and with His essence; and a plurality of infinite perfections, separately realized and existing, is a contradiction in thought. Where, then, is the *objective foundation* for making the distinction between them? Not in God Himself directly, but in the creatures, in as much as we perceive wisdom and mercy and power and intelligence appearing separately in creatural beings. Hence, the objective foundation for making the distinction between these attributes in God is *imperfect.*

Another instance worthy of special attention is the distinction between *being, one, true,* and *good.* We have seen that every 'being' is 'one,' and that everything that is 'one' is a 'being.' The same will be shown later regarding truth and goodness. All these concepts are convertible. These concepts are distinct, and the distinction between them is not purely mental; but each contains the other implicitly, and they cannot be separately realized. Hence, the distinction between these concepts is a virtual distinction with an imperfect foundation in the thing.

From the above exposition it will be clear why these distinctions are styled *'virtual.'* The concepts are distinct and different. Since, however, they apply to a single reality, they do not stand for distinct physical parts in this reality, which together make a physical composition. Rather, they stand for *metaphysical parts* which are united together in a *metaphysical composition.* These parts are present in the thing *not actually* as parts, but only potentially or *virtually.*

THE SCOTISTIC FORMAL DISTINCTION

John Duns Scotus (1266 [or 1274]–1308) is famous for his deep and sharp thinking. One of his noted doctrines is his *formal distinction, actual on the part of the thing (distinctio formalis actualis ex natura rei).* Scotus did not deny any of the distinctions mentioned above; he admitted a real distinction, a virtual distinction, and also a purely mental distinction. But he contended that there is still another distinction which must be placed between a real distinction and a virtual distinction; it is not as great as a real distinction, and it is greater than a virtual distinction which has only a 'foundation' in the thing.

Scotists claim that there are not only 'entities' present in an object, between which there is a distinction of thing and thing (real distinction), but an object also has certain *realities* or *formalities* which are *actually,* though not really, distinct from each other. A 'real' distinction would thus be a distinction between *things,* and a 'formal' distinction would be one between *formalities.* By a 'formality' (*ratio formalis*) Scotus understood a positive thought-content or reality, objectively different from another, which in the individual under consideration is so essential to it that the thing cannot exist without it, nor can this thought-content exist except in this individual. An illustration will help to understand the Scotists' meaning.

Man is a rational animal. 'Rationality' and 'animality' are present in man's nature. These are two completely different concepts or *formalities:* 'animality' is one, and 'rationality' is another formality. Although both thought-contents represent one thing in man, they are two entirely different 'formalities' or, in other words, diverse concepts. This, they say, will be clear from a simple comparison. The 'animality' of man is the same as the 'animality' of the lion or of any other animal. But the 'animality' of a lion is *actually* distinguished from 'rationality.' Consequently, the 'animality' of *man* must also be *actually* (though not really, as between thing and thing) distinguished from his 'rationality.' Since, therefore, 'animality' and 'rationality' are not distinct as different entities and things, they are not really distinct in man; but they are *actually distinct* in man as *formalities,* independent of any mind. Hence, there exists between 'animality' and 'rationality' in man, due to his nature and independent of any mind, a formal distinction, actual on the part of the thing.

We must *reject* this Scotistic formal distinction as invalid, because it is impossible for a distinction to be *actual* without being also *real.* If something is actually distinct from another, *independent of the mind,* it must be *ontologically* distinct from this other, i.e., distinct in its being or entity. The Scotists themselves admit that a formal distinction is 'actual on the part of the thing (*ex natura rei*),' and that implies that the distinction is not logical, but ontological. Since every distinction involves plurality, an actual (or formal) distinction involves an ontological plurality, i.e., a plurality in being or entity. Hence, if these 'formalities' bring in an actual distinction in the nature of the object, independent of the mind, they thereby also bring in an ontological plurality, and this can only be a *plurality of entity.* But a plurality of entity means not one thing, but 'different things'; and between one thing and another thing, between entity and another entity, there is a *real* distinction. Therefore, if the formal distinction is 'actual on the part of the thing,' it is a 'real' distinction and no longer merely 'formal.' In other words, the whole conception of the 'formal distinction' is invalid, because it amounts to a 'real distinction.' And since it is clear that 'animality' and 'rationality' (and all other metaphysical grades of being) are not really distinct, but form a single reality in man, the fact of the separate realization of 'animality' in the brute (e.g., in the lion) is merely the *foundation* for a difference of concepts on the part of the thinking mind. But this means a 'virtual' distinction with a foundation in the thing. It is obvious, then, that there is no special distinction, formal or other, midway between a real and a virtual distinction.

In the view of some modern Scotistic scholars, the interpretation of the Scotistic formal distinction, as given above, is based upon a misunderstanding of the true meaning of Duns Scotus. According to their opinion the formal distinction coincides essentially with the virtual distinction with a foundation in the thing. The former stresses the objective factors in the thing which give rise to the mental distinction, while the latter emphasizes the subjective factors of the mind which expresses the single (but equivalently multiple) reality with two or more distinct concepts. "Because of the well-known difference in mental temperament St. Thomas, the Intellectualist, saw and felt the distinction primarily as a mental distinction, and so defined it as a *distinctio rationis,* admitting, however, that it has an antecedent and independent foundation in reality, whereas Scotus, with his more realistic temperament, was more powerfully impressed by the objective factor and so emphasized the fact that it is a *distinctio a parte rei;* adding, however, that it was not simply a real distinction between thing and thing, but only a distinction between a *res* and its *realities* that is, between a thing and its intrinsic modes (*formalitates*), and consequently admitting that it is a mental distinction in so far as we have two mental concepts representing one thing of nature."[1]

If this view can be upheld, much of the opposition to the Scotistic distinction must be dropped. Most scholars, however, are convinced that Scotus maintained a 'formal distinction' which occupies a position midway between a 'real' and a 'virtual' distinction; such a distinction, as shown, must be rejected.

SUMMARY OF CHAPTER XII

Identity is the *sameness* (*oneness*) among two or more concepts or things. *Distinction* is the *absence of sameness* (*oneness*) among two or more concepts or things.

1. *Real Identity.* It is the *sameness* (*oneness*) *of things in themselves,* independent of the mind. It is a 'metaphysical' identity, when a thing is one with itself so that it can absolutely not change in any manner. It is a 'physical' identity, when it is one with itself so that it does not change in its essential reality. It is a 'moral' identity, when it is one with itself so that the change which takes place in its essential being is successive and gradual.

2. *Logical Identity.* It is the *sameness* (*oneness*) *of things* based upon the *same concept* of the mind. This is an 'essential' identity, if it is based upon a similarity of essence. It is an 'accidental' identity, if it is based upon a similarity of accidents.

3. *Real Distinction.* It is the *absence of sameness* between things *different in their reality,* independent of the mind. This is a 'major' real distinction, when the absence of identity between things is such that they are distinct from each other as entities. It is a 'minor' real distinction, when it is the absence of identity between a thing and its mode. A real distinction is an 'adequate' real distinction, when things are distinct in their total being. It is an 'inadequate' real distinction, when the things are distinct as part and whole. A real distinction is a

---

[1] Berard Vogt, O.F.M., "Note on the 'Formal Distinction' of Scotus," in *Franciscan Studies*, Vol. 3, August, 1925, p. 40.

'positive' distinction, when the distinct things are real (positive) entities. It is a 'negative' distinction, when there is a non-entity either on one side or on both sides of the distinction.

4. *Logical Distinction.* It is the *absence of sameness between concepts* of the same reality. A 'purely mental' distinction is the distinction between different concepts of one and the same reality, without a foundation in the object itself for making the distinction.

A 'virtual' distinction is the distinction between different concepts of the same reality, with a foundation in the object itself for making the distinction. The virtual distinction will have a 'perfect' foundation in the object, when these concepts are objectively different in content. The virtual distinction will have an 'imperfect' foundation in the object, when these concepts include each other implicitly.

5. *The Scotistic Formal Distinction.* It is a distinction, maintained by Scotus and his followers, that has a position midway between a real and a virtual distinction: it is *actual,* though *not real.* By 'formality' in a thing is understood a positive thought-content or reality, objectively different from another, which in the individual under consideration is so essential to it that the thing cannot exist without it, nor can this thought-content exist except in this individual. Such 'formalities' are the metaphysical grades of being, like 'rationality' and 'animality' in man.

This formal distinction is *invalid,* because an *actual* distinction is a *real* distinction. Whatever is actually distinct from another, independent of the mind, must be *ontologically* distinct, i.e., distinct in its being and entity. Distinction involves plurality, and actual distinction must, therefore, involve an ontological plurality, i.e., a plurality in being and entity. That, however, means a 'real' distinction. Consequently, the Scotistic formal distinction is a *real* distinction.

READINGS

Coffey, P., Ch. IV; Rickaby, J., Bk. I, Ch. IV; Hugon, Ed., Tr. II, Qu. I, art. 3; Mercier, D. Card., pp. 451, 452; Aristotle, *Metaph.,* V.

Chapter XIII

BEING AND TRUTH

EVERY BEING, considered in its inner constitution, is undivided and one. Unity or oneness is a transcendental attribute of being as such. Every being possesses this attribute absolutely and essentially; it is a unit in itself, even though no other being existed. As a matter of fact, however, no being is a completely isolated reality, because there is a vast multitude of beings in existence. This induces numerous relations between beings and beings.

Among these various relations, two are *transcendental* for every being: *truth* and *goodness*. Every being in its very nature has a relation to intellect and will, in virtue of which it is 'true' and 'good.' The will can only strive for something in so far as a thing is apprehended by the intellect as good; consequently, a being has a relation to the intellect before it has a relation to the will. Now, the relation of a being to the intellect is the *relation of truth,* because it is the purpose of the intellect to acquire truth. The truth of a being is, therefore, logically prior to its goodness. Hence, we must treat of the transcendental attribute of truth in a being before we treat of its goodness.

CONCEPT OF TRUTH

Truth always has a reference to the mind or intellect. Truth is an attribute of something that is *known,* and it is the mind or *intellect* that knows. Naturally, being what we are, truth exists *for us* primarily in our own intellect, and we come to understand the nature of truth by observing our own mental operations.

By 'truth' we ordinarily mean *true knowledge,* and by 'true knowledge' we mean *true judgments.* Ideas are more in the nature of a prerequisite for knowledge than real knowledge itself; they must be united in a judgment in order to be knowledge, and then this judgment is either true or false. To have the ideas 'weather,' 'warm,' 'cold,' and 'freezing' in the mind, is not a complete form of knowledge, nor can we say that such ideas are true or false. But if we make a pronouncement about the weather and assert that 'The weather is warm,' we have a mental judgment, and this judgment either agrees with the actual conditions of the weather or it does not; if the weather actually is warm, our judgment is 'true,' and if the weather is not warm, our judgment is 'false.' Correspondingly, we have 'truth' or 'falsity (error),' and both reside in the *judgment of the intellect* in so far as the intellect agrees or disagrees with the thing about which it judges. Here, then, truth is seen to be an attribute of our knowledge and judgment.

Truth, however, can be taken in a different sense. We also speak of the *truth of things.* It is a matter of everyday experience to hear people apply truth to things, but they may use the term 'genuine' instead of 'true.' People, for instance, speak of 'true friends' and 'false friends,' 'true (genuine) diamonds' and 'false diamonds,' 'true (genuine) money' and 'false (counterfeit) money,' etc. The *objects themselves* are thus declared to possess truth or falsity. The meaning is obvious. Man has an idea of a thing in his mind, and this idea of the thing is expressed in a definition or mental judgment. This idea forms the type, the standard, the norm to which the object must conform in order to be 'true.' If the object under consideration actually agrees with this type-idea, it is 'true'; otherwise it is 'false.' In such a case, truth is an attribute of the thing and resides *in the thing.*

The truth-relation between a thing and the intellect is thus seen to be such that either the intellect agrees with the thing or the thing with the intellect. Both forms of truth have this in common that there is an agreement between intellect and thing. *Truth in general,* therefore, is the *agreement (conformity) between intellect and thing.* This is truth in its widest and most fundamental meaning. The definition does not state whether the intellect must agree with the object or whether the object must agree with the intellect. And this formulation of the definition is purposely expressed in such an indefinite manner, because truth may be had either way. The definition must cover both forms of truth, that of the intellect and that of the thing. Reversely, of course, *falsity (error) in general* is the *disagreement (disconformity) between intellect and thing.*

Our concept of truth and falsity, it will be observed, is evolved out of the relation which exists between objects and our own *human* intellect. This is simply due to the fact that we are directly aware of no other mind but our own. It would be wrong, however, to think that truth exists only in the relation of an object to our own intellect. Truth must exist in the knowledge of *any intellect,* whether divine or creatural, because, wherever there is an intellect, there can be an agreement between it and an object.

From what has been said so far, it will be manifest that we must distinguish between truth and truth. This brings us to the *kinds* of truth.

KINDS OF TRUTH

Truth may be *ontological, logical,* or *moral.* The essential ideas underlying this classification have already been expressed in the foregoing exposition of the concept of truth, but an explanation of these kinds of truth will be of assistance in acquiring a better understanding of the nature and extent of truth.

Ontological (metaphysical, objective) truth is the *agreement of a being with the intellect.* It is of the nature of ontological truth that the intellect possesses an *idea* of the thing which is taken as the norm, the standard, the pattern, the type of the thing; and with this idea the thing must agree. In so far as the object agrees with the type-idea which the intellect has of this object, it is said to be 'true' — ontologically true. Ontological truth, therefore, resides in the *objects,* because they must conform to the intellect and its idea of the object. A few examples will illustrate the matter.

An artist desires to paint a picture of the Madonna. He has not seen her, but he has within his imagination an image or type which he intends to reproduce on the canvas. He paints the image. If the picture agrees with the image previously present in his mind, it will be ontologically true, because it is in conformity with the image as conceived before the painting was made. An architect plans a building, and an engineer designs a bridge; if the building and the bridge are erected according to plan and design, they agree with the preconceived idea of them and as such are ontologically true.

In the case of man, ontological truth can have only limited scope. Whenever man makes things agree with his intellect, he must take existing materials and fashion them into something which conforms to his plan. They are products of his ingenuity and skill, like buildings, machines, clothes, furniture, instruments, etc. In all these things, however, he does not make the intrinsic essence of the objects he assembles ontologically true, because they must already exist before he can use them for his purposes. The *intrinsic essence* of things is ontologically true because they are in conformity with the ideas of God who created them; He made them agree with His eternal ideas of their being.

Logical (mental) truth is the *agreement of the intellect with a thing.* Here the relation between intellect and thing is reversed: the thing is prior, and the idea posterior. This relationship constitutes *true knowledge* of a thing. It is obvious that every being has its own peculiar entity and reality, independent of the intellect which thinks of it; things are what they are, even though no mind forms an idea of them. When, however, a mind does form an idea of a thing in order to have some knowledge of it, this knowledge will either correspond ideally with the reality or not; if it corresponds, it is 'true,' otherwise it is 'false.' The mind has knowledge of a thing when it forms ideas of its reality and unites them in a declarative judgment regarding this reality. Ideas represent reality. Truth can be had in affirmative as well as in negative judgments, so long as the fact expressed corresponds to the fact existing.

Besides ontological and logical truth, there is also *moral* truth, and it is defined as the *agreement of speech with thought*. When we make a judgment in our mind regarding a certain thing or fact and then make a statement in speech which expresses this judgment in words, we have 'moral' truth, because our speech agrees with our thought; but when our speech disagrees with our judgment, the discrepancy constitutes moral falsity (falsehood, lie). Thus, when a person is called upon to 'say the truth,' the meaning is that he should state, according to his understanding of the matter, what he judges to be the fact. He may, of course, be mistaken as to the real nature of this fact, but that is not the point. So long as his verbal statement agrees with his mental judgment, he says the truth, even though his statement does not actually agree with objective reality. On the other hand, if his verbal statement is the opposite of his judgment, he will be telling a lie, even though the falsehood happens to correspond to objective reality; in such a case the falsehood is intentional, while the objective truth is merely accidental.

Moral truth may be considered as a form of *ontological* truth, if we view it solely from the standpoint of an agreement between intellect and thing. The mind's knowledge is the standard in ontological truth, and the thing must conform to it in order to be true. In moral truth the mind's knowledge is also the standard to which the verbal statement, as a thing, must conform in order that the verbal statement may be considered true.

Of the three kinds of truth, *ontological truth* mainly concerns us here. Ontology treats of being in general in its supreme determinations, attributes, and categories. Ontological

truth, like oneness, is a metaphysical and transcendental attribute of being and as such belongs to ontology proper. This
cannot be asserted of logical and moral truth; they are not
attributes of being in general. Logical truth involves the validity of our knowledge and belongs to epistemology, while
moral truth has its proper place in ethics.

THE ULTIMATE FOUNDATION OF TRUTH

Because things are known by a mind, the mind possesses
logical truth. The only reason, however, why the mind's
knowledge about things is logically true is due to the fact that
things consist of positive elements of being which the mind
recognizes to be present in the things: things are 'knowable'
by their positive elements of being, and it is by these elements
that things are 'known' by the mind. *Logical truth,* therefore,
has its foundation in the *being* of the things known, because
man's mind presupposes the being of the things 'knowable'
before it can actually become 'known.'

With regard to *ontological* truth, the relation of the human
mind to the things is reversed. Here the knowledge of the
mind is the type or standard to which the things must conform
in order to be true. This abstract knowledge is expressed in the
definition, and this *definition* then becomes the standard or
type to which a particular object must conform in order that
it can be styled 'true.' The type-idea in the human mind, however, does *not constitute* or *make* the things; the beings in the
world are what they are, independent of the type-idea present
in the human mind. Consequently, the ultimate foundation of
the ontological truth of the things in this world is not found
in the human mind.

This will be clearer when we consider the fact that human
knowledge varies from mind to mind concerning the true
nature of things; regarding most things, man has *no accurate*
and comprehensive knowledge at all; and of numberless beings
in this world the human mind has *no knowledge* whatever.
Man's knowledge is at best extremely fragmentary and subject

to many errors, even in the most ordinary things. It is evident, then, that the ultimate foundation of the ontological truth of the things in this world cannot reside in the relation of agreement which these things have to the human mind. Water was 'true' water, and gold was 'true' gold, and the solar system was a 'true' solar system, long before a human mind existed to know them. But if these things possess ontological truth in their being *after* a human mind comes to know them, they must have possessed a *fundamental* ontological truth *before* a human mind came to know them. Obviously, then, the type-ideas of the human mind are not responsible for the ontological truth of things, so as to be the ultimate foundation of their ontological truth.

Nevertheless, there can be no ontological truth in the things except in so far as they conform to an intellect and its type-ideas of these things. Since the intellect in question cannot be the human intellect, there must be some *intellect other than human* to which all things must conform; they will then owe their ontological truth to their agreement with this intellect. Ontological truth, as we have seen, lies in the *intrinsic reality* of the things; that intellect, then, will be the ultimate foundation of their ontological truth which is the ultimate foundation of their intrinsic reality. We thus see that the very reality and nature of all the things in this world demands an intellect over and beyond the world itself, and that is the Divine Mind. God gave all things their intrinsic reality by creating them. He created them according to the *exemplars* or *type-ideas* which He had of them before He gave them existence. These exemplars were, therefore, antecedent to the existence of the things created. By being created, the creatural things were made to *conform to God's ideas* of them, and therein consists the *ontological truth* of their being.

Even God's *infinite essence* possesses *ontological truth*. He is a being, a reality; as such, He is a 'true' being, 'true' reality. The agreement of His essence to His mind is an absolute agreement, because it is identical with it. God, therefore, is Truth.

God *is* absolute, eternal, infinite ontological Truth; creatures *have* relative, temporal, finite ontological truth. And this applies as well to all *possible* beings: they possess ontological truth, because they are in conformity with the type-idea which God has of them in His mind. Ontological truth, therefore, is an essential attribute of all being, divine and human, actual and possible, necessary and contingent. Consequently, *the ultimate foundation of all truth consists in the essential conformity of all things to the Divine Mind.*

CONVERTIBILITY OF BEING AND TRUTH

'Being' and 'truth' are convertible. This is to say: Every 'being' is 'true,' and whatever is 'true' is a 'being.' That should be clear from what has just been said.

Every being is either potential or actual; it is either finite or infinite. The *finite* being, whether actual or potential, has its actual or potential reality only because God can think it and make it. God, however, can think it and make it only because it is in some manner an imitation of His essence. But by imitating His essence they imitate His ideas, because His essence and ideas are identical in reality, due to the infinite perfection of His being (as will be shown in theodicy). Finite beings, therefore, whether actual or potential, have reality only by agreeing with the ideas of God. To agree in their reality with God's ideas means to agree with His intellect; and that means to be ontologically true. Consequently, every finite being is ontologically true.

God is *infinite* essence. There is a conformity of His essence with His ideas, because His essence is identical with His ideas; and this is the most exalted and perfect conformity possible. God's infinite essence, therefore, is ontologically true. Now, God's infinite essence and all finite beings, actual and possible, comprise all being. Consequently, all being is ontologically true, and *ontological truth is a transcendental attribute of being as such.*

We may even speak of all things as *ontologically* true in

their relation to the *human* mind. This, of course, does not mean that the human mind has the correct idea of all things or even has a knowledge of all things; that would obviously be false. What is meant is simply that all beings, by the very fact that they are entities, have positive elements of essence and as such are intellig*ible,* even though they are not actually known by the human mind. The mind *can know* them. So far as their reality is concerned, they are such that the human mind can make true *ideas* and *definitions* of them, to which they will always conform. Hence, even with regard to the human mind, things possess a *potential* and *fundamental,* if not an actual and formal, ontological truth.

Every being, then, is true. In order that 'being' and 'truth' be convertible, it will also be necessary to show that everything which is 'true' is a 'being.' The proof is simple. We have just shown that every being is true. Ontological truth is, therefore, a transcendental attribute of being. As an attribute of being, this ontological truth must be something. If it were not something, it would be 'nothing,' and 'nothing' cannot be the attribute of anything. But if ontological truth is not 'nothing,' it partakes of the nature of 'being.' Consequently, whatever is ontologically 'true' is a 'being.' Ontological truth and being are thus seen to be convertible and identical: they are the same reality, viewed from two different standpoints.

THE EXISTENCE OF FALSITY

By falsity we understand the disconformity between thing and intellect. As there are three kinds of truth, there are also three kinds of falsity: moral, logical, and ontological.

Moral falsity is the disconformity of speech with thought or judgment. It is also called falsehood or lie. That lies are told, needs only be mentioned. *Logical* falsity is the disconformity of the intellect to the thing. 'Error' is another name for it. That logical falsity is often present in the mind is palpably demonstrated by all the mistakes, confused opinions, and conflicting systems of thought existing throughout the world at all times. The very fact that we change our views and correct our judgments is the surest indication that logical falsity occurs frequently in our judgments about persons, things, and events. There can be no question about the occurrence of moral and logical falsity.

The matter, however, is very different when we speak of the occurrence of *ontological falsity,* the disconformity of thing to intellect. Can we really apply ontological falsity to *things?* We certainly speak of false peace, false culture, false diamonds, false friends, false ideals, false teeth, and so on. In order to avoid confusion, we must distinguish between ontological falsity in an absolute and in a relative sense.

In an *absolute sense* there can be *no ontological falsity.* A thing that is ontologically true cannot be ontologically false; that would be a contradiction in terms. But every being is ontologically true, as we have just proved. Consequently, no being or thing can be ontologically false. In order to be ontologically false in an absolute sense, it would be necessary that such a being disagree with every possible intellect; if it agreed with a single intellect, it would no longer be ontologically false, but ontologically true. Now, every being, in so far as it has any reality at all, must always agree with the intellect of God, because it could not be what it is unless it agreed with His intellect: it is what it is, because God created it according to the type-ideas in His intellect. Hence, every being is ontologically true with regard to the ideas of God.

In a *relative sense* we may speak of ontological falsity, namely in relation to the *human mind.* That we do not always succeed in making the products of our skill and art agree with the plan or type we have in our mind, is a matter of almost daily occurrence. An artist is seldom satisfied with the work of art he produces. A typist intends to make an error-free copy, but all too frequently she will find a mistake. A builder seldom erects an edifice which is perfect in every detail of the plan. The mechanism which an inventor constructs does not always perform as smoothly as the genius of its maker expected. In the case of imperfect *artificial products,* therefore, we may legitimately speak of relative ontological falsity.

We do not, however, restrict the term 'ontological falsity' to artificial products made by man; we apply it very often to *natural things.* Thus, we speak of German silver as 'false silver'; or we say that it is not true, not genuine silver. What do we mean? We mean that it has the general *appearance* of silver, and the mind in consequence is apt to judge that it is true silver. This, of course, would be a *false judgment,* since German silver is only an alloy of copper, nickel, and zinc. Hence, by means of an extrinsic denomination or analogy we transfer the falsity, which is really only in the judgment (logical falsity), over to the object itself (ontological falsity). But German silver is really and truly what it is, namely copper, nickel, and zinc, agreeing perfectly at all times with God's type-idea of it; and so it is always ontologically true with reference to God's mind. As a matter of fact, even with reference to man's intellect German silver cannot be said to be really ontologically false, because not all human minds will be deceived into judging it to be true silver; this is proved by the fact that we actually do know the composition of German silver as an alloy of copper, nickel, and zinc. If it were *really* ontologically false with reference to the human mind, no human mind would be able to discover its component elements.

No matter, then, what the appearances of things may be to man, they have an *intrinsic constitution* which is always ontologically true, at least so far as the mind of God is concerned; for man they may, of course, be the *occasion* of false judgment. 'False diamonds' are 'true paste'; 'false teeth' are 'true porcelain'; 'false virtue' is 'true vice'; 'false gold' is 'true pyrite'; 'false economy' is 'true waste'; 'false faces' are 'true masks': their true nature *can* be known by man and is known always by God. In an absolute sense, therefore, ontological falsity does not apply to any being; in a relative sense, namely with reference to man, ontological falsity may be said to exist in a limited manner. Ontology, since it views all things from a metaphysical standpoint, treats of things in their intrinsic reality, without regard to the impression they may produce upon a fallible human mind; considered metaphysically, all beings, of whatever kind and nature, are and must be *ontologically true* under all circumstances.

SOME CHARACTERISTICS OF TRUTH

Truth is *primarily in the intellect,* not in the things. The whole import of language testifies to the fact that truth is considered to be principally a qualification of *knowledge.* Knowledge is 'true,' and knowledge is 'false'; judgments are 'true,' and judgments are 'false.' Even when speaking of God, truth is primarily predicated of His knowledge and His mind, not of His essence. Only secondarily, by means of an analogy, is truth attributed to the reality of things. For created minds the reality of things is the cause of logical truth, in as much as this reality makes an impression on the mind and enables it to conform to the thing; for this reason we call things 'true,' and this analogy is an analogy of attribution, just as food is called 'healthy' because it causes health in a body. *Ontological, transcendental truth,* however, is not applied to things fundamentally for the reason that they are the 'cause' of true knowledge. With regard to created minds this is clear, because every being is transcendentally true, independent of all created minds. Nor can we say that their transcendental truth is due to the fact that they cause God's knowledge to be true, because things cannot produce any effect in the Infinite Being; God's knowledge of them is true antecedent to their existence, and they possess ontological, transcendental truth precisely because they agree in their reality with the knowledge of them which exists in God's mind from eternity. They are made to conform to God's intellect, and because of this essential conformity of their reality to God's intellect, they are said, by an *analogy of proportion,* to be ontologically 'true.' True knowledge, and therefore truth itself, is primarily an attribute of God's intellect and only secondarily an attribute of things. Hence, truth is primarily in the intellect, not in the things.

It is frequently asserted that *truth is eternal*. Is this assertion correct? If we speak of *God* as the First Truth, it is evident that it must be eternal, because it is identical with His essence. If we speak of *created truth,* we must distinguish. *Logical* truth in creatural minds is not eternal in itself, because these minds are not themselves eternal, but temporal, and logical truth resides in these created minds as a qualification of their knowledge; this logical truth is, therefore, also temporal in character. Neither is the *ontological* truth of created beings, considered in itself, eternal; their ontological truth consists in their entity, viewed as conforming to (God's) intellect, and since their entity is created and temporal, their ontological truth must also be created and temporal. Considered, however, from the standpoint of God's eternal knowledge and power, created truth can be said to be *eternal with a sort of extrinsic eternity*. This means, that things are eternally true, not because they possess any reality in themselves which would be eternal (for that is created and temporal) but because their reality (whether possible or actual) is eternally in conformity with God's eternal knowledge of them. Thus, it is eternally true that man is a 'rational animal,' because that is God's eternal idea of 'man,' even if as a matter of fact man himself is a created and temporal being so far as his existence is concerned.

This will also explain in what sense it can be said that *truth is immutable*. If something is eternally true, it is also immutably true. As 'things' things change, and their ontological truth changes with them. But if we consider their conformity to God's ideas of them, all created beings (whether possible or actual) are immutably true, because they must always agree with God's knowledge of them, even when they change in their being from moment to moment.

THE TRUTH OF CONTINGENTLY FUTURE EVENTS

Can judgments or statements about contingently future events be styled 'true' or 'false'? The question raises an interesting problem. In order to understand the issue properly, it will be necessary to explain the meaning of *contingently future events*.

It is *not* a question here of future events which are *predetermined* in their physical causes, so that they must and will happen according to the laws of nature. Such future events would be, for example, eclipses of the sun and moon. Events of this sort are in themselves predictable, provided one has a sufficient knowledge of the causes which will produce this particular effect. The judgment that 'A solar eclipse will take place at 10:00 a.m. on July 4, 1960' is at this very moment definitely true or false. There either will be an eclipse at the time designated, or there will not; if there will be, the statement is true, and if there will not be, the statement is false. Such events of the future are not contingent; they are *determined* events, and there is no question about the truth of their occurrence or non-occurrence, even if we do not know them.

It is a question of *contingently future events*. A contingent event is one that can, but need not, occur; and if the event is a matter of the future, it is a contingently future event. It is an event which may or may not take place in the future, and the doubtfulness of its occurrence results from the fact that it is *not predetermined* in its cause. Rather, the cause is of such a nature that, although every requisite for action is present, it can act or refrain from action. This will be the case when an action or event is dependent on the decision of a *free will*. In the presence of all conditions necessary for action, a free will can perform the action or omit the action. For example: Shall I walk to the library tomorrow? This walk is a contingently future event, because it depends on my free choice. I myself do not know at the present moment whether I will or will not take this walk. Two statements are possible here: 'I shall walk to the library tomorrow' and 'I shall not walk to the library tomorrow.' These are contradictory statements, and one of them should be true and the other false.

Some philosophers claim that 'truth' and 'falsity' cannot be applied to contingently future events of this character. Neither of these two statements can be styled 'true' or 'false' *at the present moment;* they can become 'true' or 'false' only after the will makes its decision at the time of the event's occurrence, but not before. Other philosophers contend that one of these two contradictory statements is true and the other false *at all times,* whether present or past, and even from eternity. Who is right? Having specified the problem as given above, we must say that contradictory statements of contingently future events which depend on the free will are simply, as future events, *definitely true or false in themselves.* As such they are known to God from all eternity. And now for the demonstration.

Let us take the two contradictory statements given above, namely 'I shall walk to the library tomorrow' and 'I shall not walk to the library tomorrow.' Since these statements are contradictory, one of them will be *definitely true tomorrow* and the other definitely false. Supposing, as a matter of fact, I actually do walk to the library tomorrow afternoon. Then, as I walk, my walking to the library is a *present definite occurrence,* and the first statement is *then definitely true;* the second statement will of necessity be definitely false. In that case, however, if anyone states *today* that 'I shall walk to the library tomorrow,' he is making a statement which is also *definitely true today,* even though he is speaking of an event which is contingently future today and will only occur tomorrow. But if a contingently future event is definitely true at the present moment, it was also definitely true yesterday and last year and from all eternity. And since God, who is infinitely perfect in His knowledge, must know all truth, He also knows all contingently future events, i.e., those dependent on the choice of free will.

The same argument can be formulated in a slightly different

way. That I am writing *at this moment,* is an event which is dependent on my free will; I decided to write, and I am writing now. *Yesterday* my present writing was a contingently future event. Since, however, my writing is here and now a definitely true event, I can obviously make the definitely true statement that 'I am writing.' If, then, I had made the statement yesterday that 'I shall write tomorrow,' it would have been a definitely true statement yesterday; on the other hand, the contradictory statement would have been a definitely false statement. But if it was definitely true yesterday, it was definitely true for the whole past and from all eternity.

A *past* event is definitely true in itself, irrespective of whether its occurrence is due to a necessarily acting or freely acting cause; and since it occurred, the statement of its occurrence is definitely true, simply because of the entity and existence which it *then had in itself.* A *present* event can also be expressed in a definitely true statement, even if it be due to the free will, simply because of the entity and existence which it *now has in itself.* And for the same reason a *future* event, whether necessary or free, is definitely true in itself and can be expressed in a definitely true statement, simply bcause of the entity and existence which it *will then have in itself.* When the future event actually happens, it will be a fact; consequently, it is even *now* a true future fact and can, absolutely speaking, be expressed in a statement which is also true. That man, in the weakness and limitation of his knowledge, cannot know these contingently future events, is beside the point: future events being future facts, God must know them simply because they *will* happen.

God's knowledge of contingently future events does not in any way militate against the freedom of their causes in acting. Such events will not happen because He knows them; He knows them because they will happen. Knowledge, whether past, present, or future, does not necessitate any action, because it is not the cause of the action. If an event is produced through a necessary cause, God will know the event as such, and if it happens as the result of free choice, God will also know that as such. All events without exception possess *ontological truth* in themselves and must conform to the intellect of God, because His mind encompasses everything that is true. That all contingently future events really possess ontological truth, is obvious: in all contradictory statements regarding such events (for instance, 'I will walk' and 'I will not walk'), one of these statements must agree with the actual event which will happen in the future, for it is impossible for both to happen and for neither to happen, due to the Principle of Contradiction and Excluded Middle; and the one alternative of the contradiction, the event which will actually occur in the future, will have reality and existence, and as such has ontological truth. Since, however, all ontological truth agrees with God's intellect, God knows it before it happens.

Such is the nature of truth. It is a transcendental attribute of all being, creatural and divine, possible and actual, necessary and free, past and present and future.

SUMMARY OF CHAPTER XIII

Just as every being is 'one,' so it is also 'true.' Truth is a transcendental attribute of being as such.

1. *Concept of Truth.* We arrive at the concept of truth from our own experience. Truth is true knowledge and consists in true *judgments,* in so far as our judgments agree with reality as it is in itself.

There is also truth in *things.* The definition of a thing is the norm or type to which things must conform in order to be called 'true.' Truth in general, therefore, is the *conformity between intellect and thing.* Falsity is the disconformity between intellect and thing.

2. *Kinds of Truth.* There are three kinds of truth: ontological, logical, and moral. *Ontological* truth is the conformity of a thing to the intellect. *Logical* truth is the conformity of the intellect to the thing. *Moral* truth is the conformity of speech

to thought. Ontology is mostly concerned with ontological (metaphysical, objective) truth.

3. *The Ultimate Foundation of Truth.* *Logical* truth depends on the positive elements of being present in a thing, because it is the conformity of the intellect to the thing; its foundation, therefore, is the being of the thing known. *Ontological* truth, since it is the conformity of thing to intellect, must have its ultimate foundation in that intellect which is the ultimate foundation of the intrinsic reality of things. This is not the human intellect, but the intellect of God, according to whose type-ideas all things have been created. Even God's essence conforms to His intellect, because it is identical with His intellect. Hence, the *ultimate foundation* of all truth, logical and ontological, consists in the essential conformity of all things to the *Divine Mind*.

4. *Convertibility of Being and Truth.* Finite beings and also the infinite essence of God are all in conformity with His mind and as such are ontologically true. Therefore, every being is 'true.' Truth is a transcendental attribute of being, as just shown; since an attribute is not nothing, it must be something, and as such it partakes of the nature of 'being.' Consequently, all being is true, and whatever is true is a being.

5. *The Existence of Falsity.* That moral and logical falsity (lies and errors) occur, is a matter of daily occurrence. In an *absolute* sense, *ontological* falsity cannot exist, because all beings are transcendentally true and agree at least with the Divine Mind. In a *relative* sense, i.e., with regard to the agreement of things with the human mind, things may be ontologically false in a limited way; products of skill and art often deviate from the plan in man's mind. If natural things are called 'false,' it is only because their appearance is the occasion of false judgments for man.

6. *Some Characteristics of Truth.* Truth is *primarily in the intellect,* not in the things. Truth is primarily considered to be a qualification of knowledge. Ultimately all things are true

because they agree with God's knowledge; truth, therefore, resides primarily in God's knowledge and secondarily in the things.

Truth can be said to be *eternal* in so far as God's knowledge, with which all things must agree, is eternal. And in so far as God's knowledge is immutable, the truth of things is also *immutable*.

7. *The Truth of Contingently Future Events.* Events are contingently future when they are dependent on a free-acting cause; the free will of man is such a cause. Can such events be termed 'true' or 'false'? They can. Contingently future events can be expressed in two contradictory statements, one of which must agree with the event that will happen; this statement will be true and its contradictory false. Since the future event will have ontological truth when it happens, it must agree with God's knowledge. God's knowledge being eternal, the contingently future event must be known by God from eternity.

READINGS

Coffey, P., Ch. V; Rickaby, J., Bk. I, Ch. IV; Hugon, Ed., Tr. II, Qu. I, art. 4 et 5; Aristotle, *Metaph.,* II, VI; St. Thomas I, q. 16, a. 1–8; Urráburu, J. J., *Disp.* II, cp. III; Mercier, D. Card., pp. 459–463; McCormick, J. F., Ch. V, pp. 72–78.

CHAPTER XIV

BEING AND GOODNESS

SO FAR we have considered two transcendental attributes or properties of being, namely, unity and truth. Being, considered in itself, in its inner constitution, is undivided, one; it has the property of oneness or unity. This is an absolute property of being, because it pertains to every being, irrespective of the fact whether other beings exist or not. Being, considered in relation to a knowing intellect, is true; it has the property of truth. Truth always involves the relationship of intellect and thing, and truth is, therefore, not an absolute but a relative property of being. And just as being always has a relation to intellect and thus is true, it also has a relation to appetency and as such is *good*. 'Goodness,' with 'unity' and 'truth,' is a transcendental property or attribute of all being.

THE CONCEPT OF GOODNESS

Like the concepts of 'being,' 'one,' and 'true,' the concept 'good' is a primary and fundamental concept of the human mind. It is more easily recognized in the concrete than analyzed in the abstract. We can point it out more readily than define it. We can, of course, define it in a descriptive manner, but the defining terms will, as a rule, hardly be more clear than the term to be defined. We must, therefore, begin by consulting our experience of the 'good' and end by formulating our experience in a descriptive definition.

When are things said to be 'good'? *Aristotle* gives this definition: "Good is what all desire."[1] A thing is good in as much as

---

[1] Καλῶς ἀπεφήναντο τ'ἀγαθόν, οὗ παντ' ἐφίεται. Lib. 1, *Eth. Nic.* c. 1.

it is appetible or desirable; goodness, then, consists in the appetibility or desirability of a thing. Now, this is really a definition of the good by its *effect* in another being, namely, by the desire engendered by it in some being. This does not tell us anything about the thing itself, *what* in it is such that others should desire it. Why do things desire something? Evidently because this something is considered to be 'good' for it. Desirability or appetibility, therefore, presupposes *something in the thing* which is 'good' and on account of which it is actually desired or is at least desirable. There must be something positive in a being which influences another and causes this other to desire it as 'good,' and it is precisely this characteristic which must constitute its 'goodness.' What is it?

What a thing desires or seeks as good in another, depends entirely on the sort of individual the thing is. A magnet seeks iron, an ionized atom seeks a stray electron, a bee seeks honey, a lion seeks food, a plant seeks sunlight, a man seeks knowledge, etc. It would be useless to attempt to discover the various kinds of 'good' which each individual being strives for in the course of its existence. We must attempt to discover the *general feature common to all* things that are styled 'good,' if we wish to arrive at a fundamental concept of goodness. Viewed in this light, we find that a being strives for something as good because the latter satisfies some need, some demand, some exigency, some natural tendency or aptitude; it helps it in some way, or completes it in some fashion, or gives it pleasure in some form, or actualizes some potentiality of its nature, or has the capacity to realize some end and purpose in it. These various viewpoints express the one fundamental fact that a thing is good because it agrees with some natural tendency or appetency. *Goodness,* therefore, is the *suitability of a thing to a natural tendency or appetency.*

'Natural tendency' or 'appetency' is used here in a very wide sense and includes every kind of *striving power.* This striving power may be a conscious appetency, as we observe it in man (rational appetite) and in the animal (sensuous appetite); or it may be unconscious, as we perceive it in the affinity of chemical elements. The affinity between protons and electrons to form an atom, or between chlorine and sodium to form salt, or between hydrogen and oxygen to form water, is as manifestly an instance of 'natural tendency' as is the striving of a cat for milk or of a man for knowledge. In each case we have the satisfaction of some natural need and demand, of some 'appetency,' but in different ways. It is obvious, too, that in each case the one is 'good' for the other for that very reason.

By the very fact, though, that beings have such tendencies and appetencies, it is clear that they cannot have their *complete actuality* from the beginning. If they had all their entity, if they possessed all the reality they are capable of receiving, they would no longer tend toward, or strive for, anything. To do so means that there is still some potentiality in their being which needs and demands realization. And in so far as something is suitable for this fuller realization and actualization of a being, it will be 'good' for it. What, in particular, is suitable to a being, will naturally depend upon what this being *needs* and what the other being has *to offer* for the satisfaction of this need. To designate each particular need of a being and its corresponding good, would require a detailed description of each individual being — a task both impossible and unnecessary. This will explain why the definition of 'goodness' is worded so vaguely as the 'suitability of a thing to some natural tendency or appetency.' To define a good more closely would require a catalogue of individually suitable realities, and that would reach far beyond the scope of ontology which seeks to determine the 'good' in its widest and most fundamental concept, applicable to every type of specific and individual 'good.'

The general concept of 'good,' therefore, consists in this that something is suitable to a thing. Now, all beings have a nature or essence peculiar to themselves as members of a class and as individuals. And each such nature has a very real and definite *purpose or end within itself* which it tends to bring to full completion and *perfection*. A thing is perfect when it has everything that it is supposed to have according to the exigencies of its nature. Perfection, then, is the full actualization of a being according to the exigencies of its nature relative to the purpose or end of its essence. This may be taken absolutely or relatively. *Absolute* individual perfection would be the complete and final actualization of a being in its *totality; relative* individual perfection would be the actualization of a being at a particular *stage of its development* as demanded by it at this point. In either case it would at the moment have as much reality as its nature demands.

For instance, a chemical element has a limited nature whose purpose or end reveals itself in its tendency to unite with other related elements so as to form a definite compound with them. A plant has the natural purpose of developing as a vegetant body into a mature plant. A brute has the natural purpose of realizing itself as a sensuously conscious animal to the full extent of its powers. Man, being a rational animal, has the natural purpose of actualizing himself as a fully developed sense-organism and rational person. What serves man's natural end or purpose would not necessarily be good for a being in a lower order; and what serves the purpose of a chemical compound or plant need not be good for a brute or man. Each nature thus implies a specific natural tendency within itself, and things will be 'good' for it in so far as they suit its nature. Nothing, however, will suit the nature of a being more than the very *entity of this nature;* that is an 'intrinsic' good for a being. Consequently, all natures or *essences are good* for the individuals who possess them. On the other hand, any *outside beings* which help to develop or actualize their natures or natural tendencies will be good for them; they are an 'extrinsic' good for a being. Sunshine, for example, is an extrinsic good for a plant: food, for the bodily welfare of man.

In the light of this analysis of the data of our experience we find that the concept of 'good' and 'goodness' has a very wide range of application. And thus we may eventually define the *good* as any *reality which suits the nature of the being which strives for it.* This definition would fit the nature itself which desires and strives as well as the reality which this nature strives for and desires. 'Goodness' in the abstract would then be defined as the suitability of a reality for the nature of the being which strives for it.

CLASSIFICATION OF GOODNESS

There are various standpoints from which we may view the good, and correspondingly we may distinguish between different kinds of good. The main divisions are as follows:

Ontological, Physical, Moral Good. A thing is an *ontological* good, when it is a good in its very *entity* or *reality.* Every being, since it possesses a certain amount of entity or reality, is an ontological good; this is due to the fact that its entity or reality is suitable for the tendency of its own nature to be what it is and to perfect itself and to retain its perfection. In as much, too, as things are good in themselves by possessing their own entity, they are capable of being desired and striven for, so as to perfect the nature of some other thing. Ontological goodness is also called 'transcendental' or 'metaphysical' goodness, because, like unity and truth, it is convertible with being. All beings are thus an ontological good, considered in themselves and for themselves.

A thing is a *physical* good, when it satisfies the demand of the *nature of a being.* Each being has its own specific and individual nature, and as such it has a very definite end and purpose. The physical exigencies of man, for instance, differ from those of a horse, a cow, a cat, an oak, or an apple. He is supposed to have a head, a trunk, two arms, and two legs; two eyes, two ears, two hands, two feet; well-functioning organs of sense, digestion, locomotion, etc. These things, for man, are physically good, and none of them may be missing or defective, if man as a whole is to be considered physically good. And so it is with every physical being.

A thing is a *moral* good, when it has everything demanded of it by the *moral law.* An action may be ontologically and physically very good, but it may be morally very bad. An example will clarify this statement. A soldier defends his country in a just war. In an attack by the enemy, he kills an enemy soldier with his rifle. On another occasion an enemy soldier comes toward him, carrying a flag of truce; him he also kills with his rifle. In both cases his action kills a human being: in so far as the action is an entity, it is ontologically good; in so far as his aim is true and physically successful for the purpose of man-killing, it is physically good. But there is a difference in the morality of the action in the two cases. In the first it is justifiable homicide and morally good, because it is in accord with the moral law which demands of him the defense of his country as a duty; in the second it is murder and morally bad, because the moral law requires that he respect the enemy's person when he carries a flag of truce.

Absolute and Relative Good. This is another division of 'good.' An *absolute* good is anything which is suitable *to a being itself,* irrespective of other beings. Any reality which a being possesses, whether substantial or accidental, is an absolute good. A *relative* good is anything which is suitable *to another being.* Thus, human nature, including every part and function which belong to this nature, is an absolute good for man. Food, drink, clothes, shelter, etc., are a relative good for man. Absolute and relative *good,* however, must not be confused with absolute and relative *perfection;* the concepts are by no means synonymous. Perfection always implies that a being have everything that it is supposed to have according to the requirements *of its nature,* either its complete and final actualization (absolute perfection) or that amount of actualization which it requires at a particular stage of its development (relative perfection). But the actualization of any nature is an absolute good for itself; hence, perfection, whether absolute or relative perfection, is a subdivision of 'absolute good,' and it cannot be a 'relative good,' since the latter is always a good for another. Again, a being may be good without being perfect. For example, if a man is blind in one eye, his vision is still an absolute good for him, but this vision is imperfect, because man is supposed to have vision in both eyes. It may be well to remember, however, that terms like 'perfect' and 'perfection' admit of a variety of interpretations, and in many instances 'goodness' and 'perfection' are used more or less synonymously; the context of the discussion will then fix the meaning of the terms employed.

Objective and Subjective Good. By *objective* good we mean anything that is good *in itself.* Any absolute or relative good, as just defined, is an objective good in this sense. By *subjective* good we mean the actual possession of an objective good. Thus, a diamond ring, considered in itself, is an objective good; the ownership and possession of it is a subjective good for the one who owns and possesses it.

Real and Apparent Good. A good is *real,* when it is judged to be good for a being, and it *actually is* good for that particular being. Such is physical well-being for an animal, knowledge for man, sunlight for a plant, rain for the soil, etc. It is an *apparent* good, when it is judged to be good for a being, but it is *actually not good* for it. Food may seem a 'real' good for a critically ill patient, but it may be very harmful; under the circumstances it is an 'apparent' good. Pleasure is a physical good; but if its enjoyment is in opposition to the moral law, it is an 'apparent,' rather than a 'real,' good. This does not mean, of course, that such things are not ontologically or physically good *in themselves;* as such each is a real good. Relative *to another,* however, they may do harm; viewed from this standpoint, they are an apparent and not a real good. The difference of standpoint for the judgment should be carefully noted; the difference is often overlooked, resulting in a serious confusion of ideas and ideals. Thus, love of country, when it engenders in the citizenry a great spirit of service and sacrifice for the welfare of all, is a lofty patriotism and a real good; but when it urges national aggrandizement at the cost of right and justice, it is a false ideal and only an apparent good.

The distinction between real and apparent good is especially important in the case of man as a composite being of *body and soul*. He is a rational animal. This composite nature of man gives rise to conflicting tendencies and needs. As an animal or sentient being, he may crave for satisfactions in a multitude of ways. As a rational or moral being, he may desire and demand satisfactions of a sort at variance with those of his natural body. The result will be a conflict between his 'higher' and 'lower' tendencies, and in this conflict tendencies of a rational and moral character must obtain primary consideration, because man is distinctively 'human' in consequence of his rational and moral nature. A proper balance must be struck between these opposing tendencies and needs. To accede to the lower demands at the expense of the higher would be irrational and immoral. *For man,* therefore, considered as a rational and moral being, much that is a physical good for his body must be adjudged an 'apparent,' and not a 'real,' good for his person.

Disinterested, Delectable, and Useful Good. A *disinterested good (bonum honestum*) is any good considered merely as *giving perfection,* irrespective of any pleasure derived from its possession. The perfection which the disinterested or upright good is capable of conferring may be physical, intellectual, or moral in character. Health, knowledge, and virtue are such. A *delectable good (bonum delectabile*) is a relative good which gives *pleasure* and enjoyment to another. What is really desirable here is the thing itself which gives pleasure; oftentimes, however, the pleasure itself becomes the object of desire. Food, drink, and the proper use of sex are delectable goods; in many instances, though, the pleasure which accompanies these things becomes the sole object of the will. A *useful good (bonum utile*) is a relative good which is desired as a *means* to acquire perfection or pleasure. There is always an ulterior end in view when a good of this kind is striven for. Examples are: clubs, balls, and links, for a game of golf; automobiles, trains, airplanes, and boats, as means of transportation.

GOODNESS AND VALUE

Much is written by modern philosophers on *value* and the metaphysical nature of value. In so far as we are interested in a thing, care for it, desire it, seek it, strive for it, this thing shows itself to be invested with 'value,' to be 'valuable.' Wherein precisely does the 'value' of a thing consist? Why is it considered 'valuable'?

Obviously, to be 'valuable' and to be 'good' are closely related terms; for something is said to be 'good' when it is the 'object of desire,' when it is 'suitable' for a being, and that, as will be observed, is practically equivalent to saying that it possesses 'value.'

The immanent and final end and purpose of every being is its own *perfection*. All things which a being desires and seeks are desired and sought in order to realize this ultimate end and purpose. Whatever, then, helps to perfect it, is in so far 'good' and 'valuable' for it; it is viewed as means to this end. Ultimately, of course, this perfection is also desired and sought and so becomes the ultimate, intrinsic 'good' and 'value' for the being.

Value, therefore, can be viewed either as an end or as means. As the ultimate and intrinsic end it is the perfection of a being. As means it is the capacity or suitability of a thing to perfect another. 'Value,' then, is either perfection itself or the ability to give perfection; whatever is perfect or is perfective, is thereby 'valuable.' Hence, we can define *value* as that which is *perfect or perfective*.

What, then, is the *relation* between 'goodness' and 'value'? Value, considered as perfection, coincides with the absolute or intrinsic good, because it is identical with the reality, substantial and accidental, which a being possesses. Considered as perfective, it is the relative or instrumental good, because its perfection is a good for another being. Everything, therefore, has value in so far as it is a good for itself or for another.

'Goodness' and 'value' are thus seen to be synonymous terms, when viewed in their metaphysical implications.

THE CONVERTIBILITY OF BEING AND GOODNESS

Goodness, like unity and truth, is a transcendental and metaphysical attribute of being and as such convertible with it. That is to say: Every being is good, and whatever is good is a being.

Every being is good. This, of course, must be rightly understood. It means that every being is *ontologically* good; every being, in so far as it is a reality at all, is good. An individual nature need not be a perfect specimen of its class; it may be very imperfect and even defective in many respects. Nevertheless, the entity that it actually possesses is ontologically good. The correct sense of the thesis, therefore, is this: Every being, in so far as it is a positive reality, possesses intrinsic or *ontological goodness.*

Every being is either a substance or an accident and as such has its own individual nature and essence. Whatever is suitable for a nature and essence is good. But nothing could be more suitable for the nature and essence of any thing than the very *entity* of this nature and essence. The entity, however, of the nature and essence of a thing makes this thing to be a 'being.' Consequently, every being, i.e., every substance and accident, is entitatively or ontologically good. Hence, every being is good.

St. Thomas Aquinas formulates his argument in the following manner: "Every being, in as much as it is being, is in some way perfect, because every actuality is a certain perfection. But what is perfect involves the idea of 'appetible' and 'good.' Hence it follows that every being as such is good."[2]

Besides, all beings are the object of Divine Omnipotence and therefore also of the Divine Will, in as much as God either directly wills them or indirectly permits them to exist and have their being. Hence, they agree with His appetency or will. But for anything, in its existence and being, to agree

---

[2] *Summa theol.,* I, q. 5, a. 6.

with God's appetency or will, means that it is ontologically good. Hence, all things are good.

And just as every being must be an ontological good, so also *whatever is good is a being*. This hardly needs demonstration. The 'good' is certainly not nothing, but something; it is something desirable, something suitable. 'Nothing' is not suitable for anything and as such cannot be the object of an appetency. Consequently, whatever is good is a being. The concept of the 'good' always implies the concept of something positive, some reality or actuality, something that can perfect its possessor. This, however, implies that whatever is good is a 'being.' Hence, every good is a being.

THE CONCEPT OF EVIL

Evil is the antithesis of good. As the good in general means the suitability of a thing for an appetency or appetent being, so *evil* is the *unsuitability of something for a natural tendency or appetency*. This definition might seem to indicate that 'something' can itself be an evil, so that evil would be a positive reality of some kind. That would be a misunderstanding of the meaning.

Evil is no being, but it is not a mere absence of being. It is the absence of a reality which ought to be there, of a *reality due a thing;* it is a defect, a *privation of reality*. An example will make this clear. There is an absence of sight in a stone; the stone is 'sightless.' This sightlessness is the absence of a reality in the stone, but is no evil for it. When there is an absence of sight in a man, he is said to be 'blind,' not merely 'sightless' like a stone. This blindness in man is not a mere absence of a reality; it is an 'evil' for him. What is the difference between a stone and a man in this absence of sight, so that the former is considered to be merely 'sightless,' while the latter is declared to be 'blind'? Why is sightlessness for the stone a mere absence of perfection or reality, and for man an evil? The difference is this: sightlessness in man is the *direct defect* of a good which *ought* to be there, and that constitutes it an evil for man; the stone, however, is not supposed to have sight, and consequently its absence is no direct defect or evil for it, but only the absence of a reality not due its nature.

It will thus be observed that the concept of 'evil' does not imply a positive reality, but a *strict privation* or defect, namely, the privative lack of an entity due a being. Since evil is essentially a privation or defect of entity, it must be obvious that it cannot exist for itself but always *presupposes a subject* which lacks something which the subject ought to have; as such it is always something *relative,* i.e., relative to the individual nature in which the defect is found. But, if evil needs a subject which it affects, is then evil not an 'accident'? It is not. An accident is a positive reality inherent in a subject, contributing some positive entity or determination to its subject, while evil is a defect of a being in its subject: between the two lies the difference between an 'entity' and a 'privative nothing.' Evil, therefore, can also be defined as the *privation of a required good* (*privatio boni debiti*).

KINDS OF EVIL

Since evil is the privation of a good, there will naturally be as many kinds of evil as there are kinds of good. The following are typical.

Ontological, Physical, and Moral Evil. An *Ontological* (metaphysical, transcendental) evil is the *privation of an ontological good.* Strictly speaking, this means that a thing, *as a being,* is evil in itself. The question, whether an ontological evil as such can exist, will be treated shortly; at present we are concerned only with its concept and definition.

A *physical* evil is the *privation of a physical good.* Thus sickness is a physical evil, because health, of which sickness is the privation, is a physical good. The absence of any member, organ, or function, which normally belongs to a being of a certain class, will be a physical evil. Such would be the absence of a finger or an arm in man, of a tail in a dog, the loss of sight or hearing in a mammal. This applies, of course, merely to the individual member, organ, or function considered for itself. That the removal of an inflamed appendix or other part of a body may be, indirectly and relatively, a physical good for the organism *as a whole,* is obvious; the physical good of the whole always supersedes the physical good of a part of the whole. For the organism as a whole, general debility, sickness, or death would be physical evils.

A *moral* evil is the *privation of the proper relation* between an action or its omission and the *moral law.* If the moral law demands a certain action and this action is unduly omitted, the omission is a moral evil. Man, as a creature, for example, is obliged to recognize the sovereignty of God and adore Him; if he fails to do this, the omission is a moral evil. On the other hand, the moral law may forbid a certain action; if the action is performed nevertheless, it will be a moral evil, because the proper relation between the law and the action is not maintained. The cashier of a bank, for example, may withdraw his own money from the bank and spend it, but if he takes other people's money and spends it, he is guilty of a crime. All lies, thefts, robberies, sexual irregularities, unwarranted personal injuries to one's self or others, etc., are a departure from the demands of the moral law and are evil. In Christian ethics such violations are styled 'sin.' Violations of the laws of society or of a government are not always violations of the moral law; some of these laws are merely penal laws, and their transgression involves no moral evil.

Absolute and Relative Evil. The term 'absolute' can be taken in different meanings. Here it is taken in the sense in which it was used when speaking of 'absolute good.' An *absolute* evil, then, is the *privation of an absolute good,* and an absolute good is anything which is good for a being itself, irrespective of other beings. When a being is deprived of such an absolute good, this privation is said to be an 'absolute' evil. The two arms which man has are an absolute good for him; to be deprived of one or both, is then an absolute evil. Sight is an absolute good for a cat; to be blind, is an absolute evil for it. Life is an absolute good for every organism; death is, therefore, an absolute evil for it. A *relative* evil is the *privation of a relative good,* and a relative good is anything that is good for another. Food and drink are a relative good for man; to be deprived of sustenance is a relative evil for him. A leash on a dog is a relative evil, because it deprives him of freedom of movement. A red-hot rod of iron, when grasped by the hand, is a relative evil, because it burns and causes pain.

Objective and Subjective Evil. An *objective* evil, as the term indicates, is the *privation of an objective good,* and the latter is anything that is good in itself, whether absolutely or relatively. Examples will be found in the preceding paragraph. A *subjective* evil is the *privation of a subjective good,* namely, the privation of the actual possession of an objective good. Thus, the loss of the possession of an automobile, of a house, of health, of sight, or of any other objective good, considered as a state or condition of the former possessor, is a subjective evil.

Real and Apparent Evil. A *real* evil is the *privation of a real good,* of something that is judged to be good for a being and actually is good for it. Examples are: a broken wing for a bird, disintegration for an element, vice for a human being. An *apparent* evil is the *privation of an apparent good,* the privation of something that is judged to be a real good for a being but is really not good for it. In an apparent evil, therefore, we have the privation of a real evil, since an apparent good is actually an evil; the net result is the cancellation of the evil, leaving a 'real good' in the being. Food for a critically ill patient, for instance, is an apparent good, but a real evil; to deprive such a patient of food in such circumstances, is an 'apparent evil,' but it is actually a 'real good.' A sharp knife as a plaything is an apparent good for an infant, though it is actually a real evil; to take this knife away from the infant, therefore, is an 'apparent evil,' but it is actually a 'real good.'

It should be fairly obvious that our judgment of evil as real or apparent, will depend upon the standpoint from which we view an evil. Depending upon the circumstances of the case, an evil may be 'real' from one standpoint and 'apparent' from another. The removal of a gangrened arm is a real evil, if we consider the loss of the arm as such; since, however, this removal may be necessary to save the life of the patient, the loss of the arm under the circumstances is more an apparent evil than a real evil. Physical suffering, taken by itself, is a real evil; but if it is the occasion of strengthening the character of the suffering person, it is rather an apparent evil.

THE EXISTENCE OF EVIL

Evil and its existence has always been a serious problem for religion and philosophy. In all ages there have been those who have asserted that evil exists as a sort of perverse positive reality. Evil, however, is a privation of some good, a 'privative nothing.' This matter must now be examined a little closer. Since all evil can be reduced to an ontological, physical, or moral evil, we can restrict ourselves to the problem of the existence of these three forms of evil.

The Existence of Ontological Evil. Can a being, *as a being,* be evil, and can ontological evil thus become a fact? This is the crux of the whole problem. A little reflection should convince us that an ontological evil in the true sense of the term cannot exist. Good is a transcendental property of all being: every being is good, and whatever is good is a being. But if every being, *as a being,* is transcendentally good, it is *ontologically* good, because then it is good precisely in so far as it is a *being,* and that is what is meant by saying that something is 'ontologically' good. If every being, however, is an ontologically good being, no being can be an ontologically evil being. Now, only a 'being' can exist; consequently, since every being is ontologically good, no ontologically evil being can exist. Hence, ontological evil (concretely, an ontologically evil being) cannot exist. It follows then, that every being, in so far as it has *any reality* at all, is good. Evil, therefore, can consist only in the privation of some reality; as such it is essentially a privative non-entity, and a non-entity, of course, is incapable of existence.

But is the above not open to a serious objection? Tuberculosis, for instance, is a disease caused by germs; these germs are, therefore, an evil. But these germs are beings. Hence, some beings are an evil. These germs exist; therefore, some evil beings exist. Certainly, the germs exist and are an evil. But are they an evil *in themselves?* Or are they an evil *for another,* e.g., for the lungs of man? In order that they be adjudged ontologically evil, it would be necessary that they be an evil in themselves. That, however, is not the case. All germs are organisms, and as such they are beings with a very definite nature of their own. Their nature is good *for the germs;* it is as good for the germs as man's nature is good for himself. Germs have their proper place in the scheme of things; their essences have their own particular purpose and end. The material of man's lungs is food for them and is a good for them. That this material happens to be taken from man's lungs, makes them an evil *for man.* They are thus an evil for another (relative evil), but they are good in themselves (ontological good). The same is true of all germs, tumors, cancers, etc. As living cells they are good in themselves; relatively, of course, they may be an evil for other beings. This line of thought can be applied to anything that could possibly be conceived as an ontological evil, and it will be found that it is, for itself and in itself, ontologically good. Hence, no being can be, strictly speaking, ontologically evil.

Are not *Satan* and the *evil spirits* ontologically evil beings who actually exist? It is doubtful whether philosophy, with the use of reason alone, unaided by divine revelation, could prove their actual existence. However, accepting their existence as a fact on the authority of Christian revelation, we must remember that even Satan and the evil spirits are not entirely evil. They are created beings and, so far as their nature and essence is concerned, they were *ontologically good when created.* They did not lose this nature and essence when they sinned; they still possess the same nature and essence which they received from the hand of God in their creation. Consequently, they *still are* ontologically good in their nature and essence. Whatever evil is in them resides in their depraved will, in as much as their will is in eternal disconformity with the will of God, and that is a moral, not an ontological evil. As existing beings, therefore, even Satan and the evil spirits are not ontologically evil.

The Existence of Physical Evil. Physical evils are an established fact in the world. Many beings lack some reality which they ought to have. Sickness and injuries deprive living beings of that physical integrity which their essence naturally demands. But it must be borne in mind that beings are physically evil only in so far as some *entity is missing* in them. Whatever entity they possess is in itself good. Thus, a tubercular lung is a physical evil only because certain portions are infected or missing; the remaining parts are good. A severed arm is a physical evil for a man, because he is now deprived of a portion of his being. But the rest of his body is not a physical evil; nor is the severed arm itself, considered from the standpoint of its constituent elements, physically evil: it is the privation of the proper relation between body and arm that is an evil, and this privation is not an entity in itself. Physical evil, therefore, consists in the *privation of being,* relative to an individual's needs, not in any positive reality as such.

The Existence of Moral Evil. That moral evils are present among men is all too evident. Sin is an undeniable fact. Crime is an everyday occurrence. But here again, it would be false to consider a moral evil as a positively existing entity. In fact, the sinful action as an action is ontologically good, because it is a being; and if the action is performed in a manner conducive to the natural purpose of the act, it is also physically good. Since, however, this ontologically and physically good act is not in accordance with the requirements of the moral law, it is morally evil. There is no morally evil *entity* here, but rather the defect or *privation of an entity,* namely, the defect of the proper relation between the act and the demands of the law. A child, for example, is playing. The mother calls the child into the house, but the child disobeys and keeps on playing. If the act of playing was ontologically and physically good before the mother's call, it is still ontologically and physically good after the call, because the act has not changed in this respect. But the attitude of the will has changed, in as much as it is disobedient to the properly constituted authority. Nothing in the *entity* of the act has changed, but there is now a *defect of proper relation* between the entity of the act and the law which governs it; the entity as such still remains good. Moral evil, therefore, does not consist in a positive entity or reality, but in privation; whatever there is of entity in the action, is in itself good.

SOME THEORIES OF EVIL

Evil is not a primary concept; it presupposes the good as the primary concept, because evil is the privation of a good. The good must exist first, before there can be a privation of it; evil can only follow the good. For the same reason the presence of evil is always dependent on the presence of the good; where there is no good there can be no privation of it and therefore no evil. The good can exist without evil, but evil cannot exist without the good. First, then, was the good. Evil came later. These principles should enable us to pass a correct judgment on some theories of evil which have become prominent in the course of time.

Pessimism, as a philosophic theory, maintains that evil predominates over good, because the world at large is essentially bad. Conscious life, particularly in man, is a constant struggle, fundamentally and inescapably painful in character, so that life is not worth living and consciousness is in itself a state of misery; the best escape from it is in unconsciousness and death. Such are the main tenets of *Buddhism* and of the modern pessimism defended by philosophers like *Schopenhauer, von Hartmann,* and *Nietzsche.* That pain and suffering are facts of life, no one denies; but that life, consciousness, and the world in general are intrinsically evil, cannot be admitted.

Whatever is, is good; evil is only incidental to the good. That our limited knowledge cannot fathom completely the *Why* of evil is no valid argument against the essential goodness of the beings which constitute the world. When beings are limited in nature and action and are mutually dependent on each other for the full actualization of their inherent reality, it is inevitable that the gain of one involves loss for another. Evil is thus relative, not absolute; the scheme of things as a whole is harmonious and ontologically good.

Excessive Dualism is another false theory. In this view all the good present in the world is due to a supreme Principle of Good, and all the evil to a supreme Principle of Evil. These two principles are independent of each other and are usually conceived as being co-equal, co-extensive, and co-eternal. Such is the theory of *Zoroastrianism*. According to *Zoroaster* (or Zarathustra), a Persian philosophic religious reformer who lived in the seventh or sixth century B.C., the forces of good and evil are waging a constant battle for supremacy in the universe. The supreme Principle of Good is Ahura-mazda (Ormuzd), and the Supreme Principle of Evil is Anra-mainyu (Ahriman); the former is the source of all good in the world, and the latter the source of all evil. In the third century A.D., *Manes* introduced this doctrine and founded the sect of *Manicheism*. God is the supreme Principle of Good, and 'matter' the Principle of Evil. His interpretation of 'matter' as the Principle of Evil harks back to the doctrines of some of the earlier Greek philosophers. In every theory of excessive dualism the Principle of Evil is conceived as a *positive being,* either conscious or unconscious. This, of course, is an erroneous conception, because evil is a privation of being, not a positive reality; it cannot be present except in so far as it is a privative defect affecting some ontological good. Besides, we know, from what has been said before, that every existent being is an ontological good in its nature and essence. Consequently, also this supreme Principle of Evil must be ontologically good, because it possesses a nature or essence; as such it must derive its ontological goodness from the supreme Principle of Good; in that case, however, it cannot be co-equal and co-eternal with the Principle of Good, but must be dependent on the latter. The Principle of Evil, therefore, is contradictory in its very concept.

Summing up our investigation of the transcendental properties of being in general, we arrive at the following results: Being, one, true, and good are convertible ideas. Every 'being' is one, true, and good. Every 'one' is being, true, and good. Every 'true' is being, one, and good. Every 'good' is being, one, and true. These realities are inter-identical; they include each other implicitly. Between them there exists only a virtual distinction with an imperfect foundation in the thing.

SUMMARY OF CHAPTER XIV

Goodness, like unity and truth, is a transcendental attribute of being.

1. *The Concept of Goodness.* Good is what all desire. Something is good in so far as it is suitable to a natural tendency or appetency. The 'good' can be defined as any reality which suits the nature of the being which strives for it.

2. *Divisions of Goodness.* The following are typical divisions of the good, viewed from different standpoints:

Ontological, Physical, and Moral Good. Something is an *ontological* good, when it is a good in its very entity or reality. It is a *physical* good, when it satisfies the demand of the nature of a being. It is a *moral* good, when it has everything demanded of it by the moral law.

Absolute and Relative Good. An *absolute* good is anything which is good for a being itself, irrespective of other beings. A *relative* good is anything which is suitable to another.

Objective and Subjective Good. An *objective* good is anything that is good in itself. A *subjective* good is the actual possession of an objective good.

Real and Apparent Good. It is *real,* when it is judged to be good for a being, and it actually is good for it. It is *apparent,* when it is judged to be good for a being, but it is actually not good for it.

Disinterested, Delectable, and Useful Good.   A *disinterested* good is any good considered merely as giving perfection. A *delectable* good is a relative good which gives pleasure to another. A *useful* good is a relative good which is desired as a means to acquire perfection or pleasure.

3. *The Convertibility of Being and Goodness.* Every being is good, and whatever is good is a being. Every being is in some way perfect, because every actuality is a certain perfection. But what is perfect, even in a limited way, is appetible and therefore good. Whatever is good is also a being; this is clear from the fact that it cannot be 'nothing,' since 'nothing' is not suitable to anything.

4. *The Concept of Evil.* Evil is the absence of a reality which ought to be present; it is the privation of a required good.

5. *Kinds of Evil.* There are as many kinds of evil as there are kinds of good. In each case the evil will be the privation of the respective kind of good. For example, an *ontological* evil is the privation of an ontological good, a *real* evil is the privation of a real good, etc.

6. *The Existence of Evil.* Evil is not a positive reality; it is the *privation* of a required good and as such a privative nonentity. Pessimism, which considers all things as essentially evil, is therefore false. So, too, are Zoroastrianism and Manicheism, since they maintain the existence of a supreme Principle of Good and a supreme Principle of Evil.

READINGS

Coffey, P., Ch. VI; Rickaby, J., Bk. I, Ch. IV; Hugon, Ed., Tr. II, Qu. I, art. 6 et 7; Aristotle, *Ethics* I; *Metaph.*, V; Urráburu, J. J., *Disp.* II, cp. IV; Ward, Leo R., *Values and Reality,* Ch. IV; Mercier, D. Card., pp. 463–471; St. Thomas, I, q. 5, a. 1–6; McCormick, J. F., Ch. V, pp. 78–84.

CHAPTER XV

BEING AND BEAUTY

BEAUTY IS a most elusive quality. Its nature is so tenuous that it always seems to escape in the very moment of its capture. There is hardly a term in any language which is used more and abused more than 'beauty.' The conflicting varieties of its definition are truly amazing — a sure indication of the complexity of its nature and of the many-sided character of its appeal. Beauty manifests itself in so many and in such divergent forms that it is extremely difficult to discover the general element common to them all.

The concept of the beautiful is closely related to the concepts of unity, truth, and goodness, the transcendental attributes of being; it is even considered by some philosophers to be a transcendental or quasi-transcendental property. Like all fundamental and primary ideas, it is more easily recognized in a concrete experience than abstractly defined in words. The best method of acquiring a serviceable knowledge of the beautiful will be to analyze our experience of the beautiful and thus gradually enucleate a more formal definition.

OUR EXPERIENCE OF BEAUTY

Beauty pleases. Universal experience and judgment show this. We do not consider that to be beautiful which displeases and annoys us, at least not under this particular aspect of being 'beautiful.' Whatever is beautiful, whether it be a poem, a painting, a melody, a piece of sculpture, or an architectural structure, is always considered to be such that it pleases, gratifies, and gives enjoyment.

Beauty gives *disinterested* pleasure. The pleasure derived

from beauty is styled 'aesthetic pleasure.' We do not consider
our pleasure to be aesthetic when our main concern on seeing
an apple is to eat it; this is a selfish food-pleasure, and it is not
founded on the beauty of the apple. We experience aesthetic
pleasure, when we derive pleasure from *beholding* it. If a man
owns a painting and takes pleasure in it because he knows he
can sell it at an advantage, he is not said to have aesthetic
pleasure; but if he is satisfied to *contemplate* it and thus enjoy
it, then he is enthralled with its beauty. There is beauty in the
seas, in the stars, in the sunrise, in the waterfalls, in the mountains; but there is no selfish enjoyment in these things. The
agreeable and pleasurable feelings engendered in us through
the mere possession of an object or through the satisfaction of
the lower sentient appetites, are not aesthetic, for they are too
organic and *selfish*. Things may taste and smell and feel
'agreeable,' but such pleasure is not the delight encountered
in the enjoyment of the beautiful.

The *primary object,* therefore, of desire in beauty is not the
pleasure derived from profit, consumption, possession, or even
use, but the pleasure aroused through the *contemplation* of
the beautiful. Hence, the *ear,* the *eye,* and the *imagination*
are the sense faculties properly engaged in the production of
aesthetic delight, and they are mainly perceptive in character.

Beauty gives disinterested *intellectual* pleasure. The intellect
is necessary for the enjoyment of beauty. Man is the only
animal which appreciates beauty. Brutes do not contemplate
the beauty of the flowers, the hills, the woods, the sunsets, etc.,
nor do they manifest anything of the joy that we feel in the
contemplation of these things. They remain indifferent in the
presence of all the beauty of nature and are concerned with
beautiful objects only in so far as they are of assistance to them
in the struggle for existence. The reason why brutes cannot
enjoy beauty in any true sense is plain: *order, proportion,
unity, appropriateness, the agreement between the ideal and
the real,* are fundamental elements of beauty, and the knowledge of these elements rests upon a more or less conscious

comparison of the parts in themselves and with the idea expressed in the whole. This, however, is a matter of rational judgment, and an intellectual being alone has the faculty for this. Beauty, therefore, must have an *intelligible content*.

Beauty gives a disinterested *intellectual-sensuous* pleasure. The intellect is necessary for the perception of the beautiful, because beauty has an intelligible content. But the intellect perceives it through the mediation of the senses. The intelligible, supra-sensible quality or 'idea' must be perceived in a *sensibly pleasing appearance* in order to be beautiful. It is a universal demand that the artist pleasantly impress the senses with images and plastic forms. Naked thoughts leave us cold. Ideas alone, free from the beauty of form, are found in science, mathematics, and philosophy; but no one looks upon these as being the proper medium and vehicle of beauty. We go to art and to the artist for beauty and its enjoyment. Hence, the idea, or truth, alone does not suffice to make a thing beautiful; the idea, or truth, must be embodied in a sensibly pleasing form before we can consider it beautiful. The scientist, the mathematician, and the philosopher may present the idea, or truth, in a far clearer and more convincing manner than the artist; they enlighten, but they do not, strictly speaking, give us aesthetic delight. The artist may express the same idea, or truth, less exactly, but he clothes it in form and figure; and we are impressed, animated, delighted, pleased.

The reason is this: Like pleases like, *simile simili gaudet*. As we are one in essence, consisting of mind and body, so the beautiful is *one* in nature, consisting of *idea* and *form*. The way of art is therefore twofold: the idea may be first and then the form, or the form may be first and then the idea: true idealism and sound realism, the idealized real and the realized ideal. It is the happy combination and fusion of idea and form which constitutes beauty, corresponding to the composite nature of man. Consequently, there must be an *equilibrium* established between the *intellectual* and *sensible* elements. An overcharge of idea or a lack of form would mean a lack of beauty, abstractness, too much intellectuality; an overcharge of form or lack of idea would mean shallowness and extravagance.

Beauty gives a disinterested intellectual-sensuous pleasure due to the *radiant perfection of a thing*. Most philosophers acknowledge that beauty is not purely subjective in character, but that it has its foundation in the things themselves and that we experience the delight of beauty in consequence of some *objective factors* present in the objects.

Beauty is not mere appropriateness. The arrangements of a barn may be very appropriate, but the ordinary barn can hardly be said to be beautiful. Nor is beauty the inner perfection of a thing, considered as such. Many ugly things are intrinsically perfect, for instance, the caw of a crow, the bray of a mule, a toad, a factory, a three-legged stool; but these are seldom considered to be beautiful.

Beauty is the *perfection* of a thing manifested in a *pleasing, happy manner*. Just as light, splendor, radiance, and color produce a pleasing impression on the eye, so also we call beauty in general 'resplendent, radiant perfection.' That perfection and goodness are fundamental properties of beauty, is shown by the fact that beauty pleases. Now, something that pleases is desirable, and the desirable is, as such, good.

Beauty gives a disinterested intellectual-sensuous pleasure due to the radiant perfection of a thing, primarily in so far as it exerts an *appeal to our cognitive faculties* and not to our will. Order, harmony, rhythm, unity amid variety, etc., are essential elements of beauty, and their appeal is evidently to the *perceptive* powers of the mind. Experience proves this. Things like a colorful landscape, a symphony of Grieg, a poem of Francis Thompson, a drama of Shakespeare, a Madonna of Raphael, a cathedral of Rheims, or a statue of Praxiteles, produce in us primarily a satisfaction of intellect and imagination. Their apprehension and appreciation afford us the pleasure peculiar to beauty; but apprehension and appreciation are acts of the cognitive faculties, not of sense-appetency or will.

It is only after we have apprehended and appreciated the inherent beauty of something, that aesthetic pleasure follows as a natural result.

St. Thomas Aquinas furnishes us with a succinct elucidation of these points. "Since that is good which all desire, it belongs to the concept of the good that the appetency come to rest in it. But it pertains to the concept of the beautiful that the appetency come to rest in its contemplation or knowledge (*in ejus aspectu seu cognitione*). Whence it happens that those senses are primarily concerned with the beautiful which are mostly cognitive in character, namely, sight and hearing in the service of the mind; for we speak of beautiful sights and beautiful sounds. Concerning the objects of the other senses, we do not use the term 'beautiful'; for we do not speak of beautiful tastes or odors. And thus it is clear that the beautiful adds to the good the relation of the cognitive faculty, so that we call that good which directly agrees with the appetitive faculty, and beautiful that whose apprehension pleases."[1] He summarizes the beautiful in the following terse expression: *"Things are beautiful which please when seen."*[2] The context shows that by 'seen' he meant as much as 'known, apprehended, imagined, perceived, contemplated': which agrees with our contention that beauty appeals primarily to our perceptive powers and not to our sense-appetency and will.

If we now analyze the data of our experience, we perceive that whatever is 'beautiful' possesses certain *objective elements.*

OBJECTIVE ELEMENTS OF BEAUTY

By the objective elements of beauty we understand those *elements or factors in the object itself* which enable us to recognize the object as 'beautiful.' Some of these factors are more general and others are more particular. The *general elements* of beauty agree to a great extent with the transcendental attributes of unity, truth, and goodness; but not altogether.

---

[1] *Summa theol.*, Ia, IIae, q. 27, art. 1 ad 3.
[2] *Idem.*, Ia, q. 5, art. 4 ad 1: *Pulchra dicuntur quae visa placent.*

There is a close relation between *beauty and unity*. Unity amid complexity is a perfection and aids the intellect in grasping the underlying meaning of things without distracting its attention and weakening its vigor of activity. The grace of line in an Apollo Belvidere, the magnificence of St. Peter's in Rome, the charm of a Bach minuet, the grandeur of Michelangelo's *Last Judgment,* the glory of Homer's *Iliad* — is not a goodly amount of their imperishable beauty due to the proportion, the harmony, the rhythm, the symmetry of their manifold and intricate details? But to admit this is to admit that beauty is intimately connected with 'unity.'

Beauty, however, implies more than mere unity. We find unity also in a mathematical theorem, in a scientific deduction, in a philosophic syllogism, and in a mechanical contrivance; but these are not necessarily beautiful on that account. We may acknowledge their unity and still not experience any delight in their knowledge. It takes more than unity to make a thing beautiful.

There is also a close relation between *beauty and truth*. The appeal of beauty, as just shown, is mainly to the perceptive powers, and especially to the intellect. The fact that animals show no appreciation of beauty in the strict sense, is alone sufficient to prove this. All beauty possesses an *intelligible* quality which transcends the ordinary realm of sense-perception. It is not sufficient to 'perceive' beauty; beauty must also be 'apprehended' and 'understood' in order to be appreciated. This shows that there is an element of truth in everything beautiful.

Again, however, beauty must not be identified in every respect with the true. Truth as such merely commands our assent, but it does not necessarily afford us aesthetic delight. In many instances truth may even displease, annoy, and pain. The truth of statistical facts is aesthetically barren. The truth of a chemical analysis leaves us cold. The truth of an algebraic calculation is devoid of the emotional response associated with the contemplation of beauty. Truth as such is not beauty.

Similarly, there is a close relation between *beauty and good-ness*. Beauty satisfies, pleases, delights; and satisfaction, pleasure, and delight have a natural reference to an appetency, because an object which has these characteristics is a delectable good. Such emotional releases are, of course, a subjective element in the enjoyment of the beautiful, but they are elicited by the object itself when contemplated by the observer. The element of goodness, therefore, is also present in the beautiful.

On the other hand, there is a difference between beauty and goodness. The good satisfies the appetency directly, as something to be acquired, possessed, and retained, not because it is known and perceived. Beauty, however, is the good in so far as it delights the beholder through its perception and contemplation. The good is always something suitable to a striving power, and for that reason it is desired by an appetency; an appetency, therefore, is somewhat selfish in its trend. But beauty gives satisfaction and pleasure through the simple contemplation of it, without the presence of any acquisitive tendency. One can be thrilled while listening to a selection by Kreisler or Paderewski, and never desire either their gifts or their instruments of music.

The general elements of unity, truth, and goodness are thus seen to be present in the beautiful; but beauty is not a transcendental attribute of being, so that every being would of necessity also be beautiful. *Being and beauty are not convertible concepts,* like being and unity, being and truth, being and goodness. Everything beautiful is a being, but the converse statement is not true. While these concepts are undoubtedly closely related, they are not identifiable: there is a difference between beauty and unity, truth, and goodness.

Turning now to the *particular elements* or factors of beauty, we find that a number of properties must be present in an object in order that it may be styled 'beautiful.' Beauty elicits joy and delight in the beholder, and these emotions are the concomitant result of the normal, healthy, full, vigorous exercise of any faculty. The joy and delight engendered by the beautiful will, therefore, be supreme when all the faculties involved in the contemplation and appreciation of the beautiful are aroused to such an exercise of their powers. Three fundamental properties are required for this.

Integrity or completeness is the first. Any noticeable defect or mutilation in a thing makes an unpleasant impression on the beholder. The mind is dissatisfied with this incomplete condition and makes an effort to restore the missing part in its imagination; this effort disturbs its poise and hinders it from coming to a proper state of rest and calm in its contemplation. As a result of this mental disturbance the aesthetic enjoyment is marred by a certain amount of annoyance and irritation. We observe this when contemplating a dilapidated building, a damaged painting, a crippled body, an awkward dance; or when listening to a melody out of tune and to the badly memorized lines of a drama; or when reading the poorly constructed verses of a mediocre poet. Of course, in some instances the defects may be so completely overshadowed by the resplendent beauty of the object as a whole, that small mutilations or blemishes escape our notice almost entirely; in that case we would experience the full enjoyment of beauty by simply concentrating our attention on the object as a whole. But defects, as defects, detract from the beauty of an object; and if these defects force themselves constantly on our attention, the object cannot be said to be really beautiful.

Proportion or balance is another requisite. It is the index of a mind which works in an orderly fashion. Just as the mind experiences pleasure in evolving order out of confusion, so it also experiences aesthetic pleasure in detecting an orderly arrangement in what at first seems to be chaotic confusion. A mere jumble does not please. A heap of stones is not an aesthetic object; but if they are arranged in the orderly construction of a building, provided there be symmetry and balance in the arrangement, they form an object of beauty. An orchestra tuning its instruments is a mere confusion of irritating noises; but when the instruments weave the same sounds into the intricate harmony of an operatic overture, we have beauty of a high order. Irregular daubs of paint are unaesthetic; when these colors, however, are applied by an artist to a canvas, they become an immortal masterpiece of exquisite beauty. The secret is proportion, balance, harmony, symmetry — in a word, *unity amid variety*. Unity without variety is not beautiful, because in that case the energy of the perceptive faculty will be exercised in an unbroken, unrelieved strain; and that would produce tension and fatigue, but not pleasure. Variety without unity is not beautiful, because then the mind's energy would be scattered and spent without being able to come to rest; and that would disturb and hinder the normal, healthy, full, vigorous activity of the faculties. Unity amid variety acts like a focus, concentrating the attention along certain definite lines, bringing harmony into the manifold elements and making of them a simplified whole; this facilitates the mind's activity, gives it a feeling of restful completeness, and thereby produces in it the joy and delight so characteristic of beauty.

Clarity or splendor is the third requirement. To be beautiful, an object must have a certain amount of compelling force; it must be impressive; it must possess a vivid presentation; it must attract and charm through its very appearance. Only then will it be able to call forth a vigorous activity on the part of the contemplating person. The elements of beauty may not be obscure or hidden, otherwise they will demand undue labor and effort of the mind to discover them; and that would beget strain and pain, not joy and delight. Joy and delight must be spontaneous, must spring up in the heart like a fountain and overflow into the emotions; and that will be the case only when the clarity of beauty exercises the perceptive faculties in such a way that they function with ease and liveliness. That is why all the arts use contrast as an effective technique to set the splendor of beauty in a sharper light; the elements of aesthetic value then fairly leap into the central position of attention and thereby give the mind the proper perspective which enables it to survey the parts and the whole in a comprehensive glance.

Such, it would seem, are the main objective elements present in objects which are called 'beautiful.' Many individual qualities have been pointed out and analyzed in the various kinds of natural and artistic beauty; upon examination, however, they all appear to be reducible to these fundamental attributes and qualities. In some forms of beauty the one or the other attribute or quality is embodied in a predominant manner, but every form of beauty contains them all in some measure. Beauty, of course, never appears in absolute purity, for the simple reason that no finite thing is perfect. There will always be an overstressing or understressing of some particular element, so that it is next to impossible to find any object which is altogether beautiful.

THE DEFINITION OF BEAUTY

To define beauty adequately is a most difficult task. Beauty manifests itself in such a multitudinous variety of forms, that an enucleation of its fundamental and essential character is well-nigh impossible. The history of aesthetics proves this. From Socrates to the present day beauty has been the subject of analysis and discussion. Never, however, has any philosopher, scientist, or artist been able to formulate a definition of beauty capable of satisfying everybody. The definitions range all the way from expressions of the crudest naturalism to those of the loftiest idealism.

How, then, shall we define beauty? From what has been said, we venture to propose the following definition: *Beauty is a blending of the unity, truth, and goodness in a thing, characterized by completeness, proportion, and clarity of presentation in an intellectual-sensuous form, so as to produce a disinterested emotional pleasure in a rational perceiver.* If this

definition seems complicated, it at least attempts to do justice
to the subjective and objective elements involved in the perception of beauty.

This definition, of course, views beauty from the standpoint
of *man's* nature. The reason is obvious. The beauty which we
know is the beauty which appeals to us, and we are human
beings consisting of body and soul, animality and rationality.
The nature of beauty *for us* must, therefore, partake of the
nature of man: it must be intellectual and sensuous, the embodiment of an intelligible *idea* in a material *form*. Its appeal
must be an appeal to the whole man in his composite nature,
not merely to the one or the other side of his being. What the
objective elements of beauty would be for a pure spirit or for
God, we have no way of knowing. No doubt, they will be
purely spiritual in character. God must be infinite, transcend-
ent, absolute Beauty. For spiritual beings beauty consists perhaps in the full agreement of reality with its thought-ideal.

Will the definition of beauty given above enable us to point
to a particular object and immediately recognize it as beautiful
or not beautiful? Hardly. The reason for this distressing defi-
ciency in every definition of beauty lies in the fact that we
first intuitively feel something to be beautiful and only then
attempt to discover the elements which make it beautiful.
Aesthetic pleasure as a sensation is an *ultimate psychological
experience incapable of complete analysis*. It is found to be
present, and must be accounted for. The enjoyment of beauty
is as much a subjective affair as it is objective. It is precisely in
the subjective field of man's emotions that so much diversity
occurs, due to differences of individual temperament, educational standards, and cultural environment. This accounts for
the extreme fluctuations of opinion regarding beauty in general and beautiful things in particular, and this condition finds
expression in the oft-repeated phrase: There is no accounting
for tastes, *de gustibus non est disputandum*.

Nevertheless, the definition may be of service in acquiring
a fuller understanding and a deeper appreciation of beautiful

things when we experience the aesthetic pleasure which accompanies the contemplation of beauty. Perhaps St. Thomas' definition of the beautiful is after all the best: *Pulchra sunt quae visa placent,* 'things are beautiful which please when perceived.'

SUMMARY OF CHAPTER XV

Beauty is an elusive quality of things. Our experience of beauty must guide us in acquiring a proper conception of beauty.

1. *Our Experience of Beauty.* Beauty, as experience shows, gives a disinterested intellectual-sensuous pleasure due to the radiant perfection of a thing, primarily in so far as it exerts an appeal to our cognitive faculties and not to our appetitive faculties. "Things are beautiful which please when seen."

2. *Objective Elements of Beauty.* There are general and particular elements present in things called beautiful. The *general* elements are unity, truth, and goodness. Beauty, however, does not coincide completely with these transcendental attributes of being. Being and beauty are not convertible ideas. The *particular* elements of beauty are integrity or completeness, proportion or balance, clarity or splendor.

3. *The Definition of Beauty.* From the above, beauty can be defined as a blending of the unity, truth, and goodness in a thing, characterized by completeness, proportion, and clarity of presentation in an intellectual-sensuous form, so as to produce a distinterested emotional pleasure in a rational perceiver. Perhaps the definition of St. Thomas Aquinas is after all the best: "Things are beautiful which please when perceived (seen)."

READINGS

Coffey, P., Ch. VII; Rickaby, J., Bk. I, Ch. IV; Hugon, Ed., Tr. II, Qu. I, art. 8; Mercier, D. Card., *Ontologie,* nn. 266–282, *Manual,* pp. 564–570; McCormick, J. F., Ch. V, pp. 84–90.

PART III
THE SUPREME CATEGORIES

CHAPTER XVI

THE CATEGORIES

ONTOLOGY TREATS of being in its most general aspects. The various particular kinds of beings belong primarily to the special sciences; they are considered by ontology only in so far as they exhibit characteristics which pertain to being in general.

The first part of our investigation examined being and its primary determinations. This included an elucidation of the concept of being, the contraction of being to its inferiors, the supreme principles based on the concept of being, act and potency, change and the principle of change, and essence and existence. The second part treated of the transcendental attributes of being which are always present whenever being is present. These are the attributes of unity, truth, and goodness. Though different in concept from being as such, they are in reality identical with it.

In this third and last part of ontology we must investigate the different modes in which real being is found to be actualized and determined in nature. Since, however, philosophy is interested only in the 'ultimate' reasons, causes, and principles of things, ontology seeks to know the ultimate and *supreme modes of being*. This leads us to a consideration of the *categories* or *predicaments*.

THE CONCEPT OF THE CATEGORY

Aristotle coined the term 'category,' as it now is used in metaphysics. Originally, the term had application only in a court of law or in a forum (Gr., κατηγορεῖν, to accuse, charge, demonstrate, attribute; κατηγορία, accusation, attribution), and referred to the accusation or charge lodged against someone in a judicial tribunal. In making a charge, something is always attributed to the accused. Aristotle perceived a similarity between a court of law in its verdict and the mind in its act of judgment ('judgment,' as will be observed, is also a forensic term), in as much as the mind in its judging attributes something (the predicate) to another (the subject). The mind acts like a judge and passes judgment on the matter under consideration. Thus, when the mind states that 'Man is a rational animal,' it attributes the predicate 'rational animal' to the subject 'man,' and the result is a judgment and sentence. Due to this similarity of attribution in the judgment of the court and in the judgment of the mind, Aristotle transferred the term 'category' to philosophy and gave it a logical meaning, namely, the *logical attribution* of a predicate to a subject. In a technical and philosophic sense, then, Aristotle understood the categories to be the *supreme and ultimate genera or classes of predicates,* as found in our judgments and sentences. The philosopher *Boethius* translated the Greek term into the Latin *praedicamentum,* from which we derive the English term *predicament.* The term 'predicament' does not, of course, mean anything like a perplexing or embarrassing situation; it is used here in the technical meaning of a 'class of predicates.' 'Predicament' and 'category' are synonymous terms.

It will be noted that Aristotle employed the term 'category' or 'predicament' primarily in a *logical* sense, as a classification of the predicates used in our judgments. In as much as the predicates are direct, universal ideas applied to individual subjects, he considered the categories or predicaments to be the ultimate and supreme classes or groups of direct universal ideas. Taken in this sense, the categories belong to logic.[1] Aristotle, however, did not restrict the meaning of 'category' to this logical sense; he also used the term in an *ontological* sense, and that with just reason. Ideas stand for things, objects, beings; an idea is the intellectual representation of a thing. And that is also true of judgments; judgments represent facts

---

[1] See the author's *Science of Correct Thinking,* p. 49 ff.

about things. Ideas and judgments express *reality*. When we say that 'Air is transparent,' we do not merely wish to state that the idea 'transparent' is a predicate which the mind in its judgment attributes to the idea 'air' as a subject; we mean to state that 'transparency' is a physical quality which belongs in reality to the physical substance 'air' as it exists in nature, independent of the ideas and judgments of our mind. Ideas and judgments thus express things and facts about things.

Since our universal ideas represent real beings, the categories must be classifications of real beings just as well as they are classifications of universal ideas. Besides the *logical* meaning, we thus have also the *ontological* meaning of categories or predicaments: they are not only the ultimate and supreme classes of *predicates,* but also the ultimate and supreme classes of *beings.* And since 'being' is the proper subject matter of ontology, the categories must receive special treatment in this department of philosophy. From an ontological or metaphysical standpoint, then, the *categories* or *predicaments* are defined as the *ultimate and supreme modes of real being.* These modes are expressed in the predicates of our judgments, and these predicates attribute various 'modes of reality' to the things designated by the subjects; in this manner our judgments are an interpretation of reality and form the basis of true knowledge.

Consider, for instance, judgments like the following: 'This man is a *substance;* he is *white;* he is *five feet and eight inches tall;* he is the *father* of a two-year-old son; he *works* hard; he has been *injured;* he lives in *Chicago;* he was born in *A.D. 1900;* he owns a *beautiful home.'* Each one of these predicates expresses a mode of being or reality as it is found in this individual and gives us information about him. The items of information which could be predicated of an individual are incapable of complete enumeration, because they change and multiply from moment to moment. Something could be said about every single portion of his being during every single moment of his existence. The result would be a total confusion of ideas, unless order can be brought into this itemized information. To reduce this chaotic multiplicity of ideas about a thing to *order* and *system,* is the purpose of the categories. At the same time, the categories will arrange the manifold *modes of reality,* which determine a being, into the order and system of a few *supreme classes,* so that our mind is able to survey all reality from a few general viewpoints. This systematization and classification of real being will be a great aid to understanding and interpreting the things of this world.

This leads us naturally to the question: How many categories are there? Or, to put it in a different way: What are the supreme classes or modes of real being?

THE PRINCIPLE OF THE CATEGORIES

Since it is the purpose of the categories or predicaments to bring order and system into our knowledge of reality as we experience it in and around us, the number of categories should *be neither too small nor too large.* If too small, the categories would give us little aid in clarifying our knowledge, since too many divergent kinds of reality would be grouped under a single class. If too large, the categories would defeat their purpose, because the mind would be confused in contemplating a multitude of classes. Whatever the number, it should not be arbitrary, but natural, i.e., based on the things themselves as they are found in nature; the categories must be *natural divisions of the modes of being,* the result of observation and experience. Again, the categories must contain a *complete classification* of being. Every being and every determination of being must be reducible to the categories; they would fail in their function if any real being or mode of being would find no place in the system. Such are the requisites of a truly serviceable list of categories. Of course, if the nature of real being, as actually found in the world, would lead us to a very small or a very large number of categories, we could do nothing but accept them; in that case, however, we could derive little benefit from them.

The categories, then, possess a double purpose and function: the ultimate division and classification of our 'ideas,' and the ultimate division and classification of the 'modes of being.' This double purpose and function of the categories will show us the *principle of division* according to which we can arrive at the proper *number* of categories. Now, 'being' and its 'modes' can be found only in individual beings, since only individual beings can have actual existence. *Individual being,* therefore, is the basis and principle of all predication in our judgments; and it must, for that reason, also be the basis and *principle for the division* and number of the categories.

Because of this close connection between the different kinds of predicates and the different modes of being, the most natural method of discovering the proper number and order of categories will be to investigate the *fundamental questions* which can be asked about an individual being. The answers to these questions will give us the ultimate classes of predicates attributable to the subject, and these predicates will in turn give us the ultimate modes of being according to which the individual being is determined and actualized in nature. In this manner we arrive at the *ontological categories*.

The categories are a challenge to the ingenuity and resourcefulness of the philosopher. Aside from the fact that a list of categories is a working necessity for science and philosophy, the very difficulties involved in such a selective list have been a constant spur to the philosophers to devise a system of categories which will be both serviceable and correct.

THE CATEGORIES OF ARISTOTLE

Before the time of Aristotle, the problem of a list of categories does not seem to have occurred to the minds of the early philosophers. We find certain classifications of things, but they hardly deserve the name of 'categories.' Perhaps the closest approach to anything resembling the categories, as we understand them, was made by the Hindu philosopher *Kanâda* (sixth century B.C.). He enumerates six classes of existence:

substance, quality, action, genus, individuality, and concretion or co-inherence. The crudeness of this list is apparent. The *Pythagoreans* (sixth century B.C.) had a list of ten classes of opposites: light and darkness, one and many, good and evil, rest and movement, masculine and feminine, right and left, finite and infinite, even and odd, straight and curved, square and oblong. *Plato* made no attempt at an enumeration of categories, although he seems to divide all things into being, rest and motion, same and other.

The genius of *Aristotle* (384–322 B.C.) attacked the problem in a definite manner. He distinguishes *ten* distinct categories: substance (οὐσία) and nine accidents (συμβεβηκότα). The nine accidents are: quantity (ποσόν), quality (ποῖον), relation (πρὸς τι), action (ποιεῖν), passion or reaction (πάσχειν), where or place (ποῦ), when or time (ποτέ), posture (κεῖσθαι), habitus or external condition or state (ἔχειν). In the fourth chapter of his *Organon,* Aristotle enumerates them as follows: "Of things incomplex enunciated, each signifies either substance or quantity or quality or relation or where or when or position (posture) or possession (habitus) or action or passion. But substance is to speak generally, as 'man,' 'horse'; quantity, as 'two' or 'three cubits'; quality, as 'white'; relation, as 'greater'; where, as 'in the forum'; when, as 'yesterday'; position, as 'he sits'; possession, as 'he is shod'; action, as 'he cuts'; passion, as 'he burns.' " Each of these ten categories expresses an attribute that can be predicated of a subject, and as such also represents some distinct mode of being which can be found in an individual. Each category is an answer to a question that can be asked about a thing. In order to understand properly this list of supreme modes of being, a brief explanation of the single categories may not be amiss.

Substance is any being which exists in itself, needing no other as a subject in which to exist. Examples: man, lion, tree, stone. It is the answer to the question: 'Who or what is this thing?' For instance: 'The oak is a *plant;* iron is a *metal.*'

Quantity is an attribute of the material (determinable) element in a being; extension, number. Examples: weight, size. It is an answer to the question: 'How big or how much is it?' For instance: 'The pole is *ten feet long;* it weighs one hundred *pounds.'*

Quality is an attribute of the formal (determining) element in a being. Examples: intelligence, strength, health, warmth, color, faculties of body and mind. It is an answer to the question: 'What sort of thing is it?' For instance: 'The rose is *red;* man is *intelligent.'*

Relation is the bearing of one being to another, a bond connecting concepts or things. Examples: paternity, equality, superiority, likeness. It is an answer to the question: 'To what or whom does it refer?' For instance: 'He is *older,* or younger, than —; the two are *equals.'*

Action is the production of an effect in another; it is expressed by the active, transitive verb. Examples: painting, baking, shooting, sawing. It is an answer to the question: 'What does it do?' For instance: 'The dog is *gnawing* a bone; the man *drives* his car.'

Passion (reaction) is the reception of an effect from another, in the sense of 'bearing, enduring, suffering, receiving, being acted on'; it is expressed by the passive voice of the transitive verb. Examples: being heated, being killed. It is an answer to the question: 'What is happening to it?' For instance: 'The anchor is *dropped;* the man is *shot.'*

When is situation in time. Examples: today, tomorrow, soon, in the beginning. It is an answer to the question: 'When, at what point of time?' For instance: 'He was there *last year;* the ship is docking *now;* the train will arrive in *five minutes.'*

Where is position in space. Examples: upstairs, in the country, on the table, at home. It is an answer to the question: 'Where is it?' For instance: 'He is *downtown;* he lives *in New York;* the book is *on the shelf.'*

Posture is the disposition of parts among themselves, in the sense of 'attitude'; immanent or intransitive action expressed

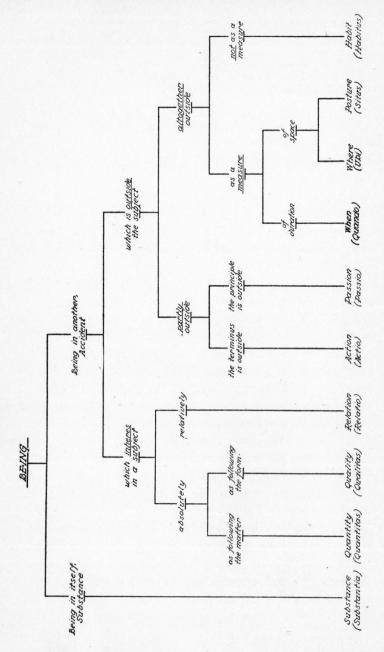

by an intransitive verb. Examples: walking, sitting, upright, standing, sideways, flat. It is an answer to the question: 'In what attitude?' For instance: 'The tower is *leaning;* the dog is *running;* the tree lies *prone* on the ground.'

Habitus is the condition resulting from clothing, equipment, physical adjuncts; or a condition or state, expressed by the reflexive verb. Examples: clothed, shod, hatted; praising one's self, hurting one's self. It is an answer to the question: 'How surrounded, equipped; how conditioned?' For instance: 'He *wears gloves;* he is *disgusted with himself.*'

In surveying this list, it is but natural to ask what *line of reasoning* Aristotle used so as to arrive at this particular number. We do not know. Nowhere in his writings does he explain his method of selection. Again, *must* there be just *ten* categories? Aristotle himself at times omits one or the other from his enumeration.[2] He gives the impression that he was not always sure in his own mind as to the necessity of this exact number. Eventually, however, he seems to have settled definitely on the list as given previously. Since Aristotle does not give us his reasons for this classification of the supreme categories, other philosophers have attempted to show that they are *grounded in nature* and have a foundation in things as we experience them; they have, then, objective value and are not the result of an arbitrary arrangement or of an *a priori* deduction. St. Thomas Aquinas offers the following explanation[3] for the Aristotelian categories:

Being either exists in itself, without inhering in a subject, and then it is *substance;* or being merely affects and modifies a substance, and then it is an *accident.* Accidents modify a substance intrinsically or extrinsically. Among those accidents which affect a substance 'intrinsically,' some may inhere in the substance relatively, and then we have *relation.* Others may inhere in the substance absolutely; if such an absolute accident follows the matter of the physical substance, we have *quan-*

---

[2] For instance, in his *Physics,* Bk. V, Ch. I, 225b, he omits posture and habitus.
[3] *In Metaph.,* lib. 5, lect. 9.

tity, and if it follows the form, we have *quality.* Among those accidents which affect a substance 'extrinsically,' some are partly extrinsic and others are altogether extrinsic. Among the 'partly extrinsic' modifications, the term of activity may be outside the substance, with the principle of activity within the substance, and then we have *action;* or the principle of activity may be outside, with the term of activity within the substance, and then we have *passion* or reaction. Among those accidents which are 'altogether extrinsic' modifications, some will affect the substance as a measure of its duration, and then we have *time;* or they will affect it as a measure of its place in space or as a measure of the disposition of its parts relative to themselves and to space, and then have either *place* or *posture.* Other 'altogether extrinsic' modifications are not a measure of the substance at all, but merely affect it as belonging to its surroundings and conditions, and then we have *habitus.* The diagram on page 228 gives a schematic arrangement according to the ideas of St. Thomas.

This searching analysis shows that Aristotle was justified in drawing up his list of ten categories. They flow naturally from the very concept of being. The number is neither too small nor too large; and the compactness and complexity, the unity and flexibility of the list is such that it is serviceable for all practical purposes. It establishes order in our knowledge, by giving us a systematization and classification of the ideas attributable as predicates to the subjects in our judgments and of the various modes of being attributable to individual things as they occur in our experience. The Aristotelian categories have been accepted through the centuries, with some exceptions, as the finest set devised by the mind of man. In general, the scholastic philosophers of the Middle Ages and of modern times have embodied them in their system without alteration.

Some philosophers, as must be expected, are not altogether satisfied with the ten categories of Aristotle. They claim that some of them are not mutually exclusive and irreducible. Causal change, for instance, viewed from the standpoint of the agent, is 'action,' and viewed from the standpoint of the recipient, is 'passion' or 'reaction'; action and passion are thus only two phases of one and the same process. While this is true enough, it must not be overlooked that in most cases the agent and the recipient are two really distinct entities, and the causal change affects each one differently; there is reason, then, for making the distinction. In a real sense, too, 'quantity' enters into the concept of 'time,' 'place,' and 'posture.' Nevertheless, there is a difference in these concepts, and this difference seems large enough to warrant the placing of these ideas and modes of being in the list as separate categories. Even though only a *logical,* and not a real, *distinction* exists between some of these concepts, that should be sufficient, as long as there is a *foundation in the things themselves* for making the distinction. A 'real' distinction hardly seems required, because it is the purpose and function of the categories to classify 'being,' not in an absolute sense, but according to the various modes in which it is attributable to some individual and according to the various ideas as predicated in our judgments. We must remember that Aristotle intended the categories to be primarily a system of *concepts* (universal ideas), and here a distinction in concepts suffices to list them as separate categories; only secondarily, in as much as concepts represent modes of being, did he intend them to be *ontological* categories. Hence, a logical distinction between the various categories, as long as there is a foundation for the distinction in reality itself, should suffice to give them a separate standing in the list.

In modern times, various attempts have been made to improve or supplant the categories of Aristotle. None were successful. The most ambitious of these substitutes are the categories of Kant. The objections against the categories of Aristotle are not of enough weight to offset the eminently practical division of all beings in the world as exemplified in this classification. Besides, tradition has sanctioned their use to such an extent that they have become almost an integral part of our language and mode of thought.

THE CATEGORIES OF KANT

Emmanuel Kant (1724–1804) sought to stem the tide of phenomenalism and skepticism which was running strong in his day, due to the philosophy of Hume. Kant's philosophy ended in a phenomenalism even worse than Hume's. It is not within the province of ontology to give an exposition of Kant's principles; that belongs to epistemology.[4] Suffice it to say, that he distinguishes between things-in-themselves and their phenomena. The things-in-themselves, or noumena, are the objects in the real world, independent of our thinking; but of these the mind can know absolutely nothing. The noumena excite our sensibility into action, and the result of this action is the production of phenomena or sense-intuitions through the subjective, innate sense-forms of 'space' and 'time.' These phenomena are the only things we can know, but they bear no resemblance to the things-in-themselves. The subjective forms of 'space' and 'time' are *a priori* present in the mind, anterior to all experience, and it is through them that experience becomes possible.

In order to obtain *intellectual knowledge,* our intuitions or phenomena must be brought under certain concepts or *categories* of the understanding; only in this manner can these intuitions become intelligible to us. The 'categories,' just like 'space' and 'time,' are subjective, innate, *a priori* forms of the understanding, and they must be united to the phenomena in order to make judgment and thought possible. These categories, therefore, are not derived from experience in any way; they are given with the mind itself and proceed from the mind. The things-in-themselves do not prompt the mind to form judgments about things by means of these categories. The application of the categories to the representations contained in the phenomena is altogether the action of a *subjective law* of the mind, and the resultant judgments tell us nothing about

---

[4] See the author's *Reality and the Mind*, p. 108 ff., and 272 ff.

the things-in-themselves and their modes of being; the latter are forever excluded from our knowledge.

Such is, in brief, Kant's doctrine of the categories. There are *twelve categories,* and for each there is a specific type of judgment. They are:

Categories	Judgments	Example
Quantity:	Quantity:	
(1) Unity	(1) Singular	This S is P
(2) Plurality	(2) Particular	Some S is P
(3) Totality	(3) Universal	All S is P
Quality:	Quality:	
(4) Affirmation	(4) Affirmative	S is P
(5) Negation	(5) Negative	S is not P
(6) Limitation	(6) Infinite	S is not-P
Relation:	Relation:	
(7) Substantiality	(7) Categorical	S is P
(8) Causality	(8) Hypothetical	If A is B, S is P
(9) Reciprocity	(9) Disjunctive	S is either P or Q
Modality:	Modality:	
(10) Possibility	(10) Problematic	S may be P
(11) Existence	(11) Assertoric	S is P
(12) Necessity	(12) Apodictic	S must be P

A glance at these Kantian categories will reveal the difference between them and the Aristotelian categories. The difference is fundamental and essential. The Kantian categories are *a priori mental forms,* absolutely independent of, and anterior to, all experience and the knowledge derived from experience. The Aristotelian categories are supposed to classify our knowledge of *reality* as it exists outside the mind and as it is acquired through experience.

The Kantian categories have value *only for the mind* and its subjective operations. They merely bring the sense-intuitions or phenomena into a scheme of unity and give them necessity

and universality. Since, however, the sense-intuitions or phenomena contain only knowledge which is purely subjective in
character and does not reach to the noumena or things-in-
themselves, the categories cannot tell us anything about the
noumenal reality which lies outside and beyond the mind.
Hence, the Kantian categories are not supreme classes of universal ideas and modes of being, but classes of *judgment-forms*
and *modes of mental relations.* These categories give us no information about the objective content of the predicates or of
the modes of being present in the things-in-themselves.

Kant calls these mental forms 'categories,' but the term is a
misnomer. The notion of 'category' was clearly defined by
Aristotle, and the term thereby acquired a definite technical
meaning. This meaning had been accepted in the sense given
by Aristotle for a period of over two thousand years and as
such became fixed and traditional in the history of philosophy.
For Kant, then, to use the term 'category' in the way he did,
amounted to a distortion and falsification of philosophic language. This was unwarranted and unjustifiable, because the
new meaning attached to the term 'category' was bound to
produce a confusion of ideas. Aristotle and Kant simply do not
mean the same thing, when they speak of 'categories.' As such,
therefore, Kant's categories must be rejected as *arbitrary.* In no
way can they be considered a satisfactory substitute for the
categories of Aristotle.

Following the subjectivistic trend of Kant's philosophy,
modern theories of knowledge are more or less phenomenalistic or idealistic. Quite naturally, these theories of knowledge
affect the entire outlook on the external world. Many scientists
and philosophers contend that we can know only the *appearances* of things, without being able to penetrate to the real
nature of things. Notions like 'substance,' 'causal action and
reaction,' 'time,' 'space and place,' and so forth, are undergoing
radical changes. In consequences of such views the Aristotelian
categories no longer carry the same meaning for many thinkers
of our day as they did in times gone by. What the final out-

come of these tendencies will be, no one can foretell. Up to the present, however, the categories of Aristotle can still be considered the best classification of the modes of being, and it is unlikely that they will be superseded.

PLACEMENT IN THE CATEGORIES

All things and modes of being must belong under some category, and it must be possible to place them there. This does not mean that all things and modes of beings, *as we conceive them in thought,* can be brought under a category directly. Due to the abstractive power of our mind, we often separate things in our thought which are united in reality and combine things in our thought which are not united in reality. Hence, it happens that we frequently conceive things to be different than they really are, and this difference is manifested in our concepts and language. The 'family,' for instance, is considered as a unit in our concept, but in physical reality it consists of individual, really distinct beings. This general fact must be borne in mind, when we attempt to place something under a definite category. Philosophers, therefore, distinguish three different ways in which something may be placed in a category: *directly, indirectly,* and *reductively.*

In order that something fall under a category *directly,* a number of conditions are required. First of all, it must be a *real being.* It is the purpose of the categories to classify the modes of being which determine an 'individual being,' and it is only a 'real' being that can be an individual being. It is not necessary that a being actually exist, in order to be 'real,' because a possible or potential being is also 'real.' An actual or possible being belongs directly under a category; but a conceptual or logical being does not, because such a being is not a thing that can, as such, have reality except in the mind. Concepts like 'vacuum,' 'illness,' 'blindness,' 'paralysis,' etc., cannot be brought directly under a category; but concepts like 'man,' 'stone,' 'water,' 'iron,' 'body,' etc., are brought directly under a category.

Another condition demands that a thing must be, not an accidental, but a *natural unit* in its being; it must be a single essence, either simple (e.g., a pure spirit) or compound (e.g., a man). The reason for this condition is that what is not a natural unit in its being contains parts which may fall under more than one category. This condition excludes *collective* ideas, like 'family,' 'army,' 'flock,' 'library,' etc.; *complex* ideas, like 'paleface,' 'historian,' 'yellow orange,' 'black cat,' etc.; and *concrete adjectives* used as substantives, like 'sage,' 'American,' 'Indian,' etc. There is a double element in every such concept which hinders it from belonging to a single category. Thus, the term 'historian' involves two distinct concepts: a 'man' (category: substance) who has a 'knowledge of history' (category: quality). But orange, man, dog, cat, water, wood, etc., are things with a natural unity in their physical being, as expressed by the concept itself, and they fall directly under the category of 'substance.' When, however, accidents are taken *abstractly,* like 'whiteness,' 'philosophy,' 'history,' 'warmth,' 'paleness,' etc., they belong directly to a category, because in such cases the concepts express only a single element or essence.

Furthermore, for direct placement in a category, a thing must be a *complete being,* and not a mere part of another being. We consider things here principally as they do, or can, exist as individuals. This condition excludes all *integral* parts of things, such as hands, feet, head, wings, heart, etc.; all *substantial* parts, like matter and form, body and soul; the *generic* element (e.g., 'sentiency,' in man) and *specific difference* (e.g., 'rationality,' in man), taken by themselves; and *modifications of accidents* (for instance, the 'intensity' of heat, the 'pitch' of sound, the 'voltage' of electricity, etc.). Complete beings, like man, horse, tree, gold, fish, bird, etc., are placed directly under a category.

Finally, only *finite beings* can be brought directly under a category. Only things, in which the term 'being' is used *univocally,* are predicamentally alike and belong together in the same category. It would be a case of logical violence to place

God and creatural beings together in the same class of 'substance,' because the distance which separates the infinite from the finite is immeasurable. The concept of 'being' or 'substance,' as applied to God and creature, is not univocal, but analogical. God is indeed a 'substance,' but a substance infinitely superior in every way to the substantiality of His creatures and as such infinitely beyond the category of creatural substance. The categories apply to beings of the *same order* only; consequently, they must be restricted to beings in the finite universe. God belongs to no category.

Such are the conditions for direct placement in the scheme of categories. Although not all realities can be brought directly under a category, they can be brought under them either *indirectly* or *reductively*. The differences which distinguish the *genera* and *species* of substances fall 'indirectly' under the category of 'substance.' Such would be concepts like 'rationality,' 'sentiency,' 'vegetancy,' 'materiality,' and 'spirituality.' *Parts* of things, beings with an *accidental* or *artificial unity,* and also *logical entities,* are brought 'reductively' under their corresponding categories. Thus, 'hands,' 'feet,' etc., 'family,' 'army,' etc., 'sage,' 'American,' etc., belong to the category of 'substance'; the 'intensity' of heat, the 'pitch' of sound, etc., to 'quality'; 'blindness,' 'illness,' 'paralysis,' 'toothache,' etc., to 'quality'; 'mathematical point,' 'curve,' triangularity etc., to 'quantity.'

It might be asked: Why are not the nine categories, distinct from the category of 'substance,' placed under the *common genus of 'accident,'* so that there would be but two supreme categories, namely, *substance* and *accident?* For one reason, the number would be too small, and the system of categories would no longer be serviceable in this abbreviated form. It would still be necessary to subdivide 'accident' into the other nine, in order to introduce a proper differentiation among the various concepts and modes of being. Besides, the concept of 'accident' cannot be said to apply univocally to the nine modes of being characterized by the various categories. An accident is defined as a being which needs a subject (substance) in which to inhere in order to exist. The common element in all accidents is that they 'inhere' in a substance. But this 'inhesion' is quite different in the various types of accidents. 'Thinking' and 'willing,' for instance, confer a distinct and new entity upon man; but 'place' and 'time' cannot be said to do that. Hence, the concept 'accident' applies only *analogically* to the various modes of being expressed by these nine categories. In that case 'accident' is not a true genus, and it is better to retain the separate standing of each category. However, even though one were to consider 'accident' a true genus, with a univocal application to everything that is not a substance, the practical purpose of the categories would still demand their separate enumeration.

After this general explanation it should be fairly obvious that the Aristotelian categories form a valuable framework for the classification of our knowledge of being and its modes.

SUMMARY OF CHAPTER XVI

The third part of ontology will treat of the ultimate and supreme modes of being. These are the *categories* or *predicaments*.

1. *Concept of the Category.* Aristotle changed the term 'category' from an expression in a court of law to a technical expression of philosophy and used it in the *logical* meaning of a supreme class of predicates in our judgments. Since, however, the predicates represent reality, he also gave the categories an *ontological* meaning. The ontological categories are the *ultimate and supreme modes of real being*.

2. *Principle of the Categories.* The number of categories must be neither too small nor too large; they must be natural divisions of the modes of being; and they must contain a complete classification. Since they are the supreme classes of the modes of being, and since 'being' and the 'modes of being' can be found only in individual beings, *individual being* must be the principle for the division and number of the categories.

3. *The Categories of Aristotle.* Aristotle distinguishes *ten categories:* substance, quantity, quality, relation, action, passion, place, time, posture, and habitus.

4. *The Categories of Kant.* Kant's so-called 'categories' are not categories in the accepted and traditional sense. They are *judgment-forms* and *modes of mental relations.* They are innate mental forms which tell us nothing about noumenal reality or things-in-themselves, since, according to Kant, our knowledge is restricted to phenomena, and phenomena are only subjective constructs of the mind.

5. *Placement in the Categories.* All beings and modes of being can be placed in the categories either directly, indirectly, or reductively. For a *direct* placement the following conditions must be observed: the thing to be placed must be a 'real' being; it must be a 'natural unit' in its being; it must be a 'complete' being; it must be a 'finite' being. *Indirectly,* the differences which distinguish genera and species fall under a category. *Reductively,* parts of things, beings with an accidental or artificial unity, and logical entities are brought under categories.

READINGS

Aristotle, *Categories;* Urráburu, J. J., Disp. IV, cp. II; Coffey, P., Ch. VIII; Pesch, Tilmann, nn. 1433–1454; Osgniach, Augustine J., *The Analysis of Objects,* Ch. I, II, III.

Chapter XVII

SUBSTANCE AND ACCIDENT

HAVING EXAMINED the general nature of the category and the reasons underlying its division into ten, we must now turn our attention to the single categories. The first and most important of these is *substance*. The other nine can, in a broad sense, be placed under the common heading of *accident,* for whatever is not a 'substance' is classified as an 'accident.' The division of all beings into 'substances' and 'accidents' is traditional in philosophy, but this tradition must be justified and cannot be taken for granted without proper proof. It is the duty of the ontologist to investigate the matter and furnish the reasons which prompt philosophers to divide all things in this manner.

CONCEPT OF SUBSTANCE AND ACCIDENT

A *substance* is a *being whose nature it is to exist in itself and not in another as in a subject.* An *accident* is a *being whose nature it is to exist in another as in a subject.* In order to obtain a better understanding of these definitions and of the nature of substance and accident, it will be necessary to analyze them somewhat more in detail.

From the *logical* standpoint of experience and knowledge, we first come to know the accidents of quantity, quality, and activity of things: namely, size, shape, weight, color, heat, odor, flavor, motion, growth, and similar realities. Then, observing the relative permanence and identity of the thing, notwithstanding the manifold modifications and changes which occur in it, we come to know the underlying subject or substance. The substance, therefore, is conceived as being the underlying subject or support (Lat., *substantia, sub-stans,* from *substare,* to stand under, bear, support) of the accidents, while not being supported in its being and existence by another. The accident (Lat., *accidens,* from *ad* and *cadere,* to fall to or upon, to rest on) is conceived as being something which requires a subject to inhere in, so that it has the necessary support for its being and existence, because it cannot exist except in another being. From the *ontological* standpoint of being and existence, the substance is first and the accident follows, because the accident is only a modification of the substance and therefore presupposes the presence of the substance before it can itself have being and existence in the substance.

A substance, then, is a being which possesses sufficient entity of its own to exist independently, so that it does not exist in another as *in a subject* which must support it in existence. The meaning is: Among beings and realities existing in the universe, substances are mutually independent beings, each capable of existing in itself as a self-contained thing, without the need of another being in which it must inhere in order to have existence. Shape and size, for instance, exist in man as in a subject; but man himself is an ultimate thing which does not again exist in something else.

We may look at 'substance' in two ways: as a thing in itself, and as a support of accidents. Obviously, the *primary* concept of substance is that it is a *thing in itself;* it is a secondary concept to consider it as a subject of modifying accidents. It is but natural that a thing must be something *in itself* before it can be something *for others.* Even if it had no modifying accidents at all, it would have its own entity and as such would be a true substance, because it would still be a thing existing in itself. In this manner God, who has no accidents in His being, is a substance *par excellence,* because He already possesses in the infinite perfection of His substance whatever entity accidents could possibly confer upon Him. Accidents necessarily presuppose the concept of 'substance,' but substances do not postulate the concept of 'accident.' Consequently, we do not define 'substance' as the subject of accidents, but as a being whose nature it is to exist in itself and not in another as in a subject.

The *accident* is defined as a being whose nature it is to exist in another as in a subject. The categorical accident always presupposes a subject of which it is a modification, and this subject is ultimately a substance. 'Ultimately'; because it would be erroneous to think that every accident must inhere immediately in the substance. One accident may inhere *in another accident* as in its *direct* subject; shape, for example, is an accident directly modifying quantity, and quantity is an accident directly modifying a material substance, so that shape modifies the substance only indirectly. Ultimately, of course, shape modifies the substance and must inhere in the substance as its fundamental subject and support.

Every accident demands inherence in a substance. However, one must avoid a too crude conception of this *inhesion*. Accidents are not a sort of outside coating or covering for the substance, nor are they to be considered as foreign and extraneous realities attached to the substance or permeating its being. Accidents are rather *determinations* and *differentiations* of the determinable and indifferent substance. The substance has certain *potentialities* which demand development and actualization, and the accidents are the *actualizations* of these potentialities. To give some examples. The human soul possesses an intellect, but the intellect needs the determination of active 'thinking' in order to become actualized; this active 'thinking' is, therefore, a perfecting accident of the intellect. Man also has the power or potentiality of sense-perception, but this potentiality must be actualized before it can be of any use to man; this actualization takes place in the acts of sight, touch, hearing, etc., and these acts of sensation are accidents which bring the power of perception to its natural completion. Thus all accidents are a fuller realization of the substances which they modify.

The definition of accident was formulated in such a manner that it was said to be 'a being whose *nature* it is to inhere, etc.' It was advisedly not stated to be a 'being *which inheres* in another.' Strictly speaking, it is not essential to an accident to *actually* inhere in another as in a subject. Science and philosophy, it is true, know of no case where accidents exist outside their substance. Nevertheless, the essence of an accident would still be the same, and an accident would always remain an accident, even if it were to exist outside its subject, provided its *nature* requires that it normally exist in a substance. To exist outside its subject would indeed be an abnormal condition for an accident. This, however, would not change its essence, because it would retain the *natural necessity* and *aptitude* to inhere in a subject. It could never lose this ordination toward its substance. The essence of an accident naturally demands inhesion and this demand would accompany it even outside its subject; it would, therefore, never become 'substantialized' by the mere fact of being detached from its substance.[1] Hence, this 'aptitudinal inherence' is an essential characteristic of an accident, but the 'actual inherence' is only a normal condition for it; God's omnipotence could detach an accident from its substance without destroying its essence.

KINDS OF SUBSTANCE

Substance can be viewed from different standpoints. A number of divisions of substance can be made, each representing a different *kind* of substance. We will now examine the main classes.

Primary and Secondary Substance. For a proper understanding of this division of substances, we must go back to the days of Plato and Aristotle. *Plato* (427 or 428 to about 348

---

[1] This distinction between *actual* and *aptitudinal* inherence of an accident in its substance is of great importance in the doctrine of the Holy Eucharist, where the accidents of shape, color, extension, etc., are deprived of the natural support of the bread-substance and wine-substance after consecration and are preserved by divine power outside any substance. Because of the natural aptitude and exigency of inhesion, they are still 'accidents' and do not become 'substances.'

B.C.) made a serious attempt to account for the universality and necessity of our scientific knowledge. Since our scientific knowledge is supposed to be universal and necessary in its scope, it must be a true representation of *reality;* as such, then, the reality, from which our knowledge is derived and which our knowledge represents, should itself be 'universal' and 'necessary.' Plato could find no such universal and necessary realities anywhere in the physical world as we observe it: all things are individual, not universal; and they are not necessary, but in a continuous process of generation and dissolution. The things of this world, therefore, Plato contended, cannot be the reason for the universality and necessity of our knowledge. Since, however, the 'concepts' or 'ideas' of our mind represent the essence of things, he concluded that the 'concept' or *Idea* is the only reality which is permanent and unchangeable. The Idea must, then, be the very essence of the reality of 'being' and of the reality of scientific 'knowledge.' Such Ideas would have to be universal and necessary, existing independently for themselves, apart from the concrete things in the world and from the concepts of our mind; they would be the patterns or exemplars according to which these concrete things and our concepts are fashioned. The physical objects would be faint copies of these Ideas, and our concepts would be intellectual copies of these same Ideas. These Ideas exist in a world of their own as essences and substances, unchangeable and eternal. Hence, these *Ideas* are the *primary substances* and the *individual substances* are *secondary substances.*

Aristotle attacked Plato's 'world of Ideas' as fanciful, poetic, and superfluous. He contended, and rightly, that we derive our universal ideas of things from our observation of the *things themselves,* not from a contemplation of eternally existing Ideas. When we form the universal idea 'man' as applicable to the whole class of men and to every individual man, we do so through a process of mental abstraction; we leave aside the individuating characteristics which differentiate one individual man from another and select ('abstract') those elements which all individual men have in common with each other. In this manner we arrive at the universal idea of 'man' or of a 'rational animal'; it applies to all men as a class (e.g., *'Man* is mortal') and to each individual man (e.g., *'This man* is mortal'). Aristotle is correct in his view that we derive our universal ideas through abstraction from individuals.[2] The concept 'man,' therefore, applies primarily to the individual human being and only secondarily to the species or class. Therefore, the *individual* ('this man') is the *primary substance,* and the substance expressed by the *universal idea* ('man' in general, as a species or class) is a *secondary substance.*[3]

Every individual substance is a primary substance: every single inanimate body (every bit of gold, paper, wood, air, etc.), every single plant (every rose, elm, bush, grapevine, etc.), every single animal (every dog, elephant, etc.) and every single man (Washington, Napoleon, Lincoln, etc.). *All universal ideas,* representing substance as a class, are secondary substances: man, animal, organism, body, substance, plant, fish, bird, etc., taken as a species or genus.

Complete and Incomplete Substances. All primary substances are either complete or incomplete. A substance is *complete* when it exists in such a manner that its nature demands no further union with a substantial co-principle. When a substance is complete, it possesses everything that its constitution and essence requires for its existence and for the proper functioning of its natural activities. Thus, every human being, consisting of body and soul, is a complete substance, capable of existing and of performing its natural functions of vegetancy, sentiency, and rational life; in like manner, every brute, plant, and inorganic body are complete substances.

A substance is *incomplete* when its nature demands that it be conjoined with some other substantial co-principle, so as to constitute a complete substance. Each substantial part or principle, taken alone, would be insufficient to exist, or, at least,

---

[2] See the author's *Reality and the Mind,* Ch. XIII, XIV.
[3] *Categories,* 5.

would be insufficient for all the functions of an individual of that particular species. It must be borne in mind that we are speaking of *substantial parts,* not of accidents. Thus, man's soul alone, without his body, could not perform the functions of vegetancy and sentiency (for example, digestion and sight) which functions are also natural operations for man; man needs a material body for them. Neither could man's body alone, without the soul, perform the functions of thinking and willing; man needs an intellectual soul for them. Hence, body and soul, each considered alone and in itself, are incomplete substances; they are substantial parts or co-principles which must be united into a single whole, in order to make a compound nature capable of all the functions proper to it.

A substance may be *incomplete* in two ways; in the line of 'substantiality' or in the line of 'specific perfection.' It is incomplete in the line of *substantiality,* when it cannot perform *any* functions of the complete substance *alone;* it must always be united with its substantial co-principle. In this way, the brute soul and plant soul cannot exist outside the matter which they inform and cannot, therefore, be active in any manner unless united with matter; the functions of these types of being are such that they are dependent on matter at all times for their existence. Matter, the other co-principle, is incapable of performing any activity of its own, because it is altogether indeterminate and cannot exist except in conjunction with a substantial form or soul. Matter and form are the two substantial co-principles which unite to constitute a bodily substance; and in every bodily substance below the level of man these substantial co-principles are incomplete in the line of substantiality.

A substance is incomplete in the line of *specific perfection,* if it can, when alone, perform *some* but *not all* activities proper to the complete substance. Thus, the human soul, being spiritual (as will be shown in rational psychology), can survive the dissolution of the body and in this disembodied condition perform some functions proper to man, for instance, thinking and willing. This is possible because such functions are spiritual and as such intrinsically independent of matter. Other operations, however, like nutrition and sense-perception, demand the participation of bodily organs and cannot be performed by the soul alone. Man, as man, though, must be able to perform all three types of activities — vegetancy, sentiency, and rationality. Hence, man's soul is complete in the line of 'substantiality,' because it is independent of the body in its existence; but it is incomplete in the line of 'specific perfection,' because it cannot perform *all* human operations independent of the body.

Simple and Composite Substances. All complete substances are either 'simple' or 'composite' in their nature. They are *simple,* when they do *not* consist of entitatively distinct *substantial parts.* Such simple substances are called *pure spirits,* for instance, angels or God. Complete substances of this kind are 'absolutely simple.' However, one can speak of certain substances as 'naturally simple' in a wider sense of the term 'simple.' By 'naturally simple' substances one would then understand substances which consist of parts which are material and entitatively distinct, but naturally indivisible and inseparable. The ultimate physical components of the universe (perhaps protons and electrons) would be 'naturally simple' in this sense; and also, according to the view of some aristotelian-scholastic philosophers, the forms or souls of plants and animals.

A *composite substance* is a complete substance consisting of incomplete *substantial parts,* entitatively distinct among themselves, in such a manner that their union results in a single, *unified nature.* In a composite substance neither of the incomplete part-substances inheres in the other as in a subject of inhesion; they complement each other, making a single principle of natural functions through their union. Man, for instance, is a composite substance consisting of body and soul. The soul does not inhere in the body, as an accident inheres in its subject; nor does the body inhere in the soul. Neither do soul and body merely co-exist side by side, as if each were independent of the other in its functioning. Soul and body form a natural unit, a *single nature,* so that man is not two things, but *one substance;* in consequence of this substantial composition man, as a unit, is capable of spiritual and material vital activities. Our consciousness testifies to the fact that we are not two things or substances, but one. Man, therefore, is a composite substance. So, too, is every animal and plant; they possess not only chemical and physical properties and activities, but also properties and activities which are immanent and therefore vital. Whether chemical elements (e.g., radium, helium, hydrogen, oxygen, etc.) and chemical compounds (e.g., water, carbohydrates, carbon monoxide, etc.) are composite substances with a single substantial form, is a mooted question. The theory of matter and form (hylomorphism) belongs properly to cosmology and will be treated there.

Every composite substance is, then, a *substantial unit* (*unum per se*), not an accidental unit (*unum per accidens*). A thing is said to be an 'accidental unit,' when it consists of two or more complete substances collaborating in a unified combination and action, while each component retains its substantial entity in the arrangement of the whole. A few examples will clarify this notion. A 'hive' of bees is a unit; since, however, each bee remains a complete substance in itself, a colony of bees is only an accidental unit. Soldiers and officers form an 'army' with a unified action; but an 'army' is only an accidental unit, because the soldiers and officers are obviously not merged into a single substance and nature. The difference between such an 'accidental unit' and a man or an animal or a plant as a 'substantial unit' is evident: the compound of body and soul in man and animal and plant is such that they are a single principle of action, a single nature, a single substance; their functions proceed from the *whole* as a *unit,* and that 'whole' is not accidental or artificial, but substantial and natural.

KINDS OF ACCIDENTS

Accidents, like substances, can be viewed from different standpoints and classified accordingly. The following are the main *kinds* of accidents.

Relative and Absolute Accidents. By 'relation' we mean the bearing which one thing has to another. There are always two terms to a relation: the 'relative' or thing relating, and the 'correlative' or thing related to. A *relative accident,* therefore, is an accident that has its being in a subject only because of the *bearing* which one thing has to another. More will be said about relative accidents in a subsequent chapter.

An *absolute accident,* on the other hand, is one that confers a *real perfection* upon its subject. *Extension* or quantitative dimension is such an accident. To be 'large' or 'small' is a matter of comparison with another object, but no object can be styled 'large' or 'small' in any sense unless it inherently possesses quantitative dimensions *in itself,* so that it can be compared with the quantitative dimensions of other objects. It is because of such dimensions (extension) that a body occupies space, is measurable, and can be divided; but all this presupposes parts beside parts in the object. Such parts are a real perfection for a thing. Again, *qualities* are absolute accidents. The potential energy of physical bodies; the power of nutrition, growth, and reproduction in plants; the faculties of sensation in the various sense-organs of an animal; intellect and will in man: all these things are a perfection for these respective substances. Furthermore, *activities* are absolute accidents. The physical actions of bodies as effected through kinetic energy, the vital functions of plant, animal, and man — these are accidents which confer perfection upon the substance performing these activities. When we walk, digest, see, hear, feel, think, and will, our nature actualizes its powers and acquires perfection thereby.

Strictly Absolute and Modal Accidents. There are two kinds of absolute accidents: strictly absolute and modal. A *strictly absolute accident* is one which affects a substance in such a manner that it actually confers upon it some *positive* and *new entity*. Such an accident, though it inheres in a substance and needs the substance as a support for its existence, possesses an entity of its own, distinct from the entity of the substance. Such would be the various types of accidents mentioned above in the preceding paragraph.

A *modal accident* or accidental mode is the definite *disposition* or *determination* of an indifferent and determinable entity, without conferring any positive and new entity upon the substance. It is something real, but it does not possess any entity of its own, distinct from the entity of the substance itself. Shape, being in motion or rest, being in time (quandocation) and place (ubication), and posture belong to this class.

Such modes are something *real;* they are not 'nothing,' nor are they logical entities existing only in the mind. It makes a difference in the real order, whether a thing have this or that shape, whether it be at rest or in motion, whether the motion be straight or curved, whether it be in a high or a low place, whether its movements occur today or tomorrow, whether it have this or that posture. These modes *change* in the real order of things, and that shows that they are neither 'nothing' nor a mere logical entity.

Intrinsic and Extrinsic Accidents. Intrinsic accidents are such as affect the *being* of the subject in some way or other; as such they are internally united to the subject and modify it entitatively. Absolute accidents are of this kind. The quantity of a 'body' as manifested in its three dimensions of length, breadth, and depth, is a positive accidental entity affecting the being of the material body. All qualities, whether material or spiritual, have the same character. All actions of bodies, immanent as well as transient, also belong to this class of accidents.

The case of *extrinsic accidents* is very different: they are accidents which do *not* affect the *being* of their subject; but they affect it indirectly by modifying the subject's immediate surroundings. *Habitus* is such an accident. It makes a difference to a person to be clothed or unclothed, to be barefooted or booted, etc. It is obvious, however, that such modifications are entirely *exterior* to the person and do not affect his being as such in any direct and intrinsic manner.

KNOWLEDGE AND SUBSTANCES

David Hume (1711–1776) denied the existence of all substance, material and spiritual. "I would fain ask those philosophers, who found so much of their reasonings on the distinction of substance and accident, and imagine we have clear ideas of each, whether the idea of *substance* be derived from the impressions of sensations or reflection? If it be conveyed to us by our senses, I ask, which of them; and after what manner? If it be perceived by the eyes, it must be a color; if by the ears, a sound; if by the palate, a taste; and so of the other senses. But I believe none will assert, that substance is either a color, sound, or taste. The idea of substance must therefore be derived from an impression of reflection, if it really exist. But the impressions of reflection resolve themselves into our passions and emotions; none of which can possibly represent a substance. We have, therefore, no idea of substance, distinct from that of *a collection of particular qualities,* nor have we any other meaning when we talk or reason concerning it."[4]

Hume's argument for the sole validity of our knowledge of phenomena underlies many modern theories of knowledge. The only means of contact that man's mind has with the outside world is the system of his senses. Consequently, the mind of man can know nothing but phenomena. For the mind to attempt to penetrate beyond the phenomenal world is a futile and illegitimate procedure. We must deny the existence of anything beyond phenomena, or, at least, we must treat that which lies beyond as the 'unknown and unknowable.' Phe-

---

[4] *Treatise on Human Nature*, Part I, 6. (Italics mine — Author.)

nomenalism may admit the existence of motion, weight, color, extension, action, thought, volition, and similar realities of a passing character; but there is *no thing underlying them* which moves, is heavy, is colored, is extended, acts, thinks, wills, etc. If we still think of some 'hidden substance' as the support of these phenomena, this is but a creation and fiction of the mind. The concept of 'substance' has no objective value.

What are we to think of this argument and its implication? Is it conclusive? Is our mind irrevocably restricted in its knowledge to the phenomenal? Is there no way of penetrating the veil of appearances? The array of opposing opinions is certainly formidable and must not be treated lightly.

We admit that our senses, as such, do not and cannot perceive 'substance,' but only the *qualities* of things or phenomena. In this sense it is true to say that we do not *experience* that which we call 'substance.' If our knowledge is absolutely circumscribed by 'sense experience,' we must admit that we can have no knowledge of 'substance.' However, is this truly so? Empiricists, sensists, materialists, and phenomenalists in general all assert this to be the case. We deny this most emphatically. Unfortunately, the entire question of the validity of human knowledge plays an essential part in the solution of this problem. The problem of human knowledge, however, is the problem of epistemology, not of ontology. The ontologist presupposes the validity of human knowledge as already definitely established. Hence, a few remarks must suffice in this connection.

Man's knowledge is not restricted to experience; it is based on *experience* and *intellection*. Man has not merely a number of senses, but also *understanding* and *reason*. Reason is as much a part of man's mental equipment for acquiring knowledge as the senses are. Knowledge for man begins in sense experience, but is completed, extended, and perfected by reason. There can be no science or philosophy without the use of reason; the senses alone are inadequate for this. Animals have sense experience like man; but, unlike man, they manifest no signs of science or philosophy. Reason must be accepted as a *legitimate source of knowledge*. To deny this means to deny the legitimacy of all sciences and philosophy. But in that case the phenomenalists refute themselves, because their theories are not 'experience' but 'philosophy.' They use their *reason* to arrive at the conclusions of their theory of knowledge: they do not taste or smell or see or hear or feel them. Now then, reason either is a legitimate means of knowledge, or it is not: if it is, phenomenalists are wrong in restricting our knowledge to sense experience and phenomena; if it is not, their theories must be rejected as futile, because they are based on the conclusions of their reason.

As a matter of fact, no one can deny the legitimacy of reason and reasoning without falling into universal skepticism. Reason must *interpret* the data of sense; only in this manner can we have science and philosophy. Though our senses can directly perceive nothing but the qualities or phenomena in nature, our *reason can draw necessary conclusions* from the data of these qualities or phenomena. *Science* does this continually. It deduces the laws of nature from phenomena and expresses them in exact mathematical and logical formulas. These laws and formulas, however, are not objects of sense in any manner; they are conclusions of reason, based on the data of sense. As such they go 'beyond and behind' the phenomena which are perceived in sense experience. If this procedure is illegitimate, then science itself is illegitimate. And in that case all thinking and reasoning is illegitimate. That, however, would be skepticism and the bankruptcy of all knowledge. The legitimacy of reason and reasoning, therefore, must be upheld and maintained as a means of knowledge.

If, then, reason forces us to the conclusion that the phenomena alone are an insufficient explanation of the facts as revealed in sense experience, we must follow the dictates of reason to its logical conclusion. And if this means that reason demands the existence of an underlying substrate or 'substance' for the phenomena, in order that we can account for the existence of these phenomena themselves, we must perforce accept the existence of 'substance.' To refuse to accept such a 'substance' would then do violence to reason, and that would be the suicide of reason and the destruction of our knowledge in all its departments. *Sense and reason,* experience and intellection, must go hand in hand and guide us in our investigation of the problem. Experience without intellection would give us merely a chaotic mass of facts, but not the systematic interpretation of science and philosophy; intellection without experience would give us a world of abstract and speculative ideas, but would tell us nothing of the universe around us. Hence, the problem of the existence of 'substances' in the universe can only be solved by our *reason,* applying itself to the data furnished by *sense experience* and drawing the necessary conclusions.

THE EXISTENCE OF SUBSTANCE

In proving the existence of substance it should be borne in mind that it is not essential for a substance to possess accidents inhering in it; so long as it exists in itself and not in another, it must be designated a 'substance' in the traditional sense.

Our first argument is based on *reality and the concept of substance* as just given. All that we presuppose for this argument is the concept of 'substance' and 'accident' and the existence of actual beings. The existence of *actual beings* cannot be denied. We ourselves, at least, exist. Were anyone to deny his own existence, he would prove his own existence by his very denial: for no one can possibly make a denial, if he does not exist. And as long as one admits one's own existence, one cannot logically deny the existence of other beings. Actual beings, therefore, must be admitted, otherwise there would be no sense in arguing about the reality of 'substances' and 'accidents.' The opponents all admit the existence of phenomena; there is only a question about the existence of substances. The argument is really quite simple:

Actual beings exist. Whatever exists, exists either *in itself* and not in a subject, and then it is a substance, or not in itself but *in another,* and then it is an accident. This exhausts every possible way of existing. To admit the first alternative settles the question, because one thereby admits that substance exists. Hence, if phenomena exist without underlying subjects, they are simply 'substances' in the sense defined. The opponents, in denying the existence of substances, have no other choice but to say that whatever exists must exist in another. But this, too, ultimately proves the existence of substance. Since it exists *in an-other,* they must necessarily postulate this 'other' in which it exists as in a subject; this 'other,' however, supporting it in its existence as a subject of inherence for it, is a 'substance' thereby. Hence, substance exists.

Their only means of escape from this conclusion would be to assert that every accident (quality, phenomenon) exists in *another accident* (quality, phenomenon), and this second in a third, and so on; we would thus have a *series* of supporting accidents. This series, however, is either finite or infinite. If *finite,* there must be a last one at the end of the series; this one, being the last in the series, has no other to exist in; it must exist in itself and not in another; and it is, in consequence, a substance supporting the other accidents, because it fulfills the conditions contained in the definition of a 'substance.' If *infinite,* then we have an infinite number of accidents inhering in each other serially. However, the assumption of an infinite number of accidents piled upon each other, simply to explain the red color of a rose or the round shape of a ball or the incandescence of a filament, is really too absurd. Besides, an actually infinite number, as will be shown later, is self-contradictory. But if the opponents still insist on an infinite number of accidents, one inhering in the other, then the following point can be urged. Does this infinite series exist in itself or in another? If *in itself,* it is a being which exists in itself and not in another as in a subject; as such it would be a substance, and thus a 'substance' would again exist. If *in another,* this infinite series of accidents would presuppose this 'other' as the subject of its inherence; this 'other' must be a substance and cannot again be an 'accident,' since there would then be an 'accident' which is *outside* the infinite number (series), giving a number which would be *one plus* the infinite number. This is absurd, because it is impossible to have a number greater than infinite: in that case the supposedly 'infinite' number never was infinite, but finite. Since an infinite series of accidents inhering in each other is thus seen to be impossible, the number can only be *finite;* a finite number of accidents, however, demands an ultimate subject for the series, and this ultimate subject is a 'substance.'

Since, in short, things do exist and not all can be accidents, some must be substances. Hence, substances exist.

Our second argument is based on the *conscious Ego and the concept of substance.* Our consciousness, as was indicated above, is a clear witness to the fact that our Ego is the permanent subject of our willing, thinking, walking, resting, working, eating, smoking, growing, pleasure, pain, anger, love, etc. This means that the Ego, our 'self,' is the subject of all these changes, modifications, and qualities, bodily and mental. We perceive not merely the presence of these phenomena or passing states as existing realities; we recognize them undeniably as *our own,* i.e., that our *Ego possesses* them. This is evident from the way we speak of them. We say: '*I* think,' '*I* walk,' '*I* love,' etc. If the Ego were not the underlying subject of inhesion for these various states and activities, we could have a knowledge of their 'existence' only; our conscious experience should never prompt us to refer them to a non-existent Ego as the one to whom they belong and in whom they occur.

And this Ego as subject is also recognized as a *substantial* subject of these phenomenal realities. We know through self-consciousness that the Ego is not an act or a state or a modification of some *other* subject underlying itself; it is an *ultimate* reality, existing in itself. The Ego never refers its states and activities to an ulterior being beyond itself as to their subject.

All the functions of mental life, like thinking and willing and emotional states, are referred to the Ego; so, too, are the bodily activities, like walking, eating, and growing. The Ego is the ultimate reality to which they are referred as their *possessor,* and nothing is experienced which could be designated as the ulterior possessor of the Ego. Hence, our Ego must be adjudged 'a being existing in itself and not in another as in a subject.' Since we may not doubt the testimony of our consciousness, the Ego must be a *substance,* because the definition of 'substance' applies to it.

Now, just as we must conclude that the Ego is a real substance, we must conclude that there are subjects for the changes and modifications (phenomena) in the world about us. There can be no 'extension' in the world outside without there being 'something extended'; there can be no 'squareness' or 'roundness' without there being 'something square' or 'something round'; there can be no 'motion' or 'action' without there being 'something moving' or 'something acting'; there can be no 'heaviness' or 'solidity' without there being 'something heavy' or 'something solid.' These qualities are phenomena; but the *'something qualified'* must be a *substance*. This is a legitimate conclusion, based on our own internal experience and carried over to the field of our external experience.

Since the days of Locke, it has become customary to think of 'substance' as some sort of hidden, inert, inactive core upon which the qualities rest. This is a misconception. It is *no such inert, inactive being*. Water may flow, boil, freeze, turn to steam. Just what is the 'substance' here? It is the very 'water' itself. Gold is a metal, yellow, malleable, ductile, heavy. What is its substance? The 'gold' itself, which is actualized as metal, yellow, malleable, ductile, heavy. The substance is the intrinsic *nature* of things, considered as the source of the various states and activities which we perceive. *Something* certainly remains *constant* and *permanent* in such changes and activities; it is the 'nature' of the thing, and this 'nature' is the 'substance.'

Again, opponents labor under a misconception when they speak of substances as something 'unknown and unknowable.' Of course, if they mean that we do not have direct sense-apprehension of substance, they are correct. But neither do we have a direct intuition of atoms, electrons, and similar things; yet we know a great deal about them through their *effects*. The same is true of 'substances.' Every physical body is a substance, and science tells us many things about bodies. Everything we know concerning the quantity, quality, and activity of a thing is a manifestation of its substance, because they are the *actualizations* of the substance. What things *do,* tells us what they *are*. After all, the knowledge of science is, to a very great extent, just this kind of knowledge. For example, our knowledge of the energies of nature consists entirely in what they can or cannot perform; and such, too, is our knowledge of the molecular, atomic, and sub-atomic world. Molecules, atoms, protons, electrons, and kindred realities, are substances. Needless to say, all bodies like minerals, metals, solids, gases, fluids, chemical compounds, plants, animals, men, and stars, are substances. No one can say that such things are unknown and unknowable. In calling them 'substances,' we merely wish to indicate the *manner and mode of their existence,* namely, that they are beings which exist in themselves and not in another as in a subject. The distinction, therefore, between such things (substances) and their modifications (accidents) simply adds one more important item of information to our store of knowledge concerning them. If the opponents understand anything else under the terms of 'substance' and 'accident' than this traditional definition and explanation, they place a false interpretation upon them and are guilty of fighting straw men of their own making.

EXISTENCE OF ABSOLUTE ACCIDENTS

Descartes denied the real distinction between accident and substance, contending that there are no *absolute accidents,* i.e., no accidents which communicate a positive and new perfection or entity to the substance which the latter would not already possess as a substance. His view, and that of his followers, was that accidents are only 'determinations' of substance which consist in a difference concerning the *position* and the external connection of the *parts* in a substance, or in a difference concerning the *bearing* of one substance toward another. This would mean that there are only *relative accidents*.

This view is *erroneous*. Certainly, many accidents are merely relative; for instance, those of 'similarity' and 'equality' between two individual substances. The mere fact that two persons or trees are five feet and ten inches tall, does not give to either of them any positive and new perfection or entity beyond what they already possess; their 'equality' in height consists entirely in this 'point of comparison' or relation. The same applies to the 'similarity' between a horse and a cat, because they resemble each other in this that both are 'white' in color. But not all accidents are of this kind. *There are absolute accidents*. In proving this statement, we will restrict ourselves to facts revealed by our own internal experience, because no philosopher can doubt this evidence without destroying the ultimate possibility of all valid knowledge.

Our *internal experience* testifies to us that there are various modifications within us, like thinking, willing, seeing, hearing, feeling, walking, working, and various kinds of productive activity. To deny these activities is to make an illusion of our internal experience as a source of knowledge. These activities are a *reality,* distinct from our fundamental essence or substance. They are present for a time and then disappear; we exert ourselves to increase or decrease their intensity; we are actively engaged in bringing them forth or stopping them. These activities confer a new perfection and entity upon us which was not there before. Would anyone assert seriously that a blind and deaf person does not lack something which one who sees and hears possesses through the activity of sight and hearing? Or, that a healthy person does not possess a perfection and entity which a critically ill person has lost? If so, then there is no real distinction between blindness and sight, deafness and hearing, health and illness; but that is obviously false. However, while these activities come and go, we still retain our *essential identity* as an abiding and permanent reality throughout the origin and passing of these transient modifications. But this proves that we are a *substance,* while these acts are a positive perfection and entity consisting in something more than the mere relation of one thing to another; more, for instance, than the relation of 'similarity' between the light of an electric lamp and the light of a star.

Knowledge, too, is more than an accidental relation. If it were nothing real superadded as an entity to the mind, then the mind with knowledge would not be really different from the mind without knowledge. Ignorance and knowledge would really amount to the same thing for a mind. But the mind undergoes a *change,* when it passes from a state of ignorance to a state of knowledge, as our consciousness clearly testifies. Change, however, implies that something is actually acquired (or lost) in the process. Reversely, when we forget or are the victims of amnesia, we realize that we have lost something definite in the line of a perfection for our mind; not the mind itself, of course, because that we still possess, but something that the mind had and now is deprived of. If knowledge were not a real perfection, we would *acquire* nothing when we learn, and we would *lose* nothing when we forget; there would then be no real distinction between the erudition of a great thinker and the vacuity of an idiot. Hence, knowledge is some*thing* that can be acquired and lost, an accident that is a reality distinct from the mind. The *effort* we put forth in order to learn proves the same thing. It takes no effort on our part to be similar to another in the color of our complexion or equal to another in our size. But to acquire a knowledge similar or equal to that possessed by another, demands distinct effort and labor. And this proves that knowledge is more than a mere relation or relative accident; it is an absolute accident.

This brief examination of the various kinds of substances,

accidents, and modes should give us a better understanding of the different ways in which 'being in general' is realized in the things which constitute the totality of the universe.

SUMMARY OF CHAPTER XVII

The division of all beings into 'substance' and 'accident' is traditional in philosophy.

1. *Concept of Substance and Accident.* A *substance* is a being whose nature it is to exist in itself and not in another as in a subject. An *accident* is a being whose nature it is to exist in another as in a subject. This 'aptitudinal inherence' is the essential characteristic of an accident, while 'actual inherence' is its normal condition.

2. *Kinds of Substances. Primary* and *secondary* substances. The former are the individual substances; the latter are the class-substances (e.g., species and genus) expressed by universals. *Complete* and *incomplete* substance. The former is one which demands no further union with a substantial co-principle; the latter demands a union with a substantial co-principle in order to constitute a complete substance. *Simple* or *composite.* The former does not consist of entitatively distinct substantial parts; the latter consists of incomplete substantial parts, entitatively distinct.

3. *Kinds of Accidents. Relative* and *absolute* accidents. The former have their being in a subject only because of the bearing which one has to another; the latter confer a real perfection upon their subjects. Absolute accidents are either *strictly absolute* or *modal.* The former confer a positive and new entity upon the substance; a mode is the definite disposition or determination of an indifferent and determinable accidental entity in such a manner that it does not confer a positive and new entity upon the substance. *Intrinsic* and *extrinsic.* The former affects the being of the subject in some way; the latter merely affects the subject's surroundings, but not its being.

4. *Knowledge and Substance.* Hume and the phenomenalists contend that we can know nothing of 'substances,' because

our senses can reach only the qualities of things. Reason, however, is also a legitimate source of knowledge. Science and philosophy are based on *experience* and *intellection*. Hence, if reason demands the acceptance of 'substance,' we must conclude that 'substance' exists.

5. *The Existence of Substance.* Actual beings exist either *in themselves* or *in another*. If in themselves, then 'substance' exists, because that is what is meant by the term. If in another, then this 'other' is the subject supporting the former in their being and existence; in that case, 'substance' exists, because this 'other' exists in itself and not in another as in a subject. It is impossible for all beings to exist in another serially, because that involves an infinite number, and an infinite number, actually existing, is absurd.

Our *conscious* Ego is the *possessor* of all internal states of our being. The Ego is the ultimate subject to which all such states are referred, but the Ego itself is not referred to any ulterior subject. Hence, it exists in itself and not in another as in a subject; and that is the definition of a 'substance.'

6. *Existence of Absolute Accidents.* Not all accidents are relative; some are absolute. Our *internal experience* testifies that we actually acquire a positive and new perfection or entity through thinking, sense-perception, and other activities.

READINGS

Coffey, P., Ch. VIII; Rickaby, J., Bk. II, Ch. I; Hugon, Ed., Tr. III, Qu. I, art. 1, 2, 3; Qu. III, art. 1, 2, 3; Aristotle, *Metaph.,* IV, V, VII, IX; Urráburu, J. J., Disp. V, cp. I; Phillips, R. P., Ch. VI, VIII; Mc-Cormick, J. F., Ch. VI; St. Thomas, *De Ente et Essentia;* Osgniach, A. J., Ch. IV–VII.

Chapter XVIII

ESSENCE, NATURE, HYPOSTASIS, PERSON

A NUMBER of concepts are closely allied to that of 'substance.' Their meanings are so very much alike that they are frequently used synonymously. These concepts are *substance, essence, nature, hypostasis,* and *person.* It would be incorrect, however, to consider them as strictly synonymous; there is a distinction between them which it is important to note. These terms have occurred many times in the preceding chapters, with the exception of 'hypostasis.' We must now give them serious attention, in order to see in how far they agree in meaning and in how far they disagree. In the course of the history of philosophy these terms have given rise to some problems which have occasioned considerable controversy; these we must attempt to solve.

SUBSTANCE AND ESSENCE

We have already discussed the meaning of *essence* (see Chapter X). In a general sense, it is defined as that through which a being is just what it is. Taken in this general sense, every being of whatever kind has an 'essence,' because every being without exception 'is what it is,' and there must, therefore, be that in it which makes it to be 'what it is.' And since all being must be either 'substance' or 'accident,' it follows that every substance has an 'essence' which makes it to be a 'substance,' and every accident must have an 'essence' which makes it to be an 'accident.'

In a concrete, individual being it is the *substance* which makes it to be '*what* it is.' Accidents have no being and existence of their own, except in so far as they receive it from the substance of which they are a modification and actualization. The substance can exist without the accidents, but the accidents cannot exist naturally without the substance; the substance, therefore, is the primary reality in a being, while the accidents are only secondary realities in it. That, however, 'through which a being is what it is,' is the *primary* reality in it, namely, the essence. In concrete, individual beings the 'essence' must be, in this stricter sense, the *ultimate intrinsic principle of being*. And since this definition applies only to the substance, and not to the accidents, the 'essence' of a concrete, individual being consists in its 'substance.' It follows from this that 'essence' and 'substance' are, so far as their reality is concerned, identical.

However, though really identical in a concrete, individual being, 'substance' and 'essence' are *conceptually distinct*. The concepts of both are somewhat different, which can be seen from their definitions. The definition given in the preceding paragraph is the definition of 'essence,' not that of 'substance.' The essence, considered in itself, is this 'ultimate intrinsic principle of being'; considered in the *mode* of its being and existence, it exists 'in itself and not in another as in a subject,' and that is the definition of substance. While really identical, 'essence' and 'substance' are thus conceptually different.

SUBSTANCE AND NATURE

A similar situation prevails concerning the concepts of 'substance' and 'nature.' The term 'nature' is taken in many meanings. Very frequently it is used to designate the totality of all objects in the universe, or the sum of all the forces operating in bodies according to the laws controlling these bodies. In ontology, however, we do not speak of 'nature' in this sense, except incidentally. Here we speak of the nature of a concrete, individual thing, and the term applies to immaterial as well as to material things. In this ontological sense, we understand *nature* to be the *ultimate principle of all operations* in an individual being.

The kind of activities a thing can perform depends upon the kind of being it is: action follows being (*agere sequitur esse*). Specifically different beings have specifically different activities. Water does not act like gold, nor gold like iron, nor iron like radium, nor radium like argon, nor argon like hydrogen. As long as a thing remains what it is, its activities must remain specifically the same. It is because of this fact that the inductive process of reasoning employed by scientific investigators is a valid form of inference and leads to a valid knowledge of physical laws: since the nature of a specific type of bodies remains the same, their activities must, under identical conditions, produce identical results, i.e., these bodies must act according to a definite physical law. Given the same cause, the same effect must follow.

The activities of things do not simply happen; they are determined by some principle within the thing itself. Since an infinite regress within the being of a concrete thing is impossible, there must be an *ultimate intrinsic principle of activity*. This determining principle is called its *nature*. And since there is but one single ultimate principle in each being, namely, the 'essence,' this 'essence' is the 'nature' which determines all the activity of the thing. The essence of a thing, however, is identical with its 'substance.' Hence, the 'nature' of a thing is in reality identical with its 'substance,' because two things, identical with a same third, are identical with each other.

But here, too, there is a *conceptual distinction* between 'nature' and 'substance.' The same essence, considered as the 'ultimate principle of operation' in a thing, is called its 'nature'; and the same essence, considered as something which 'exists in itself,' is called a 'substance.' The three concepts differ in meaning and definition, although they are identical in their reality.

SUBSTANCE AND HYPOSTASIS

Another concept, closely allied to substance, essence, and nature, is that of *hypostasis* (Gr., ὑπόστασις). In Latin it is called *suppositum.* There is no equivalent term in English, although the word *'supposit'* is employed at times. We will use the Greek word 'hypostasis.'

It has been shown that accidents belong to their substance and inhere in it; accidents, therefore, do not exist completely in themselves. Secondary or universal substances, as expressed in concepts designating species and genera, are communicated to, and predicated of, the individual substances; they also do not exist completely in themselves. Substantial parts belong to the whole of which they are parts; they, too, do not exist completely in themselves. But an *individual, concrete substance* exists completely in itself. By this we mean that it is incommunicable to any other being; it does not belong to another; it is the whole or unit containing all the parts; it is the ultimate reality to which all functions, powers, and perfections of that particular being are referred; it is the possessor of its entire nature; it is self-contained and autonomous, i.e., it controls its own actions independent of any other individual (creatural) being; it is complete in the order of its essence and in the order of its existence: it is, in a word, *sui juris* ('of its own right'), its own possessor.

For example, I perform my own acts and my Ego is the ultimate reality from which they originate and to which they must be referred; my actions are 'mine' and belong to no one else. Hence, I act 'of (in) my own right'; my Ego is *sui juris.* This sort of existence has a special name; it is called 'subsistence.' The phrase *'sui juris'* may be rendered in English as 'self-contained and autonomous.' *Subsistence,* therefore, is that mode of existence in virtue of which a thing is self-contained and autonomous in its operations. When we speak of a *suppositum* or *hypostasis, we mean a complete individual substance which has subsistence,* i.e., a substance which is self-contained and autonomous (*sui juris*) in its operations. This definition applies to every individual substance as it actually exists in the universe, including every inorganic body, plant, brute, and man.

The fundamental reason why such beings are 'subsistent' is

that they are a *single* 'substance,' 'nature,' and 'essence.' It is because of this that they are self-contained and autonomous in their being and existence. Hence, it follows that a hypostasis is nothing but the 'substance' considered as *sui juris,* i.e., as subsistent. And since it is identical in its reality with 'substance,' it is also identical with the 'nature' and 'essence' of the thing. Hypostasis, however, differs in concept from these three, because it includes within its concept the mode of *subsistence,* namely, that the 'substance,' or 'nature,' or 'essence,' is self-contained and autonomous; 'subsistence' is not included in the concept of these others. We see, therefore, that we may call a concrete individual being a 'substance,' an 'essence,' a 'nature,' and a 'hypostasis': they are conceptually distinct, but in reality identical.

SUBSTANCE AND PERSON

The term 'person' is peculiar. There is no question as to what or to whom the term applies; but there is considerable controversy among modern philosophers as to what actually *constitutes* 'personality.' In this connection we do not take 'personality' in its popular sense as the sum of those qualities of temperament and character which distinguish one human being from another. In philosophy we understand by 'personality' that particular mode of being which makes an individual to be a 'person.' The important question, then, is this: *What specifically constitutes a person?*

The term has been in constant use, and for centuries there never has been any ambiguity in its use and application. In this respect the term 'person' is not vague like the terms 'substance,' 'essence,' and 'nature,' which are rather loose in meaning and are applied in a variety of meanings to many diverse types of things, being used at times in a stricter and at times in a wider sense. When used by philosophy, these terms must always be narrowed down to a specific meaning and defined accordingly, so that they will apply to a very definite group of beings and to no other. In the case of the term 'person,' its use has become restricted to a definite group of beings and to no other. Although the group to which the term is thus definitely known, the exact meaning implied in the term 'person' is far from clear. To arrive at a distinctive definition of 'person,' we must consider the *type of beings* to which the term is invariably applied and, by means of a careful analysis of their nature, discover in them the *specific element* which constitutes their 'personality.'

It is an easy task to designate the *types of beings* to which the term 'person' is or is not applicable. *Inorganic* beings like gold, silver, carbon, are never styled 'persons.' Neither do we use the term 'person' when speaking of a *plant,* like a rose, a geranium, a pumpkin. No *brute* is called a 'person,' no matter how highly developed in the scale of life; thus, no amoeba, fish, reptile, bird, or ordinary mammal, is a 'person.' These types of beings do not possess that specific element which we invariably associate with the concept of 'person.'

Every being, however, *above the level of brute animality* is styled a *person.* Every *human* being is a 'person,' irrespective of age, sex, color, or condition. A child, even though unborn, is a 'person' in the strict sense of the term, and the courts of law recognize it as a potential heir to an estate. That an octogenarian or centenarian is still a 'person,' need hardly be mentioned. Even deformed and insane people are real 'persons.' A corpse is not called a 'person,' because it is no longer a human being. Hence, from the universally accepted use of the term we must conclude that *living human* beings are 'persons' and possess that specific element which constitutes 'personality.'

God and *spirits* are also 'persons.' It is true that God, in the meaning of the pantheists, of the absolute idealists, and of some pragmatists, can hardly be said to be a 'person'; but these philosophers are a small minority in comparison with the vast bulk of Christian and other peoples and philosophers who have considered God and the angels real 'persons' in a truly philosophic sense. In the traditional sense, and that is the one taken here, God is a 'person' in the highest degree.

From the above it is clear that any kind of being below man is not a 'person,' while man and all beings higher than man are 'persons.' This being the case, the specific element of 'personality' must consist in something absent in the former and present in the latter; and although men, spirits, and God are so diverse in nature, there must be an element common to them which constitutes them as 'persons.' What is this *common element,* present in man, spirits, and God, which is absent in inorganic beings, plants, and brutes?

It cannot be *materiality*. The spirits and God are not material beings, though man has a material body. It cannot be *life*. Plants and animals possess life, but they are not 'persons.' It cannot be *simplicity of nature*. God and the spirits are simple in nature, while man is a compound of body and soul; yet all are 'persons.' It cannot be *immortality*. God and the spirits are immortal in their essence, while man is mortal. It cannot be *infinite perfection*. God is infinitely perfect, but the spirits and man are entirely finite. It cannot be *substance* or *essence* or *nature* or *subsistence*. All individual beings, from inorganic bodies up to and including God, possess these degrees of reality. Then what is it?

The only discoverable element which is distinctive of God, spirits, and man and which is lacking in all beings below the level of man, is *intellectuality*. Of course, the intellectuality of God is of an infinitely higher order than that found in spirits or man; it is one with all His other perfections, and all His perfections are a single, identical, infinite reality. Nevertheless, the perfection of intellectuality is truly present in God. We are now in a position to state what specifically constitutes a person: a *person* is an *intellectual hypostasis, i.e., an individual, complete, subsistent, intellectual substance*. It is customary to define a person as a *'rational* hypostasis.' The term 'rational,' however, means 'having reason' or 'having the faculty of reasoning,' and as such does not apply to God; God is an 'intellectual,' but not a 'rational,' being. On the other hand, 'intellectuality' is an attribute which is applicable to God, spirits, and man. We therefore use the term 'intellectual' rather than 'rational' in our definition.

It will be clear from the above that hypostasis may be either non-intellectual or intellectual. If it is *intellectual,* it has the special name of *person.* Every person is thus a hypostasis, but not every hypostasis is a person. The subsistence of a person has a greater perfection than that of an ordinary hypostasis, because an *intellectual* being is to a far greater extent the possessor and master of itself and of its operations. Since, however, every person is a hypostasis and every 'hypostasis' is really identical with 'substance,' 'essence,' and 'nature' in an individual being, it follows that 'person' is only conceptually distinct from them in man, spirits, and God.

From the definition of 'person' it is evident that the *human soul,* considered by itself, cannot be called a 'person.' The soul is only a substantial part of man, the formative principle in the human compound of body and soul. Only a *complete* intellectual substance is a 'person,' and the soul is an *incomplete* substance. This is also true of a disembodied soul after death. It will always remain an essentially incomplete substance, since its essence demands that it exist together with matter to form the complete substance of man as a compound of body and soul. Hence, *man* himself, but not his soul, is a 'person.'[1]

The concepts elucidated above lead to some important *prin-*

---

[1] These distinctions should enable us to obtain a deeper understanding of the 'nature' and 'personality' of Christ, as expounded in Christian theology. The human nature of Christ is a complete nature, viewed from the standpoint of substantiality and specific perfection; it lacks nothing of the entity found in any other human nature. But it does *not subsist;* it has not that mode of subsistence in virtue of which it is 'self-contained and autonomous' or *sui juris.* The human nature of Christ does not exist in itself and it is not the ultimate possessor of its operations. The Logos or Second Person of the Trinity has assumed this nature and taken possession of it, so that the Logos is the real possessor of all its functions. Hence, Christ's human nature is a complete substance, but not a 'hypostasis' or 'person.' There is only *one subsistence or one personality* in the God-Man, and that is the divine personality of the Logos. The human nature of Christ is united 'hypostatically' or 'personally' with the divine nature of the Logos, so that both together are only *one person.* Christ, therefore, consists of two distinct natures in one person.

ciples which occur quite frequently in philosophic discussions, especially among scholastics.

Actions belong to the hypostasis or person. The 'nature' of a being is the principle of all its actions. But the nature of an individual, concrete being, as it actually exists in the universe, is always a hypostasis and, if it is intellectual, a person. This fact is clearly expressed in our judgments and statements about things. We seldom refer actions to the faculties or parts from which they proceed immediately, but to the ultimate possessor of the nature. We say 'I see, I hear, I digest, I think, I drive the car,' although it is the eyes that see, and the ears that hear, and the stomach that digests, and the intellect that thinks, and the hands that hold the steering wheel. Actions are thus attributed to the hypostasis or person. The hypostasis or person is the principle *which* (*principium quod*) performs the action, while the nature is the ultimate principle *by means of which* (*principium quo*) the hypostasis or person performs the action.

Actions participate in the dignity of the person. This means that an action has a higher perfection or value, if performed by a person of a relatively higher nature, and a lower perfection or value, if performed by a person of a relatively lower nature. The intellection of a pure spirit is more perfect than a man's, and God's intellection is infinitely more perfect than a creature's, because the 'person' in each instance is greater in perfection. This is natural. If the actions belong to the person, then the dignity of the person is reflected in everything that proceeds from the person, and the actions participate in the dignity of the person.[2]

---

[2] For this reason the infinite dignity of the Logos or Second Person of the Trinity confers an *infinite* dignity or value upon the actions of His *human* nature. This does not mean that the physical actions of the finite human nature of Christ ever become physically or entitatively infinite; but it does mean that the entitatively finite actions of Christ have an infinite *value,* because performed by an infinite Person.

This also explains why it is possible to predicate seemingly contradictory things of the person of Christ. It is the *person* which possesses the *nature* and, through the nature, the *actions.* Hence, the activities and attributes of both the divine and human natures in Christ must be predicated of the selfsame person, the *Logos,*

THE CONSTITUTION OF PERSONALITY

The specific element which constitutes a 'person' has become one of the most mooted questions in modern philosophy. The classic and traditional explanation through the centuries up to recent times has been that a 'person' is an intellectual hypostasis, i.e., a complete, individual, intellectual substance, self-contained and autonomous (*sui juris*). Philosophers and psychologists of a phenomenalistic trend object to this view very strongly.

Phenomenalists admit the existence of phenomena, but deny the objective validity of the concept of 'substance.' Of course, if there are no substances in this world, a person is not a substance and the definition of 'person' as a substance is wrong. Driven by their denial of the reality of substance to seek a different explanation of 'person' and 'personality,' they could find nothing in man to constitute 'personality' but his *internal, mental states*. And since man is a person, while the brute is not, the mental states which constitute personality must be such as are found only in man, namely, the self-conscious states. Man is conscious of his Ego, while the brute manifests no self-consciousness. Hence, most modern philosophers, aside from the scholastics, claim that 'personality' consists in *self-consciousness,* in the *conscious Ego*. As William James puts it: "The passing thought is itself the thinker."

We reject this view as unsatisfactory. In connection with this problem it must be borne in mind that the real question is: What *meaning* must be attached to the term and concept of 'person' and 'personality'? One thing is certain from the start: every human being is called a 'person.' This is universal usage,

---

and the Logos, therefore, is theandric, both God and man. The Logos as God, is eternal, immutable, infinite; as man, temporal, mutable, finite. As God, He cannot suffer and is immortal; as man, He suffered and died. He suffered and died in His human nature, not in His divine nature. Of course, these things cannot be proved on philosophic grounds; but neither can they be disproved. These facts rest on revelation, not on experience.

and we must find the precise element in man which constitutes his 'personality.' We contend that 'self-consciousness' or
the 'conscious Ego' is not this distinctive element.

Evidently, if that which *constitutes* 'personality' is absent
from a being, then that being is not a 'person.' The opponents
assert that personality consists in self-consciousness. Consequently, if a human being lacks self-consciousness, it is not a
person. A human being, however, is not always conscious of
self. Children, during the entire prenatal state, and after birth
for a considerable period of time, have no reflex knowledge of
themselves; they are not conscious of self or Ego. Perpetually
insane people and idiots of an extreme type have no real consciousness of self. Human beings under the influence of some
strong narcotic are totally unconscious and have, therefore, lost
their self-consciousness for the time being. Deep sleep and
intense distraction deprive people of all conscious contact with
their surroundings and also of the consciousness of their Ego
for a while. Similarly, sickness or traumatic shock often render
human beings oblivious of themselves for weeks and even
months at a time.

Now, if 'personality' were really and formally constituted
by 'self-consciousness' or the 'conscious Ego,' we would be con-
strained to conclude that human beings in such conditions are
not persons, because the *constitutive element* of 'personality' is
absent. This, however, would do violence to the concept of
'personality.' Only a desperate extremist would assert that a
child before birth and up to probably two or more years of age
is not a 'person.' It is certainly false to claim that normal
human beings are 'persons' *only when awake,* and cease to be
'persons' for the period of sleep or intense distraction. Every
human being is a 'person' *as long as he lives.* This is clear
from the fact that the subject of law is the human 'person,'
and the law applies to every human being, whether born or
unborn. Only 'persons' can demand a reparation for injury or
damage done to them by their fellow men. Shall we then

maintain that people in sleep or under an anaesthetic may be injured with impunity for the mere reason that they are not self-conscious and are, therefore, not 'persons'?

Furthermore, *self-consciousness* is an *operation, a function.* According to our opponents, this passing state or function would constitute 'personality.' They must assert this, because they do not admit the existence of anything like a substance. However, we have already shown that *substances exist.* The reason for their opposition, therefore, is nullified. We have also shown (and it will be shown more clearly in psychology) that underlying all internal states and functions there is a substantial basis, a substance, which *possesses* these transient modifications and to which they must be ultimately referred as to their originating principle. These mental states and functions are phenomena, accidents; as such they must inhere in an *Ego,* and this Ego is the ultimate reality within us, identical and permanent amid all changes. The Ego is, therefore, a *subsisting substance,* existing in itself and not in another as in a subject.

This idea of a *subsisting substantial Ego* alone coincides with our concept of a 'person.' The difference between the brute and man as subsisting substances lies in this that man is a 'person,' while the brute is not. This difference between man and brute is an *essential* one; and, being essential, it is not merely an accidental difference, but a substantial one. The difference between them cannot consist in 'subsistence' as such, because both are subsistent and both are substances. The essential difference between man and brute consists precisely and formally in this, then, that man is an intellectual subsistent substance, while the brute is a non-intellectual subsistent substance. That is the *specific difference* between them; and this difference is not accidental, but essential. But what does this mean, if not that man is a 'person,' because he is an individual, complete, *intellectual* substance, self-contained and autonomous? That, however, is the meaning we attach to the term 'person' from the beginning of the discussion.

This interpretation alone will avoid the absurdities of the theory of self-consciousness as constituting 'personality.' Man, then is a 'person' by the very fact that he is a man; and he remains such as long as lives, from the first moment of his life until the moment of his death, whether he be born or not, whether he be conscious or unconscious of self. Hence, the concept of 'personality' is identical with that of an *intellectual subsistence,* and the concept of 'person' is identical with that of an *intellectual hypostasis.*

Some philosophers attempt to evade these conclusions by asserting that a human being may remain *habitually* self-conscious and thus remain a 'person' at all times, even if he lose actual self-consciousness through sleep, disease, narcotics, etc. This view, however, will not remove the difficulty. Something is said to be 'habitual' when it is based on a habit, and a habit is usually the result of frequently *repeated separated acts.* However, can an unborn child be said to have 'habitual' self-consciousness? This would presuppose that it had performed repeated acts of self-consciousness from the very first moment of its existence and had thereby *acquired* habitual self-consciousness. This is a necessary conclusion, because even an unborn child is a true 'person.' But who will not understand that such an assumption is purely arbitrary? No one can reasonably assert that an unborn child performs such acts. Besides, a habit that is acquired through repeated acts can also be *lost* through the omission of such acts; then a human being would cease to be a 'person.' That, however, is contrary to the universal conviction that *every* human being is a person at *all* times. Hence, habitual self-consciousness cannot constitute a 'person.' Consequently, the thesis stands: *A person is an intellectual hypostasis,* i.e., it is an individual, complete, *intellectual* substance, self-contained and autonomous.

To sum up: in a concrete, individual being, as it actually exists, the distinction between 'essence,' 'substance,' 'nature,' 'hypostasis,' and (in the case of man, spirit, and God) 'person' is only *conceptual, not real.* In reality they are one identical entity. Since, however, there is a foundation in the beings themselves for making a distinction between them in concept, they differ from each other by a *virtual* distinction with a foundation in the reality itself.

SUMMARY OF CHAPTER XVIII

The concepts of 'substance,' 'essence,' 'nature,' 'hypostasis,' and 'person' are closely akin in meaning.

1. *Substance and Essence.* In a *general* sense, 'essence' is that through which a being is just what it is. Since substances and accidents are beings, each accident as well as substance has its own essence. In a *strict sense,* we take the concrete, individual being, consisting of a substance and numerous accidents; and in this sense, the *substance alone* is the essence of the thing, because the accidents of such a being are not absolutely required and are not absolutely sufficient to make this being to be what it is. 'Essence' is, therefore, identical in reality with 'substance,' with a virtual distinction between the two.

2. *Substance and Nature.* By 'nature' we mean the ultimate principle of all operations in a concrete, individual being. Since the individual being is a natural unit of entity and activity, it can have but one ultimate principle of both its entity and its activity. This is the 'essence,' which is identical with the substance of the thing. Hence, in reality 'nature,' 'essence,' and 'substance' are identical, with a virtual distinction between them.

3. *Substance and Hypostasis.* Neither the accidents, nor secondary substances, nor substantial parts, exist completely in themselves; they exist in the concrete, individual substance, and it is the latter which exists completely in itself in such a manner that it is self-contained and autonomous, i.e., *sui juris.* This mode of existence is called 'subsistence.' A *suppositum* or *hypostasis,* therefore, is a complete, individual substance that has subsistence, i.e., one which is self-contained and autono-

mous. And since it is the 'substance' or 'essence' or 'nature' which has being and existence, the 'hypostasis' is in reality identical with them, with a virtual distinction between them.

4. *Substance and Person.* The term 'person' is never applied to any being lower in nature than man. Men, spirits, and God are always considered to be 'persons' and to have 'personality.' That which constitutes a 'person' must, therefore, be some specific element found in men, spirits, and God. The only discoverable element found in men, spirits, and God, and absent in inorganic bodies, plants, and brutes, is *intellectuality*. Hence, a 'person' is an *intellectual hypostasis,* i.e., a complete, individual, subsistent, intellectual substance. Every person is thus a hypostasis, but not every hypostasis is a person. From this it follows that 'person,' 'hypostasis,' 'substance,' 'essence,' and 'nature' are identical in their reality, with a virtual distinction between them.

Two principles are important: actions belong to the hypostasis or person; actions participate in the dignity of the person.

5. *The Constitution of Personality.* Modern philosophers, especially psychologists of a phenomenalistic trend of thought, contend that *self-consciousness* or the *conscious Ego,* as a passing mental state, constitutes 'personality.' This is erroneous. If this were the formal, constitutive element of personality, then, this element being absent in a being, this being could not be called a 'person.'

Man is a 'person' at all times and in all conditions; but man is not always conscious of self or Ego. This is the case with infants, especially those as yet unborn; with perpetually insane people and idiots of an extreme type; with human beings under the influence of a strong narcotic, of sleep, of intense distraction, of sickness, and of traumatic shock. Hence, self-consciousness is not the constitutive element of 'personality,' because these people are real 'persons.'

Furthermore, self-consciousness is a *function* which is *possessed* by the *Ego*. The function is a passing mental state, the

Ego remains. Hence, the Ego is an intellectual hypostasis. 'Intellectuality' is the specific difference between man, spirit, God, and the lower forms of brute, plant, and inorganic body. A 'person,' therefore, is an *intellectual hypostasis*.

READINGS

Coffey, P., Ch. IX; Rickaby, J., Bk. II, Ch. II; Hugon, Ed., Tr. III, Qu. I, art. 4; Urráburu, J. J., Disp. V, cp. II; Phillips, R. P., Ch. VII; McCormick, J. F., Ch. VI, pp. 109–112; Aristotle, *Metaph.*, V.

CHAPTER XIX

QUALITY

ONTOLOGY DOES not treat of all the single categories of accident. Ontology is *General* Metaphysics and as such concerns itself with those phases of being which are, as a rule, found in both material and immaterial beings. Accidents found in material beings only or in immaterial beings only do not belong to ontology proper. Immaterial reality, such as the human soul, belongs to psychology; corporeal reality, such as quantity, place, time, posture, and habitus, belongs to cosmology. 'Quantity,' for example, presupposes material parts side by side in a body; 'place' and 'space' rest upon the quantity and extension of bodies; 'time' is the element of successive duration in bodily movements. These accidents, therefore, belong to cosmology, the philosophy of bodily or material beings. 'Posture' and 'habitus' are also accidental determinations of bodies, and their treatment is thereby excluded from ontology; from a philosophic standpoint, however, they are so unimportant that they hardly deserve special treatment.

It is different with the remaining accidents of *quality, relation, action* and *reaction* (passion). They are really general in character, because they affect immaterial as well as material beings. These will be examined in the following chapters.

THE CONCEPT OF QUALITY

Strictly speaking, quality *cannot be defined*. The only proximate genus which could be used in such a definition would be 'accident.' But, as was intimated before, the concept of 'accident' can hardly be predicated of its inferior members in a strictly univocal manner; it is, rather an *analogous concept.*

Taken in a *wide* sense, 'quality' means any kind of modification. The term is used in a very loose way to signify almost anything, even though it be a part of the essence, which can be predicated of a subject in an adjectival form. Thus, we say the 'Man is rational.' Here 'rationality' is considered as a quality of man, although it is really essential and one with man's concrete substance. Similarly, we say that 'a brute is sentient, a plant is living.' Here, too, 'sentiency' and 'life' are predicated of their subjects in an adjectival form as qualities, but they are not qualities in the sense of 'quality' as a categorical accident. In this wide sense all *specific differences,* distinguishing one species of substance from another, are considered to be qualities. In fact, since *any kind of accident* is, in a way, a modification and qualification of substance, all accidents, even quantity, are frequently spoken of as being 'qualities' of things. This, of course, is not the meaning of quality when we speak of it as a separate and distinct *category*.

Taken in a *strict* sense, quality is a category distinct from the category of substance, quantity, relation, and the others. *Aristotle* describes it as follows: "By 'quality' I mean that in virtue of which people [things] are said to be such and such."[1] A quality always presupposes a thing as being constituted in its proper species, as completed in the line of its substantiality and specific perfection. A quality determines a completed substance in some accidental manner, so that the substance is now 'such and such' by the addition of some modifying entity. Creatural substances have certain *potentialities* which must be actualized and completed if these substances are to attain the fullness of their being; and it is the qualities which supply, at least partly, the *actualization* and *completion* of such natural tendencies.

Aristotle's description is too vague to be of much value. Subsequent philosophers have attempted a more definite wording in their descriptive definition of quality. A definition which

---

[1] *Categoriae,* Ch. 8 b 25. Tr. by E. M. Edghill (Clarendon Press, Oxford, 1928).

serves the purpose is this: *A quality is an absolute accident completing and determining a substance in its being and in its operations.*

Aristotle[2] enumerates four distinct *types of quality:* habit and disposition (ἕξις καὶ διάθεσις); natural capacity and incapacity (δύναμις καὶ ἀδυναμία); affective qualities and affections (παθητικαί ποιότητες καὶ πάθη); form and figure (σχῆμα καὶ μορφή). He admits that there might be some qualities not included in this division, but maintains that most qualities, properly so called, will find a place in these groups.[3] It will be noticed that each group consists of two members. The four groups can readily be reduced to two main classes: *entitative* and *operative* qualities. This is indicated in the definition of quality, when we say that it modifies a substance in its 'being' and in its 'operations.'

HABIT AND DISPOSITION

A *habit* is a comparatively *permanent quality disposing a thing well or ill in its being.* When it is stated that a habit is 'comparatively permanent,' the meaning is that it must be *stable relative to the nature* of the thing which has this habit. That, of course, differs with different beings. The life, for instance, of some insects lasts but a week or even a day. Something may be relatively permanent for it in its short life, which would be relatively transient in the much longer period of life for some other being. The beauty of such an insect would be an entitative habit, perfecting and completing it in its being. If a human being's beauty lasted for a week or a day only, it would be transient. Habits, however, need not always be a perfection of the substance: they may dispose a thing *well* or *ill* in a permanent manner. Many habits dispose a thing 'well': for example, beauty and health in a human body, knowledge in the intellect, virtue in the will. Other habits dispose a thing 'ill': for example, chronic catarrh or rheumatism in a person,

---

[2] *Idem.,* Ch. 8.
[3] *Idem.,* Ch. 10 a 25.

ugliness or deformity in a body, forgetfulness in the intellect, vice in the will.

If this quality is not permanent, but *relatively transient to the nature* of the thing which possesses it, it will either dispose the thing temporarily *well,* and then it is called a *disposition,* or it will dispose it temporarily *ill,* and then it is called an *indisposition.* Thus, the easing of pain through morphine, the feeling of well-being after a meal, the rally of a seriously wounded or dying person, are naturally temporary in character and dispose the patient 'well'; this is a 'disposition.' A toothache, a headache, a sprained ankle, a carbuncle, acute appendicitis, are qualities, temporary in character, which dispose one 'ill'; they are 'indispositions.' If these dispositions or indispositions become inveterate in the course of time, so that they are difficult to remove and are comparatively permanent in the subject, they become 'habits.'

So far we have taken 'habits' and 'dispositions' in a wider sense, as permanent or temporary *entitative states. Operative habits* are 'habits' in a stricter meaning of the term. Operative habits are stable qualities disposing a being ill or well in the *operations* of its faculties. Such a habit gives a definite direction to the acts of a faculty, a determination in virtue of which the faculty *tends* to act in one manner rather than in another. Every repetition of the act increases this tendency and makes the subsequent operation of the same kind easier. What was done in the beginning as the result of conscious effort, now becomes almost automatic, and the faculties carry out their respective acts with little external stimulation or none at all. We perceive the working of operative habits in the complicated acts of walking, speaking, typewriting, playing a musical instrument, memorizing, etc. One need but recall to mind the painful efforts of the tyro on the piano and compare them with the ease, grace, and proficiency of the same person after years of diligent application to the art, in order to realize the difference between the single act and the habit.

Not all faculties are capable of being determined by habits.

The very nature of habit as a quality *determining* a faculty to a definite mode of operation shows that habit presupposes a faculty which is *indifferent to a variety of actions*. It is only when a faculty is as such indeterminate to various kinds of actions that it is capable of *further* determination from a habit. A faculty which is already determined by its very nature to act in such or such a manner can receive no further determination from a habit, because no inclination and tendency is as strong as one given through the necessity of a being's nature. Thus, the natural forces of inorganic elements and bodies work forever in the same manner. Gravity, for instance, attracts the stone with the same force after the thousandth time as at the very first time; it gains nothing by repeating the action. Chemical affinity, electricity, light, steam, magnetism, heat, etc., acquire no increased facility or tendency through repetition. So, too, plants and animals are determined in their operations by their very nature; under the same conditions they will, if left to themselves, act in the same way.

Hence, only such things can properly be the subjects of operative habits as are *free in their activities,* because they are intrinsically indeterminate. The *free will* is primarily capable of habits. We know from our own experience that by repeated actions we form certain habits of virtue and vice which, once they have gained a foothold, are difficult to change. The *intellect* is also capable of habit, in so far as the will can apply it in different ways to its object; we see this in the habit of knowledge. The *sensitive powers* of man, considered in themselves, are incapable of habit, because they have a necessary direction toward their respective objects. Since, however, they are under the control of the will, they are, indirectly, capable of being perfected by habit. Through intensive exercising along certain lines, man can 'train' his eye, his ear, his imagination, and so forth.

Brutes cannot acquire habits in the strict sense of the term. Their organs are directed by natural necessity toward determined acts. Their movements are regulated by sense-perception and sense-impulse, both of which have no choice in the performance of their natural functions. Under the influence of man's direction, especially through the administration of pleasure and pain, they can be 'trained' to perform actions which *of their own accord* they would never perform. But this seems to be nothing more than forcing their memory to associate certain pleasures and pains with the performance or omission of certain actions, and this pleasure or pain drives the animal *with necessity* toward the performance or omission. Hence, strictly speaking, only rational powers are capable of habits; under their influence other powers can, indirectly, also acquire habits.

Some habits are *given by nature* itself. It would be more correct to say that nature gives the *beginning* of habits, rather than habits themselves. Thus, philosophers speak of the *habitus principiorum,* the 'habit of principles,' as present in the mind from the start; they mean thereby that man's mind has a natural facility and inclination to understand and form fundamental principles of thought. Such are the Principles of Identity, Contradiction, Excluded Middle, and Sufficient Reason.

Other habits are *acquired* through the *frequent repetition* of the same acts. What has been said in general about habits, refers to this class. Examples would be the habit of language, knowledge, walking, writing, etc.; of virtue, like kindness, patience, truthfulness, chastity, temperance, etc.; of vices, like cruelty, mendacity, immodesty, laziness, drunkenness, etc. Once acquired, they are relatively stable.

Theologians also speak of *supernatural* habits. They exceed the limits of nature and can be acquired only as the gift of God. Such would be the divine virtues of faith, hope, and charity; also infused knowledge and the gift of tongues. Supernatural habits are, of course, outside the scope of philosophy.

CAPACITY AND INCAPACITY

By *natural capacity* we understand the *proximate accidental principle of operation, toward which (operation) it is specifi-*

cally directed. It is a 'principle' of operation, because it produces the operation. It is a 'proximate' principle, in order to
distinguish it from the remote adequate principle of operation,
which is the nature or substance. Both nature and natural
capacity are principles of operation in a thing, but in a different
way. The nature or substance is the ultimate principle of operation, in as much as the operation flows directly from the
capacity or faculty and the capacity or faculty is the immediate
principle 'through which (*quo*)' the nature or substance acts.
The natural capacity is a 'principle' of action, and that distinguishes it from a 'habit.' The capacity or faculty is the immediate source of activity, while the habit merely modifies the
faculty in such a manner that the faculty performs its operations with greater ease and speed. Without the faculty there
can be no operation and no habit; but without the habit, the
faculty would still be capable of performing its operation,
though not with ease and speed. A natural capacity is said to
be an 'accidental' principle of operation, so as to distinguish
it from a substantial part in a being; thus, the hand is an instrument of action, and as such a principle of operation,
although it is not a faculty or capacity. By 'operation' we mean
the act which the faculty performs. This may be transient, as
when a ballplayer throws a ball; or immanent, as when the
intellect thinks and the will desires. The capacity or faculty
must be 'specifically directed' toward a certain action, in order
that it may be said to be the faculty of this action. Thus, the
will is specifically directed toward appetitive acts and not
toward intellectual acts, although the will frequently commands the intellect to act; the will, therefore, is not the faculty
for intellectual acts, but for appetitive acts. Faculties or natural
capacities thus make a nature prepared and fit to act, even
though it does not actually exercise them; man, for instance,
has an intellect and will capable of action, irrespective of the
fact whether he actually thinks and wills or not.

Inorganic beings have many natural capacities. Such are
gravitational attraction, electromotive power, chemical affinity,

cohesion and adhesion, flexibility, elasticity, etc. In *vegetative* beings we observe the powers of nutrition, growth, and reproduction. *Sentient* beings have these vegetative powers and also the special faculties of sense-perception, sense-appetition, and locomotion. *Rational* beings have the spiritual faculties of intellect and will; and man, since he is a rational animal, also possesses the vegetative and sentient powers characteristic of plants and animals. What has been termed 'subjective' or 'real' potentiality in the previous discussion on 'potency' and 'act,' belongs to this class.

More or less in opposition to these natural capacities are the incapacities. By an 'incapacity' we do not mean the total absence of a faculty, because that would no longer be a faculty of action. By *incapacity* we understand an *existing faculty in a weakened or unfit condition*. The worn spring of an automobile, having lost a great amount of its resilience, would be an incapacity. A weak dry cell in a flashlight would be another instance of incapacity. A drooping flower, a drought-affected tree, a mildewed patch of grain, manifest a diminished power of vegetative function; but they still are living beings. Lameness of limb, astigmatism of the eyes, and other functional deficiencies, do not deprive the animal completely of its faculties and their use, but they render it more or less unfit for action. Psychopathic conditions, like insanity, idiocy, and sexual perversion, are at times the result of physiological abnormalities; they are incapacities which hinder the intellect and will in their proper functioning.

AFFECTIVE QUALITIES AND AFFECTIONS

Affective qualities and affections are qualities which *produce, or result from, some accidental sensible alteration*. If this alteration is relatively permanent, it is an *affective quality;* if it is more or less ephemeral in character, it is an *affection*. The term 'affection,' as should be obvious from the context, does not mean love or devotedness; it is used in the sense of 'affecting' or 'being affected by' something. It was stated in the definition above that affective qualities and affections 'produce' or 'result from' alterations. Both types may be the *cause* or *effect* of such alterations in a sense-organism. Hence, any sensible alteration involved in sense-perception or sense-appetition belongs to this class. This includes the sensible qualities of bodies, like color, flavor, odor, sound, temperature, the feel of smoothness and resistance, etc.; the sensible passions and emotions, like anger, lust, pleasure, pain, etc.

Taking the terms in the above-mentioned meanings, a *permanent* red color of the cheeks, due to a systemic condition of the body, would be an 'affective quality'; such, too, would be the natural color of the skin in the various races of mankind, the blue color of the violet, the sweetness of sugar, the sourness of the lemon, the fragrance of the rose, the obnoxious odor of asafoetida, etc. If such qualities are temporal and *transient,* they are 'affections.' The blush of shame, the pallor of fear; heat, color, moistness, dryness, hardness, softness, etc., when of short duration or easily removed; the states of sensation, as they exist in the organs of sight, hearing, taste, etc.; brief spells of anger, fear, grief, hunger, thirst, and so on: these are various kinds of 'affections.'

It was stated that these terms apply to accidents which *cause* such changes as well as to accidents which are the *effects* of such changes. This will be noted in the illustrations enumerated. Thus, the 'red' of the rose and the 'sweetness' of the sugar cause the sensation of 'vision of red' and of the 'taste of sweetness' in the perceiver; they are the *causes* of corporeal changes in the perceiver and are affective qualities for that reason. On the other hand, the 'perception' of red and of sweetness is the *effect* of the red color in the rose and of the sweetness in the sugar, in as much as the qualities of the rose and of the sugar produce sensations in the organs of the perceiver; this 'perception' is, therefore, an 'affection.' And this holds true of the other affective qualities and affections.

The *soul* also has its affective qualities and affections. According to Aristotle: "That temper with which a man is born and which has its origin in certain deep-seated affections is called a quality [affective quality]. I mean such conditions as insanity, irascibility, and so on; for people are said to be mad or irascible in virtue of these. Similarly, those abnormal psychic states which are not inborn, but arise from the concomitance of certain other elements, and are difficult to remove, or altogether permanent, are called qualities, for in virtue of them men are said to be such and such. Those, however, which arise from causes easily rendered ineffective are called affections, not [affective] qualities. Suppose that a man is irascible when vexed: he is not even spoken of as a bad-tempered man, when in such circumstances he loses his temper somewhat, but rather he is said to be affected. Such conditions are therefore termed, not [affective] qualities, but affections."[4]

What Aristotle here remarks about one or the other quality of the soul, is especially true of the *temperaments* of people. Four types of temperament are usually mentioned — a division that is more convenient than accurate. They are: the choleric, the phlegmatic, the sanguine, and the melancholic. *Choleric* persons are energetic and vigorous in action, strong-willed, ambitious, tenacious of purpose, not easily discouraged, capable of overcoming great obstacles, quick-tempered, and opinionated. *Phlegmatic* persons are unhurried in their movements, lethargic in disposition, slow of decision, unruffled in temper, indolent, difficult to arouse, unimaginative, easily discouraged in the face of difficulties. *Sanguine* people are lively, enthusiastic, imaginative, witty, sociable, quick in movement and speech, eager for novelty, prone to flightiness, easily led by appeal, adventurous, and inclined to follow romantic ideals. *Melancholic* persons are introspective and brooding, sad of disposition, inclined to see the dark side of life, given to discouragement, easily hurt in their feelings, unforgiving and unforgetting, suspicious of motives, obdurate in judgment, ec-

---

[4] *Categoriae*, Ch. 9 b 35; 10 a 1-10.

centric in conduct, aloof in social life. The very complexity of temperaments is an indication that they rest upon a variety of affective qualities which are partly bodily and partly mental. While the general types are fairly clear and plainly recognizable, there is in the vast majority of cases a blending of temperamental characteristics; this again is due to the fact that they are the composite result of a number of affective qualities existing in an individual person.

In all instances of affective qualities and affections, a certain amount of *sensible alteration* or change is noticeable. This is but natural, since chemical, physical, and mechanical energies play a prominent role in all operations of sense-perception and sense-appetition, either directly or indirectly, either as causes or as effects. Sentient life is strongly influenced by these energies and is also instrumental in releasing these energies. But wherever energy is at work, alterations or changes are bound to be involved. Hence it happens that affective qualities and affections either *produce* such alterations or *result* from them.

FORM AND FIGURE

Form or *figure* is the *quality resulting in a body from the arrangement of its quantitative parts.* There is no real difference between the concepts of 'form' and 'figure,' except that the term 'figure' is used of the shape of a *geometrical* quantity, while the term 'form' is used of the shape of a natural body in its *physical* quantity as it exists in nature. In geometry, for instance, we speak of the 'figure' of a circle, of a triangle, of a square, of a cube, of a rhombus. But when speaking of actually existing bodies, we say that the 'form' of an orange is spherical, that of a pyramid is triangular, that of a shaft is cylindrical, etc. 'Form' as a quality is altogether different from 'form' as the determining substantial principle which unites with matter in a composite substance; 'form' as a quality is here taken in the sense of 'shape' and is but an accidental modification of a bodily substance. It is well to remember, however, that in ordinary language the terms 'form' and 'figure' are

sometimes used synonymously, as when people say that 'So-
and-so has a beautiful figure.'

Some *physical forms* are given by *nature* itself. The atomic
structure of chemical elements possess a definite form. Many
inorganic substances arrange themselves into crystals of sharply
defined configurations. All plants, from bacteria to the giant
sequoias, assume a form characteristic of their genus and
species. The roots, stems, branches, flowers, and fruits follow a
distinct pattern, notwithstanding the almost infinite number
of variations found among the individuals of a species. This is
also true of animals. Though unlike each other in many minor
points, the individuals of a class can always be recognized by
the distinctive forms of their bodies; they all conform to type.
There are, of course, sports in nature which deviate from this
type, but even they have a permanent form in which the general pattern can be recognized.

Other physical forms are *artificial,* the result of man's ingenuity and art or of nature's forceful activity. Man can mold
and arrange the objects found as crude materials into a multitude of forms. Stones, woods, and metals are shaped to suit his
manifold needs and to give expression to his aesthetic tastes.
He erects buildings, constructs machines, carves statues, paints
pictures, fashions clothes, landscapes gardens, builds highways, prints books. Nature by means of wind and weather and
earthquakes, raises the mountains towering to the skies, levels
the plains, digs the valleys, places the rivers and oceans in their
beds, directs the seasons, and in general gives shape to the
world. The individual objects in none of these instances would
assume these forms of their own accord and in virtue of their
intrinsic nature; they do so because of the interplay of natural
forces impressed upon them from without.

Whatever the individual form, whether the result of the
intrinsic nature of the being itself or imposed upon it by an
outside agency, the object must have within itself the *quality*
which enables it to *obtain and retain* a definite form. Without
such a quality things would flow from one amorphous condi-

tion of change into another, indistinct and indistinguishable as
to form. The very fact that all things are built up ultimately
of protons and electrons arranged into an atomic structure
and a system, shows that the quality of form is inherent even
in the smallest particles of material substance.

CHARACTERISTICS OF QUALITY

Qualities have *characteristics* which, though not properties
in the strict sense of the term as something which emanates
necessarily from the essence, are more or less *general*.

Qualities have contraries. Contraries are realities which are
extremes under the same genus and cannot co-exist in the same
individual. 'Being' and 'non-being,' 'life' and 'death,' and
similar pairs of concepts, are not contrary, but contradictory,
and there is no common genus for such pairs, because the one
member is the utter negation of the other and contains no
positive reality which could be placed under the positive reality
of a genus; hence, such pairs are not contrary. Qualities can
be contrary, because both extremes are positive realities under
a common genus. 'White' and 'black,' for instance, are the two
extremes under the genus of 'color'; color is thus a quality
which admits of contraries. 'Justice' and 'injustice,' though
seemingly contradictory, are really contraries, considering them
as *habits* affecting the will; 'moral habit' is the genus for both.
So, too, 'health' and 'disease,' 'science' and 'ignorance,' considered as *states* of being, are contrary qualities. *Not all* qualities, however, have contraries. There are, for instance, no contraries to operative powers or faculties; one either possesses an
intellect and will, or one does not. Neither are there contraries
to form or figure; there is nothing contrary to the square or
circular or triangular shape in an individual, because a
'triangle' is simply a 'triangle' and can be nothing else.

Qualities are susceptible of degrees. Many qualities can be
present in varying degrees of intensity or reality. Some people
have a greater capacity for knowledge than others, just as some
people acquire more knowledge than others. Virtues and vices

can be intensified by habits. Some habits are more deeply rooted in an individual than others, and the particular habits are increased or diminished in an individual in the course of time. Dispositions and indispositions may be present in greater or lesser degrees; thus, the feeling of well-being may be more marked at one time than another, and neuralgia has many degrees of painfulness. Some operative powers increase and decrease in efficiency, as we observe in eyesight, hearing, locomotion, and so on. On the other hand, form and figure admit of no variations. Nothing can be more a square or less a square; a 'square' has an absolutely specified shape, and any deviation from it would make the object cease to be a 'square.'

Qualities are the foundation for similarity and dissimilarity. When things are one in substance, they are identical; when they are one in quantity, they are equal; but when they are one in quality, they are similar. In order that things can be said to be 'similar,' it is necessary that the *same kind* of quality be present in them. Two roses are similar, when both are white or red or yellow. Two patients are similar, when both have the same kind of illness. Human beings in general are similar, because their bodily form is alike. Saints are similar, because they possess virtue in a heroic degree. Since only those things are said to be (accidentally) similar which are characterized by the same kind of qualities, quality is the foundation or basis of the relation of similarity and dissimilarity; and since this is peculiar to quality, it is a *property* of quality.

MATERIALISM AND QUALITIES

Qualities have always been the bugbear of *materialistic* scientists and philosophers. In their view, the universe of bodies consists ultimately of atoms (or protons, electrons, etc.) which are indivisible and unchangeable. Elements and bodies originate through a mere arrangement and configuration of these ultimate particles; substantial change is an illusion and abstraction. Whatever happens is the result of *mechanical motion* and gives rise to nothing more than a shift of *local relations* of a *quantitative* character among masses, molecules, atoms, and electrons and protons. These ultimate material particles are homogeneous in nature; that is to say, they are absolutely alike in essence, so that they differ only in size and shape. Hence, everything in the universe can be explained by means of quantitative structure and spatial motion, and our knowledge of things is complete when we can express them in a mathematical formula of quantitative measurement. There is no place for 'qualities' in such a materialistic and mechanistic conception of the universe; *matter in motion* is the sum-total of all objects and events. Thus, what common people and philosophers term 'quality' is reducible to 'quantity.'

The opposition of materialists to 'hidden qualities' is based on the same grounds as their opposition to 'hidden substance': our knowledge is solely a knowledge of sense-perception, and the sense *cannot perceive qualities;* hence, qualities are unknowable and as such can have no claim to existence.

When materialistic scientists advance the claim that matter and motion or energy are sufficient to explain the events of nature, they overlook the fact entirely that the *mental life of man* is also an event in the existing universe. Man is just as much a part of nature as is the atom, the proton, and the electron; and man's mind is just as much a reality as is his body. Hence, the mental processes of man's mind must be accounted for and explained in a manner satisfactory to the demands of reason. These mental processes, however, can never be adequately explained on the mere basis of matter and the mechanical, spatial relations of motion. The energies and motions of matter, as materialists view them, are inorganic, while the mind and its processes are decidedly more than that.

Take, for example, *sense-perception,* the experience of which plays such an all-important part in the theory of materialism. All that we know of sense-perception we know through consciousness; and all we know of the world outside us we know through sense-perception: hence, all that we know about the world and ourselves rests on the ultimate testimony of our consciousness. Now, consciousness tells us that sense-perception is more than mere matter and motion. Certainly, motion accompanies all processes of sense-perception (although we are not directly conscious of this), and this motion is quantitative and can be measured. But there is much more than this to perception. *We perceive things,* not processes, with our senses. This perception itself, *precisely as 'perception,'* is something totally different from the inorganic movements of dead particles of matter: it is a *cognitive* process, a process of *knowing,* and that cannot be explained by the mechanical dance of the molecules, atoms, electrons, and protons which make up the material structure of the sense-organs. These 'perceptions' are as real as the particles of matter and the sub-atomic movements of these particles. These 'perceptions,' however, are something *over and above* the mechanical movements of such particles: they are real *affections* in man's mental life, distinct from matter and mechanical motion, and as such are *qualities.* Furthermore, since these 'perceptions' cannot be explained by matter and mechanical motion, nor by the material energies present in inorganic nature, they must proceed from some *other principle* present in the mind itself. Hence, sense-perception demands a principle or power or faculty of its own, distinct from the common mechanical energies of inorganic nature, for each kind of sense has a different kind of 'perception.' But these powers or faculties we name *qualities.* Consequently, qualities exist.

Similarly, our consciousness testifies to the fact that we *think* and *will*. It would take an enormous stretch of the imagination to reduce 'thinking' and 'willing' to some form of mechanical, inorganic motion. No one can seriously assert that the formation of ideas, judgments, and inferences are motions due to cohesion, adhesion, electricity, gravitational attraction, or to any other form of energy known in the world of physics or chemistry. Nor can anyone honestly claim that love and hatred, desire and aversion, joy and sorrow, are merely forms of attraction and repulsion in a physical and chemical sense. But if not, then they, too, must emanate from principles distinct from the ordinary energies of inorganic matter present in nature. We call the principle of thinking the 'intellect' and the principle of willing the 'will.' *Intellect* and *will,* therefore, are powers or faculties; and such powers or faculties we style *qualities.* Consequently, qualities exist.

The same line of argument applies to every kind of *vital activity* found in *plant* or *animal* or *man,* in so far as they are distinctive of these classes or species. There are, of course, activities and motions present in them which are mechanical, physical, and chemical; and they can be measured according to quantitative standards. But in every organism there is a *residue of activity* which cannot be explained on the basis of matter and motion. Reason, therefore, demands that these vital activities proceed from *vital* powers or *faculties.* And since all faculties are qualities, qualities exist.

As a matter of fact, the materialistic scientists themselves admit unwittingly that qualities exist. They speak constantly of *energy* in nature. Most of them insist that phenomena like cohesion and adhesion, attraction and repulsion, light and heat, etc., are the results of various forms of energy, though many incline to the theory that all phenomena are the results of one fundamental energy, namely, electromagnetic energy. But *energy in some form* is accepted, together with *matter.* Even such a crass materialist as Büchner admitted the existence of *Kraft und Stoff* (Force and Matter). But what is 'force' or 'energy,' if not the 'power or capacity to do work' in some form or other? Energy is not the work itself that is done, but the *power or capacity* to do work. 'Power,' however, is what we call a *quality.* To refuse to accept the existence of 'quality,' while they accept the existence of 'energy,' is an inconsistency which ill becomes them; because 'energy' is not a datum of sense-perception at all, but something which reason demands as an adequate explanation of existing phenomena as we perceive them. Here again, as in the case of 'substance,' materialistic scientists admit the *thing,* though they will not admit the *name.* Moleschott, for example, accepted 'chemical affinity' as a fact of nature. F. A. Lange accused him with fine irony of inconsistency, in the following words: "Here we find Moleschott deep in scholasticism; his 'relationship' [between oxygen and potassium] is the prettiest *qualitas occulta* [hidden quality] that can be wished for. It sits in the oxygen like a man with hands. If potassium comes anywhere near, it is laid hold of; if none comes, at least the hands are there, and the wish to get hold of potassium."[5] And so the arguments of materialists simmer down to a quarrel of words.

In a discussion of this kind it is sufficient to prove that *one* quality exists; it settles the argument. Once the existence of a quality of any kind is proved and accepted, there should be no trouble in accepting the various kinds of qualities. While any serviceable division is satisfactory, Aristotle's division has the advantage of compactness and completeness. We have therefore followed him in his enumeration of qualities: habit and disposition; natural capacity and incapacity; affective qualities and affections; form and figure. Something might have been said of the 'relative' character of some of the qualities, but 'relation' is a separate category which will be treated in the next chapter.

SUMMARY OF CHAPTER XIX

Quality is the first of the categorical accidents with which ontology is concerned; the category of 'quantity' will be treated in cosmology.

1. *The Concept of Quality.* 'Quality' admits of no strict philosophical definition, because 'accident' is not a univocal term and thus cannot be used as a proximate genus. 'Quality' can be described as an absolute accident, completing and determining a substance in its *being* and in its *operation.* Aris-

---

[5] *The History of Materialism,* tr. by Ernest C. Thomas, 3rd ed., Harcourt, Brace, and Co. (Kegan Paul, Trench, Trubner and Co.), 1925, Bk. I, Sect. 2, Ch. II, p. 377.

totle enumerates four *types:* habit and disposition; natural capacity and incapacity; affective quality and affection; form and figure.

2. *Habit and Disposition.* A *habit* is a comparatively permanent quality disposing a thing well or ill in its being. A *disposition* is a relatively transient quality which disposes a thing well or ill. An *operative* habit disposes a thing well or ill in its operation. Strictly speaking, only a free faculty is capable of habit; such is the will of man. Indirectly, under the influence of the will, other faculties can be said to acquire habits. Some habits are natural, others acquired; there are also supernatural habits.

3. *Natural Capacity and Incapacity.* A natural *capacity* is the proximate accidental principle of operation, toward which (operation) it is specifically directed. All beings — inorganic, vegetative, sentient, and rational — possess natural capacities. An *incapacity* is an existing *faculty* in a weakened or unfit condition.

4. *Affective Qualities and Affections.* An *affective quality* is a relatively permanent quality which produces, or results from, some accidental sensible alteration. If such a quality is more or less ephemeral in character, it is an *affection.* The 'sensible qualities' of color, sound, etc., and also their 'perception,' belong to this class. The *soul* also has affective qualities and affections. Chief among the affective qualities of the soul are the *temperaments.* A temperament may be choleric, phlegmatic, sanguine, or melancholic.

5. *Form and Figure.* Form or figure is a quality resulting in a body from the arrangement of its quantitative parts. Geometrical shapes are called 'figures'; physical shapes are called 'forms.' Some physical forms are natural, others artificial.

6. *Characteristics of Quality.* Qualities have contraries. Qualities are susceptible of degrees. Qualities are the foundation for the relation of similarity and dissimilarity.

7. *Materialism and Qualities.* Generally speaking, materialists try to explain all things in the universe as *matter in motion.*

They are opposed to 'hidden qualities,' because qualities cannot be perceived by the senses. However, sense-perception is not the only source of knowledge; *reason* is a valid source, otherwise scientific *induction* is invalid.

Matter, force, energy, atoms, protons, and electrons, accepted by materialists, cannot be perceived by the *senses;* their existence is guaranteed by *reason.*

The *perception* of things, as cognition, demands a mental principle or faculty. *Thinking* and willing are not mechanical; they demand the faculties of intellect and will. The same is true of all *vital* functions. *Energy,* as a *capacity* for work, is a quality. Hence, qualities exist.

READINGS

Coffey, P., Ch. X; Hugon, Ed., Tr. III, Qu. IV, art. 1 et 2; Aristotle, *Categ.,* c. 6–8, *Metaph.* V, c. 14; Mercier, D. Card., nn. 161 ff.; Urráburu, J. J., Disp. VI, cp. I; McCormick, J. F., Ch. VIII; Osgniach, A. J., Ch. XI.

Chapter XX

RELATION

'RELATION' AND the 'relative' are concepts which play a very important part in modern philosophy. The *relative* stands in opposition to the *absolute*. One can safely state that in the past century and a half philosophers have written more about these two concepts than about any other two concepts within the whole range of philosophy. Modern philosophy has been, and still is, chiefly concerned with the problem of human knowledge, and in this problem the 'relative' and 'absolute' are the key-ideas. These concepts are the foundation for entire systems of thought. This alone shows the importance of the category of 'relation.'

THE CONCEPT OF RELATION

What constitutes a 'relation'? Three factors or elements are necessary and suffice to constitute a 'relation': the subject, the term, and the foundation. The *subject* of the relation is the thing *that* is related to another. The *term* of the relation is the thing *to which* the subject is related. The *foundation* of the relation is the basis, the ground, the *reason why* the subject is related to the term. The 'subject' and the 'term' are also styled the *extremes,* because the 'foundation' is the connecting link or bond which unites the subject and term together and places them 'in relation' to each other.

From this it should be plain that one thing alone, taken for itself, can never form a relation; relation must exist *between two or more* things taken in reference to each other. The essence of 'relation,' considered formally as such, consists in the *'esse ad,'* the *'being-toward'* of one thing to another; it is the bearing, the reference, the attitude, the ordination of one to another due to some foundation which is a common bond between them. The *foundation* is the necessary *condition* for a relation, but it is not the 'relation' itself. The foundation is present in both the subject and the term, and it is because of this foundation that the subject and the term are connected, giving each a 'respect toward' the other, so that they are thereby 'related' or 'in relation.' Two white horses, for example, are similar to each other in their white color; their whiteness is not the relation of their similarity; but it is the reason or foundation of their relation of similarity; as such, then, they stand to each other in a 'relation of similarity' because of the white color present in both. The 'relation,' therefore, *results from* the presence of a common foundation in a subject and term and is considered to be, at least conceptually, distinct from the foundation, the subject, and the term.

No strict definition of 'relation' can be given. The only concept which could be used as its proximate genus in such a definition would be 'accident.' But 'accident,' as was pointed out before, is not used univocally of its inferior members; it can be applied to the various categories only in an analogous sense. Using a descriptive definition, we define *relation* as the *bearing* (reference, respect, attitude, ordination) *of one thing to something else.*

KINDS OF RELATION

All relations can be grouped into two main classes: *logical* and *real*.

Logical Relation. A logical relation is defined as a relation *made solely by the mind and placed by the mind between entities.* Such entities may exist outside the mind, or may be concepts, judgments, and inferences existing in the mind itself. The foundation for such a relation is an *ens rationis,* a logical entity. There is no real foundation in the extra-mental things themselves for making such a relation; the relation, therefore, is strictly a product of the mind's thinking. Thus, we systematize our ideas and in this manner bring them into relation with one another, when we study a certain branch of knowledge: such relations are logical. Between every subject and predicate in a sentence there exists a certain relation of comprehension and extension: this is also a logical relation. So, too, there is a definite relation of sequence between the premises and conclusion of an inference; and also between a number of inferences in an extended argumentation: such relations, however, are logical, because they exist solely in the mind and its operations.

In a similar manner, we often place relations between objects *outside the mind,* although these relations have no reason or foundation in the properties of the things themselves. The relation between the little black marks of print on this page and the ideas which they represent and convey to the reader, is purely logical, because these black hooks and dots have no significance except in so far as the mind selects and designates them to have a meaning. A scepter represents royal dignity; a palm, victory; a red light, danger; a flag, a country: but the relation between these things is purely of the mind's own making and has no foundation in the things themselves.

Real Relation. A real relation is defined as a relation which exists *between things, independent of the mind and its thinking.* The subject and the term are real entities in nature; the foundation of the relation is present in them *objectively* and is not merely conceived by the mind as being there. There is thus a connection or bond between real things, due to something present in them, independent of all thought; and this connection or bond would exist, even if there were no mind adverting to it. Such a relation exists, for instance, between parent and offspring, between plant and flower, between two pups of the same litter, between two trees of equal height, between two houses of the same architectural style, etc.

A real relation may be either essential (transcendental) or accidental (categorical, predicamental). An *essential* (or *transcendental*) relation is one in which the very *essence* of one thing has a relation or bearing toward something. This relation will, therefore, always be present as soon and as long as this essence is present; the essence cannot exist without this relation. Thus the relation between every being and an intellect and will, making this being 'true' and 'good,' is essential and transcendental, because it is an essential and transcendental attribute of all being to be true and good. Every creature owes its entire essence and existence to the Creator, and the relation of the creature to the Creator is thus an essential one. The relation between body and soul in man is an essential relation, because both are ordinated toward each other to form a composite substance, and this ordination lies in their very essence. A similar condition obtains between every incomplete substantial part and the substantial whole of which it is the part.

An *accidental* (or *categorical,* or *predicamental*) relation is one based upon an *accident* as its foundation. The accident which serves as the foundation for the relation is something superadded to the essence and its absence would not destroy the essence itself. Two children have blond and curly hair; in this respect they stand to each other in the relation of similarity. Two men are six feet tall; they are related to each other through the equality of the quantitative measurements. Obviously, 'blond and curly hair' and the equal 'height of six feet' are accidental modifications of these persons and do not belong to their essence.

From another standpoint relations are divided into *mutual* and *non-mutual.*

A relation is *non-mutual,* if its foundation is *real or logical in one of the extremes only.* A case in point would be the relation of knowledge between the knowing subject and the known object. The foundation or basis of the relation is the transition from a state of non-knowledge to a state of knowledge with regard to some definite object; this transition involves a real change. It is obvious, however, that only one extreme undergoes this transition and change, namely, the knowing subject which acquires the knowledge. The relation of knowledge is real only on the part of the knower; on the part of the thing it is only logical.

On the other hand, a relation is *mutual,* if its foundation is *real or logical in both extremes.* If two horses are white, the foundation of the relation of their similarity, namely, 'white color,' is present in both horses. In children of the same parents the relation of origin is present in each, and this relation is mutual. When two poles have a length of ten feet, the foundation of their equality in length, namely, their quantity, is found in each pole, because each one is ten feet long, independent of the other; the relation, therefore, is mutual.

A mutual relation is said to be one of the *same denomination* or *symmetrical,* when the foundation in both extremes is of the *same nature* and *degree.* The whiteness of the horses, the common origin of children in the same family, the equal length of the poles, as mentioned in the preceding paragraph, are of the same denomination, because the foundation is of the same nature and degree in each.

A mutual relation is said to be of *mixed denomination* or *asymmetrical,* when the foundation present in both extremes is of a *different nature* or *degree.* Father and child are related; but the father is the cause, while the child is the effect. This means a difference of foundation in both and consequently also a difference in relation of the one to the other, because filiation implies a state of dependence of the child with respect to its father, while paternity implies a state of independence of the father with respect to his child. Many relations are of this kind; for example, that between husband and wife, master and servant, physician and patient, lawyer and client, judge and criminal, teacher and pupil, superior and subject, king and people, and so on.

The examples given above for mutual relations pertain to *all* relations which are mutually present in both extremes, whether of the same or of a mixed denomination. Mutual relations, however, may also be purely *logical.* Such mutual logical relations would rest upon a foundation which is conceptual or logical in *both extremes*. Thus, all relations existing between concepts, judgments, and inferences rest upon foundations which have no existence except in the mental order, because the concepts, judgments, and inferences themselves are logical entities and as such have no existence outside the mind. Such would be the relation between subject and predicate in a sentence, all relations of grammatical construction, etc. Formal logic, or the science of correct thinking, is practically a treatise on mutual logical relations.

THE FOUNDATION OF RELATION

The foundation of relation, as was stated before, is the basis, the ground, the *reason why* one thing is related to another. Almost anything can be taken as the point of comparison, so as to establish a relation between things. Every category contains such foundations.

Substance contains the foundation for *specific identity* and *diversity*. Two flasks of water, two elm trees, two sparrows, two men, etc. (the two members of each pair being compared together), are identical in species; and each pair, compared with another pair in this series, is different in species. We thus have the relation of specific identity existing among all the individuals of a certain species, and the relation of specific diversity among the individuals of different species.

Quantity contains the foundation for the relation of *equality* and *inequality*. Things that have the same weight, size, volume, shape, or dimensions are equal to each other on account of their quantity, while things which differ from each other in these respects are unequal. Two globes of the same diameter have the relation of equality; a quart and a gallon of wine have the relation of inequality.

Quality contains the foundation of *similarity* and *dissimilarity*. For example, we speak of two painters as being similar or dissimilar in their technique; of two philosophers as being similar or dissimilar in their opinions; of two dogs as being similar or dissimilar in their behavior.

Action and *passion* (*reaction*) contain the foundation of the relation of *cause* and *effect*. We observe this relation extensively in mechanical, physical, and chemical agencies. Salt is the effect of the combination of sodium and chlorine, and as such it is in relation to these two chemicals. Iron is attracted to a magnet; the two are thus related. Electricity produces light and heat; these are, therefore, related to electricity as effects to their cause.

Time contains the foundation for *priority, simultaneity,* and *posteriority* in successive duration. The murder of Julius Caesar is in the relation of priority to the death of Napoleon; the murder of Julius Caesar, however, is in the relation of posteriority to the death of Aristotle.

Place contains the foundation of the relation of *distance, nearness,* and relative *position*. The moon is nearer to the earth than to the sun; between the moon and the earth, therefore, there is the relation of comparative nearness. The positions of north, east, south, and west, or right and left, or before and behind, or up and down, or inside and outside, etc., give rise to relations among objects.

Posture and *habitus* contain the foundation of the relation of *similarity* and *dissimilarity* between things, but in a different manner than the qualities. To be prone, or to be erect, makes objects either similar or dissimilar; thus, there is a relation of dissimilarity between one man lying down and another man standing. So, too, to be clothed or not clothed, shod or not shod, etc., makes two persons either similar or dissimilar.

From this it will be seen that every category contains items which may be the foundation for various sorts of relations between things.

SOME AXIOMS CONCERNING RELATION

Correlatives are simultaneous in nature. By this we mean that related things, precisely and *formally* as in relation to each other, must exist at the same time and the one cannot exist before the other. Thus, 'mother' and 'child' are correlatives. Obviously, the mother as a 'woman' or 'human being' exists before her child. But as a 'mother' she must have a 'child,' and she cannot be a 'mother' before she has a 'child'; at the very moment when her child begins to exist she is a 'mother,' and not a moment sooner nor a moment later.

Correlatives are simultaneous in knowledge. This means that the knowledge of one extreme as 'relative' always involves the knowledge of the other extreme as 'correlative.' And in truth, it is impossible to know what 'parent' is without also knowing what 'offspring' is. If we know that the Washington Monument is smaller than the Empire State Building, we must have a knowledge of the size of each.

Correlatives connote each other. This means that the intelligibility of the one extreme is dependent on the intelligibility of the other; they can be understood only in reference to each other. This follows from the foregoing principle. The concept of 'offspring' involves the concept of 'parent,' and *vice versa.* That two figures are similar to each other in their triangularity implies that the understanding of the 'triangular shape' of the one involves the understanding of the 'triangular shape' of the other; otherwise it would be impossible to know that they are similar. Hence, no relative term, strictly as 'relative,' can be defined without bringing the correlative term into the definition, because they cannot be understood except in reference to each other.

EXISTENCE OF REAL RELATIONS

The philosophy of relations gives rise to a very serious problem. Are relations merely the product of our minds and their relating activity, so that things are 'conceived' as related to each other simply because the mind has a natural tendency to arrange and classify all things in conceptual groups? Or, are relations also present in nature, among the things existing in the universe, so that these things are related to each other, even though no mind be thinking of them? In short, are relations merely conceptual and *logical,* or are they actual and *real?*

Many philosophers deny that relations are real and maintain that all relations are *purely mental and logical* in character. Modern phenomenalists and idealists are especially persistent in their view that the entire conception of order in the universe is *projected* into it by the mind. *Kant,* for example, maintains that our knowledge is the result of applying certain innate mental forms to the chaotic manifold of sense-intuitions, thereby bringing order and definite relations into them. The monistic idealists, like *Fichte, Hegel,* etc., contend that our *knowledge is constitutive of reality* as we experience it. If this were true, all relations would, of course, be purely mental and logical, because all knowledge would then be completely mind-made: in this view, the mind would not acquire its knowledge by conforming itself to the things, but things acquire their reality by being conformed to the mind. It is not the purpose of ontology to prove the existence of a physical world which is independent of the mind; this is a fact which epistemology must vindicate.[1] Here we accept the reality of the physical world and maintain that some *relations are real* and independent of the mind.

In order that a relation may be real and not merely logical, the following *conditions* must be fulfilled: the subject of the relation must be real; the term must be real; the foundation in the subject must be real; the foundation must be really distinct from the term. In other words, there must be a real, individual subject, a real, individual term, and a real foundation existing in both extremes.

First of all, the *natural sciences* teem with demonstrations of real relations in nature. The scientific classification of plants and animals is based upon *structural similarity.* The only reason why science can arrange plants and animals in a hierarchical order of kingdoms, phyla, classes, orders, families,

---

[1] See the author's *Reality and the Mind,* Ch. IX and X.

genera, species, and individuals, is because each individual is similar to others in certain well-marked properties and peculiarities. These properties and peculiarities are real in each individual, independent of the mind which recognizes them. Certainly, no one would seriously claim that science first made these structures similar. Hence, if there is structural resemblance among plants and animals in nature, real relations exist in nature.

Again, there is *dependence* in nature. Plants are dependent on various things in nature for their existence and substance: air, soil, light, warmth, moisture. Animals need plants for food, and man needs both animals and plants. In the case of bi-sexual forms of plants and animals, the sexes are dependent upon each other for the propagation of their kind. This dependence is without question a real fact of nature, and is not a product of our thinking. But 'dependence' of one upon another is a reference, an ordination, of one thing to another. And since this is the relation of a real dependence of one real being upon another real being, real relations exist in nature.

Nations with their governing and governed classes, international commerce, diplomatic service, wars, peace contracts, industrial and agricultural difficulties, cultural, social and religious contacts, etc. — these and similar things are realities in human society and in the world, independent of our thinking. They constitute real relationships among real people.

Furthermore, physics and astronomy assure us that all beings in the universe, from the electrons and protons in the atoms to the interstellar nebulae and star-galaxies, are continuously in motion and are drawn toward each other in virtue of gravitational attraction. All this implies a 'reference of one to the other' with regard to *distance, position,* and relative *motion.* The only way to deny the fact of their real relation would be to deny the fact of their real existence; only a confirmed subjectivist, however, would do that.

Then, too, *active production* is a universal fact of nature. Leaving the formation of chemical compounds aside, there can be no question that living beings produce living things. This is true of plants and animals, as well as of men. If so, then the relation of *offspring to parent* is a real relation. It would assuredly be ridiculous to assert that plants and animals propagated their species only after man's mind adverted to them. But if plants and animals did propagate before the coming of man, the relation of offspring to parents was a fact in nature before man's mind was present to 'relate' them. But a relation between real beings, based upon a real foundation like generative production, is a real relation, independent of man's mind and its thinking.

Hence, if we accept the existence of a real world outside the mind, we must also accept the existence of real relations among the things of this world. No thing can exist together with other things, without some real relations being established between them.

THE ENTITY OF REAL RELATION

Every relation contains three factors: a subject, a term, and a foundation. The 'relation,' considered strictly as such, is not the 'subject' itself nor the 'term' itself, because the relation is the *bond* which connects and links the extremes together, so that there is a reference or ordination of each to the other. Nor is the relation, considered strictly as such, the 'foundation.' The foundation is the basis, the ground, the reason for the relation. The foundation is always some reality, essential or accidental, which is either a 'being-*in*-itself' or a 'being-*in*-another'; the relation, however, is formally a 'being-*toward*' something. Hence, there is no question that there is a distinction between the concept of the 'relation' and the concept of the 'foundation.'

Is the *distinction* between the 'relation' and the 'foundation' *real* or only *virtual*? If we maintain a *real* distinction between them, we must consider the 'relation' to be an *accidental entity or mode* superadded to the entity of the foundation in the extremes. This would mean, for example, that, besides the quality of 'whiteness' which makes two horses similar, there would be a distinct entity or mode of 'similarity' added (as a relation) to the 'whiteness' in each horse. If we maintain only a *virtual* distinction between them, the 'relation' would be no *new entity or mode* added to the extremes besides the foundation itself. This would mean, in the example given, that the relation of 'similarity' between two white horses would be in reality identical with the quality of 'whiteness' present in each horse. We maintain that only a *virtual distinction* exists between the relation and the foundation. In order to prove this, we appeal to the following principles and facts.

If the 'relation' were really distinct from the foundation, it would follow that the 'relation' would be a real entity or mode which would be *acquired* when a relation is established, and *lost* when a relation is discontinued. However, to acquire or lose a real entity or mode involves a *real change,* and that could be accomplished only by some positive *action producing* the change. Hence, if it can be shown that relations are acquired or lost without a real change occurring in one or both of the extremes, it will be shown thereby that the relation does not consist in a real entity or mode. But this can be shown.

To take an example. In South Africa there exists a pole fifty feet in height. A man in Alaska erects a pole which is also fifty feet in height. The poles are now related to each other through the 'relation of equality.' If this relation be a real entity or mode, the pole in South Africa acquires a new entity or mode which it did not possess before; it has undergone a real change thereby. What possible agency can have introduced this change and given it a new entity or mode? It seems incredible that the mere erection of a pole in Alaska should be able to effect a real change in a pole in South Africa. Since no conceivable real change took place in the latter, we must conclude that a 'relation' does not add any real entity or mode to the extremes which would be distinct from the entity of their foundation.

Again, *substance* and *accident* are *correlatives;* they are 'related.' The inhesion of the accident in the substance is the
foundation connecting them. If this relation were a real entity
or mode, distinct from the entity of the extremes and the
foundation, this entity or mode of the 'relation' would also
be an *accident,* an accidental reality; and as such it, too, would
'inhere' in the substance. Thereby a second 'relation' would be
established. This second relation, being an accident also, establishes a third 'relation' between itself and the supporting substance. This third must bring a fourth 'relation' into existence,
for the same reason. The fourth must produce a fifth, and so
on, into infinity. Thus, an *infinite number* of entities or modes
would be introduced into a substance, simply because we maintain that the relation is a real entity or mode, distinct from the
entity of the extremes and their foundation. An infinite number being impossible, the 'relation' cannot be a real entity or
mode.

Finally, an *immense aggregation* of real entities or modes
would exist in each individual being, if we maintain that a
'relation' is an entity or mode distinct from the extremes and
the foundation. Not only between every individual being as a
whole and every other individual being in the universe, but
also between every single atom of every being and every other
atom in the universe, there exist relations of specific identity
or diversity, of similarity or dissimilarity, of equality or inequality, of distance, time, position, action, etc. Thus, an in-
calculable multiplicity of real entities or modes would be introduced into each being, shifting and changing from moment
to moment. By merely crooking my finger, I would actually
produce a *physical change* (change of relation, due to distance, position, etc.), throughout the universe. This, however,
seems incredible. It is an unnecessary *multiplication of beings,*
and beings should not be multiplied without sufficient reason.
Such a view involves a *power of activity* in each and every
being far beyond the exigencies of their nature, because this
active power of change would reach to every being within the

utmost bounds of the world. Hence, we must conclude that relations are not real entities or modes.

If, however, a relation is *not really distinct* from the extremes and the foundation which constitute the factors of a relation, then the reality of a 'relation' must be somehow *identified with* the extremes and the foundation. The question, therefore, arises: With which factor is the relation identified, with the subject, the term, or the foundation? Or, is it identified with all three factors? The 'relation' is *not identifiable* with the *subject* and *term*. The subject and term (extremes) are not the 'relation,' because they are the things which *become related* through the connecting bond of the relation. And how do they 'become related'? What is the connecting bond which makes them 'related' to each other? It is the 'foundation' which places them 'in relation' to each other. It follows that *the entity of the relation is one with the entity of the foundation*. In reality, then, the 'relation' and the 'foundation' are identical so far as their entity is concerned, and there is no real distinction between them.

Nevertheless, there is a *virtual distinction* between 'relation' and 'foundation.' The foundation is conceived as that reality in things 'because of which' a relation exists between the things; hence, in concept there is a distinction between the foundation and the relation, because the relation 'follows out of' the foundation. An example will make this clearer. Two globes are 'similar' to each other because both are 'white.' The first globe is 'white,' and the second globe is 'white.' This 'whiteness' exists in each, independent of the other; and it is a real accidental entity present in each. There are, therefore, two 'whitenesses' in existence, and these *two* 'whitenesses' (one in each globe) are the foundation for the *one relation of similarity*. Since the relation is one, while the foundation is twofold, and since the foundation (whiteness) exists *in* the globe, while the relation (similarity, due to the whiteness) exists *between* the white globes, it is obvious that a virtual distinction exists

between the 'foundation' and the 'relation.' This distinction
between the two concepts being grounded in the objects themselves, due to the twofold foundation, we come to the final
conclusion that the distinction between the reality of the
'foundation' and the reality of the 'relation' is a *virtual distinction* with a foundation in the thing (*distinctio virtualis cum
fundamento in re*): they are identical in reality, but distinct
in concept, and the ground for the distinction is not purely
mental, but is present in the things themselves.

THE ABSOLUTE AND THE RELATIVE

It has become almost a commonplace in modern philosophy
to say that all being and all knowledge is only 'relative.' The
reason for this spurious axiom lies in the fact that anything,
in order to be known, must enter into a relation with the
mind and as such must be 'relative to mind.' It is, of course,
true that nothing can be known unless it enter into a relation
with the mind, because 'knowledge' in its very concept and
essence implies such a relation. But this only means that a
thing, *when known,* has a relation to the mind and that the
knowledge of the thing is dependent on this relation; it does
not mean that the thing, *as existing,* is dependent on the
mind and its knowledge-relation, so that the *existence* of the
thing would be dependent on our knowing it. A thing must
exist before it can become known; as such, it must be 'absolute'
before it can become 'relative' to our mind.

All creatural beings are, in a true sense, 'relative.' They are
dependent on God as their First Cause for their being and
existence; and 'dependence' is a form of relation. This relation
of the creatures to the Creator is essential to them, and they
can never free themselves from it. Taken in this meaning,
only God is 'absolute,' because He alone is without dependence
on any other being.

Creatural beings are also related in many ways *among themselves.* All, compared to each other, are similar or dissimilar,

equal or unequal, acting or acted upon, specifically identical or diverse.

While relations, therefore, exist among all beings, it would be an erroneous view to hold that there is nothing 'absolute' in things. *Things are both 'absolute' and 'relative.'* That all things can be said to be 'relative,' we have just seen. That they are also 'absolute' in some form, is also true.

A thing is said to be *relative,* when it is taken *in reference to something else;* it is *absolute,* when it is *taken in itself and on its own account.* A relation always implies the three factors of subject, term, and foundation; and the relation, formally considered as 'relation,' is conceived as something 'existing between' the subject and the term due to their common foundation. The 'subject' and 'term' must be distinct in entity. No being is said to be 'related' to its own self; it is always 'in reference to *something else.*' Consequently, both the subject and the term must be 'something in itself and on its own account' before either can have a reference to the other. If they had no being or existence of their own, they could never have a reference to anything. But to have a being and existence of its own means to be 'something in itself and on its own account,' and that means to be *absolute.* Things, therefore, cannot be 'relative' unless they are first 'absolute.' From this it is clear that creatural beings in the universe are both absolute and relative.

But is this not a *contradiction in terms?* Certainly, if it were stated that something were 'absolute' and also 'relative' from the same standpoint and in the same respect, a contradiction would be involved in the statement. A thing, however, can very well be 'relative' from one standpoint and 'absolute' from another; there is no contradiction then. And that is precisely the case in the question under consideration. Considered in themselves and for themselves all things have a being and existence of their own, independent of the being and existence of other things; viewed from this standpoint they are *absolute.* Compared, however, with other things, they are either similar or dissimilar, equal or unequal, etc.; viewed from this stand-point, they are in relation to these others with which they are compared, and as such they are *relative*. As a matter of fact, they can be 'relative' *to others* only because they are 'absolute' *in themselves*. Hence, there is no contradiction in stating that things are both 'absolute' and 'relative,' because the standpoint is different for each designation.

It should now be easy to solve the problem: Can the mind of man *know the 'absolute' or only the 'relative'?* Many modern philosophers claim it can know nothing but the 'relative.' *Sir William Hamilton,* for example, accepts "the great axiom that all human knowledge, consequently that all human philosophy, is only of the relative and phenomenal. In this proposition, the term *relative* is opposed to the term *absolute;* and, therefore, in saying that we know only the relative, I virtually assert that we know nothing absolute — nothing existing absolutely; that is, in itself and for itself, and without relation to us and our faculties."[2] *Herbert Spencer* speaks in a similar vein: "Thinking being relationing, no thought can ever express more than relations."[3] Such views are false. To know that a relation exists, we must know that certain *things are related*. If we do not know these things as they exist in themselves and for themselves, we cannot know the 'foundation' in them which makes the one to be the 'subject' and the other the 'term' of the relation. But this we can and do know.

When we perceive two houses built according to the same plan, we perceive three things: the first house, as it is in itself and for itself; the second house, as it is in itself and for itself; and the identity of plan in each, on account of which they are said to be related as 'similar.' If we did not first perceive each house and its plan separately, as *an entity distinct in itself and for itself,* we could never recognize the 'similarity' which exists between them. But to perceive each house in this manner is to perceive each one as it exists *absolutely*. Only then do we per-

Lectures on Metaphysics, Lect. VIII.
[3] *First Principles,* Part I, Ch. IV.

ceive their similarity and with it the 'relation of similarity' which exists between them, so that they can be said to be 'related to each other.' Hence, the knowledge of things as 'relative' presupposes the knowledge of them as 'absolute': we must always know the terms of a relation before we know the relation itself. Consequently, *the knowledge of the absolute is prior to the knowledge of the relative.*

We may summarize our doctrine of relation in a few sentences: Not all relations are logical in character; some relations are real in nature; the entity of the 'relation' is really identical with the entity of the 'foundation' in the extremes, with a virtual distinction between them; a knowledge of the 'absolute' is necessary before a knowledge of the 'relative' is possible.

SUMMARY OF CHAPTER XX

Much of modern philosophy is based on the concept and category of relation.

1. *The Concept of Relation.* Three factors are involved in relation: subject, term, and foundation. Relation is the bearing (reference, respect, attitude, ordination) of one thing to something else.

2. *Kinds of Relation.* All relations are either logical or real. A *logical* relation is one made solely by the mind and placed by the mind between entities. A *real* relation is one which exists between things, independent of the mind and its thinking.

A real relation is either essential (transcendental) or accidental (categorical, or predicamental). It is *essential,* when the very essence of one thing has a relation toward something. It is *accidental,* when the relation is based upon an accident as its foundation.

Relations are also mutual or non-mutual. It is *non-mutual,* if its foundation is real or logical in one of the extremes only. It is mutual, if its foundation is real or logical in both extremes. A mutual relation is of the same denomination, when the foundation in both extremes is of the same nature and degree; otherwise, it is of mixed denomination.

3. *The Foundation of Relation.* The foundation is the *reason why* one thing is related to another. Almost anything can be taken as the point of comparison. Every category contains foundations for relations.

4. *Axioms Concerning Relation.* Correlatives are simultaneous in nature. Correlatives are simultaneous in knowledge. Correlatives connote each other.

5. *Existence of Real Relations.* Not all relations are purely logical; some are *real in nature.* The systematization of science (e.g., botany and zoology) is based on structural similarity among things as they exist. There is dependence of one thing on another in nature. Nations and human beings in general have real relationships. The production of living beings through generation is a fact of nature. Our consciousness testifies to the fact that the things themselves impose the knowledge of their relations upon us.

6. *The Entity of Real Relation.* A 'relation' is not an *entity or mode* superadded to the entity of the foundation in the extremes. No such entity or mode is required in order to explain the presence of a relation; the existence of the *extremes* and their *foundation* automatically makes the extremes related. If the relation were a new entity or mode, things would be changed with a real alteration without any action. An infinite number of relations would exist in each individual. Things would actively influence every being throughout the universe. This is incredible. Hence, there is only a *virtual* distinction between the 'relation' and the 'foundation.'

7. *Absolute and Relative.* All things are related in some way; in this sense it is true to say that all things are 'relative.' In order, however, that things can be 'relative' *to others,* they must be 'absolute' *in themselves;* that is, they must be something in themselves and for themselves, before they can have a reference to other things. We cannot know that things are

'similar,' 'equal,' etc., to each other, unless we know them first as they are in themselves. Hence, the knowledge of the absolute is prior to the knowledge of the relative.

READINGS

Coffey, P., Ch. XII; Rickaby, J., Bk. II, Ch. IV; Hugon, Ed., Tr. III, Qu. IV, art. 3, 4, 5; Aristotle, *Categ.,* c. V; Urráburu, J. J., Disp. VI, cp. II; McCormick, J. F., Ch. IX, pp. 132–138; Aristotle, *Metaph.,* V; Osgniach, A. J., Ch. IX, X.

Chapter XXI

ACTION, REACTION: CAUSE, EFFECT

IN PASSING from the categories of quality and relation to those of *action* and *reaction* (*passion*), we approach one of the profoundest problems of metaphysics, the problem of *change* and *causality*. This problem, perhaps more than any other, turned the minds of the early Greek thinkers toward a discussion of the origin and constitution of the physical world. That was the beginning of Greek philosophy.

It would be an erroneous view of the world to think of it as an unchanging, static reality *in facto esse,* i.e., in a condition of completed development. And it would be just as erroneous to consider it as an altogether non-permanent, dynamic reality continually *in fieri,* i.e., in a process of ceaseless change and becoming. The fact is, changes occur in things relatively permanent by means of action and reaction.

CONCEPT OF CAUSE AND EFFECT

Whenever a change takes place, it proceeds from an *operative potency,* from an active power or faculty. The exercise, or operation, of an operative potency (active potentiality, power, or faculty), is called *action;* and the being which possesses this operative potency, is called the *agent.* By means of the action of its operative potency the agent produces a change in itself or in another as the recipient of the action. The *reception* of the action on the part of the recipient is called *reaction* (*passion*); the recipient is called the *reagent* (*patient*). Every change, therefore, presupposes an active potentiality in the agent and a passive potentiality in the patient. The active potentiality of the agent acts and produces a change, while the passive potentiality of the patient is acted on and undergoes the change. By means of its action the agent actualizes the passive potentiality of the patient, and therein consists the 'change.' The change, therefore, as it *proceeds* from the agent, is the *action;* this same change, as it is *received* by the patient, is the *reaction* (*passion*).

In all *transient* actions, the agent and patient are individual beings, really distinct from each other. The wind which agitates the water of a lake is really distinct from the agitated water; the burning wood which cooks the food is really distinct from the food itself; the jigsaw which carves the wood is really distinct from the carved wood. But in *immanent* actions the agent and patient are entitatively the same individual, and there is on that account only a virtual distinction between the agent and patient. Nutrition, for instance, is an immanent action in an organic being, perfecting this organic being itself. Thinking and willing are immanent actions which actualize the faculties of intellect and will in the rational being itself, so that this rational being is both agent and patient. The action, since it is the exercise of an operative potency (power, or faculty), is *really* distinct from this operative *potency* and from the *agent*. The power, or faculty, remains in the agent, while the action comes and goes. Active thinking, for example, proceeds from the faculty of the intellect in repeated actions, but the intellect itself, whether active or inactive, remains in the soul as a permanent operative potency.

What has been said here of action and reaction refers to *creatural beings*. In an *analogical* sense action is also attributed to *God*. God, however, being infinitely perfect and totally substantial, has no operative faculties and actions in the meaning just given, otherwise there would be accidental potentiality and accidental actuality in His being. In our limited understanding of the divine perfections, we have no intuitive knowledge of God's being. The best we can do is to attribute the perfection of action, as we observe it in creatures, to God, after we have removed the imperfection of potentiality from it, and then deny all limitation and composition of this perfection. In God essence and action are absolutely identical and infinitely perfect, while in creatures agent and action are really distinct and very limited in perfection. When, therefore, we attribute 'action' to God, we must always bear in mind that the term is used only in an analogical sense.

As found in creatural beings, action always implies a change, and change implies *causality*. The 'agent' is the 'cause'; the 'action' of the agent producing the change is the 'causality'; the 'change' produced in the patient as reaction is the 'effect.' But this is the meaning of 'cause' in the restricted sense of an efficient cause. The term 'cause' has a much wider significance than this.

In the traditional view a *cause* is defined as *that which in any way whatever exerts a positive influence in the production of a thing*. Three factors enter into the concept of 'production': that which produces, or the *cause;* that which is produced, or the *effect;* and the positive influence of the cause in the production of the effect, or the *causality*. Everything depends upon this positive influence in the production, in order that a thing may be called a 'cause.'

For this influence to be really 'causal,' it must *affect the being* of a thing *in its production*. There is no causality unless there is a 'production,' and 'production' means the bringing of a substantial or accidental thing from a state of potentiality (actual non-existence) to a state of actuality (actual existence). Such a production evidently affects the 'being' or entity of a thing in some productive manner.

This *productive influence* on the being of a thing is the most important factor in causality. Mere *external sequence* or connection on the part of two things is not sufficient to bring them into the relation of cause and effect. The fact, for example, that one train follows another along the tracks, establishes no causal relation between them, because the connection between them is purely extrinsic.

For the same reason a purely *logical influence* of one thing on another is insufficient to constitute causality. The Principle of Contradiction, for instance, exerts a tremendous influence upon all our thinking. Its influence, however, is 'logical,' not 'causal'; this principle does *not produce* our thinking, nor does it confer anything toward the production of the *entity* of our thought. It is the intellect which actually produces our thought and as such is its 'cause.' The influence of the cause may be either corporeal (seed, for example, producing a plant) or spiritual (the intellect, for example, producing thought); but in order that such an influence partake of the nature of causality it must be *productive of being* in some manner. This will become clearer, when we compare the concepts of 'principle' and 'cause.'

PRINCIPLE AND CAUSE

In general, *a principle* is defined as *that from which something proceeds in any manner whatever*. In order that something be a 'principle,' it is required: that the principle be *prior* to that which proceeds from it; and that this priority be grounded in the things themselves because of some *special connection* existing between them.

There are two main kinds of priority: the priority of *reason,* and the priority of *reality*. These are also called *logical* and *real* priority. 'Logical' priority is attributed to a thing which, although it precedes another neither in time nor in nature, has within itself the ground on account of which our mind conceives it as preceding the other. Thus, according to our human way of thinking, the 'essence' of God is prior to His 'attributes' of intelligence, omnipotence, etc., because the essence is the ultimate ground of being in anything. Hence, we consider God's essence to be the 'principle' of His attributes.

'Real' priority, or the priority of reality, can be threefold: one of *time,* or of *nature,* or of *origin*. A thing is said to have priority of *time,* when it has existence before that which proceeds from it. A mother, as a human being, exists before her child. A thing has priority of *nature* with regard to another when this other presupposes the natural entity of the first for its own entity, even if the existence of both be simultaneous. Thus, a substance is prior in nature to its accidents, even though it have no priority of time with respect to its accidents; the ground for this priority of nature lies in the fact that the 'substance' is the necessary support for the entity of the accidents inhering in it. A thing has priority of *origin,* when it precedes another in such a manner, that there is a procession of the one from the other without any strict and real dependence.[1]

It should now be clear that we must distinguish between a 'principle' and a 'cause.' *Every cause is a principle, but not every principle is a cause.* A cause is always a 'principle,' because it is a thing from which another (the effect) proceeds. A 'cause,' however, is that which exerts a positive influence in the *production* of a thing; and that does not apply to every 'principle,' because there are some principles (for example, logical principles) which do not produce anything. The concept of 'principle' is thus seen to be wider than that of 'cause.' Hence, we may also define *cause* as a *principle of production,* and this definition is only verbally different from the one given above.

For something to be a real cause or principle of production, *three conditions* must be fulfilled. First of all, the cause must be a real and positive *entity;* a negation or privation is never given the name of a 'cause.' A negation or privation is the absence of entity and as such is actually nothing; but what is actually nothing cannot exert a positive influence in the production of anything. Then, the cause must really contribute some *influence* in the production of the effect. This also follows from the fact that a cause is conceived as a principle of

---

[1] Thus, in the Blessed Trinity, as theologians explain, the Logos proceeds from the Father, and the Holy Spirit proceeds from the Father and the Son (Logos). Due to this procession, the Father is prior in origin to the Son, and both the Father and the Son are prior in origin to the Holy Spirit. Since all three divine Persons possess the same nature, there is no priority of nature among them; and since this procession is eternal, there can be no priority of time.

production. The effect is the result of a production which originates in the cause. If the cause exerted no positive influence,
this production could never originate, and the effect would
never come into being. Hence, a mere precedence in time or
place is not sufficient to constitute a cause. Finally, the effect
must be *really distinct* from the producing cause. The cause
'produces' the effect; it must, therefore, produce something
distinct from itself. The cause must evidently exist, in order
to produce something; if the effect were not distinct from the
producing cause, the cause would of necessity *produce itself,*
although it has existence already. That, however, is impossible:
if it 'exists,' so as to be able to produce an effect, it can no
longer produce itself in order that it 'obtain existence' as the
effect of its productive act. Hence, the effect and the producing
principle must be diverse.

THE MAIN KINDS OF CAUSES

Two main theories have attempted to give an adequate explanation of the facts of change in the universe: *mechanism*
and *naturalism.* The theory of materialistic mechanism, as was
pointed out on a former occasion (Chapter XIX), maintains
that the ultimate constituent particles of matter are homogeneous in character, actuated by purely mechanical forces which
produce only local movement. According to this mechanistic
explanation of change and production, the only causes existing
in nature are efficient causes. The theory of *naturalism,* as advocated by Aristotle and the scholastics, maintains that the
beings possess a 'nature,' in virtue of which they are specifically
distinct substances with specific properties and activities. Each
nature existing in this physical universe is a compound, consisting of a 'material' and a 'formal' element as its constituent
causes. By means of their powers and actions they change other
beings, either in an accidental or substantial manner, thereby
acting as 'efficient' causes in changing these beings. Such
changes, however, do not occur in an entirely haphazard
manner. On the contrary, the hierarchical arrangement of

natural beings according to a definite plan and the constant functioning of natural forces according to physical laws, seems to show clearly that all things in the universe follow certain tendencies and ends; hence, 'final' causes also operate in the changes which take place in the world. According to the theory of naturalism, therefore, four distinct types of causes account for the 'how' and 'why' of all beings: *material, formal, efficient,* and *final.*

Aristotle, the first to attempt a thorough analysis of cause in all its phases, gives the following explanation of the number and character of the four causes just mentioned. "We aim at understanding, and since we never reckon that we understand a thing till we can give an account of its 'how and why,' it is clear that we must look into the 'how and why' of things coming into existence and passing out of it, or more generally into the essential constituents of physical change, in order to trace back any object of our study to the principles so ascertained.

"Well, then (1) the existence of *material* for the generating process to start from (whether specifically or generically considered) is one of the essential factors we are looking for. Such is the bronze for the statue, or the silver for the phial. [Material causes.] Then, naturally, (2) the thing in question cannot be there unless the material has actually received the *form* or characteristics of the type, conformity to which brings it within the definition of the thing we say it is, whether specifically or generically. Thus the interval between two notes is not an octave unless the notes are in the ratio of 2 to 1; nor do they stand at a musical interval at all unless they conform to one or other of the recognized ratios. [Formal causes.] Then again, (3) there must be something to initiate the process of the change or its cessation when the process is completed, such as the act of a voluntary agent (of the smith, for instance, [making a bronze statue, as mentioned in Bk. II, Ch. II]), or the father who begets a child; or more generally the prime, conscious or unconscious, *agent* that produces the effect and starts the material on its way to the product, changing it from what it was to what it is to be. [Efficient causes.] And lastly, (4) there is the *end* or *purpose,* for the sake of which the process is initiated, as when a man takes exercise for the sake of his health. 'Why does he take exercise?' we ask. And the answer 'Because he thinks it good for his health' satisfies us. [Final causes.] Then there are all the intermediary agents, which are set in motion by the prime agent and make for the goal, as means to the goal. Such are the reduction of super-fluous flesh and purgation, or drugs and surgical instruments, as means to health. For both actions and tools may be means, or *'media,'* through which the efficient cause reaches the end aimed at. This is a rough classification of the causal determi-nants of things."[2]

If we seek to determine why there are just *four causes,* no more and no less, we can find the *necessity* for this number in the following reasons. A cause is something on which the production of a being depends. This caused being can be con-sidered in a twofold way. If we consider it absolutely, the cause of the being, making it to be actually what it is, is its *form* (*formal* cause). If we consider it as a potential being becoming an actual being, two factors are necessary to reduce it from potency to act. There must be the material factor, or *matter,* which is reduced from potency to act (*material* cause); and there must be the *agent* which, by means of its action, reduces it from potency to act (*efficient* cause). Since, however, an agent can act only according to the tendency of its own de-termined nature, and a tendency implies a definite direction or end, this *end* also determines the production of the caused being (*final* cause).[3]

To put the subject in a different way: There are four ques-tions which can be asked of a thing, in order to explain the 'how and why' of its being. If we ask *'By what* is it made?'

---

[2] *Physics,* Bk. II, Ch. III, tr. by P. H. Wicksteed and F. M. Cornford, 1929, Will. Heinemann, London (Harvard U. Press).

[3] St. Thomas Aquinas, *In Physic.,* II, lect. 10.

the answer is 'By the efficient cause.' If we ask *'Out of what* is it made?' the answer is 'Out of its material, its material cause.' If we ask *'Through what* is it made?' the answer is 'Through its form, its formal cause.' And if we ask *'On account of what* is it made?' the answer is 'On account of the end or purpose which induced the agent to act.' By answering these questions with respect to a thing we obtain the various determining factors which explain the production of the thing and make it to be what it is. Since these answers explain the whole thing in its being and in its production, we have all the causes which account for its 'how and why' and these causes are just four in number.

In order that these four determinant factors really deserve to be called 'causes' it is necessary that they actually be *principles of production* for the being of the thing said to be the 'effect.' That they actually are such, will now have to be shown. 'Material' and 'formal' causes belong properly to cosmology and psychology; hence, they will be treated in brief fashion, mainly for the purpose of obtaining an understanding of these terms.

THE MATERIAL CAUSE

It is through the process of *change* that we arrive at the concept of material cause. A thing is said to 'change' when it passes from being one sort of thing into being a different sort of thing. There are two kinds of change: *accidental* and *substantial*. Both are common occurrences. When water changes from a solid to a liquid or to steam, it still retains its nature as 'water'; this is an accidental change. When a block of marble is carved into the figure of George Washington, it undergoes a change, since it is now something different from what it was before; but this change of shape does not affect the nature of marble as 'marble,' and so the change is accidental. Many changes, however, alter the very nature and *substance* of things. A plant, for instance, will absorb various kinds of elements from the soil and change them into living tissue, so that these elements unite into organic compounds and perform functions more or less contrary to their natural tendencies; such a change is substantial. Again, animals will take inorganic elements and the organic compounds of plants, assimilate them through a digestive process, change them into animal tissue, and utilize them in the cognitional process of sense-perception in a manner far superior to their own natural propensities; such a change in the elements, when compared to their original nature, is truly substantial, because they are now integral parts of a higher substance, having changed from non-living to living beings. Reversely, too, when living tissues break down in the organism, or when plants and animals die and decay, a substantial change of an opposite character takes place, because living compounds thereby become non-living.

Whether a change be accidental or substantial, there is always a *substratum* or *base* present which persists throughout the process of change, which passes *from potency to act*. This substratum is something indifferent, potential, receptive, passive, determinable, actualizable; it is that which is changed, determined, actualized. This substratum is that out of which something becomes or is made; and this is called the *matter* or the material cause.

In an *accidental* change this matter or material cause is the *complete substance* acquiring some accidental 'act' or 'form.' A block of marble, for example, has the potentiality of receiving the shape of a statue, a column, an urn, a fountain, a bench, a table, etc. It is the 'matter' or 'material' out of which any of these things can be fashioned.

In a *substantial* change there must also be a material factor or matter. Whenever there is a change of one substance into another, as when non-living substance is changed into living substance, a *substratum* passes through the whole process. This substratum is the *primal matter*. It is present in the inorganic elements; it is also present, when the elements are changed into the living substance of the plant; and it remains present, when the plant substance is digested by the animal and becomes animal substance. Hence, primal matter has the capacity or potentiality of being changed from one kind of substance into another, depending on the kind of agent which acts upon it. Hence, primal matter is a true cause, because it is that *out of which* something is made.

THE FORMAL CAUSE

The formal cause is the correlative of the material cause: matter and form always go together, because they are related to each other as *act* and *potency*. Matter is indifferent; the form is definite. Matter is passive; the form is active. Matter is receptive; the form is that which is received. Matter is potentiality; the form is act. Matter is determinable; the form determines it. Matter is actualizable; the form actualizes it. Matter is that 'out of which' something is made; the form is that 'through which' a thing is made to be what it is.

Since changes may be accidental or substantial, the form acquired in the change will be either an *accidental* or a *substantial form*. An accidental form is some reality determining the complete substance, such as quality or quantity, or a modification of quality or quantity. When a drop of water freezes, the crystalline structure is an accidental form or act communicated to the water. When a lump of clay is modeled into different shapes, these shapes are accidental forms or acts determining the indifferent clay. When the mind thinks, these thoughts are accidental forms or acts perfecting the perfectible mind. When a child grows to full stature, this growth is an accidental form or act affecting its quantity. In all these cases, the substance as such remains intact throughout the change.

But in substantial changes, the *nature* or *substance* is transformed into a new nature or substance through the access of a new substantial form. The substantial form unites with primal matter to constitute a *specific nature*. It is that essential and constitutive principle which makes a man to be specifically a 'man,' a lion to be specifically a 'lion,' a dog to be specifically a 'dog,' a rose to be specifically a 'rose,' and so forth. Primal matter is common to all these beings; and if matter were the only essential principle present in them, there would be no specific difference between them. What makes them specifically different among themselves, is the specifically different substantial form present in them, determining the indifferent primal matter to be just this kind of being and no other. When the substantial form changes, the species changes. The substantial form is united intrinsically to primal matter and takes away from the latter all its indifference and indeterminateness.

An example will perhaps make this relation between matter and form clearer. Take, for instance, a piece of beef. The matter in it is indifferent to becoming any particular kind of new being. It may be eaten by a lion, or a tiger, or a jackal, or a dog, or a cat, or a man. Whatever animal eats this meat, breaks down the beef tissue into minute particles, and by a process of assimilation turns it into flesh of its own kind. The inherent indifference of the primal matter is thereby removed, and this matter receives specifically new characteristics, due to the action of the new being into which it passes. There must, then, be a specifically different formative principle or 'form' in each of these types of animal. Such a substantial form must exist in the lion, making it to be just a 'lion' and nothing else; and that also applies to the tiger, the jackal, the dog, the cat, and man. That the beef ceases to be 'beef' and becomes lion flesh, or tiger flesh, etc., must be due to a substantial form, peculiar to the species, found in each individual of the type or class; and this formative principle then actualizes and determines the indifferent primal matter by depriving the meat of its beef form and substituting its own as the actualizing agency.

This substantial form is truly a *cause,* because it assists intrinsically in the production of a being by means of a positive influence. Together with primal matter it is a *constitutive principle* of the composite substance, determining it essentially in the line of substantiality and specific perfection: it actualizes the potentiality of primal matter and makes it to be a definite substance of a definite species. All corporeal beings are thus essentially composed of substantial matter and substantial form. This theory of the composition of bodies is the *hylomorphic* theory (ὕλη, matter, and μορφή, form) of Aristotle and the scholastics.

THE EFFICIENT CAUSE

The efficient cause is that *by which* something is produced. A being of one kind is changed into a being of another kind by means of *action*. The agent or efficient cause acts upon another being and effects a change in it, thereby producing a new act or form. When scientists speak of 'causes' in physical phenomena, they refer to these efficient causes and their action.

In our discussion so far, we have spoken of 'production' in the sense of change of one kind of being into another kind of being, as it occurs mainly in corporeal beings; in such changes a pre-existing matter or material cause is presupposed. It would be erroneous, however, to restrict the action of efficient causes to such a production. *Creation* is also 'production,' and it demands an efficient cause to bring a non-existent being into existence; in this case, however, no pre-existing matter is present out of which, as out of a passive potentiality, the new thing originates.

Of all the causes which assist in the production of an effect by means of a positive influence, the efficient cause is most readily recognized as being a *true cause*. Its influence is unmistakable. When a mason builds a brick wall, his action certainly influences its making, and he is the efficient cause of the wall. When the expansive power of steam drives a locomotive along the rails, its action produces the motion and it is the efficient cause of this motion. When hydrogen and oxygen are brought together under proper conditions, their action upon each other results in the formation of water; they are the efficient cause of the new compound. And so with other agencies in nature. Since a real production takes place, the agent responsible for it is an efficient cause.

THE FINAL CAUSE

The final cause is that *for the sake of which* an efficient cause acts. It is the end, the purpose, the intention, which dominates and determines the action of the efficient cause in its production of something. This purpose *induces* the agent to act and determines the *kind* and the *manner* of action, so that the end or purpose may be achieved. The concept of a final cause or 'purpose in view' involves the concept of a plan of action and the use of the proper means to attain the end.

That man does things for a definite purpose or end, is a matter of daily occurrence. When a carpenter intends to make a table, he selects the wood, cuts it into proper lengths, each piece having a definite shape and thickness, nails them together according to a plan determined by the particular kind of table he desires, and in this manner achieves the purpose he had in mind before he began to work. That the end or purpose positively influences the action of the efficient cause, is clear; the end or purpose is thus seen to be a *true cause*. It is called the *final* cause or end-cause.

Of the four causes here mentioned, two are intrinsic and two are extrinsic. The two *intrinsic causes* are the material and the formal cause. Matter and form are constitutive principles of things, entering into the very composition of their being. This is especially the case with corporeal beings or physical bodies where substantial matter and substantial form are the essential part-substances which combine to constitute the corporeal compound. Since the nature and constitution of physical bodies is the special object of investigation in cosmology, matter and form will be discussed at length in that department of philosophy; nothing further will be said of them in ontology.

The two *extrinsic causes* are the efficient cause and the final cause. They do not enter into the composition of the being of things, but act upon them 'from without.' These two types of causes are found in material as well as in immaterial beings; their nature is, therefore, more of a metaphysical character. Hence, we must now treat of efficient and final causality a little more in detail.

SUMMARY OF CHAPTER XXI

Changes occur in things relatively permanent by means of *action* and *reaction* (*passion*). Action and reaction are the basis of causality.

1. *Concept of Cause and Effect.* Change proceeds from an operative potency. The exercise of this potency is 'action.' The reception of this action in the subject is 'reaction' or 'passion.' By means of this action the agent actualizes the passive potentiality of the patient, and therein consists the 'change.'

A *cause* is defined as that which in any way whatever *exerts a positive influence in the production of a thing.* Causality must affect the being of a thing in its production.

2. *Principle and Cause.* A principle is that *from which something proceeds* in any manner whatever. The two main kinds of *priority* involved in a principle are the priority of reason (logical priority) and the priority of reality (real priority). Every cause is a principle, but not every principle is a cause. The cause is a principle, because something (the effect) proceeds from it. But not every principle is a cause, because some principles (e.g., logical principles) do not produce anything. Hence, a cause can also be defined as a 'principle of production.'

For something to be a cause or principle of production, *three conditions* must be fulfilled: the cause must be a real and positive entity; it must influence the production in a real manner; the effect must be really distinct from the producing cause.

3. *The Main Kinds of Causes.* There are four main kinds of causes: *material, formal, efficient,* and *final.* They explain the 'how and why' of a being. The material cause is that 'out of which' something is made. The formal cause is that 'through

which' something is made. The efficient cause is that 'by which' something is made. The final cause is that 'on account of which' something is made.

4. *The Material Cause.* Changes are either accidental or substantial. There is always a *substratum* or *base* present which persists throughout the change. This is the *matter* or material cause *out of which* the thing is made.

5. *The Formal Cause.* Matter is that 'out of which' something is made, while the 'form' or 'formal cause' is that *through which* a thing is made to be what it is. In accidental changes this form is some accidental reality determining the complete substance. In substantial changes this form unites with primal matter to constitute a *specific nature.* When the substantial form changes, the species changes. Matter and form are the constitutive principles of a composite substance, determining it essentially in the line of substantiality and specific perfection. This theory is called the *hylomorphic theory.*

6. *The Efficient Cause.* It is that *by which* something is produced. A being of one kind is changed into a being of another kind by means of the action of the agent or efficient cause. Creation is also a kind of efficient causality. When scientists speak of natural causes, they mean efficient causes.

7. *The Final Cause.* It is that *for the sake of which* an efficient cause acts. It is the end, the purpose, the intention, which dominates and determines the action of the efficient cause in its production of something.

The material and formal causes are *intrinsic* to the things produced, while the efficient and final causes are *extrinsic.*

READINGS

Coffey, P., Ch. XIII; Rickaby, J., Bk. II, Ch. III; Hugon, Ed., Tr. IV, Qu. I, art. 1–4; Qu. II, art. 1 et 2; Aristotle, *Metaph.,* IV, V; *Phys.,* II; Urráburu, J. J., Disp. VI, cp. III; Mercier, D. Card., pp. 527–533; McCormick, J. F., Ch. IX.

Chapter XXII

EFFICIENT CAUSALITY

SCIENTISTS AND philosophers often speak a different language, when they discuss questions referring to 'cause' and 'causality.' The scientist, as a scientist, is not supposed to be a philosopher and metaphysician. He is not interested in the ultimate explanation of things, but in those which are relatively proximate in character. In his proper field of research the term 'cause' has a different meaning for him than it has for the metaphysician who seeks to penetrate into the deeper reasons of things. What the scientist calls 'physical causes' are but the necessitating and indispensable *conditions* or *antecedents* of physical events, not the 'producing agencies' which exert a positive influence in bringing things from non-existence to existence through a process of productive change or through creation. Thus, John Stuart Mill says: "The causes with which I concern myself are not *efficient,* but *physical* causes. They are causes in that sense alone, in which one physical fact is said to be the cause of another. Of the efficient causes of phenomena, or whether any such causes exist at all, I am not called upon to give an opinion."[1]

As long as the scientist restricts himself to this negative attitude, the philosopher need not quarrel with him. But sometimes the scientist surreptitiously turns metaphysician and denies the validity of the concept of efficient causality as proposed by the philosopher. According to him the 'physical causes,' in the sense just indicated, are the *only* true causes; 'efficient causes' simply do not exist in nature. It thus becomes

---

[1] *System of Logic,* III, V, § 2.

imperative to vindicate the validity of the concept of 'efficient causes' and 'efficient causality' in a philosophic sense.

CAUSE, CONDITION, OCCASION

In order to arrive at a better understanding of the problem, it will be necessary to recall what has been said about the nature of an efficient cause, as outlined in the foregoing chapter, and compare it with 'condition' and 'occasion.' These concepts are closely allied.

A *condition* is something *required in order that an efficient cause can act,* but it does not contribute any positive influence toward the production of the effect itself. That the filament of an electric bulb may become incandescent, it is necessary to push the button of the switch, so that the electric circuit will be closed; but the pushing of the button does not make the filament glow. Clear weather is a condition for effective artillery action; but the weather has in itself nothing to do with shooting off a cannon.

If a condition is so necessary that the efficient cause cannot produce its effect under any circumstances without it, it is called a *conditio sine qua non,* i.e., 'a condition without which the cause does not act.' Thus, the knowledge of a good is the *conditio sine qua non* for an appetitive faculty to strive for the good. Light is the *conditio sine qua non* for the act of seeing. It is obvious, however, that the intellect itself does not 'strive' for the good, but the appetitive faculty; nor does the light 'see,' but the eyes.

Sometimes the 'condition' consists merely in the *removal of an obstacle* for the cause; the presence of the obstacle hinders the cause from acting. Thus, if a person's feet are tied, it is a necessary condition for walking that the impediment be removed. If a person is locked in a room, the door must first be unlocked before he can leave the room. The rope and the locked door are obstacles which must be removed; but that the person actually walks, that is due to the person's own efficient causality.

An *occasion* is a *circumstance* or combination of circumstances *which affords an opportunity for an efficient cause to act*. A crowd is an occasion for a pickpocket to ply his trade. A tavern may be the occasion for a drunkard to indulge his pet vice. Election time is the occasion for political oratory. The meeting with a friend may be the occasion of a confidential chat. The difference between an 'occasion' and a 'condition' should be fairly obvious. A condition is such that its fulfillment or presence is *required* in order that an efficient cause can act; an occasion is not a requirement for action, but its presence is something which merely gives the *opportunity* for action. Thus, the presence of a tavern gives a drunkard the opportunity to obtain the liquor needed to get intoxicated, and the tavern is for this reason an 'occasion' for intoxication; but the possession of a quantity of liquor, sufficient to become intoxicated, is required, and this possession is, therefore, a 'condition' for intoxication.

Neither a condition nor an occasion amounts to the causality of an efficient cause. They exert an indirect influence on an agent to act, but it is the *action of the agent* which positively influences the production of something; and *efficient causality* consists precisely in this productive action of the agent. To take the example just mentioned; it is neither the presence of the tavern (occasion) nor the possession of the liquor (condition) which makes the drunkard intoxicated, but the actual drinking (action) of the man himself (agent).

KINDS OF EFFICIENT CAUSES

Efficient causes may be viewed from a variety of standpoints. This gives rise to a number of classifications.

First Cause and Second Cause. By 'First Cause' we understand one whose causality is *absolutely independent* of any other cause or being, and on which all other causality depends. This is God. God is the uncaused Cause of all things. Since He is the source of all being, He must be independent of all beings in everything He is. And since all beings owe their essence and existence to Him, their causality is ultimately dependent on Him. By 'second cause' we understand one whose causality is *dependent* on some other cause or being. Since all creatural beings are dependent in their essence and existence on God, the First Cause, their causality is also dependent on Him. Hence, creatural beings are 'second causes.'

Physical and Moral Cause. A 'physical' cause is one which produces an effect by its own *direct action*. For example: the carpenter who makes a table, the boxer who defeats his opponent by knocking him unconscious, the boy who throws a snowball through a window, the violinist who draws his bow across the strings, the philosopher who thinks, the orator who gives a speech. A 'moral' cause is one which *inclines a free agent to act;* this may be done by an appeal, by a threat, by a promise, etc. The politician is a moral cause, when he induces an official to give him a position by paying him a sum of money. A criminal who extracts money from his victim by means of blackmail, is a moral cause. The detective who wrings a confession from a suspect by threats of the 'third degree,' is a moral cause.

Principal and Instrumental Cause. A 'principal' cause is an efficient cause which produces an effect *in virtue of its own power*. An 'instrumental' cause is an efficient cause which produces an effect *in virtue of the power of another cause*. Principal and instrumental causes are correlatives; the one implies the other. A carpenter uses a saw to cut a board; the saw is the instrumental cause, the carpenter is the principal cause. A hunter kills a deer by shooting it with his rifle; the rifle is the instrumental cause performing its action under the direction and control of the hunter. It should be noted that both causes exert their own peculiar causality. The saw cuts and the rifle shoots; but they would not act at all and not in this particular manner, were it not for the direction and control of the principal cause.

Cause per se and Cause per accidens. A cause is said to be a cause *per se,* if it has the *natural tendency* to produce a particular effect or, if it be a free agent, if it *intends freely* to produce it. It is a cause *per accidens,* if it produces an effect toward which it has *no natural tendency* and which the free will (if that be the cause in question) does *not intend.* When I take a hammer and deliberately drive a nail into a board, I am the cause *per se* that the nail enters the wood; but if I thereby hit my finger, I am the cause *per accidens* for that, because I did not intend that particular effect as the result of my attempts at carpentering.

Proximate and Remote Causes. A 'proximate' cause is one which produces its effect *directly,* in virtue of its own action, without using the action of some intermediate cause. When I walk, eat, push a cart, swing a stick, catch a ball, etc., I am the proximate cause of these effects, because they are the results of my own direct action. In melting snow, in boiling water, in making a piece of iron glow, in expanding the mercury in a thermometer, etc., heat is the proximate cause, because these phenomena are the direct result of the heat's action. A 'remote' cause is one which produces an effect through the direct action of some *intermediary cause* or causes. When my finger pulls the trigger of a rifle and explodes the charge of the cartridge, a bullet is ejected which travels through the air and kills a deer at a considerable distance; the bullet is the proximate cause of the death of the deer, while the exploding charge, the action of my hand and arm, and the deciding influence of my will, are the remote causes of the killing. Naturally, the ultimate cause in this particular chain of causes is my will.

Total and Partial Cause. A cause is said to be the 'total' cause, when the *entire* effect is produced by its action; if only a *part* of the entire effect can be attributed to a particular cause, it is a 'partial' cause. The masons, carpenters, plumbers, plasterers, etc., who assist in the construction of a building, are all part-causes of the construction. But when I lift a plank, push a table, walk a mile, dig a hole, throw a ball, etc., I am the total cause of these effects.

Univocal and Equivocal Cause. A 'univocal' cause is one which produces an effect *similar to itself in nature.* Thus, the oak produces an oak, the maple a maple, the dog a dog, the robin a robin, man a man. Living beings, therefore, which reproduce their own kind, are univocal causes in this respect, because these effects are similar to themselves in nature. An 'equivocal' cause is one which produces an effect *dissimilar to itself in nature.* When a dog, for example, gnaws a bone, the splintering of the bone is an effect dissimilar to the nature of the dog; the dog is the equivocal cause of this effect. When a robin builds a nest, the robin is an equivocal cause of the nest. A painter is the equivocal cause of his paintings, a writer of his writings, a builder of his buildings, because the effects are different in nature from himself as their cause.

Necessary and Free Cause. A 'necessary' cause is a cause which is *determined by its nature* to produce a certain effect, provided the requisite conditions are present. If I throw a stone into the air, gravity must pull it back to the earth, because gravity is a necessary cause and is determined to a definite line of action without choice. A 'free' cause is a cause which is *not compelled to act,* even though all the requisite conditions for action are present. Thus, man is free in very many of his actions, like walking, eating, smoking, playing, etc. He can perform them or omit them, as he chooses.

After this brief enumeration and explanation of the various classes of efficient causes, as handed down to us by the traditions of philosophy, we must turn our attention to the far more important question of the existence of such efficient causes. In considering this question, we must accept the term 'efficient' cause in the meaning previously given: as something which, through its positive action, produces something.

THE EXISTENCE OF EFFICIENT CAUSES

Briefly, the status of the question is this: Is there really a *causal connection* between things? Does the being and existence of things really depend intrinsically upon other things?

Does one reality actually *produce* another reality? In a word, are there efficient causes in the universe?

Phenomenalism in its various guises denies the existence of efficient causes. It contends that we cannot possibly know anything of the reality of 'causes.' 'Cause' is an obscure metaphysical notion without any objective foundation in the things or in the events of nature. Our knowledge is restricted to sense-perception; and the senses can contact only the phenomena or appearances of things, but not their inner nature or energy. Hence, according to phenomenalistic philosophers, the only facts accessible to our knowledge are objects in a *local* and *temporal sequence:* things are perceived as following each other; that is the total extent of our valid knowledge. We perceive *antecedents* and *consequents,* nothing more. Man arbitrarily changes this local and temporal sequence in serial happenings into an imagined 'causal connection,' in virtue of which the later phenomenon is considered to be 'produced' by the earlier.

David Hume attacks efficient causality in the following words: "When we look towards external objects, and consider the operation of causes, we are never able, in a single instance, to discover any power or necessary connection; any quality, which binds the effect to the cause, and renders the one an infallible consequent of the other. We only find, that the one does actually, in fact, follow the other. The impulse of one billiard-ball is attended with motion in the second. This is the whole that appears to the *outward* senses. The mind feels no sentiment or *inward* impression from this succession of objects: consequently, there is not, in any single, particular instance of cause and effect, any thing which can suggest the idea of power or necessary connection."[2] He then takes the case of the will commanding bodily members to act, and argues: "The motion of our body follows upon the command of our will. Of this we are every moment conscious. But the means, by which this is effected; the energy, by which the will per-

---

[2] *An Enquiry Concerning Human Understanding:* Section VII, Part I, § 50.

forms so extraordinary an operation; of this we are so far from being immediately conscious, that it must for ever escape our most diligent enquiry."[3] *John Stuart Mill* agrees with this view of Hume: "The Law of Causation, which is the main pillar of inductive science, is but the familiar truth, that invariability of succession is found by observation to obtain between every fact in nature and some other fact which has preceded it; independently of all considerations respecting the ultimate mode of production of phenomena, and of every other question regarding the nature of 'Things in themselves.' "[4]

For *Kant* and his disciples, a knowledge of efficient causes in the world is also impossible, but for a very different reason. According to the traditional view, these efficient causes would be the things-in-themselves, as they exist outside the mind in the universe. The mind, however, according to Kant, cannot know such things-in-themselves. 'Causality' is a *category* of the mind, and the 'category' is an innate, *a priori* mental form which acts as a regulative principle in arranging our judgments. But the category of causality is not derived from our experience of things and events as they actually exist in nature, and as such tells us nothing about the efficient causality of such things. The causal connection which we place between things and events is purely mind-made and has value only for the mind and its operations.

The *occasionalists,* like Malebranche and some others, accept the efficient causality of God, but *deny* it altogether of *creatures.* God is the only efficient cause in existence. If creatures seem to produce effects, this is only a mistaken notion on our part: it is God alone who acts, using the creatures as His instruments.

In opposition to these views, we contend that the concept of efficient cause is an objectively valid concept, based on the data furnished by *experience* and demanded by *reason* as the only

---

[3] *Loc. cit.,* § 52.
[4] *System of Logic,* III, 5, § 2.

true explanation of the facts. What we must prove, of course, is, that a mere 'invariable sequence of antecedents and consequents' is not sufficient to account for our concepts of 'cause and effect,' but that there exists the *actual production* of one thing or event by another thing or event.

PROOF FOR EFFICIENT CAUSALITY

In proving the existence of efficient causality among things, it will be necessary first to show that the *assumptions* which underlie the position of the opponents are unwarranted; then it will be necessary to adduce the *positive evidence* which supports the view that efficient causality actually is present in nature.

The opposition against the existence of efficient cause is based primarily on an adverse *theory of knowledge,* and not on the facts themselves. As such, the denial is made primarily on epistemological grounds. *Kant,* since he maintained that we can have no knowledge of things-in-themselves, naturally had to deny any knowledge of efficient causality as existing among these things-in-themselves. It is the purpose of epistemology to vindicate the sources of our knowledge, among them being sense-perception, consciousness, and reason. In this connection we will restrict ourselves to one consideration. If Kant's fundamental assumption were correct, we could know nothing of the existence and activity of *other minds* beside our own, because these 'other minds' are evidently things-in-themselves. But we have *a knowledge of other minds.* This is proved conclusively by the fact of *language,* whether spoken or written or printed. We do not use language to converse with ourselves; conversation is essentially a dialogue between our mind and 'other minds.' Hence, we can and do acquire knowledge of things-in-themselves, as they exist in themselves, through the medium of language. Kant's fundamental assumption is, therefore, incorrect. Consequently Kant is wrong, when he asserts that we could know nothing of efficient causality,

if it existed among things. If we can show that efficient causality exists *in ourselves,* we prove that efficient causes exist in
nature, because we ourselves are a part of nature.

Hume, Mill, and others, denied efficient causality because of
their *phenomenalism.* According to their assumption, all we
can perceive are the phenomena, and phenomena are revealed
to us in our senses merely as events in 'invariable sequence.'
Whenever, then, we perceive phenomena as invariably succeed-
ing each other in place and time, we are prompted by habit
and the association of ideas to imagine a *causal connection* to
exist between them, so that the earlier event is the 'cause' and
the later event the 'effect.' This is, in their view, the origin
within our mind of the concept of efficient causality.

This is a deplorable error. The fact is, we clearly distinguish
between mere 'invariable sequence' and 'real causality.' We
notice, for example, an invariable sequence between day and
night every twenty-four hours, and we are convinced that this
sequence has been maintained throughout the ages; at any rate,
we have never experienced a single exception in this sequence.
We also notice, when the day is hot and humid, and a sudden,
decisive drop in temperature occurs, that a rainstorm develops;
this sequence, however, is by far not as invariable as the
sequence between day and night. No one, however, dreams of
considering day and night as being in any causal connection,
as if the day 'produced' or 'caused' the night. On the other
hand, we certainly are convinced of the existence of a causal
connection between the states of the weather, although the
occurrence has by no means the invariability of the sequence
we observe between day and night. Hence, the fundamental
assumption of the phenomenalists, that our observation of 'invariable sequence' is the basis of our concept of 'efficient causality' is opposed to fact. In accordance with their principle, the
phenomenalists must maintain a parity in all cases of invariable sequence. We, however, do not judge the cases to be
the same. There must, then, be some other reason why we

judge a causal connection to exist between phenomena, between things and events.

Besides this, we clearly distinguish between *conditions* and *causes,* even if there be an invariable succession between them. We know by experience that we are unable to see objects except in the presence of light. In the dark all objects are invisible; light must first be admitted before we can see. There is an invariable sequence between the presence of light and the seeing of objects. According to the phenomenalists' principle, therefore, we should judge that light is the 'cause' of vision, because its presence invariably precedes vision. But we do not so judge. We consider light to be the *condition,* not the cause, of vision, although vision must always 'follow after' the admission of light in sound eyes. And so it is with all 'conditions.'

It is entirely untrue to assert that we obtain our concept of cause and effect from the observation of the frequency of an occurrence through habit and the association of ideas. We judge of the presence of causality even *in single cases.* When the first steam engine, or the first telephone, or the first automobile, went into operation, no one waited for the hundredth or thousandth appearance or operation in order to apply the principle of causality; this was done immediately. Similarly, when an accident or disaster occurs, we do not wait until it occurs frequently before we think of cause and effect; we look for the causal connection as soon as it occurs. On the other hand, though we see a million automobiles follow each other down the highway, we never think of the one being the cause of the other, due to association of ideas or habit.

Hence, mere sequence, no matter how frequent and invariable, is not the principle which forces us to accept the concept of efficient cause and causal connection as valid in nature. The *facts* themselves compel our *reason* to judge that the relation of cause and effect exists between things.

Our experience proves causality. A critical analysis of our internal states and of external nature convinces us of its reality.

Internal consciousness is an indubitable witness to the fact that our mental activities not only take place *in* us, but that they are also produced *by* us. Such are the activities of thinking, imagining, desiring, willing. They are clearly observed to be 'produced' by ourselves, and this production is observed to be due to *our own action,* so that their existence is intrinsically dependent on this productive action. Thus, we are conscious that we deliberately set about to solve a certain mental problem by combining ideas into judgments, judgments into inferences, and a whole chain of inferences into an extended argumentation. With the help of our imagination we work out poems, essays, melodies, pictorial scenes, machines, etc., before they ever appear outside the mind. We desire certain things and consciously will them; and we are fully aware that we are the responsible agents of these desires and acts of the will, because we produce them by direct action. No one can deny these facts; they are present for anyone to observe. But if the conscious knowledge of ourselves as the active agents in the production of these internal activities is unreliable and false, all our knowledge, of whatever character, must be adjudged an illusion, because knowledge rests ultimately on the testimony of consciousness. In that case, however, universal skepticism is the logical outcome, and that means the bankruptcy of all science and philosophy. Hence, our consciousness is a trustworthy witness to the fact of efficient causality within us.

External experience proves the same. We speak. Language is an external expression of our internal ideas. It is impossible for us to doubt that we actually produce the sounds of language which express our own thoughts. We *intend* to express these thoughts in conversation, and we actually *do;* and we are conscious of the fact that we are the agents in this process. If I am a painter, I set up my canvas, mix the paints, apply the colors, and with much effort project my mental images upon the canvas in form and color; I know that all this is not a mere 'sequence of events,' but a production of something in virtue of my own actions. So, too, if I take pen and ink and write something on paper, I not only perceive one word following the other, but I am also convinced beyond the possibility of any rational doubt that I am the 'author' of the words appearing on the paper. Neither Hume, nor Mill, nor any other phenomenalist, disclaimed the authorship of the books which appeared in their name, nor would they refuse to accept royalties from their publishers on the plea that they were not the efficient causes of these books.

Again, we are convinced that many bodily actions are of a *voluntary* nature. I move my hand, my arm, my head, and I know that these members move because I make them move. If I am set for a sprint, and the gun goes off, I jump into action. But I am conscious that there is not a mere sequence between the shot and my running; and I am also conscious that the shot does not make my limbs move so rapidly: it is I myself who decide to run and who deliberately produce this action of running. This is all the more obvious to me, when I compare this sort of action with the action of the heart or of the liver, etc., over which I have no control. I clearly distinguish between 'sequence' and 'causality.' Hume, as we have seen, claims that we cannot know of this causal connection between our will and our bodily movements, because we cannot 'feel' the energy involved in this operation. This merely proves that we do not observe the *whole* process. Of the fact of causation itself we are most assuredly aware, and we are also aware of the *exertion* and *fatigue* involved in producing these effects; but if we 'produced' nothing, or if there were no energy expended in the production (for instance, in walking, working, running, making a speech, etc.), why should we feel exertion or fatigue? And thus our external experience also testifies to the fact that we ourselves are efficient causes which produce definite effects.

In order to disprove the opponents' contention, no more is required than to prove *a single case of causality*. We could, therefore, rest our case with the above argument taken from the internal and external experience of our own selves. However, we contend that the existence of other efficient causes in nature is also capable of proof.

Reason demands efficient causality in nature. If reason demands that we admit the existence of efficient cause acting in the universe, the philosopher cannot refuse to accept the verdict of reason, because science and philosophy are based on the operations of reason. Now, if I am convinced beyond doubt that I am the cause of the picture I paint, what am I to conclude, when I see someone else paint a picture? I must conclude that *he* is doing what *I did,* when I went through the same series of actions. Of course, all that my senses can observe is a 'sequence' of actions; my *reason,* however, demands that he, too, must be the 'producer' of his picture, just as I am of mine. This is common sense and sound logic. And the same principle applies to all actions performed by others, when I observe them doing the same things that I do or have done: if I am an efficient cause, they must be efficient causes for the same reason. There is a complete parity between my actions and their actions, and so I know, through a conclusion of reason, that real causality exists in nature in these and similar cases.

It is only a short step from instances of such activities to *productive activities in the world* at large. A farmer places seed into the soil. After a period of time it sprouts, grows, and eventually matures into an abundant harvest. Here something new has originated. And so with animals and men. We were not here a hundred years ago; but we are here now. We perceive new living beings coming into existence daily. They are new realities. But if they did not exist always and do exist now, they must have *received existence.* Consequently, they must either have given themselves existence, or some other being did. In either case their existence is a 'produced' existence, a 'caused' reality, because they were brought from nonexistence to existence. That, however, which exerts a positive influence through its action in the production of another, is an efficient cause. Here again, scientists admit the thing, though some of them will not admit the name. In general, of course, scientists do not deny the existence of efficient causality.

Efficient causes, therefore, exist in nature. We must, then, reject phenomenalism as false and accept efficient causality as the only adequate interpretation of the facts as observed.

THE PRINCIPLE OF CAUSALITY

The Principle of Causality is formulated in a variety of ways: Nothing happens without a cause; whatever begins to exist must have an efficient cause for its being and existence. One might put it into the following form: *Whatever passes from a state of non-existence into a state of existence, must have an efficient cause for its existence.* This latter formulation includes every kind of real production, whether absolute or relative. A real production is *absolute,* if the total being passes from non-existence to existence without being produced out of the potentiality of pre-existing matter; this is 'creation.' It is *relative,* if the being is produced out of the potentiality of pre-existing matter, or if it passes from one kind of being into another kind of being; this is substantial or accidental 'change.' In either case the principle demands an efficient cause to account for the real production.

The validity of the Principle of Causality has been rejected by only a few philosophers. Among these is *Hume.* He says: "The true state of the question is, whether every object, which begins to exist, must owe its existence to a cause; and this I assert neither to be intuitively nor demonstratively certain."[5] The position of Hume and of the phenomenalists is logical, when we consider that they deny the existence of efficient causes in general and admit nothing but an invariable sequence of events in time and space.

The majority of scientists admit that there must be a cause for every effect. In this sense, the Principle of Causality is the basis of all sciences. Unfortunately, however, for the interests

---

[5] *Treatise on Human Nature,* Bk. I, Part III, § 3.

of harmonious thought and understanding between philosophers and scientists, the latter at times understand by the 'Principle of Causality' something different from the traditional interpretation as given above. A perusal of the writings of modern physicists might lead the unwary reader to the view that these scientists reject, or at least doubt, the principle that every effect must have a cause. They speak of the necessity of 'reformulating' or 'reinterpreting' the 'Principle of Causality.' Some even assert that its validity has been disproved by modern physics. A careful examination of their views, however, will show that they are speaking of the purely *scientific,* not philosophic, Principle of Causality.

What is the *scientific Principle of Causality?* Briefly, it can be stated thus: When a future event can be predicted with complete certainty from the occurrence of a previous event, they are connected in such a manner that the future event is caused by the previous event. The *predictability* of the future event is the test or criterion of causality. This does not mean, of course, that the future event is considered to be causeless, if it cannot be forecast with accuracy by the scientist; it merely means that the scientist in that case cannot be certain which particular event is the particular cause of such and such a particular effect. The scientist, therefore, attempts, with his Principle of Causality, or predictability, to *deduce* from a present event the existence of a future event, so that he can conclude *from cause to effect:* if the cause is given, what effect must follow and can be predicted? It will be seen from this that the 'scientific' Principle of Causality is quite different in meaning and scope from the 'philosophic' Principle of Causality. The 'philosophic' principle argues the other way around, namely, *from effect to cause;* if a being passes from nonexistence to existence, it must be a 'produced' being (effect) and as such demands an adequate efficient cause to bring it to existence. While the scientist is interested in deducing a specific effect from a specific cause, the philosopher is interested in discovering whether any and every effect must have a cause.

It would be wrong, therefore, to think that the scientists are in opposition to the philosophers regarding the validity of the Principle of Causality in its *philosophic* meaning. The scientists merely quarrel among themselves about the validity of their own 'scientific' principle, namely, whether effects can be accurately predicted from a scientific knowledge of the physical causes. Their question does not affect the question of the philosophic Principle of Causality in its traditional meaning.[6]

After these preliminary remarks, we must now turn to the problem and ask ourselves: Must every being passing from non-existence to existence, whether relatively or absolutely, be brought to existence through the active influence of an adequate efficient cause? The answer is *affirmative*. An analysis of the ideas contained in the Principle of Causality will make the principle evident. In other words, the Principle of Causality is an *analytical principle,* independent of observation and the inductive inferences of science.

By the very fact that a being passes from non-existence to existence, it is assumed and stated that at first it was *non-existent*. In that condition it was as such only *possible,* i.e., capable of existing. In this state of possibility the 'act' or perfection of 'existence' was not present in any form within the possible being; otherwise it would have been existent at the very time it was non-existent, which is impossible because contradictory. If and when this non-existent but possible being passed into a state of existence, it must have received the act of existence from somewhere and someone. Now, there are only three possible ways in which this being could have received its act of existence: either it received it from 'nothing,' or from *itself,* or from *some other being*.

It is impossible that it could have received existence *from 'nothing.'* Since 'nothing' possesses no entity or existence within itself, it cannot give anything and cannot account for anything. If this possible being depended on 'nothing' for its existence,

[6] See Max Planck, *The Philosophy of Physics,* tr. by W. H. Johnston (W. W. Norton and Co., New York, 1936), Ch. II.

it could never receive the act of existence and would remain forever merely possible, i.e., non-existent. Hence, it could not pass from non-existence to existence. But the supposition is that it did become existent. Consequently, it did not receive its act of existence from 'nothing.'

Could this possible being have received existence *from itself*? It could not. A possible being, from the standpoint of physical actuality and physical entity is *nothing;* this lies in the fact that it is only a *possible* being. As a possible being it is as yet in a condition of non-existence, and it becomes actual by receiving the act of existence. If it were to give itself existence, it would be necessary that it *produce itself*. A being, however, that does not as yet exist and is actually nothing, cannot produce anything, least of all itself. This is evident. To 'produce' would mean to 'act'; and to 'act' would mean to 'exist,' because no being can 'act' before it 'exists.' Hence, under the above supposition it would exist, because it acts and produces; and it would not exist, because its existence is assumed to be the effect of its own act. That is, however, impossible, because it involves a contradiction: it would exist and not exist at the same time. Consequently, a being that passes from non-existence to existence cannot receive this existence from itself.

The sufficient reason, why a possible being passes from non-existence to existence, is not found in 'nothing,' nor is it found in this possible being itself. But it is supposed to pass from non-existence to existence. Hence, by a process of elimination, it is clear that *some other being* must give to it the act of existence. To 'give the act of existence,' however, means to *produce it* by a positive influence. If it did not exert any 'positive influence,' it would not *do* anything and could not *give* anything; but in that case nothing would happen to the possible being, and the latter would remain in its condition of mere possibility, which is non-existence. This other being must, then, be an *existing* thing itself and *give existence* to the possible being by means of a *positive influence*. But to produce a being, i.e., to bring it from non-existence to existence, by the positive influence of its own action, is the definition of an *efficient cause.*

We have thus established the truth of the Principle of Causality: Whatever passes from non-existence to existence, must have an efficient cause for its existence.

AXIOMS REGARDING EFFICIENT CAUSES

Cause and effect are proportionate. The effect cannot be greater than the cause producing it. Otherwise a part of the effect would be without a cause, and that is contrary to the Principle of Causality. Again, the cause cannot have an actually exerted causality which is greater than is required to produce the effect. Otherwise the cause would (partly) not be a 'cause,' since that part of its action would not produce any effect.

No effect can be more perfect than its adequate cause. This is obvious. Otherwise there would be an effect, or part of an effect, without a cause to produce it and give it existence. This would be in violation of the Principle of Causality.

The cause must contain within itself the perfection of the effect. No being can give what it does not possess. Hence, the cause must contain the perfections of its effects either formally, virtually, or eminently.

Nothing can come from nothing; ex nihilo nihil fit. The meaning is: whatever happens must have an efficient cause to account for its happening. Nothing has nothing to give; therefore, it cannot produce anything. This follows from the Principle of Causality, as just explained.

Every agent acts in a manner similar to itself. Action flows from the nature of the agent. Since the action depends on the nature of the agent, the nature cannot give rise to an action which would be at variance with itself: the agent, therefore, can act only in a manner similar to its nature, i.e., to itself. For this reason the effect must also, in some way, resemble its cause, otherwise the cause would not have contained the perfection of the effect.

Action follows being; agere sequitur esse. All actions are the exercise of the operative powers of a thing. These operative powers proceed from the nature or being of the thing. Hence, the action of a thing must be proportionate to the being and follow the manner of this being.

SUMMARY OF CHAPTER XXII

When scientists speak of physical causes, they do not always mean efficient causes in the philosophic sense. As philosophers, we are interested in the latter.

1. *Cause, Condition, Occasion.* The nature of efficient cause has been explained in the foregoing chapter. A *condition* is something required in order that an efficient cause can act, but it does not contribute any positive influence toward the production of the effect itself. An *occasion* is a circumstance or combination of circumstances which affords an opportunity for an efficient cause to act. They differ from an efficient cause in this that the latter through its own action produces the effect.

2. *Kinds of Efficient Causes.* There are a number of classifications, depending on the different standpoints taken as the basis of division.

First Cause and Second Cause. The former is one whose causality is absolutely independent of any other cause, and on which all other causality depends; this is God. Second causes are those whose causality is dependent on some other cause or being; such are all creatural causes.

Physical and Moral Cause. A 'physical' cause is one which produces an effect by its own direct action. A 'moral' cause is one which inclines a free agent to act.

Principal and Instrumental Cause. A 'principal' cause is an efficient cause which produces an effect in virtue of its own power. An 'instrumental' cause is an efficient cause which produces an effect in virtue of the power of another cause.

Cause per se and Cause per accidens. A cause is a cause *per se,* if it has the natural tendency to produce a particular effect or, if it be a free agent, if it intends to produce it. It is a cause *per accidens,* if it has no natural tendency to produce a particular effect or if it does not freely intend it.

Proximate and Remote Cause. It is 'proximate,' if it produces its effect directly, in virtue of its own action, without using the action of an intermediary cause. It is 'remote,' if it produces its effect through the action of an intermediary cause or causes.

Total and Partial Cause. It is the 'total' cause, when the entire effect is produced by its action; it is the 'partial' cause, when only a part of the entire effect can be attributed to it.

Univocal and Equivocal Cause. A 'univocal' cause is one which produces an effect similar to itself in nature. An 'equivocal' cause is one which produces an effect dissimilar to itself in nature.

Necessary and Free Cause. It is 'necessary,' when it is determined by its nature to produce a certain effect, provided the requisite conditions are present. It is 'free,' when it is not compelled to act, even though the requisite conditions for action are present.

3. *The Existence of Efficient Causes.* There are efficient causes in nature. The *phenomenalists* claim that all we can know is an invariable sequence of events in time and space. *Kant* considered efficient causality to be merely a mental category. The *occasionalists* maintain that God alone is an efficient cause.

Kant's assumption, that we cannot know any things-in-themselves, is wrong, because we certainly know about 'other minds' besides our own. The phenomenalists' assumption is wrong, because we distinguish clearly between sequence and causality.

We prove the existence of efficient causes from our *experience, internal and external*. We are conscious of producing our own acts of thinking, imagining, desiring, willing. We are also conscious of actively producing things through external actions of our body. *Reason* demands that we conclude to a similar causality, when we see others do as we do; and it also demands causality for the origination of new realities.

4. *The Principle of Causality.* It is formulated: Whatever passes from non-existence to existence, must have an efficient cause for its existence. It is an *analytical* principle. Such a being must obtain its existence either from 'nothing,' or from itself, or from another being. Not from *'nothing';* because 'nothing' has no existence to give. Not from *itself;* because to produce itself it would have to act, and to act presupposes existence. Hence, it must receive existence from *another.* But for another to produce a being, so that it passes from non-existence to existence, means that it is an efficient cause.

5. *Axioms Regarding Efficient Causes.* Cause and effect must be proportionate; no effect can be more perfect than its adequate cause; a cause must contain within itself the perfection of the effect; nothing can come from nothing; every agent acts in a manner similar to itself; action follows being.

READINGS

Coffey, P., Ch. XIV; Rickaby, J., Bk. II, Ch. III; Hugon, Ed., Tr. IV, Qu. II, art. 3, 4, 5; Aristotle, *Phys.,* I, II; *Metaph.,* V; Urráburu, J. J., Disp. VII, cp. II; Mercier, D. Card., pp. 533–541; Phillips, R. P., Ch. IX; McCormick, J. F., Ch. IX, pp. 148–156.

Chapter XXIII

FINAL CAUSALITY

THE EXISTENCE and nature of *final causes* is one of the most controverted points in the history of philosophic thought. The prevalence of materialistic and positivistic views in modern times has accentuated the controversy. Materialists and positivists attack the validity of the concept of 'final causes.' Much of this opposition is due to bias, because the doctrine of 'final causes' seems to point too obviously toward a Supreme Intelligence as a directing influence in the physical world. The question, therefore, is important and warrants a closer inspection.

THE KINDS OF FINAL CAUSES

The general concept of a 'final cause' has already been treated in a former chapter (Chapter XXI). Here we must go more into detail as to the various kinds of final causes.

Intrinsic and Extrinsic Final Causes. The causality of a final cause is said to be *intrinsic,* if the action producing a definite effect is the result of a being's *natural tendencies.* A conspicuous example of intrinsic finality is the natural tendency present in the germ-plasm of the organic being to develop into a specific kind of organism. The germ-cell has a very definite direction in its developmental action. The fertilized ovum of man, for instance, grows into a body which is distinctly human in structure and characteristics, gradually developing the requisite organs and parts even before they can be of any immediate use; such are the head, heart, brain, lungs, nerves, ears, eyes, mouth, stomach, hands, feet, intestines, sex organs, etc. The finality of development is not impressed upon the germ-plasm from without, but is 'intrinsic' to it, because the tendency to develop in this manner is present within the cell itself and the entire action proceeds from the cell itself as from the producing agent. That is why the human ovum never tends to produce the body of a horse or a mouse or any other animal, but only the body of a human being. The same applies, of course, to any other organic being, whether plant or animal.

The causality of a final cause is said to be *extrinsic,* when it is *impressed* upon a being by some *outside directive force.* The finality given to a bowling ball, as it speeds toward the pins, is extrinsic, because it does not lie in the nature of such a ball to move in this particular manner and direction; this action of the ball is imposed on it by the player. So, too, the direction given to a bullet by a sharpshooter aiming at an enemy soldier, wounding or killing the latter, is obviously extrinsic to the bullet, because the bullet as such has no natural tendency to go anywhere in particular.

Final causes are classified also according to the *different ends or purposes* which an agent may have in view, when exerting its productive activity. The 'end' or 'purpose' is 'that for the sake of which' an agent or efficient cause acts, and therein consists the causality of the final cause. Hence, a classification of the various kinds of ends or purposes will also be a classification of the various final causes.

The End Which and the End for Which (Whom). The former is the *good itself which* is striven for as the end to be realized through the action. When a man, for instance, goes about building a house, it is the house itself which is the end he has in view as the result of his efforts in building. When a physician treats a patient, so as to restore his health, this health of the patient is the 'end which' he intends as the effect of the treatment. The *end for which* (or whom) is the *thing* or *person* that is to benefit by the acquisition or realization of the 'end which' is acquired or realized. When a man builds a house, he may build it as a home for his own family or he may build it to sell at a profit; both purposes are the 'ends for which' the house is built. The physician may have as his 'end for which' he cures a patient the payment of a fee or the increase of his medical reputation.

Proximate End and Remote End. Whenever there is a question of proximate and remote ends, two or more ends are always implied, with a relation between them of nearness or remoteness concerning the final result intended. An end will be the *proximate end,* if it is referred to some ulterior end, but has no other end referred to itself. Thus, when a physician gives his patient some medicine, the immediate or proximate end of this medicine is the health of the patient; and when a man builds a house, the immediate or proximate end is the completed house itself. An end will be a *remote end,* if one or more other ends are referred to it. And this remote end will be either an 'intermediate' or an 'ultimate' end. *Intermediate* this remote end will be, if one or more ends are referred to it, and it is itself referred to some ulterior end. This will be the case, for example, when the physician wishes to restore the health of the patient (which is his proximate end) for the sake of the fee which he will thereby acquire (intermediate end), so that he can safeguard the future of his family (ulterior end); or when a man builds a house (which is his proximate end), in order to have a comfortable home for his family (intermediate end), so that his family may enjoy earthly happiness (ulterior end). *Ultimate* this remote end will be, if it has one or more ends referred to itself, while it is not itself referred to any other end. This ultimate end may again be either 'relatively' or 'absolutely' ultimate. It is *relatively ultimate,* when it is the last purpose in some particular line; for example, the relatively ultimate end of the physician's work may be a life of affluent retirement in consequence of his amassed wealth, and for the builder of a house it may be the desire of a happy family life. It is *absolutely ultimate,* when it is the last purpose in every line, so that no ulterior end or purpose can be conceived; this, for the physician and builder and for all creatures, is the greater glory of God.

Primary End and Secondary End. An end is said to be the *primary* or principal end, when it is the main one among two or more which actuate an agent and is sufficient of itself to make the agent act. Thus, the fulfillment of his social duty may be the principal end a physician has in view in his medical practice; the primary end for a man building a house may be the comfort of his family. An end is said to be *secondary* or accessory, when it is intended together with a primary end, without, however, exerting the same potent influence on the action of the agent. For example, the physician may also strive for fame and money besides the fulfillment of his social duty; and the builder may also intend the personal enjoyment of the lake view which his house affords.

End of the Act and End of the Agent (finis operis, finis operantis). By the end of the *act* we understand the purpose which is present in the act itself and which the act tends to realize because it is this particular kind of act. Thus, the 'end of the act' of healing on the part of the physician is the restoration of the 'health' of the patient; and on the part of the builder it is the 'house' being built. By the end of the *agent* we mean the purpose which the *agent itself* (himself) has in performing this particular act. For instance, the 'end of the agent' for the physician in healing his patient may be the fulfillment of his duty, or money, or fame, etc.; the 'end of the agent' for the builder may be his own comfort, or the comfort of his family, etc.

Natural End and Supernatural End. We speak of a *natural end,* if it lies within the tendencies and powers of the nature of an agent to strive for this end and to realize it. The physician working for the cure of his patient and the builder constructing his house have a natural end in view. An end is *supernatural,* if it lies beyond the tendencies and powers of the nature of an agent to strive for this end and to realize it. For instance, that the physician and builder strive for divine grace in their labors, in order to obtain eternal happiness, is a supernatural end of their efforts.

THE EXISTENCE OF FINAL CAUSES

Are there really final causes in nature? Is there finality in the universe? Do things and beings act *in order* to realize some definite *end* and *purpose?* Or, are there merely efficient causes with their effects in nature? Whoever affirms the existence of finality and final causes in the world, advances a *teleological* or purposive explanation of phenomena (τέλος, end, purpose). One who denies finality (teleology) and final causes in nature and asserts that all effects are due to active agents and their powers without any end or purpose directing their activity, is the advocate of a *mechanical* explanation of all things.

Materialists, of course, are mechanists; their theory does not admit of any intelligent foresight working toward the realization of a definite end or purpose, and consequently they must deny the existence of final causes throughout all nature. To them the world consists but of matter and blind energy. *Positivists, agnostics,* and *empiricists* deny the possibility of knowing anything beyond the data of sense-perception; hence, since all causality is to them unknowable, final causes are also unknowable and unacceptable. According to these philosophers, final causes are fictions of the mind which man in his ingenuousness carries out into nature; in reality the activities of beings show no directive principle and no intentional effects. *Kant* and his followers also deny real finality; they consider, as was explained in the preceding chapter, 'causality' to be merely an *a priori* mental form, without objective value in nature.

In opposition to these we maintain the existence of *finality* or *teleology* in nature. This means that things are not only efficient causes, but are efficient causes with a definite direction in their action: *they tend to realize definite results.* Ontology is concerned with establishing the *general fact* that there are final causes, no matter in what form, and that the concept of finality and final causes has *objective value* and is not a mere fiction of the mind. As long as it can be proved that final causes exist at all, i.e., that some things are influenced in their productive action by ends and purposes, the existence of final causes must be considered as established.

The *proof* is not difficult. We find final causes at work in intellectually conscious, in sentiently conscious, and in unconscious, beings. We mean to prove that there are beings in each of these three groups which act with definite ends or purposes in view, so that their productive activity is positively influenced by the effects which they *intend* to realize in the future.

First, then, we find final causes at work in *intellectually conscious beings*. Such a being is man. It takes but a little reflection to see the truth of the statement that man acts under the direction of ends and purposes. When a farmer plows his field and plants seeds in the springtime, he does his work with a definite end in view: he wishes to harvest an abundant crop in the future, and this intention determines the time, place, manner, and duration of his labor, etc.

In fact, it is the exception that man acts without a definite end in view. The entire structure and operation of industry, business, commerce, art, invention, labor, governments, etc., is the result of a host of actions, all of which are directed and dominated by definite ends and purposes. All the activities of peace and war are based upon final causes. It is only the somnambulist, or the insane, or the idiot, who acts without a conscious rational end in view. Intellectually conscious beings, therefore, act in consequence of final causes or purposes, and this happens from morning until night throughout the length of their life. That this is really the case, is evidenced by the direct testimony of our own consciousness; and the validity of this testimony cannot be denied or impugned without destroying the foundations of all knowledge, science, and philosophy.

That these ends and purposes actually *influence* our productive actions in a *positive* manner, is obvious. The examples mentioned above show this conclusively. Nothing more is required as a proof for the existence of finality and final causes *in some form*. It proves that the concept of ends and purposes as 'final causes' is valid and legitimate and not merely a fiction of the mind. For the sake of completeness, however, we will extend the argument to the remaining two groups of beings.

We also find final causes at work among *sentiently conscious beings*. Brute animals are such beings. Their actions manifest finality. When a cat watches at the hole in the floor with unswerving eyes, crouches with tensed muscles, chases the mouse that unwisely comes forth, pounces upon it with exposed claws, and then devours it, is this not done for the purpose of catching her prey? When a bird flies about, seeks bits of string, feathers, straw, and twigs, brings them together to a certain tree, and then shapes them with a co-ordinated sequence of apt motions into a nest, is this not done for the purpose of fashioning a nest? Animals may not (and for that matter, do not) understand the 'rationality' of their actions, but they certainly *perceive* things, *desire* them, and *strive* for them. This is finality, or purposive action, pure and simple. Hence, sentiently conscious beings also act in consequence of final causes determining their productive actions.

Finally, there are final causes at work among *unconscious beings*. Such are the chemical compounds and physical bodies in the world at large. Here, naturally, the existence of final causes is not so obvious. It is quite evident, of course, that inorganic beings can have no knowledge of any good and in consequence of this knowledge strive for it. The question is not, however, whether they 'knowingly' strive for ends, but whether they do, *as a matter of fact,* tend to realize definite results in the future as the effects of their activities, so that these activities have a definite *direction* given to them in virtue of the effects striven for. This, we contend, is actually the case.

Inorganic beings are governed by *natural* and *necessary laws,* to which they are subject at all times. Chemical affinity, for instance, is a selective attraction existing between different kinds of elements and it controls the activity of the elements and their compounds throughout all chemical changes. This affinity, however we may conceive it in its nature and operation, is the expression of a natural *law*. But what is a natural law, if not the expression of the *inner tendencies of the nature* of such things? Chemical affinity is not a fortuitous event, occurring sporadically here and there and now and then, but a constant and regular occurrence which takes place without exception, provided the conditions are the same. Hence, elements *tend* to form specific compounds by means of a *selective tendency,* and this selective tendency runs through a *set series of changes,* until it realizes the compound as the end-result of its activity; this done, its activity ceases.

The finality existing in unconscious beings is observed more clearly in the tendencies of *vegetant* beings, as manifested in the growth and development of their *structural forms.* Attention has already been called to the 'intrinsic finality' existing in the human ovum. This applies with equal force to every *organism,* whether man or brute or plant, in the vegetative functions of its growth, beginning with one original cell and developing into a completely mature individual. Growth is an unconscious operation of living tissue. Notwithstanding the unconsciousness of the process, there is a very distinct tendency and direction in it toward a specific result. Somehow, the germ-cell contains within itself the design of the mature individual of a particular *specific type,* and it *tends* to develop this type under all conditions. The individuals vary in height, size, weight, and characteristics within certain limits; but they develop according to a well-defined plan, so as to carry out the pattern of the type. This is so obvious a fact, that the theory of evolution demands vast periods of time for the transmutation of one species into another. The development of the germ-cell into an individual of a specific type is constant, regular, natural; it is the result of an *internal driving power* present in the germ-cell and prolonged through the whole life history of the organism.

As the result of this internal principle of development, billions of cells are formed, combine together into various kinds of structural members, tissues, and organs, placed in mutual relationship as to position and function. These members, tissues, and organs have their own individual kind of activity, but they are co-ordinated and interdependent in such a manner that the well-being of the organism *as a whole* is the evident purpose and tendency of all combined. This tendency to produce and maintain the type-individual is an immense fact of nature which can be adequately explained only through *finality* and *final causes,* because the original cell has the positive tendency to produce a definite effect *in the future.*

FINALITY AND FUTURITY

There is a serious objection against the concept of final causes in general and against the concept of finality in unconscious beings in particular. In speaking of 'ends' and 'purposes' as final *causes,* are we not doing violence to the concept of 'cause'? A cause must really assist in the production of a thing through a positive influence. But surely, no being can assist in the production of something unless it really exists. The end or purpose, however, does not reach existence until the entire productive action is terminated, because it is effected or realized only as the result of the action. Since, then, the end or purpose is really non-existent as an entity at the beginning of the productive action, it seems impossible for it to exert any causality in the production. For instance, the physician intends to restore the health of a patient; this 'health-to-be-restored' is the end or purpose he has in view with his treatment; health itself occurs only at the termination of the treatment and is non-existent at the beginning of the treatment: then how can this 'health-to-be-restored' influence his action (the restorative treatment) and be a *real cause?*

It is true that the end or purpose intended (e.g., the health of the patient) does not exist in the *physical order* in the beginning; as such, therefore, it cannot exert any 'physical action' in the production of the result. But the end or purpose exists in the *intentional order,* namely, as a 'design' or 'plan' held constantly in view. As such it determines the agent (e.g., the physician) to *act* and also determines the *manner* of action (e.g., the treatment). The presence of this end or purpose sets a long chain of actions in motion, bringing into existence a decided change of events. And this means that the end or purpose is a real final *cause* in the true sense of the term.

But would the end or purpose, since it determines the action from the beginning, not presuppose some sort of *knowledge of the end or purpose* on the part of the agent, in order to strive for its realization *in the future?* Assuredly it does. With intellectually conscious beings this involves no difficulty, because they possess a faculty of knowledge. With unconscious beings and inorganic and vegetative activities the situation is entirely different. Inorganic beings and plants have no faculty of knowledge, and the vegetative functions of brutes and men are performed unconsciously; in them the tendency to produce definite effects in the future is the result of their *nature,* which directs their activities without any knowledge of the process on their part. Then how can one speak of an 'end' or 'purpose' which is supposed to be present from the beginning and work 'in order to' realize a future effect according to a certain 'plan' or 'design'? How can their nature direct a course of action of which it has no knowledge? Whence this 'tendency' and 'determination' intrinsic to their nature? The answer is that such finality in action certainly presupposes a *conscious knowledge* of the end or purpose striven for. Since, however, inorganic activity and vegetative function is not the result of conscious knowledge on the part of these beings themselves, but is the outcome of an intrinsic tendency of their nature, the finality of their actions ultimately postulates a *creative Intelligence* which intended these future results for them and gave them a nature which spontaneously tends to realize its intrinsic ends and purpose. Any other hypothesis will not account for the evident facts. This is also the only logical explanation for the *instinctive* actions so strikingly manifested in the animal kingdom.

However, no matter what we may consider to be the proper explanation, there can be no question about the *fact* that beings do act for definite ends. Final causes, therefore, do exist in some form among beings; and the concept of 'final causes' is thus not an idle fancy, but is *objectively real* in nature.

AXIOMS CONCERNING FINAL CAUSES

The end or purpose is the cause of all causes. The material cause is determined by the formal cause; the formal cause is determined by the efficient cause; and the efficient cause is determined in its action by the end or purpose in view, i.e., by the final cause. Hence, the final cause determines the other causes and is thus the cause of all causes.

Every agent acts for an end. Man acts because his will strives for some apprehended good. Animals, plants, and inorganic beings strive for things in virtue of the tendencies inherent in their nature. Consequently, all beings act, consciously or unconsciously, for an end or purpose.

Who intends the end must intend the means. Whoever effectively intends an end, must strive to realize it. But if one cannot realize it except through the use of certain means, one must evidently also intend these means; otherwise one would not effectively intend the end itself. It follows from this, that whoever uses certain means in order to attain the end, is responsible for the means which he uses in the attainment of this end. Hence, a good end will not justify immoral means.

The end is first in intention, last in execution. The end or purpose is the result to be achieved through the productive action in the future; and when it is achieved, the action ceases. But in order that the action can tend to produce this result, the action must be determined from the very beginning by this effect held in view as an end or purpose. Hence, the end is first in intention and last in execution.

The end is, in itself, nobler than the means. It is the end which determines the means to be used; the means do not determine the end. The means are used to acquire the end. Hence, the means are not striven for on account of their own goodness, but rather for the possession of the goodness present in the end.

End and means must be proportionate. Obviously. It would not do to attempt to stem a flood with a twig, nor to let loose a deluge in order to drown a fly. Major purposes demand major means, and minor purposes demand minor means. This refers as well to the importance as to the magnitude of the end in view; both demand a corresponding use of means, so as to insure the achievement of the result intended.

SCIENCE AND FINAL CAUSES

What is the attitude of science toward final causes and *finality in nature?* By 'science' we mean the 'scientists.' Their general attitude is one of negative aloofness toward the question. They do not concern themselves about the presence of final causes in nature and make no attempt to decide whether things actually strive with their actions to realize ends and purposes set for their actions as a definite goal which they are supposed to reach. As scientists, they seek to understand the phenomena which occur in nature and then seek for the efficient causes which produce them through their actions. When they have discovered this causal connection between subsequent and antecedent events, they feel that they have arrived at a *scientific knowledge* of all that science is entitled to investigate and know. Whatever lies beyond this sort of knowledge lies beyond the legitimate field of science. The philosopher may seek to penetrate more deeply into the mysteries of nature, if he can; but the scientist, as a scientist, is content to understand the operations of nature and express its operations in the formula of a physical law.

As scientists conceive science, it is primarily a *method* of investigation, based on *observation* and *experiment*. Whatever is discoverable by this method is a proper object of science. This object alone is of interest to the scientist. Hence, the changes in nature, and the corresponding activities producing them, are the field which science investigates. This means that 'efficient causality,' in a physical sense of the term, are the factors in nature which science can legitimately investigate, so as to correlate its findings in a complete body of demonstrated, scientific truths. Such are the limits of science set by the scientists themselves. Hence, scientists do not interest themselves in the intrinsic, constitutive principles of bodies, such as matter and form (material and formal causes), nor in the intrinsic tendencies of bodily actions (final causes). They are content to accept the nature of bodies as given and to study the actions as observable facts.

No one can quarrel with the scientists, if they deliberately restrict the field of scientific research in this manner, provided they do not overstep the bounds of their own restrictions. They may *ignore* the question of finality in nature as something outside the scope of their scientific investigation. But they may not, according to the rules laid down by themselves, *deny* the existence of finality in natural beings, without ceasing to be scientists and professing to be philosophers. The question of finality and final causes is a metaphysical question and belongs to philosophy, not to science as limited by the scientists. Consequently, if the investigations of the philosopher demand the existence of final causes as an adequate explanation of natural occurrences, it is not within the province of the scientist as such to dispute or deny their existence and the validity of their concept. Unfortunately, scientists sometimes contend that, because final causes are *not observable,* their existence must be *denied.* This is a false principle of logical reasoning which, if applied, must do harm to the best interests of both science and philosophy.

Unlike the scientists, the philosopher cannot ignore the problem of final causes and finality. It is his endeavor to discover the truth in things *as far as reason can reach*. He cannot rest content with a knowledge of observable data, but must apply the principles of reason to the data furnished by observation and experiment and seek a *rational interpretation* of the facts in their entirety. It is for this reason that the philosopher attempts to discover all the causes operative in nature. Among these causes are final causes. So far we have established the fact that final causes actually exist, at least in some form and to some extent.

The question is often asked: 'Do ducks fly and swim because they have wings and webbed feet, or do they have wings and webbed feet in order to fly and swim?' The scientist would answer: 'They fly, because they have wings, and they swim, because they have webbed feet': that is all that concerns the scientist as a scientist. The philosopher, if he agrees with our viewpoint, would answer: 'First of all, the ducks have wings and webbed feet in order to fly and swim, and then they fly and swim because they have wings and webbed feet.' The scientist answers by affirming the existence of *efficient* causes, while the philosopher answers by affirming the existence of both *efficient and final* causes.

Those philosophers who deny the existence of final causes in nature (except, perhaps, in the case of man, due to his intellectual capacity of preconceiving an end or purpose for his action), must of necessity contend that *blind forces* rule the world and that all things occur through 'chance,' or 'luck,' or 'accident.' Hence, some attention must be given to the possible existence of such factors in nature.

CHANCE, LUCK, ACCIDENT

Terms like 'chance,' 'luck,' 'accident,' and similar expressions are found in all languages. They show the firm conviction of people that many things happen in this world which are beyond the control of any regulative principle in nature. Such occurrences are, therefore, conceived as happening without being the result of purposive action: no end or purpose and consequently *no final cause determines their course.* What truth is there in this view?

The following are instances of the occurrences which are usually considered to be the result of 'chance' or 'luck' or 'accident.' A man spades his garden, in order to plant some vegetables, and uncovers a hidden treasure of which he had no knowledge. This is a case of 'good luck,' and he is said to find this treasure by 'chance' or 'accident'; it is also spoken of as 'good fortune.' Years after a war, a farmer plows a field which had been the scene of a battle, hits a hidden shell, and is hurt by the explosion. He had 'bad luck' or 'misfortune,' and his injury was the result of an 'accident.' Two cars, speeding along separate highways which cross each other at right angles, meet at the intersection, and a collision occurs. The meeting of the cars was 'by chance,' and the collision was an 'accident.' What is *chance,* or *luck,* or *accident?*

The Principle of Causality guarantees that no effect can happen without an *adequate efficient cause* to account for it. 'Chance' results, therefore, must never be understood in the sense that effects occur without a cause: such events would be impossible. But what is meant by chance results is that certain effects are *not intended* by the active agents under these particular circumstances. An effect may be 'intended' by directly *willing* it, if the agent is free in its activity; or it may be 'intended' because a thing has the *natural tendency* to produce a definite effect. Thus, if I deliberately throw a ball, I 'intend' the movement of the ball through the air. Gravity has the natural tendency to bring the ball back to earth; it also 'intends' this downward motion. Neither of these two movements is due to 'chance,' 'luck,' or 'accident.' When, however, a certain effect is not intended freely or naturally, as just explained, it is said to be due to 'chance,' 'luck,' or 'accident.' For instance, when I throw a ball, and the ball, without my intending it, hits a man on the head, this is an 'accident.' Because, although I freely 'intended' to throw the ball, I did not intend the man's head as the target for my marksmanship; and so, too, although gravity attracted the ball in virtue of a natural tendency and thus 'intended' its downward course, it had no natural tendency to attract the ball in such a manner that it would alight upon the man's head. That the ball struck his head was due to an unfortunate *conjuncture of causes* which was intended neither by me nor by nature.

In accidental occurrences *two distinct factors* must be considered. Each efficient cause intends a certain result, either freely or because of a natural tendency, and the causality of the efficient cause is directed and determined by an end or purpose which the efficient cause seeks to realize as the direct effect of its action; the action of each cause is, therefore, intended separately and *independently* of the other, so that there is no concerted action intended by the different causes with relation to each other. The *coincidence* of these separate and independent lines of action, therefore, is not intended by these efficient causes and lies outside the scope of their individual ends and purposes; therein lies the element of 'chance,' 'luck,' and 'accident,' because no regulative principle controls the *meeting* of these separate and independent actions: their meeting or conjuncture just 'happens.' Accidents thus occur *incidentally* to some intended action.

Aristotle therefore *defines chance,* or luck, or accident (for they mean essentially the same thing) as "the incidental production of some significant result by a cause that took its place in the causal chain incidentally, and without the result in question being contemplated." And he goes on to say: "Clearly then luck itself, regarded as a cause, is the name we give to causation which incidentally inheres in deliberately purposeful action taken with respect to some other end but leading to the event we call fortunate" [or unfortunate].[1] Aristotle's observation here is very acute and is borne out by the analysis of an accidental occurrence. Two automobile drivers take their cars

---

[1] *Physics,* Bk. II, Ch. V, 196 b 30; 197 a 5.

out into the country. One drives from east to west, and the other from north to south. Their action is purposeful; each intends to ride, and drives his car in accordance with his purpose. That the two cars, driven at their respective speeds, will meet at the intersection of the two highways at a particular moment and thus cause a collision, is something unforeseen and unintended by both drivers. Hence, the *conjuncture* of these two sets of efficient causality is only *incidental* to the purposeful action of each driver and is beyond their knowledge and control.

Since there is no finite controlling factor which brings about this conjuncture of efficient causalities, such accidental effects cannot be foreseen and foretold with any degree of certainty, except by God. *Irregularity* and *lack of constancy* are the characteristic marks of events that happen by chance. It follows that events and phenomena, which occur regularly and constantly in nature according to a physical law, cannot be the result of chance; whatever is constant, normal, and according to type, is contrary to the very concept of chance.

Is the universe, then, governed by *chance* or *purpose?* The law, order, and harmony manifest everywhere in nature is the best evidence that the universe is governed by *purposeful design.* Aristotle expresses his view on this question as follows: "In general, the theory [of chance, as the dominant factor in the universe] does away with the whole order of Nature, and indeed with Nature's self. For natural things are exactly those which do move continuously, in virtue of a principle inherent in themselves, toward a determined goal; and the final development which results from any one such principle is not identical for any two species, nor yet is it any random result; but in each there is always a tendency toward an identical result, if nothing interferes with the process. A desirable result and the means to it may also be produced by chance, as for instance we say it was 'by luck' that the stranger came and ransomed the prisoner before he left, where the ransoming is done as if the man had come for that purpose, though in fact he did not. In this case the desirable result is incidental; for, as we have explained, chance is an incidental cause. But when the desirable result is effected invariably or normally, it is not an incidental or chance occurrence; and in the course of Nature the result always is achieved either invariably or normally, if nothing hinders. It is absurd to suppose that there is no purpose because in Nature we can never detect the moving power in the act of deliberation. . . . That Nature is a cause, then, and a goal-directed cause, is above dispute."[2]

Nature, of course, has no intelligence of its own and as such cannot select the goal of its action as an end or purpose for which to strive. Nevertheless, intelligence is required in order that nature can be "a goal-directed cause," striving toward the realization of its all-encompassing purpose according to precise laws. Hence, the presence of a purpose or goal in nature demands the existence of a Supreme Intelligence outside itself. One of the most eminent of modern physicists, Max Planck, says: "The most perfect harmony and consequently the strictest causality in any case, culminates in the assumption that there is an ideal spirit having a full knowledge of the action of the natural forces as well as of the events in the intellectual life of men; a knowledge extending to every detail and embracing present, past, and future."[3]

This "ideal spirit" is God.

SUMMARY OF CHAPTER XXIII

The existence and nature of final causes is one of the most controverted points of philosophy.

1. *Kinds of Final Causes.* The concept of final cause was explained in a preceding chapter.

Intrinsic and Extrinsic Final Causes. The causality of a final cause is said to be 'intrinsic,' if the action producing a definite effect is the result of a being's natural tendencies. The causality

---

[2] *Physics*, Bk. II, Ch. VIII, 199 b 15–30 (Harvard U. Press).
[3] *The Philosophy of Physics*, tr. by W. H. Johnston (W. W. Norton, New York, 1936), p. 78.

is 'extrinsic,' when it is impressed upon a being by some outside directive force.

Since it is the 'end' or 'purpose' which is that for the sake of which an efficient cause acts, final causes are also classified according to the various kinds of 'ends' or 'purposes.' *The End Which and the End for Which (Whom)*. The former is the good itself which is striven for as the end to be realized through the action; the latter is the thing or person that is to benefit by the acquisition or realization of the end which is acquired or realized. *Proximate and Remote End*. It is a 'proximate' end, if it is referred to some ulterior end, but has no other end referred to itself; it is a 'remote' end, if one or more other ends are referred to it. A remote end will be either intermediate or ultimate. *Primary and Secondary End*. It is the 'primary' end, when it is the main one among two or more and is sufficient of itself to make the agent act; it is 'secondary,' when it is intended together with a primary end. *End of the Act and End of the Agent*. The former is the end which is the purpose of the act itself; that latter is the purpose which the agent has in performing the act. *Natural and Supernatural End*. It is a 'natural' end, if it lies within the tendencies and powers of an agent to strive for this end and to realize it; it is 'supernatural,' if it lies beyond the tendencies and powers of an agent to strive for this end and to realize it.

2. *The Existence of Final Cause*. This existence is denied by materialists, positivists, agnostics, and empiricists; we maintain *finality* (teleology) in nature, at least in some form. This means that some efficient causes *tend to realize definite results*.

Intellectually conscious beings (men) have definite ends and purposes for their action; this is a daily experience, as our consciousness testifies. *Sentiently conscious* beings (brutes) perceive things, desire things, and strive for things; instinctive actions are all purposive. *Unconscious* beings (chemicals and plants) also show finality in their actions: chemical affinity is a selective tendency which seeks to realize definite sorts of compounds; the germ-cells of plants tend toward producing individuals according to the patterns of the specific type.

3. *Axioms Concerning Final Causes.* The end or purpose is the cause of all causes. Every agent acts for an end. Who intends the end must intend the means. The end is first in intention, last in execution. The end is, in itself, nobler than the means. End and means must be proportionate.

4. *Science and Final Causes.* The attitude of scientists toward final causes in nature is one of *negative aloofness* toward the question. They are interested merely in observable phenomena and their causation. Hence, they restrict the field of scientific knowledge to efficient causes and ignore the possible existence of final causes in nature as being beyond the scope of science.

5. *Chance, Luck, Accident.* The Principle of Causality guarantees that no effect can happen without an adequate efficient cause. But many effects happen by chance, in as much as the *conjuncture* of efficient causes and their actions is not always *intended.* Chance (luck, accident) is the incidental production of some significant result by a cause that took its place in the causal chain incidentally, and without the result in question being contemplated. *Irregularity* and *lack of constancy* is the mark of chance; what happens regularly, constantly, and normally, is not the result of chance. Nature works in a manner which is regular, constant, and normal, because it acts according to *laws.* Nature, therefore, is governed by final causes, not by chance.

READINGS

Coffey, P., Ch. XV; Hugon, Ed., Tr. IV, Qu. II, art. 6, 7, 8; Aristotle, *Phys.,* II; *Metaph.,* V; Urráburu, J. J., Disp. VII, cp. III; Mercier, D. Card., pp. 541–551; Phillips, R. P., Ch. X; McCormick, J. F., Ch. IX, pp. 156–159.

GLOSSARY OF TERMS

NOTE: In the case of qualified words, always look for the word or noun qualified. For example: in seeking for *Absolute Accident,* look for *Accident, Absolute,* etc.

ABSTRACTION. A process in which the mind fixes its attention upon one or the other characteristic of a thing or upon one element common to many things, excluding others which are joined to it in the real order. *See* Precision.

ACCIDENT. A being whose nature it is to exist in another as in a subject.

ACCIDENT, ABSOLUTE. An accident which confers a real perfection upon its subject.

ACCIDENT, EXTRINSIC. An accident which does not affect the being of its subject, but modifies the subject's immediate surroundings.

ACCIDENT, INTRINSIC. An accident which affects the being of its subject in some manner.

ACCIDENT, MODAL. The definite disposition or determination of an in-different and determinable accidental entity in such a manner that it does not confer any positive and new entity upon the substance.

ACCIDENT, RELATIVE. An accident that has its being in a subject only because of the bearing which one thing has to another.

ACCIDENT, STRICTLY ABSOLUTE. An accident which confers upon its subject some positive and new entity.

ACT. Any entity of whatever kind and nature which perfects and de-termines a thing in its being.

ACT, MIXED. An act that in some form or other has an admixture of potentiality.

ACT, NON-PURE. *See* Act, Mixed.

ACT, PRIMARY. An act that is the first in a series of acts.

ACT, PURE. An act that is without the least admixture of potentiality.

ACT, SECONDARY. An act that presupposes another act in a definite series, so that it proceeds from a primary act.

ACTION. The exercise or operation of an operative potency. The produc-tion of an effect.

ACTIVITY, IMMANENT. The activity through which a living being perfects itself and makes itself the goal for the acquired actuality or perfection.

ACTIVITY, TRANSIENT (TRANSEUNT, TRANSITIVE). The activity which tends to change another object.

ACTIVITY, VITAL. *See* Activity, Immanent.

AFFECTION. A relatively transient quality which produces, or results from, some accidental sensible alteration.

ALTERATION. The change of a being from one qualitative state to another.

ANNIHILATION. The reduction of an existing being to non-existence.

ATTRIBUTES, TRANSCENDENTAL. The supreme modes necessarily connected with every being, which are different phases of the same fundamental being, but are not explicitly contained in its concept as such.

AUGMENTATION. The change of a being from one quantitative state to another.

BEAUTY. That attribute of a thing in virtue of which the thing pleases when perceived. A blending of the unity, truth, and goodness in a thing, characterized by completeness, proportion, and clarity of presentation in an intellectual-sensuous form, so as to produce a disinterested emotional pleasure in a rational perceiver.

BEING. That which exists or can exist, the existible; whatever is not nothing.

BEING, ABSOLUTE. A being which can be thought of or can exist without reference to another.

BEING, ACCIDENTAL. *See* Accident.

BEING, ACTUAL. Anything that really exists at the present moment in the physical or spiritual world.

BEING, CONTINGENT. A being whose non-existence is possible.

BEING, CONTRACTION OF. *See* Contraction of Being.

BEING, FINITE. A being whose reality is limited in perfection.

BEING, IDEAL. Any object in so far as it is known.

BEING, INFINITE. A being which has no limit in its entity or perfection.

BEING, LOGICAL. Anything that has objective being only in the mind.

BEING, NECESSARY. A being whose non-existence is impossible.

BEING, POSSIBLE. Anything that does not actually exist, but is capable of existence.

BEING, REAL. Anything that has, or can have, existence independent of man's actual knowledge.

BEING, RELATIVE. A being which can be thought of or can exist only in reference to another.

BEING, SUBSTANTIAL. *See* Substance.

CAPACITY, NATURAL. The proximate accidental principle of operation, toward which (operation) it is specifically directed.

CATEGORY. An ultimate and supreme mode of real being; a predicament.

CAUSALITY, PRINCIPLE OF. The principle which states that whatever passes from a state of non-existence into a state of existence must have an efficient cause for its existence.

CAUSE. That which in any way whatever exerts a positive influence in the production of a thing.

CAUSE, EFFICIENT. That by which something is produced.

CAUSE, EQUIVOCAL. A cause which produces an effect dissimilar to itself in nature.

CAUSE, FINAL. That for the sake of which an efficient cause acts.

CAUSE, FIRST. A cause whose causality is absolutely independent of any other cause or being, and on which all other causality depends.

CAUSE, FORMAL. That through which a thing is made to be what it is. Form.

CAUSE, FREE. A cause which is not compelled to act, even though all the requisite conditions for action are present.

CAUSE, INSTRUMENTAL. An efficient cause which produces an effect in virtue of the power of another cause.

CAUSE, MATERIAL. That out of which something becomes or is made. Matter.

CAUSE, MORAL. A cause which inclines a free agent to act.

CAUSE, NECESSARY. A cause which is determined by its nature to produce a certain effect, provided the requisite conditions are present.

CAUSE, PARTIAL. A cause whose action produces only a part of the total effect.

CAUSE PER ACCIDENS. A cause which produces an effect toward which it has no natural tendency, or which the free will (if that be the cause in question) does not intend.

CAUSE PER SE. A cause that has the natural tendency to produce a particular effect or, if it be a free agent, that intends freely to produce it.

CAUSE, PHYSICAL. A cause which produces an effect by its own direct action.

CAUSE, PRINCIPAL. An efficient cause which produces an effect in virtue of its own power.

CAUSE, PROXIMATE. A cause which produces its effect directly, in virtue of its own action, without using the action of some intermediate cause.

CAUSE, REMOTE. A cause which produces an effect through the direct action of some intermediary cause or causes.

CAUSE, SECOND. A cause whose causality is dependent on some other cause or being.

CAUSE, TOTAL. A cause whose action produces the entire effect.

CAUSE, UNIVOCAL. A cause which produces an effect similar to itself in nature.

CHANCE. The causality of agents resulting in effects not intended by the agents under these particular circumstances.

CHANGE. The transition from one positive state of being to another.

CHANGE, PRINCIPLE OF. The principle which states that whatever changes is changed by another.

COMPOSITION, LOGICAL. A union of elements which are neither objectively different in idea nor physically different as things, but merely different in the sense that the one idea contains implicitly and vaguely what the other expresses explicitly and determinately.

COMPOSITION, METAPHYSICAL. The union of elements that are objectively different in idea, but really identical in their physical being as things.

COMPOSITION, PHYSICAL. The union of elements that are objectively different in idea and physically different as things.

CONDITION. Something required in order that an efficient cause can act.

CONTRACTION OF BEING. The reduction or narrowing of the extension of 'being' to its inferiors by means of the addition of some element to the comprehension of 'being,' thereby including some definite beings and excluding others from this extension.

CONTRADICTION, PRINCIPLE OF. It is impossible for a thing to be and not to be at the same time. A thing cannot be and not be something at the same time.

CORRUPTION. A substantial change which makes a substance cease to be.

CREATION. The production of a thing from nothing.

DETERMINATIONS, PRIMARY. Primary determinations of being are those which are transcendental, i.e., those which constitute the most fundamental distinctions of 'being in general' and go beyond all the ordinary classifications of beings.

DETERMINATIONS, TRANSCENDENTAL. Those primary determinations which constitute the most fundamental distinctions of 'being in general' and go beyond all the ordinary classifications of beings.

DISPOSITION. A relatively transient quality which disposes a being temporarily well.

DISTINCTION. The absence of sameness between concepts or things.

DISTINCTION, ADEQUATE REAL. A real distinction between things so that they are distinct in their total being.

DISTINCTION, FORMAL (SCOTISTIC). A distinction, maintained by Duns Scotus, actual on the part of the thing, as between formality and formality, though not real, as between thing and thing.

DISTINCTION, INADEQUATE REAL. A real distinction in which things are distinct as part and whole.

DISTINCTION, LOGICAL. The absence of sameness between concepts of the same reality.

DISTINCTION, MAJOR REAL. The absence of identity between thing and thing to such an extent that they are distinct from each other as entities.

DISTINCTION, MENTAL. See Distinction, Logical.

DISTINCTION, MINOR REAL. The absence of identity between a thing and its mode.

DISTINCTION, NEGATIVE REAL. A real distinction in which there is a non-entity either on one or on both sides of the distinction.

DISTINCTION, POSITIVE REAL. A real distinction in which the distinct things are real (positive) entities and differ in their entities.

DISTINCTION, PURELY MENTAL. A distinction between concepts of one and the same reality, without a foundation in the object itself for making the distinction.

DISTINCTION, REAL. The absence of sameness between things different in their reality.

DISTINCTION, SCOTISTIC. See Distinction, Formal.

DISTINCTION, VIRTUAL. The distinction between different concepts of one and the same reality, with a foundation in the object itself for making the distinction.

EFFECT. That which is produced.

END (PURPOSE). That for the sake of which an agent or efficient cause acts. See Cause, Final.

END FOR WHICH (WHOM). The thing or person that is to benefit by the acquisition or realization of the 'end which' is acquired or realized.

END, INTERMEDIATE. An end to which one or more ends are referred, and which is itself referred to some ulterior end.

END, NATURAL. An end which lies within the tendencies and powers of the nature of the agent to strive for.

END OF THE ACT. The purpose which is present in the act itself and which the act tends to realize because it is this particular kind of act.

END OF THE AGENT. The purpose which the agent itself (himself) has in performing this particular act.

END, PRIMARY (PRINCIPAL). The main end or purpose among two or more which actuates an agent and is sufficient of itself to make the agent act.

END, PROXIMATE. The end that is referred to some ulterior end, but has no other end referred to itself.

END, REMOTE. An end to which one or more other ends are referred.

END, SECONDARY (ACCESSORY). An end intended together with a primary end, without, however, exerting the same potent influence on the action of the agent.

END, SUPERNATURAL. An end which lies beyond the tendencies and powers of the nature of an agent to strive for.

END, ULTIMATE. An end which has one or more ends referred to itself, while it is not itself referred to any other end.

END WHICH. The good itself which is striven for as an end to be realized through the action of a cause.

ENERGY, KINETIC. Energy of motion.

ENERGY, POTENTIAL. Energy of position.

ERROR. Disconformity (disagreement) between intellect and thing.

ESSENCE. The act of actuality which perfects and determines a thing in its species; that which makes a thing to be what it is.

ESSENCE, METAPHYSICAL. The sum of the various grades of being which constitute a thing in the abstract concepts of the mind.

ESSENCE, PHYSICAL. An essence as it exists concretely in nature, independent of the mind's thinking.

EVIL. Something that is unsuitable for a natural tendency or appetency. The privation of a required good.

EVIL, ABSOLUTE. The privation of an absolute good.

EVIL, APPARENT. The privation of an apparent good.

EVIL, MORAL. The privation of the proper relation between an action or its omission and the moral law.

EVIL, OBJECTIVE. The privation of an objective good.

EVIL, ONTOLOGICAL. The privation of an ontological good.

EVIL, PHYSICAL. The privation of a physical good.

EVIL, REAL. The privation of a real good.

EVIL, RELATIVE. The privation of a relative good.

EVIL, SUBJECTIVE. The privation of a subjective good.

EXCLUDED MIDDLE, PRINCIPLE OF. A thing either is or is not. Everything must either be or not be. Between 'being' and 'not-being' there is no middle or third thing possible.

EXISTENCE. That state of a being in virtue of which it is present as an actuality and not merely as a possibility, distinct from the mind and, if it be a produced being, distinct from its producing cause.

FALSITY (ERROR). Disconformity (disagreement) between intellect and thing.

FALSITY, LOGICAL. The disagreement of the intellect with the thing.

FALSITY, MORAL. The disagreement of speech with thought.

FALSITY, ONTOLOGICAL. The disagreement of a thing with the intellect.

FIGURE. The geometrical quality resulting in a body from the arrangement of its quantitative parts.

FINAL CAUSE, EXTRINSIC. A cause whose causal action is impressed upon it by some outside directive force.

FINAL CAUSE, INTRINSIC. A cause whose action producing a definite effect is the result of a being's natural tendencies.

FORM. The physical quality resulting in a body from the arrangement of its quantitative parts. *See* Cause, Formal.

GENERATION. A substantial change which brings a new substance into being through the corruption of another or others.

GOOD. Any reality which suits the nature of the being which strives for it.

GOOD, ABSOLUTE. Anything which is suitable to a being itself, irrespective of other beings.

GOOD, APPARENT. Something that is judged to be good for a being, but is actually not good for it.

GOOD, DELECTABLE. A relative good which gives pleasure and enjoyment to another.

GOOD, DISINTERESTED. A good considered merely as giving perfection, irrespective of any pleasure derived from its possession.

GOOD, METAPHYSICAL. *See* Good, Ontological.

GOOD, MORAL. A good which has everything demanded of it by the moral law.

GOOD, OBJECTIVE. Anything that is good in itself.

GOOD, ONTOLOGICAL. A thing as good in its very entity or reality.

GOOD, PHYSICAL. A good which satisfies the demand of the nature of a being.

GOOD, REAL. Something that is judged to be good for a being and actually is good for it.

GOOD, RELATIVE. Anything which is suitable to another.

GOOD, SUBJECTIVE. The actual possession of an objective good.

GOOD, TRANSCENDENTAL. *See* Good, Ontological.

GOOD, USEFUL. A relative good which is desired as a means to acquire perfection or pleasure.

GOODNESS. The suitability of a thing for a natural tendency or appetency.

HABIT. As a quality, it is a comparatively permanent accident disposing a thing well or ill in its being.

HABIT, OPERATIVE. A stable quality disposing a being ill or well in the operations of its faculties.

HABITUS. The condition resulting from clothing, equipment, physical adjuncts, environment; or a condition or state, as expressed by the reflexive verb.

HYPOSTASIS (SUPPOSITUM). A complete and individual substance which has subsistence, i.e., a substance which is self-contained and autonomous (*sui juris*) in its operations.

IDENTITY. A sameness between concepts or things.

IDENTITY, ACCIDENTAL LOGICAL. The logical identity of things based upon the similarity of their accidents.

IDENTITY, ESSENTIAL LOGICAL. The logical identity of things based upon the similarity of their essence.

IDENTITY, LOGICAL. The unity (oneness) of things based upon the same concept of the mind.

IDENTITY, METAPHYSICAL. The real identity of a being, in virtue of which it can absolutely not change in any manner.

IDENTITY, MORAL. The real identity of a being, in virtue of which the change which takes place in its essential being is successive and gradual.

IDENTITY, PHYSICAL. The real identity of a being, in virtue of which it does not change in its essential reality.

IDENTITY, PRINCIPLE OF. Whatever is, is; and whatever is not, is not. Everything is what it is. Everything is its own being. Being is being, and not-being is not-being.

IDENTITY, REAL. The unity (oneness) of things in themselves.

INCAPACITY. An existing faculty in a weakened or unfit condition.

INDISPOSITION. A relatively transient quality which disposes a being temporarily ill.

INDIVIDUALITY. That state of an existing being in virtue of which it is one and non-multipliable.

INDIVIDUALITY, UNITY OF. The unity of a being which is one in itself and non-multipliable.

INDIVIDUATION, ABSOLUTE, PRINCIPLE OF. That intrinsic principle which gives the unity of individuality to an existing being.

INDIVIDUATION, PRINCIPLE OF. The principle which makes an existing being to be an individual, so that its nature or essence is incommunicable to others and is restricted to this one.

INDIVIDUATION, RELATIVE, PRINCIPLE OF. The principle which determines the possibility of having a number of individuals of the same species.

MANICHEISM. A theory, originating with Manes, which maintained that God is the supreme Principle of Good and matter the supreme Principle of Evil.

MATTER. *See* Cause, Material.

MECHANISM. The theory which maintains that the ultimate constituent particles of matter are homogeneous in character, actuated by purely mechanical forces which produce only local movement.

METAPHYSICS. The science of the ultimate principles and properties of real beings.

MOTION, LOCAL. The transition of a thing from one place to another.

MOTUS. Any activity involving the transition from potency to act in a corporeal being through successive stages, i.e., a successive change in a body. The act of a being in potency while still in potency.

MOVEMENT. *See* Motus.

NATURALISM. The theory of Aristotle and the scholastics, that beings possess a 'nature,' in virtue of which they are specifically distinct substances with specific properties and activities.

NATURE. The essence of a being considered as the ultimate principle of its operations.

NOTHING. The absence of being.

NOTHING, ABSOLUTE. The total absence of being in every conceivable form.

NOTHING, NEGATIVE. The mere absence of some kind of being in a thing.

NOTHING, PRIVATIVE. The absence of some kind of being in a thing that is fit to have it and normally ought to have it.

NOTHING, RELATIVE. The absence of a definite kind of being.

OCCASION. A circumstance or combination of circumstances which affords an opportunity for an efficient cause to act.

ONENESS. That attribute of a being in virtue of which it is undivided in itself (and divided from every other being).

ONTOLOGY. The science of being in its most general aspects.

PASSION (REACTION). The reception of an effect from another.

PERSON. An intellectual hypostasis, i.e., an individual, complete, subsistent, intellectual substance.

PESSIMISM. The philosophic theory which maintains that evil predominates over good, because the world at large is essentially bad.

PHILOSOPHY. The science of things in their ultimate reasons, causes, and principles, acquired by the aid of human reason alone.

POSSIBILITY. Objective potency, or the capacity or aptitude of a being for existence.

POSSIBILITY, ABSOLUTE. See Possibility, Intrinsic.

POSSIBILITY, EXTRINSIC. The capacity or aptitude of a being for existence in virtue of the power of an efficient cause capable of producing it.

POSSIBILITY, INTRINSIC. The capacity or aptitude of a being for existence, due to the compatibility or non-contradiction of its constitutive elements.

POSSIBILITY, LOGICAL. See Possibility, Intrinsic.

POSSIBILITY, METAPHYSICAL. See Possibility, Intrinsic.

POSSIBILITY, MORAL. The possibility of free agents to do something without grave difficulty.

POSSIBILITY, PHYSICAL. The possibility due to the powers of a thing acting according to the laws of nature.

POSSIBILITY, RELATIVE. See Possibility, Extrinsic.

POSTURE. A disposition of parts among themselves in the sense of 'attitude'; immanent or intransitive action expressed by an intransitive verb.

POTENCY. The capacity or aptitude for something.

POTENCY, OBJECTIVE. The capacity of a non-existent being for existence.

POTENCY, OPERATIVE SUBJECTIVE. The capacity for doing something.

POTENCY, REAL. See Potency, Subjective.

POTENCY, RECEPTIVE SUBJECTIVE. The capacity for receiving an act.

POTENCY, SUBJECTIVE. The capacity of something existing for an act.

PRECISION. A process in which the mind fixes its attention upon one or the other characteristic of a thing or upon one element common to many things, excluding others which are joined to it in the real order.

PRECISION, FORMAL. A type of abstraction or precision in which the ideas drawn out by the abstractive process are only subjectively different, i.e., these ideas mutually include each other implicitly, though they do not expressly mention each other.

PRECISION, MATERIAL. A type of abstraction or precision in which the ideas drawn out by the abstractive process are objectively different, i.e., these ideas have a different comprehension or thought-content, so that the one does not necessarily include the other.

PRECISION, OBJECTIVE. *See* Precision, Material.

PRECISION, SUBJECTIVE. *See* Precision, Formal.

PREDICAMENT. An ultimate and supreme mode of being; a category.

PREMOTION, PHYSICAL. An antecedent physical influence (*praemotio physica*) which, according to Thomists, is required in order that the faculty of a creature can pass from potentiality to actuality.

PRINCIPLE. That from which something proceeds in any manner whatever.

PRINCIPLE OF CAUSALITY. *See* Causality, Principle of.

PRINCIPLE OF CHANGE. *See* Change, Principle of.

PRINCIPLE OF CONTRADICTION. *See* Contradiction, Principle of.

PRINCIPLE OF EXCLUDED MIDDLE. *See* Excluded Middle, Principle of.

PRINCIPLE OF IDENTITY. *See* Identity, Principle of.

PRINCIPLE OF SUFFICIENT REASON. *See* Sufficient Reason, Principle of.

PRINCIPLES, FIRST. *See* Principles, Supreme.

PRINCIPLES, SUPREME, OF BEING. Those highest principles which are immediately derived from the concept of 'being.'

PROPERTIES, TRANSCENDENTAL. The supreme modes or attributes necessarily connected with every being, which are different phases of the same fundamental being, but are not explicitly contained in its concept as such.

PROPERTY. The act or actuality perfecting and determining an essence in such a manner that the entity it gives to the being flows necessarily from its nature, without being strictly essential.

PURPOSE. *See* End.

QUALITY. An absolute accident completing and determining a substance in its being and in its operations.

QUALITY, AFFECTIVE. A relatively permanent quality which produces, or results from, some accidental sensible alteration.

QUANTITY. An attribute of the material (determinable) element in a being.

QUIDDITY. The 'whatness' or essence of a being.

REACTION (PASSION). The reception of an action on the part of the recipient.

RELATION. It is the bearing (reference, respect, attitude, ordination) of one thing to something else.

RELATION, ACCIDENTAL (CATEGORICAL, PREDICAMENTAL). A relation based on an accident as its foundation.

RELATION, CATEGORICAL. *See* Relation, Accidental.

RELATION, ESSENTIAL (TRANSCENDENTAL). A relation in which the very essence of one thing has a bearing toward something.

RELATION, EXTREMES OF. The subject and term of a relation.

RELATION, FOUNDATION OF. The reason why one thing is related to another.

RELATION, LOGICAL. A relation made solely by the mind and placed by the mind between entities.

RELATION, MUTUAL. A relation whose foundation is real or logical in both extremes.

RELATION, MUTUAL, ASYMMETRICAL. A relation in which the foundation in both extremes is of a different nature or degree.

RELATION, MUTUAL, SYMMETRICAL. A relation in which the foundation in both extremes is of the same nature and degree.

RELATION, NON-MUTUAL. A relation whose foundation is real or logical in one of the extremes only.

RELATION, PREDICAMENTAL. *See* Relation, Accidental.

RELATION, REAL. A relation which exists between things, independent of the mind and its thinking.

RELATION, TRANSCENDENTAL. *See* Relation, Essential.

SUBSISTENCE. That mode of existence in virtue of which a thing is self-contained and autonomous (*sui juris*) in its operations.

SUBSTANCE. A being whose nature it is to exist in and for itself and not in another as in a subject.

SUBSTANCE, COMPLETE. A substance whose nature demands no further union with a substantial co-principle.

SUBSTANCE, COMPOSITE. A substance consisting of incomplete substantial parts, entitatively distinct among themselves, in such a manner that their union results in a single, unified nature.

SUBSTANCE, INCOMPLETE. A substance whose nature demands that it be conjoined with some other substantial co-principle.

SUBSTANCE, PRIMARY. Any individual, concrete substantial being.

SUBSTANCE, SECONDARY. Any generic or specific substance.

SUBSTANCE, SIMPLE. A substance which does not consist of substantial parts which are entitatively distinct among themselves.

SUFFICIENT REASON, PRINCIPLE OF. The principle which states that everything without exception must have an adequate reason or ground for its being and existence, even if no production be involved.

SUPPOSITUM. *See* Hypostasis.

TELEOLOGY. The tendency of efficient causes to realize definite results through their action.

TERM, ANALOGOUS. A term applied to unlike things, partly for the same and partly for a different reason.

TERM, EQUIVOCAL. A term which is used of totally diverse things, so that it has entirely different meanings.

TERM, UNIVOCAL. A term which designates a number of things in an identical sense.

TERMINUS A QUO. The starting-point from which something proceeds.

TERMINUS AD QUEM. The goal or ending-point toward which something proceeds.

THOMISM. One of the schools of scholastic philosophy.

TRANSCENDENTAL. Something which goes beyond all ordinary classifications and categories of being.

TRUTH. The conformity (agreement) between intellect and thing.

TRUTH, LOGICAL. The agreement of the intellect with the thing.

TRUTH, MENTAL. *See* Truth, Logical.

TRUTH, METAPHYSICAL. *See* Truth, Ontological.

TRUTH, MORAL. The agreement of speech with thought.

TRUTH, OBJECTIVE. *See* Truth, Ontological.

TRUTH, ONTOLOGICAL (METAPHYSICAL, OBJECTIVE). The agreement of a being with the intellect.

UNITY. That mode or attribute of a being in virtue of which a being is undivided in itself (and divided from every other being).

UNITY, LOGICAL. The indivision of a universal idea (class) considered as a whole of which the inferiors are the part.

UNITY, MATHEMATICAL. *See* Unity, Predicamental.

UNITY, NUMERICAL. *See* Unity, Predicamental.

UNITY OF COMPOSITION. The unity of a being in such a manner that it is a whole not actually divided into the real parts of which it consists.

UNITY OF SIMPLICITY. The unity of a thing in such a manner that it does not consist of any parts into which it could be divided.

UNITY, PREDICAMENTAL (MATHEMATICAL, NUMERICAL). A unit considered as a standard for measuring mathematical or numerical quantity.

UNITY, REAL. The indivision of a thing in its entity.

VALUE. That which is perfect or perfective.

WHEN. Situation in time.

WHERE. Position in space.

ZOROASTRIANISM. An oriental theory, originating with Zoroaster (or Zarathustra), which maintains that the forces of good and evil are waging a constant battle for supremacy. Ahura-mazda (Ormuzd) is the supreme Principle of Good, and Anra-mainyu (Ahriman) is the supreme Principle of Evil.

BIBLIOGRAPHY

American Philosophy Today and Tomorrow, ed. by H. M. Kallen and Sydney Hook (Lee Furman, Inc., New York, 1935).

Aristotle, *Physics* and *Metaphysics,* tr. by P. H. Wicksteed and F. M. Cornford (Harvard University Press, 1929).

Aspects of the New Scholastic Philosophy, ed. by Charles A. Hart (Benziger, New York, 1932).

Balmes, James, *Fundamental Philosophy,* tr. by H. F. Brownson (Sadlier Co., 1875).

Bandas, Rudolph G., *Contemporary Philosophy and Thomistic Principles* (Bruce, Milwaukee, 1932).

Baschab, Chas. R., *A Manual of Neo-Scholastic Philosophy* (B. Herder Book Co., St. Louis, 1923).

Bergson, Henri, *An Introduction to Metaphysics,* tr. by T. E. Hulme (G. P. Putnam's Sons, New York, 1912).

Bowne, Borden P., *Metaphysics* (American Book Co.).

Bradley, F. H., *Appearance and Reality* (Macmillan, 1893).

———— *Essays on Truth and Reality* (The Clarendon Press, 1914).

Burtt, E. A., *Metaphysical Foundation of Modern Physical Science* (K. Paul, Trench, Trubner and Co., London, 1925).

Carr, H. W., *The Philosophy of Change* (Macmillan, 1914).

Casanova, Gabriel, *Cursus Philosophicus* (Madrid, 1894).

Coffey, P., *Ontology* (Longmans, Green and Co., 1914).

Contemporary British Philosophy, 1st series, ed. by J. H. Muirhead (Macmillan, 1924).

———— 2nd series, ed. by J. H. Muirhead (Macmillan, no date).

Conze, Eberhard, *Der Begriff der Metaphysik bei Franciscus Suarez* (F. Meiner, Leipzig, 1928).

De Maria, Michael, *Philosophia Peripatetico-Scholastica* (Philip Cuggiani, Rome, 1904).

Descartes, René, *Principia Philosophiae,* tr. by John Veich (W. Blackwood and Sons, Edinburgh and London, 1902).

Descoqs, P., *Institutiones Metaphysicae Generalis* (Beauchesne, Paris, 1925).

De Wulf, Maurice, *History of Medieval Philosophy* (Longmans, Green and Co., 1925).

——— *Scholasticism Old and New,* tr. by P. Coffey (Benziger Bros., New York, 1907).

Donat, Joseph, *Ontologia* (Felician Rauch, Innsbruck, 1910).

Dotterer, Ray, *Philosophy by Way of the Sciences* (Macmillan, New York, 1930).

Esser, Gerard, *Metaphysica Generalis* (Techny, Ill., 1933).

Felkin, Fred W., *A Wordbook of Metaphysics* (Oxford Univ. Press, H. Milford, London, 1932).

Garrigou-Lagrange, P. Reg., *Le Réalisme du Principe de Finalité* (Des-clée De Brouwer, Paris, 1932).

Geyser, Jos., *Einige Hauptprobleme der Metaphysik* (Herder, Fribourg, 1923).

Gilson, E., *The Philosophy of St. Thomas Aquinas,* tr. by Edw. Bul-lough (B. Herder Book Co., St. Louis, 1929).

Gredt, Joseph, *Elementa Philosophiae* (Herder, Fribourg, 1929).

Gutberlet, C., *Allgemeine Metaphysik* (Theissingsche Buchhandlung, Münster, 1906).

Haldane, Richard B. H., *The Pathway to Reality* (E. P. Dutton Co., New York, 1926).

Harris, C. R. S., *Duns Scotus* (Clarendon Press, Oxford, 1927).

Hickey, J. S., *Summula Philosophiae Scholasticae* (B. Herder Book Co., St. Louis, 1917).

Kleutgen, J., *Philosophie der Vorzeit* (Münster, 1860).

Lange, Fred A., *The History of Materialism,* tr. by Ernest C. Thomas (Harcourt, Brace and Co., New York, 1925).

Lehmen, A., *Lehrbuch der Philosophie* (Herder, Fribourg, 1909).

Lortie, Stanislaus, *Elementa Philosophiae Christianae* (L'Action Sociale, Quebec, 1921).

Malebranche, Nicolas, *Dialogues on Metaphysics and Religion,* tr. by Morris Ginsberg (Macmillan, 1923).

Maritain, J., *An Introduction to Philosophy,* tr. by E. I. Watkin (Longmans, Green and Co., New York, 1930).

McCormick, John F., *Scholastic Metaphysics* (Loyola Univ. Press, Chicago, 1928).

Mercier, D. Card., *A Manual of Modern Scholastic Philosophy* (Herder Book Co., St. Louis, 1916).

—— *Métaphysique Générale* (Institut Superieur de Philosophie, Louvain, 1910).

Miltner, Charles C., *Introduction to Metaphysics* (Macmillan, 1930).

Morgan, C. Lloyd, *Emergent Evolution* (Williams and Norgate, 1923).

Osgniach, A. J., *The Analysis of Objects* (J. F. Wagner, New York, 1938).

Perrier, Jos. L., *The Revival of Scholastic Philosophy* (Columbia Univ. Press, New York, 1909).

Perry, Ralph B., *Present Philosophical Tendencies* (Longmans, Green and Co., 1912).

Pesch, Tilmann, *Institutiones Logicales* (Herder, Fribourg, 1889).

Phillips, R. P., *Modern Thomistic Philosophy* (Burns, Oates, and Washbourne, London, 1934).

Philosophische Handbibliothek, ed. by Clemens Baeumker (J. Kösel, Munich, 1920–1925).

Planck, Max, *The Philosophy of Physics,* tr. by W. H. Johnston (W. W. Norton, New York, 1936).

—— *Where is Science Going?* tr. by James Murphy (W. W. Norton, New York, 1932).

Rickaby, John, *General Metaphysics* (Benziger Bros., New York).

Robinson, Daniel S., *An Anthology of Modern Philosophy* (Crowell, New York, 1931).

—— *An Anthology of Recent Philosophy* (Crowell, New York, 1929).

—— *Introduction to Living Philosophy* (Crowell, New York, 1932).

Scotus, Duns, *Summa Theologica,* ed. by H. de Montefortino (Rome, 1900).

Shallo, Michael W., *Lessons in Scholastic Philosophy* (Peter Reilly Co., Philadelphia, 1934).

Sheen, Fulton J., *Philosophy of Science* (Bruce, Milwaukee, 1934).

Sheldon, Wilmon H., "The Task of Present-Day Metaphysics," in

American Philosophy Today and Tomorrow, ed. by H. M. Kallen and S. Hook (Lee Furman, Inc., New York, 1935).

Suarez, Francis, *Disputationes Metaphysicae* (L. Vives, Paris, 1877).

Taylor, A. E., *Elements of Metaphysics* (Methuen and Co., London, 1920).

Thomas Aquinas, St., *Summa Theologica. De Ente et Essentia. Contra Gentiles.*

Tongiorgi, Salv., *Institutiones Philosophicae.*

Urban, Wilbur M., *The Intelligible World* (Macmillan, New York, 1929).

Urráburu, John J., *Institutiones Philosophicae.*

Van de Woestyne, Z., *Cursus Philosophicus* (Mechlin, 1925).

Walshe, Msgr. T. J., *The Quest of Reality* (Herder Book Co., 1933).

Ward, Leo R., *Values and Reality* (Sheed and Ward, New York, 1935).

Whitehead, Alfred N., *Process and Reality* (Macmillan, 1929).

Willmann, Otto, *Philosophische Propaedeutik* (Herder, Fribourg, 1914).

Zybura, J. S., *Present-Day Thinkers and the New Scholasticism* (Herder Book Co., St. Louis, 1926).

INDEX

Absolute, and relative, 313 ff.; as God, 109; existence of, 314; knowability of, 315 f.

Absolute accident, 249

Absolute being, 26

Absolute evil, 197

Absolute good, 190

Absolute perfection, 188

Abstraction, *see* Precision

Accident, 240 ff.; absolute, 249; absolute, existence of, 258 ff.; act of, 59; actual inherence of, 243; an analogous term, 238; aptitudinal inherence of, 243; being not a genus of, 35 ff.; definition of, 240; extrinsic, 250; in nature, as a fortuitous concurrence of causes, 370 ff.; intrinsic, 250; kinds of, 249 ff.; modal, 249; not a genus, 237 f.; relative, 249

Accidental being, 23

Accidental change, 86, 327 f.

Accidental form, 329

Accidental identity, 151 f.

Accidental relation, 302

Act, 56 ff.; and perfection, 105; and the Principle of Change, 95 ff.; as a principle of activity, 106; definition of, 56 f.; formal, 103; kinds of, 58 ff.; mixed, 60; of accident, 59; of essence, 58; of existence, 58; of property, 58; primary, 59; pure, 60; secondary, 60; virtual, 103

Action, as a category, 227, 319 ff.

Activity, chemical, 91; immanent, 90; mechanical, 91; physical, 91; transient (transeunt, transitive), 91; vital, 90

Actual, 22

Affection, as quality, 286 ff.

Affective quality, 286 ff.

Agnosticism, and final causes, 361

Ahriman, 203

Ahura-mazda, 203

Alteration, 85

Analogous, being is, 37 ff.

Andronicus of Rhodes, the metaphysics of Aristotle, 5

Anra-mainyu, 203

Appetency, and goodness, 186

Aristotle, and hylomorphism, 331; and metaphysics, 5; and naturalism, 324; categories of, 222 ff.; classification of causes, 325 f.; definition of chance, 372; definition of goodness, 185; definition of *motus,* 88 ff.; definition of quality, 280; enumeration of qualities, 281; methods of change, 95; on affection and affective quality, 287 f.; on finality in nature, 373; on the Principle of Contradiction, 52; primary and secondary substance, 244 f.

Attributes, of God, distinction between, 160; transcendental, definition of, 131; transcendental, of being, 131 ff.

Augmentation, 85

Beauty, and goodness, 212; and truth, 211; and unity, 211; definition of, 215; its experience, 206 ff.; objective elements of, 210 ff.

Becoming, 94 ff.; *see* Change

Being, absolute, 26; accidental, 23; actual, 22 f.; an analogous idea, 37 ff.; and beauty, 206 ff.; and goodness, 185 ff.; and individuality, 138 f.; and nothing, 18 f.; and truth, 166 ff.; concept of, formed by means of a subjective, or formal, precision, 15; cognitional, 28; contingent, 23; contraction of, 33 ff.; convertibility with goodness, 194; convertibility with truth, 173 f.; convertibility with unity, 136 f.; definition of, 19 f.; direct concept of, 12 ff.; finite, 24 f.; ideal, 26 ff.; individual, as the principle of division of the categories, 225; infinite, 24 f.; intentional, 28;